Desmond L. Anderson

EDITOR

Associate Dean,
School of Public Administration,
University of Southern California

Municipal Public Relations

Published for the

Institute for Training in Municipal Administration

by the

International City Managers' Association

MUNICIPAL MANAGEMENT SERIES

First edition, 1966

Library of Congress
Catalog Card No.: 66–20874

Printed in the
United States of America

Foreword

This book is the latest addition to the Municipal Management Series published by the International City Managers' Association. Each volume is a complete and separate training and reference guide dealing with one field of administration.

The nature and approach of this series can best be explained by a brief review of its origin and development. In 1934 the International City Managers' Association received the first of several special grants from the Spelman Fund of New York for the preparation and administration of in-service training courses for municipal government officials at the management level. This training program has been developed by the Association through its Institute for Training in Municipal Administration.

In its early years the Institute confined its training activities to the correspondence course method. This required the preparation of study materials, but it soon was discovered that the published texts then available were not suitable for the kinds of training for which the Institute was established. It was necessary therefore for the Institute to prepare its own training guides. By 1941 eight texts had been published, and all eight have been revised several times. These eight texts cover general management, personnel, finance, planning, police, fire, public works, and recreation.

In the past two decades the responsibilities of cities, counties, and other local governments have expanded enormously in response to population growth, technology, and rapid sociological change. This has had a dramatic effect on cities and other local governments both inter-

nally and externally—internally in the changing complexion of management, externally in the assumption of wider responsibilities.

To meet these changes, seven courses, with accompanying books and training materials, have been developed. *Supervisory Methods in Municipal Administration,* published in 1958, is designed chiefly for on-the-job training of supervisory personnel. In 1959 *Management Practices for Smaller Cities* was published to aid in special training problems for city managers, city clerks, public works directors, and other administrative officials in smaller communities. In 1961 *Administration of Community Health Services* was published to provide a guide both for chief administrators of local government jurisdictions and for public health workers.

Two new texts were added in 1964. *Local Public Library Administration* is intended for library administrators and other local government officials to provide information on library programs within the context of local government. *Case Problems in City Management* is intended for training city managers and administrative assistants to managers, department heads, and others by use of the case method of teaching.

In 1965 instructional materials for management were extended with the publication of *Effective Supervisory Practices,* a series of 15 bulletins for in-service training of foremen and other supervisors.

This volume, *Municipal Public Relations,* provides the 15th book in this series and is intended for city and county managers, department heads, and other local government administrators in the increasingly complex areas of public opinion, public attitudes, and public information.

The interest of the International City Managers' Association in public relations extends back almost 40 years to the pioneering efforts of Clarence E. Ridley to apply critical standards to annual municipal reports and to establish guidelines for city managers. Mr. Ridley, Executive Director of the International City Managers' Association from 1929 to 1956, exerted considerable influence through his annual review of municipal reports which appeared for many years in *National Municipal Review* (now *National Civic Review*), his preparation in 1939, with Herbert A. Simon, of *Specifications for the Annual Municipal Report,* and his interest in developing the total concept of public relations as an integral part of the total management job.

Over the years ICMA has devoted considerable space to articles and reports on public relations activities in its journal, *Public Management;* has included the subject in most of its annual conference programs; has issued three monographs on the subject; and has either had separate chapters or material under subject headings in most of the books in the Municipal Management Series.

The editor for this book is Desmond L. Anderson, Associate Dean, School of Public Administration, University of Southern California. Drawing upon his extensive experience in research, teaching, and administration, Dr. Anderson has conceived and directed the preparation of a volume which considers public relations as integral to the political and administrative processes. It is viewed broadly in terms of agency performance rather than narrowly in terms of certain kinds of organized governmental publicity.

This volume, as with others in the Municipal Management Series, has been under the editorial supervision of David S. Arnold, Assistant Director, Publications, ICMA.

All volumes in the series have drawn heavily on the first-hand experience of governmental administrators; all have given careful consideration to the latest developments in research and teaching; and all have been reviewed by administrators, consultants, staffs of appropriate professional organizations, and teachers and students.

Two distinguishing features of the series are traceable directly to their origin. First, these volumes approach local government from the administrative point of view—be it the responsibility of the city manager, the city librarian, the public works director, the public health officer, the police captain, the recreation supervisor, or the street maintenance foreman. They are built around the commonalities of administration—organization, management, personnel, finance, programming, and accountability.

Second, because these books are intended for in-service training, most of their content deals with the "how" rather than the "what" of administration. They are not intended as theoretical treatises, nor as detailed procedure manuals. Rather they aim to help administrators at all levels in local government organization to analyze their own duties and responsibilities within a common framework.

These training guides since 1935 have established their value both as training and reference manuals. They are widely used by universities and colleges in courses in local government administration, particularly at the graduate level. They are also widely used as the basic text for group in-service training classes for local government administrative personnel. Finally, administrators in many local governments use these volumes as reference guides in solving local problems.

ORIN F. NOLTING
Executive Director
International City
Managers' Association

Chicago
February, 1966

Preface

Man reads books to find answers. His study in the classroom and in the executive development seminar is a quest for solutions. But there are no effective patterned solutions, and answers do not come that easily. They result from a continuous process of performance, analysis, and understanding. They may come more quickly and with greater precision to the person who has cultivated an approach to problem-solving and refined his insights in a particular subject-matter field.

This is especially true with public relations. Although patterned solutions to individual public relations problems in local government may not be found within the pages of this book, it is hoped that greater insight regarding such problems may be developed through an understanding of the material contained herein and hence that resolution of public relations problems may become easier.

Thus it is the purpose of this book to provide students and local government administrators with a better understanding of public relations within the context of the governmental process and to acquaint them with some of the more sophisticated aspects of public relations as well as the practices and techniques of public information.

Public relations is a composite of relationships, both human and institutional, for all persons involved in local government. It is concerned with opinions, attitudes, information, impressions, context, and images. It is circular, interacting, and composite. It is perceived by the general public in terms of public information—news releases, radio and television programs, press conferences, and the like. It is not so well known or appreciated as a process of interaction in which facets of both program performance and public relations are inextricably involved.

In this volume public relations is examined from several points of view—that of the city council, of municipal employees in general and police in particular, of the broad spectrum of publics, and of newspaper reporters and others employed by the mass media.

Part One of the book provides the perspective for public relations in society, in government, and in administration. Chapter 1 leads off with a case study, based on an actual incident, to dramatize the importance of public relations. Chapter 2, "Public Relations and The Governmental Administrative Process," provides a definition of public relations for purposes of this book and places public relations in the context of the organization. Chapter 3 deals with research and public relations.

Part Two covers public relations from a program and policy standpoint. Chapter 4 describes the important and difficult role played by city councilmen individually and collectively in dealing with the nebulous concepts of the public interest. "The Multitudinous Publics" are dealt with in Chapter 5. Attention is given to the reciprocal flow of influence and opinion and the structure of the many publics.

Chapter 6 covers "Serving the Public," especially through continuing personal relationships between the city government and the citizens. Chapter 7 explores this concept further by review of employee-citizen relations through neighborhood meetings, citizen committees, and intergovernmental relations. "Community Group Relationships" are reviewed in Chapter 8 from the standpoint of the nature of the community and broad types of organizations.

Police work is the only municipal service that has been singled out for coverage in a chapter of its own—Chapter 9, "Municipal Police and Public Relations." This has been done because probably no other group of municipal employees is so influential in setting the tone for municipal government as perceived by the average citizen.

Part Three deals with public information in the more conventional sense. Chapters 10 and 11 cover the broad spectrum of journalism, including the role of the press, the nature and role of reporters, city hall news coverage, and interactions between the press and the city government. Chapter 12 covers the annual report, special reports, and tours and special events. Chapter 13 describes preparations for oral reports and advantages and limitations of speeches and other kinds of in-person reporting. Chapter 14 describes publications planning, printing and distribution.

Part Four deals with public relations within the administrative organization. Chapter 15 suggests organizational arrangements for public relations. Chapter 16 sets forth the rationale for public relations training together with guide-lines for training programs.

If more effective understanding and performance result from the publication of this volume it is hoped that this will be considered recompense for those many whose interest and contributions may otherwise go unacknowledged. Special thanks are due David S. Arnold, Assistant Director, Publications, International City Managers' Association, under whose general supervision the book was prepared, for his patience, good humor, and thoughtful insights which made collaboration a pleasure rather than a drudge.

Ernest E. Brashear, former city manager of Seal Beach, California, participated in the initial planning for this book. Other persons who contributed information or reviewed portions of the book are Evett N. Allen, Assistant to the City Manager, Norfolk, Virginia; Murray Brown, Editor and Manager, *Western City Magazine;* Elgin E. Crull, City Manager, Dallas, Texas; Marshall Fels, Organization and Manpower Utilization Specialist, California State Department of Mental Hygiene; George Frederickson, Assistant Professor of Government, University of Maryland; James R. Fulton, former city manager, Cuero, Texas; Truman J. Keesey, former Director of Information, District of Columbia Government; James C. MacDonald, Associate Editor, *The Toledo Blade;* Lew Price, Director, Department of Publicity, Miami-Metro, Miami, Florida; Abe S. Rosen, former Director of Public Information, City of Philadelphia; J. E. Sargent, Deputy Director, Royal Institute of Public Administration, London; Walter A. Scheiber, Executive Director, Metropolitan Washington Council of Governments; and Robert A. Stierer, City Manager, Troy, New York.

Personal gratitude is extended to a wide range of family and professional associates for ideas and inspiration. To authors of individual chapters I express appreciation not only for their contributions but for responding to my importunings, cajoling, and prodding as chapters were blue-penciled, cut, expanded, and rewritten in order to develop a consistent theme.

Notwithstanding the considerable contributions of many, I absolve all but myself for what may be considered errors of judgment, style, and content. If the citizens' desires are given more effective consideration because of this publication, then its purpose will have been served.

DESMOND L. ANDERSON

Los Angeles
February, 1966

Table of Contents

Illustration credits: Figure 5: Adapted from *Public Opinion and Foreign Policy,* by James N. Rosenau. © Copyright 1961 by Random House, Inc. Reprinted by permission. Figure 11: Adapted in part from *Taking Action in the Community* (Washington, D.C.: Adult Education Association of the U.S.A., 1955), pp. 14–15. Figures 12 and 14: Chicago Police Department photos.

Tables

Municipal
Public Relations

1

Public Relations
in Society

Brisk, chill winds whistled down the river valley as billowing white puffs of the winter's first snow cascaded along hedgerow, ditch-bank, and street. Spence Carlson tugged at his up-turned coat collar to form a better shield against the driving snow as he strode from his doorstep onto the city street. Mingling with the falling snow, autumn leaves rustled and crunched beneath his feet. Spence mused about the unseasonal and precipitous change from the golden fall of Idaho's Upper Snake River Valley to the white of winter.[1]

The potato harvest was still in full swing; pungent, earthy odors rose from the furrowed sod; the monotonous shrill of crickets resounded from meadowland and tree. On the farmlands surrounding Boulder, the valley's commercial center and principal city, the harvest was still not finished. But on this November election night, 1962, the snow continued to fall. Nature was quietly fashioning a seasonal change from the rapture of Indian summer to the rigors of winter.

Dr. Spencer B. Carlson, professor and chairman of the department of political science at Boulder University, a thriving center of education sponsored by the Seventh Day Adventist Church, had quietly eaten supper with Nancy and their children. Nan was a brick; she hadn't raised a question about Spence's pensive mood

at the supper table, which was usually a gay occasion in the Carlson household. Without saying so, they both knew that Spence was concerned about the outcome of today's municipal election. Now Spence was on his way to his neighborhood polling place. He had just enough time to cast his ballot before continuing over to College Bluff for his weekly university class in state and local government at 7:30.

"Land, I was afraid you'd miss casting your vote to retain the council-manager charter," exclaimed poll supervisor Mrs. Nielsen to Professor Carlson, as she folded up the election flag to close the polls.

"It's been a bitterly fought campaign, Carrie! Thanks for holding the clock back until I arrived."

Picking up his ballot, Spence went behind the screen, breathed a long, contemplative sigh, then marked his ballot for individual candidates and to retain the council-manager charter. Stepping through the parted curtain, he handed his ballot to an elections clerk who reported, as she placed it in the box, "Spencer B. Carlson has voted."

"Well, charming ladies, the vote's all in," commented the professor. "Now while you're helping to discover the verdict, I'll tell my students about your gallant efforts in preserving the American way of life."

Outside again, Spence quickened his pace as he moved along the boulevard which follows the edge of the "Bench" leading over to College Bluff. Below and to the right, he could see the

---

[1] This essentially is a true story which understandably has been made anonymous by use of fictitious names and places.

mercury-vapor lamps illuminating University Avenue as it proceeds westward and intersects with Center Street to mark the center of town. In the distance beyond, toward the west end of town, were the lights of the new and highly successful potato processing plants working round the clock to convert famous Idaho Russets into "instant potatoes." Less than a decade ago, with cellars crammed full of beautiful but unmarketable potatoes, the local farmers were faced with economic despair. Now, with the success of the processing plants, lured to Boulder by its first city manager, the whole valley was enjoying financial rejuvenation.

Spence recalled his first efforts almost nine years earlier in initiating the movement to change from the commission form of government to the council-manager plan. The idea soon spread from the political science faculty and students at Boulder University to the downtown businessmen. Within two years, sufficient interest had been generated to launch an election campaign for adoption of a new charter. Many of the standard slogans were used: efficiency, progress, public interest, modern life, need for a change. . . . Although the margin of victory was surprisingly slight, much less than Spence had predicted, the council-manager system was adopted by the people of Boulder. If any one person were chiefly responsible for the change it was Spence Carlson. He had been its chief proponent, having initiated the idea, formed the battle plan, and directed the successful election campaign.

Now, nearly seven years to the day later, the same question was being reconsidered by Boulder's electorate. And once again he had been deeply involved and committed, consuming most of his evenings and week-ends for the past couple of months. It was over now—except those agonizing minutes, perhaps an hour, at most two, before the verdict would be known. And somehow it was a relief to have it done. Yet his nerves tensed. Apprehension, common to persons associated with politics on an election day, overcame him.

"It *will* pass," he consoled himself. "The city manager form of government is working successfully. We now have positive leadership in Boulder. And the people of this town are aware

that the National Municipal League is considering Boulder for the 'All America City Award' this year. They simply *can't* vote back in some archaic form of local government." Spence Carlson *did* care whether the city manager charter were retained. He cared greatly!

"Hi, Doctor Carlson," rang out on the cool night air as a passing student's greeting awakened him to the physical reality of the campus. Already he had passed the university hospital and medical school, for which Boulder University is best known, and was now mounting the steps to Clarke Hall, where his class was assigned. Inside, the hallways were crowded and noisy with students rushing to 7:30 classes but the warmth of the building felt good as he shook the snow from his coat and hat. As Spence neared his classroom he heard the sounds of a toothpaste commercial. "That's fine! Dick Wright brought his portable television tonight," he reassured himself.

Entering the room, Professor Carlson took his customary seat where he could see and hear the toothpaste commercial conclude with a rousing jingle. Then Chuck Bartles, an inane local sports announcer, began to report election results. Several Idaho communities were having elections to decide numerous questions and elect city and county officials. But like most "off years" there were no national issues or offices at stake.

After announcing that early returns indicated that incumbent city councilmen in both Twin Falls and Pocatello were being reelected, Bartles reported, "We now have the returns from six of the twenty-nine precincts in Boulder showing 1,101 votes favoring the school bond and 541 against. On the city charter question there are 853 votes favoring repeal of the city manager plan and 797 against. And now for some pro basketball scores. The Syracuse Nats upended. . . ."

Dick Wright turned the volume down as everyone began talking at once. Keen disappointment cut deeply into Spence's being as he said to himself, "It looks bad." He whirled his chair around to face the class and began to speak.

"First I would like to report that our trip to Miami was very successful. Professor Chris

McCormick, from the School of Commerce, and I left last Friday morning and arrived in Miami that evening. Jim Grossman, our city manager, had most of our displays prepared to which we added the materials we had taken. In all, they made a fine presentation. Officials of the National Municipal League seemed very impressed. We had a banquet on Saturday night, after spending the day looking at the displays and applications of various other cities. At the banquet, representatives of each city were introduced.

"When we left to return on Sunday morning, both Professor McCormick and I had the distinct impression, from viewing the applications and displays, that Boulder has a better chance than most of the others to be the 'All America City,' or at least one of the top three or four."

Walt Bearing raised his hand.

"Question?" intoned Professor Carlson.

"Yes. Were any of the NML officials aware that we were having a referendum to junk the city manager plan?"

"Yes," replied Professor Carlson. "Several of them asked us informally about it. Obviously they thought it a little unusual that a city should evidence so much progress since the adoption of the plan, and then experience a strong movement to repeal it. I just don't know how this will affect our chance of getting the award. We might call it an X factor. Anyway, we assured them that, although there was to be a repeal election, we were confident that the manager plan would be retained and that the election would serve as a public vote of confidence in the present system. I suppose there is a little. . . ."

Dick Wright interrupted by saying, "It sounds as if Bartles has some more results." He turned the television sound up.

"Results are now in from fourteen precincts and the school bond issue has 2,200 voting yes and 1,692 voting no. On the proposal to repeal the manager plan there are 2,349 voting yes and 2,032 voting no. In Blackfoot it appears that their. . . ."

Professor Carlson motioned to Wright to turn the volume down. Staring out at the blackness beyond the windows for a few seconds, Spence Carlson knew now that it was all over. With calmness and deliberation he faced the class.

"Well, the trend appears quite definite. The proponents of repeal have greater strength than we suspected. There are many influences which contribute to an election verdict. I will ask each of you to submit a systematic analysis of these influences as a semester paper due at a later date. For tonight, however, while freshness of the decision is upon us, perhaps it will be worth while to review some of the developments of the last few years which have had a public relations impact upon the city manager system and may have contributed to its repeal. Any comments?"

For a brief moment there was silence. Quickly it flashed through Spence Carlson's mind that it would have been better to lecture, but it was too late.

Bruce Nicholl was speaking, ". . . the most significant thing that influenced the election was the change of city managers. When Willard was here you didn't see city hall all loused up. After Grossman took over, things started fouling up and they've been that way ever since. I think the people were voting against Jim Grossman rather than against the city manager plan."

Professor Carlson recalled, while Bruce Nicholl was speaking, that Adam Nicholl, Bruce's father, had been a fellow political science student at what was then called Boulder College 25 years ago. Bruce was no less opinionated and tactless than his father.

"These are rather serious charges, Bruce. Can you be more precise? Are you saying that Grossman isn't as good a city manager as Willard was?"

"No, that's not what I meant," Nicholl replied loudly. "I think they are both good administrators. It's just that Grossman doesn't seem to have an ability to deal with the public."

"What do you mean, specifically?" queried the professor.

"Well," Nicholl responded, "remember the Annual Fourth of July program two years ago? Well, Grossman heard the carnival outfit that was here hadn't bought a city license. So what did he do? He marched right in and told them to close up! Right in the middle of the carnival! It must have been four or five hours before the carnival people could get through the city hall red tape to get the license. In the meantime the carnival was closed and a lot of children were disappointed and parents were burned up. I'll bet Bill Willard wouldn't have closed the thing down, even though he would have required them to get a license."

"That's a good example," the professor agreed. "Grossman didn't handle that situation in a judicious manner. Even so, he could have eased the pain to the public if he had made an attempt through the paper or over the radio to explain the situation. The matter was just left with the citizens without explanation. The annoyed citizens believed the city manager was a dictator who could go in and disrupt one of the city's traditional events. There were, no doubt, some people who voted against the manager plan today because of the carnival situation. Although it was a mistake for Grossman, he might have recovered, had he known how to defend and explain his actions through the media."

"But Doctor Carlson," interceded Jack Hanson, "that wasn't the last of the Annual Fourth of July celebration problems. You know we customarily hold a huge parade spectacular along University Avenue, sponsored by the Seventh Day Adventist churches in town. Just last year, on the day before the parade, the city manager through his secretary called the parade chairman to inform him that the city was entering its four new garbage trucks in the parade entourage. He didn't ask; he informed the chairman that it would be so. Wrongly or rightly, the parade chairman did not want the trucks in the parade because it would upset his ordering of the procession. The chairman tried to get in to see the city manager but was unable to do so. He left word that he wanted to discuss the matter with him, but no word at all from Grossman. The trucks appeared in the parade. Even though Grossman is a Seventh Day Adventist, the parade chairman and sponsors were greatly antagonized by his behavior. Last year's parade chairman, incidentally, a leading clothing merchant in town, worked hard during the election to retain the city manager charter."

Marshall Bird, a top scholarship student, took the floor. "Along similar lines, Professor Carlson, I believe Grossman is not conscious of the fact that he has no front office machinery for meeting the public. I know even some of the important people in town have a hard time getting to see him. In fact, I heard once that someone went in to see Grossman and his secretary said he was busy. This person glanced through the door to the manager's office on the way out and saw him sitting at his desk reading a magazine, which annoyed the caller no end.

"I also know that Grossman spent a great deal of his time talking about and formalizing his long-range programs for the city. As a result, he was not dealing with many of the problems and interests of the important people in town. I believe some of these people led the campaign to repeal the manager plan, principally because he wouldn't talk with them.

"When Bill Willard was here, he let his assistant take care of the details of the long-range planning and made similar adjustments in his time so that he had time to meet with the people who wanted to see him. Furthermore, it seems to me that Willard has the type of personality for meeting people while Grossman does not. Anyway, his daily inability to deal with the public probably hurt Grossman as much as any single element."

While Bird was speaking, Professor Carlson found himself nodding affirmatively. "That's an excellent point, Marsh. I must agree with you. Grossman has a serious problem with access. I personally have had a heck of a time trying to see him. I never had that trouble with Willard. His staff was doing as good a job of long-range planning as Grossman is. When we had the commissioner system the mayor was easy to get hold of too. Although, I must say none of the mayors ever did any decent long-range planning.

"One more example on Grossman's accessibility may be illuminating.

"Sometime during the early spring of 1961, the more prominent farmers of Boulder were invited by Grossman to a meeting in city hall. Purpose of the meeting was to encourage the farmers and other irrigation water users to organize themselves into a citizens' irrigation

FIGURE 1. ". . . *sitting at his desk reading a magazine.*"

committee. It was believed that such a committee could serve both to channel complaints and suggestions from the citizenry to the city irrigation department, and to familiarize the people with the difficult problems facing the department at that time.

"At the appointed hour, the city manager, his assistant, the city engineer, and the city water masters were all seated in the council chambers. The farmers came in as a group and began taking seats on the opposite side of the long council table. One of the farmers approached the city manager who was seated reviewing some written material on the table before him, leaned over the table, and said in a somewhat hostile voice loud enough to be heard throughout the chambers, 'Is it true that a person has to have an appointment before he can get in to see you?'

"Grossman had been in Boulder less than a year at this time and as we have observed had not practiced any kind of 'open-door' policy. For several long moments Grossman continued

to read his papers, then slowly raised his eyes to meet those of his ruddy-faced farmer accuser. As if in retaliation to the stinging words of the farmer, Grossman at last dismissed his accuser with a cold, 'That's right,' and went back to reading his papers."

At this, Morrie Roth, son of a local department store owner, interjected: "Let's not beat a dead horse, Doctor Carlson. Grossman also had some internal public relations problems, too, or you might call them problems of management relations or human relations. Remember when Grossman fired those six linemen from the utility department? He really dropped a bomb, then."

"What do you mean?"

"Well, Grossman just doesn't seem to understand the delicate balance between the regular city departments and the utility department. He just isn't willing to give an inch on the issue of whether or not he has the power to hire and fire linemen. I think he was right, according to the charter, to take this stand. But, according to the situation, it seems to me he made a big mistake. It created a feeling among city employees, and probably among residents, too, that he has no regard for the way things are traditionally done in Boulder. Thereafter, the utilities department personnel were always suspicious of his demands and tended to oppose them just for the sake of opposition. Firing those men didn't make utilities happy but it didn't frighten them either."

"Morrie, you've now got us looking at management personnel," commented Professor Carlson. "Do you students remember the confidential poll of city employees we took earlier in the campaign? It showed that almost 80 per cent of them wanted to repeal the city manager charter.

"Dick, you helped take the poll. What were some of the reasons given by employees for favoring repeal of the manager plan?"

Dick Wright thought for a moment, then responded, "Well, let's see. As I recall, they felt that under Grossman there had been a big drop in morale. Many of them commented that their low morale was related to the constant surveys and investigations being conducted by people from the city manager's office. I know that Grossman had several personnel surveys conducted by his assistant and by a couple of other people. They handed out cards asking each employee to give his position and then describe the work he does each day, and then give suggestions regarding how this work might be improved. The reasons for these surveys were never very well explained to the employees. This caused many of them to wonder if there were some possibility that their job might be eliminated. It annoyed several supervisors and department heads, too. They figured that Grossman had just sent some of his boys down to do a little snooping. I think these surveys, plus the firing of the linemen, would have caused low morale in any outfit. I'm not surprised that 80 per cent of them wanted to get rid of the manager plan."

"That illustrates well the problems Grossman is having with the employees," Professor Carlson agreed. "Similarly, when soon after his arrival the news leaked out that the new city manager was considering a consolidation of the police and fire departments, a tremendous furor was caused among the fire and police people."

Marshall Bird raised his hand again, and Professor Carlson nodded.

"There is another thing that could possibly have annoyed the public. It seems to me that when the whole idea of a possible repeal of the manager plan started, something should have been done about it. Grossman and the city council wouldn't listen to the grievances of these people. They did everything possible to keep from discussing the real issues with the people involved. They just kept putting them off. I really think that local interest groups were forced to oppose the city manager plan because the current manager would not discuss the issues which seemed to them significant.

"In addition, when it appeared that the proponents of repeal had an adequate petition to force an election on the repeal issue, the city manager had it taken to the courts to try to prevent the election. This left a bad taste in the mouths of a lot of people. The repeal group really used this in the campaign, too, by saying that the city manager didn't even want to allow the people the privilege of voting on the kind of government the city is to have. Anyway, if Grossman would have dealt with the issues when they arose this whole repeal thing might not have happened."

"It makes interesting speculation, anyway, doesn't it Marsh?" was Professor Carlson's rejoinder.

Glancing first at his watch and then through the window into the black of night, Spence Carlson could see the snow was still falling against the window pane. Thoughtfully and deliberately he concluded, "As nature is now transforming the landscape, so too the voters of Boulder have today fashioned a change in their form of municipal government. As each season has its own beauties and special advantages, so too is it possible to have effective local government administration under a variety of organizational forms. Much depends upon the competence and diplomacy of the public officials involved—councilmen, managers, department heads, police officers, counter clerks, janitors, firemen. . . .

"Tonight, as we witnessed a voter transition from one governmental form to another, we discussed one of the more critical problems facing the public administrator—his ability to deal effectively with the public and his fellow employees.

"For your term papers, which are due two weeks before the end of the semester, I want you to analyze what you consider to be all the identifiable social, political, and economic elements which had an impact on the election for charter repeal.

"See you next week."

Spence strode quietly—and alone—out of the classroom and building and onto the quad. The storm had ended. Lights from the campus lamp posts illuminated the glistening white mantle of snow which covered all. A fresh new season had come to Boulder.

Public Relations in Historical Perspective

Although the experience in Boulder is a recent dramatic illustration of the impact of "public relations" upon individuals, organizations, and activities, it is not an isolated phenomenon in time, place, or function. Rejection of the council-manager form of government in Boulder is but a variation on a public relations theme which is universal and has no recorded beginning in time.

It should be emphasized, however, that the Boulder experience is not typical of the majority of professional city administrative officers who not only administer high quality municipal services but also perform reasonably well from a public relations point of view. While only rarely will all such events transpire in a short space of time in one jurisdiction, *as they actually did in Boulder,* at least some of the events do and will occur in nearly all jurisdictions at some time or other.

FROM ANTIQUITY

Awareness of the power of popular approval and support dates from antiquity. Much of what historians know of ancient Egypt, for example, has come from literature and art which were intended to publicize and gain public favor for the then current pharaoh. The early Romans paid tribute to the forces of public opinion with the expression *vox populi, vox Dei*—"The voice of the people is the voice of God."

During the American Revolution, men like Thomas Jefferson, Samuel Adams, Thomas Paine, and Benjamin Franklin wrote pamphlets, contributed articles to the press, made speeches, and instigated word-of-mouth campaigns to stir up public support for what at the outset was not always a popular cause. The Declaration of Independence itself states that it was composed "out of a decent respect for the opinions of mankind." The eloquence of Alexander Hamilton, John Jay, and James Madison exhibited through *The Federalist* papers and activities associated therewith urging the ratification of the Constitution, was one of the most notable examples of influencing public opinion in the history of statecraft.

While history provides abundant examples of attempts to influence public opinion—and there are numerous and diverse antecedents of modern public relations—recognition of the concept of planned public relations is of more recent origin.

Two seemingly unrelated developments during the nineteenth century were among the more significant of these antecedents of modern public relations practices: (1) the creation of press-agentry, and (2) the "public-be-damned" attitude of business tycoons of that era.

THE GENESIS OF PRESS-AGENTRY

America was in the process of explosive expansion toward the undeveloped West. Fortunes were being built in banking, railroads, mining, and steel. Newspapers flourished in virtually every community as the principal, and frequently the only, medium of mass communication.

Circus owner P. T. Barnum early took heed of the growing power of the press and soon learned to use it for the promotion of his own interests. He bought many advertisements, but it was his unusual talent for obtaining free newspaper space for publicity stories which brought most of his customers to the circus box office. Thus he became the first press agent and achieved notable success through promotion of the midget, Tom Thumb; Jenny Lind, "the Swedish Nightingale"; and many more.

Professing to believe that "there's a sucker born every minute," Barnum did not hesitate to embroider the facts or, in numerous cases, to resort to pure fakery and staged events to gain notoriety which paid off so well he was able to leave an estate of $4 million when he died in 1891.

Press-agentry spread swiftly throughout most branches of show business, into advertising, and into political campaigning. It has remained as an integral part of those fields to this day.

Meanwhile, the stage was set for the next advance toward the present concept of public relations.

—AND THE "PUBLIC-BE-DAMNED"

In the years immediately following the Civil War, the nation experienced a period of unprecedented growth and expansion. It was a time of rugged individualism which saw the rapid rise of business monopolies and great concentration of wealth in the hands of a few. It was the era of the "Robber Barons" who rode roughshod over all opposition in building a new industrial empire.

Typical of the attitude of the time was the "public-be-damned" statement attributed to young William Henry Vanderbilt, son of railroad magnate Commodore Vanderbilt. Asked by reporters about the public interest in a proposed rail schedule change, young Vanderbilt is alleged to have said, "The public be damned. . . . I don't take any stock in this silly nonsense about working for anybody's good but our own because we are not. When we make a move it is because it is in our interest to do so."

REACTION AND REFORM

By 1900, there was a mounting wave of public outcry against the ruthless tactics and cynical practices of men like Vanderbilt. Theodore Roosevelt and Robert M. LaFollette soon became the leaders of a popular antibusiness revolt among elected politicians while the "muckrakers"—Lincoln Steffens, Upton Sin-

clair, Ida M. Tarbell, and others—turned their literary guns on business with articles describing illegal practices, overcharges, and corruption throughout the business world.

Faced with imminent danger from governmental action, business leaders turned to the press agents for help. For some years there was a publicity battle between the muckrakers on the one hand, bent on exposing the foulness of the large corporation, and the press agents on the other, applying huge quantities of whitewash in an attempt to belie the charges. Business almost invariably lost out in the final accounting to the public because the whitewash, in far too many cases, failed to cover the record of facts from public view.

Establishment of the profession of city management was inspired in part by the muckrakers who attacked not only big business but graft, corruption, and inefficiency of municipal government as well. In 1904, Lincoln Steffens published *The Shame of the Cities,* a vitriolic exposé of malpractices in local government. This and other similar works undoubtedly aroused and crystallized the public demand for improvement in local affairs which in subsequent years resulted in widespread adoption of the council-manager system.

In 1906, one of the press agents, Ivy Ledbetter Lee, startled the business world by proposing an unprecedented approach. The public, he said, should not be ignored in the grand manner of the Robber Barons. Neither should it be tricked and misled in the manner common to the press agent. *The public should be informed. It should be given the truth.*

Lee had been a young reporter on the *New York Evening Journal* and the *New York Times.* He had worked as a publicity man with the Democratic National Committee and in a mayoralty campaign in New York City. In 1904 he had opened a press bureau with George F. Parker, a newsman who had served as press agent for Grover Cleveland, but they met with only meager success.

Employed by the Pennsylvania Railroad and by the anthracite coal industry to put his new system into effect, Lee issued a statement to newspaper editors that illustrated his concept of public relations.

This is not a secret press bureau. All our work is done in the open. We aim to supply news. This is not an advertising agency; if you think any of our material ought properly to go to your business office, do not use it. Our matter is accurate. Further details on any subject treated will be supplied promptly and any editor will be assisted most cheerfully in verifying directly any statement of fact. . . . In brief, our plan is, frankly and openly, on behalf of business concerns and public institutions, to supply to the press and public of the United States prompt and accurate information concerning subjects which it is of value and interest to the public to know about.[2]

Indicative of the application of the new approach was the reversal of the Pennsylvania Railroad's previous policy of news suppression when a wreck occurred in 1906. Lee carried reporters to the scene of the accident at company expense.

Lee was among the vanguard of press agents who discovered that careful presentation of the facts, rather than a patchwork of deceptive phrases, would win the confidence and columns of the editors. His new approach, boldly advocated, won him both immediate financial success and recognition as "the father of public relations."

Although Lee's solution to the problems of harrassed businessmen of the period did establish certain postulates which served as a framework for development of the new art of public relations, it should not be inferred that, with a single stroke, he transformed press-agentry into public relations. During the following decades the concepts and techniques of public relations developed at a remarkably slow pace. It was not until the forties that the rate was appreciably accelerated.

Until the advent of the muckrakers, private business was considered to be *private*, and little interest was accorded public opinion. The "public-be-damned" attitude was a logical extension of this viewpoint and developed when the public inquired into what was supposedly none of its concern.

SOMETHING MORE THAN HAPHAZARD

There were those in government, however, who had some appreciation for and understanding

of public opinion. Political leaders and candidates recognized that their success or failure depended directly on the mood of the voting populace. They developed reasonably effective means of attracting votes for their party and themselves. In the earlier years, political campaigns were considered and organized as specialized, short-term affairs, a whirlwind of activity which soared to an apex on election day and collapsed nobly or ignobly with the close of the polls. While this phenomenon still prevails, political public relations has become much more sophisticated and extensive. Commercial public relations firms conduct the major political campaigns today and serve both major national parties as permanent public relations departments. The first full-time permanent publicity bureau was organized within the Democratic Party in 1929. Both parties now regularly advise their candidates to retain individual public relations counselors and successful officeholders often name public relations people and publicity experts as their administrative assistants.[3]

In corporate enterprise, increasing reliance on public relations resulted from a variety of influences such as resentment and suspicion of business for its adverse practices and monopolistic and ruthless suppression of competition, and the anticipation of government ownership and operation of certain sectors of the economy highly vested with the public interest. Accordingly, those interests which turned first and most frequently to the newspapermen and journalists for their publicity *expertise* were the railroads, electrical utilities, the oil and gas industry, and steel and insurance companies. This trend was highly accelerated following first, the Great Depression with its social reform and accompanying criticism of business tycoons as economic royalists and second, the peculiar circumstances of World War II which demanded spectacular accomplishments of American business and industry. With these developments there has been an appreciable

---

[2] Quoted in Sherman Morse, "An Awakening in Wall Street," AMERICAN MAGAZINE September, 1906, p. 460.

[3] For the most complete account of the role and extent of professional public relations in political parties and campaigns, see Stanley Kelley, Jr., PROFESSIONAL PUBLIC RELATIONS and POLITICAL POWER (Baltimore: The Johns Hopkins Press, 1956), 247pp.

change from defensive and occasional propaganda campaigns to continuous publicity and public relations programs.

Today there is no private enterprise which does not engage in some publicity and other public relations activities and hardly any business or industry of any consequence which does not have a formalized public relations program and personnel.

Paralleling these developments were the publicity imperatives of government. There has always been a need for government publicity, if for no other reason than to inform citizens of the services available and the manner in which they may be used. With the developing complexity of government there was a corresponding increase in publicity. This function was assigned to someone, irrespective of titles and principal functions performed, whether statisticians, administrative assistants, or clerks.

Administrative agencies of government disseminate substantial amounts of information. Various governmental officials compile and prepare such data to inform the public of services available from government and of duties required of citizens by governmental regulations.

By 1913, the United States Civil Service Commission was bold enough to announce an examination for a "Publicity Expert" whose ". . . affiliations with newspaper publishers and writers is extensive enough to secure the publication of items prepared by him."[4] Although this caused a Congressional furor, the functions continued to be performed, and in 1917 President Wilson appointed George Creel as head of the Committee on Public Information. The Creel Committee operated as a large-scale propaganda agency during the war as it channeled information both externally to other countries and internally to citizens at home.

With new-found vigor bred of social change, the alphabet agencies of FDR's New Deal, beginning with the Blue Eagle of the NRA (National Recovery Administration), precipitated a flood-tide of publicists into the channels of government. The flow was only accelerated during and following World War II with the establishment of such agencies as the Office of War Information (OWI) and the present United States Information Agency (USIA) which operates as an information channel for American diplomacy.

Such activity has had its effect upon Congress which has sought, sometimes unsuccessfully, to curb especially those programs designed to influence public opinion and legislative action. These efforts have been initiated in part by Congressional fear and jealousy of the growing power of the bureaucracy. An interesting coincidence of dates occurs when it is noted that in 1913 Congress forbade the hiring of "publicity experts" by government departments and followed this up in 1919 by prohibiting expenditures for influencing Congress. This prohibition was again repeated in 1939 by a petulant Congress annoyed at some New Deal agency. Despite such prohibitions, administrative agencies not only play an important part in the legislative process but are engaged extensively in public relations activities.

Commonplace today are news releases, press conferences, myriad reports, information bulletins and other governmental publications, Post Office posters, and a vast array of armed services activities from the radio musicale to the base athletic team. Even the earlier Congressional and citizen hostility which led to the shift from PRO (Public Relations Officer) to PIO (Public Information Officer) has gradually diminished.

Similar developments have occurred in state and local governments although at a significantly slower pace. Through the land-grant university system, established and promoted by national legislation and state enabling legislation, a vast network of public relations ambassadors has been in existence for over a half-century, blending the interests of national, state, and local levels of government. Although several states on their own accord had already instituted agricultural advisers within their states, the Smith-Lever Act of 1914 established the basis of a federal system, involving cooperative effort and financing by national, state, and local levels of government.

[4] PRELIMINARY REPORT of the Select Committee to Investigate the Executive Agencies of the Government, United States Senate, 75th Congress, 1st session, pp. 531–32.

Resembling itinerant teachers initially, the county agricultural and home demonstration agents have been active for many years in every state in the union. Their role is to teach, enlighten, and assist farmers and housewives through use of the most effective techniques, publications, and recent research findings, translating the new insights and data into meaningful applications in the lives of each person contacted. Today, through the state cooperative extension services, more than 3,000 county agents are quietly improving the lives of individual citizens. This is not the typical public relations functionary, but a significant and useful prototype nonetheless.

Of the more traditional variety, Wright and Christian observed that by 1949 nearly every state in the nation had established a state-supported public relations program to lure tourists and industries to their states.[5]

At the regional level, bridging state-local interests, the Port of New York Authority in 1945 opened an office in Chicago "to promote and protect the commerce of the Port of New York" by seeking to prevent diversion of mid-western commerce to Gulf and other North Atlantic ports. This was a feature of their planned public relations program.[6]

The most systematic efforts to promote effective public relations at the local level have been undertaken by the International City Managers' Association which adopted a code of ethics for managers in 1924 and proposed a more extensive system of codes and creeds for all municipal officials and employees in 1962. Many of the ICMA training manuals have chapters on public relations, and in 1940 ICMA published a monograph by Elton Wool-pert on *Municipal Public Relations*. Although a survey by ICMA in 1962 showed that the overwhelming majority of municipalities had no formal public relations programs, many individual managers have pioneered effective public relations techniques, and a few munici-pal reports are among the most distinctive and best produced by human effort.

The role of other groups and associations also has been effective at the municipal level. For a long time the Government Public Relations Association, now defunct, through the efforts especially of Pan Dodd Wheeler, stimulated local jurisdictions to develop a conscious awareness of municipal public relations. The National League of Cities, the National Association of Counties, the various state leagues of cities and counties, all have promoted actively better public relations. Similarly influential have been the several specialized associations such as the Public Personnel Association which in 1941 published the manual, *Public Relations of Public Personnel Agencies*.

Irrespective of the extent of development of public relations in government and business, as Stanley Kelley has remarked,

No more than it can be viewed solely as a phenomenon of the business world, however, can public relations be treated as a creature cosponsored by business and government. If the public relations man has found his way into business and government, he has also found a market for his talents with almost every other contemporary institution of importance: professional groups; social service or-ganizations; charitable institutions; religious groups; schools and colleges; and state and local govern-ments.[7]

Public Relations Distinctions between Business and Government

Whatever the similarities in the applications and uses of publicity and public relations in government and business, there are certain distinctions which relate to purpose, organiza-tion, ethics and morals, and public scrutiny. These distinctions condition the impact in each case.

PURPOSE

Private business exists to make a profit by selling goods and services to the public whereas government exists to serve the people on a nonprofit basis. As a result of this distinction, business public relations programs are oriented to the *sales and profit* motive, while govern-

[5] J. Handly Wright and Byron H. Christian, PUBLIC RELATIONS IN MANAGEMENT (New York: McGraw Hill Book Company, 1949), p. 168.
[6] *Loc. cit.*

[7] *Op. cit.*, p. 16.

ment public relations must evolve from a *service* viewpoint.

Often in business the public relations program is made a part of or subservient to the sales program. Advertising, the principal means of mass salesmanship, receives a major share of the sales budget, which in itself may be a considerable portion of the entire company budget. The public relations department, except for its lobbying duties when those duties are so assigned, frequently is organized as a division of advertising by many firms. It is this emphasis on sales which sometimes leads the public relations executive to accede to or even suggest policies and practices which may boost sales at the ultimate expense of good relations with the public. Misleading advertising, tricky slogans, and the stuntsmanship of press-agentry are among these efforts and may inspire harsh criticism of public relations *per se* when, in fact, such practices are opposed by ethical public relations practitioners.

Governments, on the other hand, are differently motivated. Other than required legal advertising, most jurisdictions use little paid advertising space in print or time on the air. As a complex of public services, they usually receive substantial amounts of free advertising in the form of news stories about the services they provide. The mayor or city manager or sometimes the governor may be offered the opportunity of writing a regular column for a local newspaper. Free time on radio or television may likewise be available to officials who have a story to tell and know how to tell it.

Because there is great public interest in the activities of government, especially local government, the nation's press is willing to provide jurisdictions with newspaper space and air time which it sells dearly to private enterprise.

ORGANIZATION

The corporate enterprise is a legal entity established under and required to comply with a somewhat limited number of lawful procedures. On the other hand, all governmental levels in American democratic society are circumscribed and limited. For example, the municipal corporation is a legal entity rigidly prescribed by law, restricted to limited and specified powers, formally established procedure and method, and, in general, rigorously bound up in legalistic "red tape" in all of its principal activities. These society-imposed safeguards and restrictions make the municipality vulnerable because the public may and often does develop an impression of slowness due to inefficiency rather than legal circumscription.

Obviously, the effect on the citizen of such seeming dalliance is negative and constitutes a serious problem in public relations. This may be better viewed as a public relations challenge, however. The ordinary citizen regularly sees his local government in a deprivational role—taking his money for taxes, giving him a traffic ticket, requiring him to secure a building permit, making him maintain his property in a given way. It is no wonder that the ordinary citizen is occasionally upset with "city hall."

On the other hand, local government does a very great deal that is not deprivational. How much do the citizens know of the successful recreation program, the improved street drainage system, the reduced fire insurance rates? Is not the public official responsible for informing citizens of all local governmental activity of consequence? Clearly the majority of local governmental programs is positive and non-deprivational. The private corporation, on the other hand, need not be concerned for whatever deprivational qualities their product may have. There are none.

ETHICAL AND MORAL DISTINCTIONS

Although there is considerable evidence of evolving business ethics, it seems fair to observe that many businesses, like many individuals, comply with ethical and moral standards only as far as they are established and enforced by law. Legislation such as the Pure Food and Drug Act, Fair Trade Act, Child Labor Law, Sherman Anti-Trust Act, and many others demonstrate the need for policing, rather than morality, to serve as a guide and deterrent. Many businessmen bluntly contend that they have every right to go "as far as the law allows" in the conduct of their firm's affairs.

Government, conversely, creates and enacts legislation, enforces the law, and adjudicates charges of wrong-doing. It not only enforces the law against individuals and business firms, it also enforces the law against its own employees and, in some cases, against itself. Government is thus symbolic of fair play, law and order, and justice in both the abstract and concrete.

In the case of a municipality, every intended decision to act in an unprecedented manner must be evaluated not only as to its legal character but also with regard for ethical and moral standards. Every city government has far greater powers than it exercises. The restraint is frequently traceable to ethical or moral grounds.

The higher standards required of government are often reflected in the behavior pattern the public expects of government employees. Should a business executive be arrested for drunkenness, he would probably escape with a small fine and a razzing from fellow employees. Should a city manager face a similar charge, he would be almost certain of losing his position. Such is the double standard of expected behavior distinguishing the public servant from the businessman. Another aspect of the double standard is reflected by the fact that the citizenry not only accepts but expects the practice of publicity and advertisement by business, but regards government public information activities as wasteful of the taxpayers' money and essentially propagandistic.

Another aspect of morality in government derives from the fact that government is monopolistic while private enterprise is expected to meet competition. The city council and city manager must attempt to provide good services at reasonable cost merely because it is their responsibility to do so. There is no direct competition to the city in most of its services and therefore no means of comparing either quality or price of the service. The citizen must take what the city provides. This pessimistic note should be modified, however, by the realization that there is in fact quality comparison from jurisdiction to jurisdiction; if the local officials do not measure up to quality standards of performance and service elsewhere they should not be retained in office.

In business, the competitive factor serves to force each firm to improve products and to reduce prices to attract customers who do have a choice. Relative absence of the competitive factor makes it incumbent on public officials to maintain a high sense of public duty.

PUBLIC SCRUTINY

Although all private enterprise is affected to some degree by public interest considerations, the business world conducts its affairs in an atmosphere of comparative calm and privacy. The world of government appears to belong to another universe. As the late Paul Appleby, noted scholar and public official, observed,

Government administration differs from all other administrative work to a degree not even faintly realized outside, by virtue of its public nature, the way in which it is subject to public scrutiny and public outcry. An administrator coming into government is struck at once, and continually thereafter, by the press and public interest in every detail of his life, personality, and conduct. This interest often runs to details of administrative action that in private business would never be of concern other than inside the organization. Each employee hired, each one demoted, transferred, or discharged, every efficiency rating, every assignment of responsibility, each letter, has to be thought about in terms of possible public agitation, investigation, or judgment. Everything has to be considered in terms of what any employee anywhere may make of it, for any employee may be building a file of things that could be made publicly embarrassing. Any employee who later may be discharged is a potentially powerful enemy, for he can reach the press and Congress with whatever charges his knothole perspective may have invited. Charges of wrongdoing on the part of a government official are always news, no matter who makes the charge, for every former employee is regarded as a source of authoritative and inside information.

In private business the same employee would be discredited by the very fact of having been discharged. Government employees number far less than nongovernment employees, but the cases of discharged government workers getting into the public prints with denunciations of their former chiefs must be at least a thousand times more frequent. A person discharged is always offended. But whereas a person discharged from a private job is of little interest to the press, the dismissal of a person from a public job is regarded as public business.[8]

In municipal administration, meetings at which decisions of any consequence will be

8 Paul H. Appleby, BIG DEMOCRACY (New York: Alfred A. Knopf, 1945), p. 7.

made are ordinarily announced in advance and held in public. They are attended by the public and covered by the press. Numerous states have legislation, such as the Brown Act in California, which either prohibits or severely restricts the holding of any nonpublic meeting attended by a majority of the council members. The intent is to avert the making of private "deals" by unscrupulous councilmen.

While there are other distinctions between business and government having a public relations impact, it is clear that the philosophy and techniques of public relations are conditioned by these distinctions. Emphasizing these differences is essential because of the tendency to identify public relations with business and thus with a salesmanship approach. Perhaps the principal reason is that commercial public relations has been the dominant force in developing the public relations profession.

Political Considerations

Despite the slow development of the formal public relations functions in government, public relations has been operative in government longer than in any other field of practice. The slowness of development is attributable in considerable measure to the fact that suspicion and hostility from the public have been directed toward the elaboration of the publicity functions in government with an intensity not felt by public relations practitioners in most other areas. Historically, this hostility has been nourished by certain fundamental cleavages, such as the classical struggle for power implicit in executive-legislative relations at all levels of government, the unrelenting efforts of major political parties to gain majority control of government, and the inevitable clash between vigilant newsmen seeking to inform the public and discretionary public officials who restrain the search for news for various reasons.

Every resort to typical public relations or information activities is fraught with danger of charges that government information is invidious propaganda for the executive branch, the party in power, or a controversial program, or constitutes a screening and hence a suppression of legitimate information about the administrative agencies or the prevailing political party.

Stemming from the early political traditions of this country, Americans have always been suspicious of anything connoting propaganda, a suspicion which has been heightened by observation of the cunning success with which propaganda techniques have been utilized in other countries by dictators to gain despotic control of their governments.

The suspicion and hostility in legislative-executive forays moves in both directions. The use of an obviously edited film of the so-called student riots in San Francisco in 1960 as a vehicle to prolong the life of the House Un-American Activities Committee and the widespread charges in 1961 of administrative muzzling of the military, set off by a program of political indoctrination of American troops in Germany, are indicative of the continuing battle at the federal level. Objections to films as a form of municipal reporting, including charges of exorbitant waste of tax funds, are typical at the local level.

Current charges of Communist control and domination of "Thirteen-thirteen," including ICMA, and of the city manager profession by vocal minorities hoping to gain municipal control, are often set off by legitimate public information releases by municipalities which tend to display the city manager form of government in a favorable light. The widespread publicity, during 1961, heralding drastic changes in the application of welfare laws by the city of Newburgh, New York, evoked extensive political controversy across the nation.

The jaundiced regard of newsmen for secret or executive sessions of city councils or executive bodies of administrative agencies is frequently in evidence. Yet effective public relations and information programs at all levels of government serve to diminish antagonisms to the extent that they facilitate the expression of citizen desires regarding governmental programs and develop within the community a high regard for the integrity of those who are administratively responsible. To explore the parameters of this challenge in municipal government is the purpose of the next chapter.

2

Public Relations and the Administrative Process

A PREREQUISITE TO responsible and effective administration is understanding a function and how it fits into the administrative process. Yet the elusiveness of a precise statement of the public relations function is a barrier to effective understanding and control. In the previous chapter, without defining the term with precision, certain facets of its appearance and function were described. As will be seen in the following paragraphs, one of the major difficulties in effectively defining the term resides in the very nature of the process involved and of the difficulty of distinguishing between public relations functions and management functions.

Universality of Public Relations

Public relations is a composite of relationships, both human and institutional. It is both the reflection and the substance of public opinion. It includes all of the contacts within and extending outside an agency—personal or impersonal, direct or indirect, specific or general. The frequency, variety, and inclusiveness of such contacts indicate the pervasiveness of public relations throughout society. The handshake of the mayor, the voice of the telephone operator, the job done by the streetsweeper, all establish relationships with the public, relationships which contribute positively or negatively to the sum total of public opinion about a public jurisdiction, whether a municipality or UNESCO. Every governmental jurisdiction,

every agency within a municipality, every individual obviously has public relations. Such relations may be consistently good and resultant public opinion high, or they may be poor or otherwise with a corresponding public attitude. Wherever man is, public relations simply exists as a matter of fact, irrespective of what is done or not done and regardless of quality. In this sense, public relations is pervasive.

In a sense, all public relations is personal; thus, *an agency's public relations is a composite of relationships for all persons in the agency.*

THE INTERMINABLE DEFINITIONS

Our understanding of the meaning of public relations is still fluid—it is yet evolving and defining itself.

Broadly Construed. Several writers, in efforts to avoid misconception and inaccuracy, have concluded that public relations must be defined in broad generalities. Thus, public relations is conceived as the sum of all contacts, attitudes, impressions, and opinions, both direct and indirect, which constitute the relationships between a government and its various publics.[1] This is sometimes modified to suggest that it is the sum of the actions by which the attitudes of an organization's publics are created, changed, or reinforced.

---

[1] See, for example, James L. McCamy, GOVERNMENT PUBLICITY (Chicago: University of Chicago Press, 1939), 275pp., and THE TECHNIQUE OF MUNICIPAL ADMINISTRATION (Chicago: The International City Managers' Association, 3rd ed., 1947), p. 486.

Rex F. Harlow once described the broad scope of public relations as follows:

> . . . public relations includes all that is thought, said and done to create and maintain effective relations between an institution and its public. Public relations is a broad term which covers an enormous range of activities. . . . Necessarily, public relations rests upon the social sciences: economics, sociology, psychology, political science, history and philosophy, to mention only a few of the more conspicuously related fields. In addition, public relations is generally taken to include such working tools as the press, the radio, motion pictures, printing, public speaking and professional writing.[2]

Obviously, no individual or vocation can be expected reasonably to develop expertise in all of the areas indicated, nor did Harlow think it possible to build a profession of public relations on such a broad base. He urged a selection and limitation of scope. During the intervening years, there have been attempts to delimit, specify, and clarify, but ambiguity and dispute still remain.

With Management Connotations. Although public relations involvement in the administrative process has been obvious, appropriate distinctions have not always been clear. Wright and Christian, while recognizing that public relations is primarily good management, directed from the top but involving every person within or connected with an organization, claimed that "Modern public relations is a *planned program* of *policies* and *conduct* that will build *public confidence* and increase *public understanding.*"[3]

Among the efforts to develop a theoretical and professional base for public relations was a search for a proper definition of the term conducted by the editors of *Public Relations News*. Some 2,000 replies were received which variously characterized public relations as ". . . a science; a system; an art; a process; a function; a relationship; a humanizing genius; a term; a business; a profession; a method; an

activity; a program; a policy; a pattern of behavior; a moral force."[4]

Synthesizing the many definitions with their own insight, editors Glenn and Denny Griswold concluded that "Public relations is the management function which evaluates public attitudes, identifies the policies and procedures of an individual or organization with the public interest, and executes a program of action to earn public understanding and acceptance."[5]

Although many other definitions have been contrived, the Griswold definition has become essentially standard and has been repeated in many texts.[6] It embraces a concern for policy determination which is overlooked in other definitions. Many of the simpler definitions, for example, demonstrate a concern only for the elements of good performance and favorable recognition, which has resulted in an even simpler mnemonic formulation of:

P (for performance), plus

R (for reporting), equals

PR (public relations).

This definition, however, does not distinguish between nor identify separate spheres of action for public relations and management.

Distinguishing Some of the Facets. Caught on the horns of this dilemma, some writers have avoided its resolution simply by distinguishing among certain facets associated with the public relations function.

In his monograph prepared for the International City Managers' Association in 1940, Elton Woolpert sought to minimize confusion by distinguishing between the influences of cause and effect. He used the term "public relations" to refer to the *relationships* between the municipality and its several publics and the terms "public relations programs" or "public relations activities" to refer to *policies* and

---

[2] Rex F. Harlow, "Public Relations at the Crossroads," PUBLIC OPINION QUARTERLY, Winter, 1944–45, p. 554.

[3] J. Handly Wright and Byron H. Christian, PUBLIC RELATIONS IN MANAGEMENT (New York: McGraw-Hill Book Company, 1949), p. 3.

[4] Denny Griswold, PUBLIC RELATIONS COMES OF AGE (Boston: Boston University School of Public Relations, 1947), p. 3.

[5] *Ibid.*

[6] See, for example, Scott M. Cutlip and Allen H. Center, EFFECTIVE PUBLIC RELATIONS (Englewood Cliffs, New Jersey: Prentice-Hall, Inc., 2nd ed., 1958), p. 5, and Gene Harlan and Alan Scott, CONTEMPORARY PUBLIC RELATIONS: PRINCIPLES AND CASES (Englewood Cliffs, New Jersey: Prentice-Hall, 1955), p. 4.

activities designed to improve relationships with these publics.[7]

In their book on municipal supervision, Sherwood and Best identify in a different way two kinds of public relations which they call *operative* and *communicative*. Operative public relations involves what is done in the course of administering a program while communicative public relations is concerned with efforts to tell others what is done.[8]

The authors of a widely used text, Cutlip and Center, attempt a distinction between management and public relations roles with the terms *operating concept of management* and a *specialized staff function in management*. The first, they write, is a static, general principle which guides administrators and is the responsibility of every person identified with an enterprise, while the second is a dynamic specialized function for which managers hire skilled practitioners.[9] Although it is doubtful that their distinction is clear and unambiguous, it is useful to note that there are certain sets of tasks and activities in the administrative process which when grouped together may occupy part or all of the time of one or more employees on the management team.

Webster's New International Dictionary provides a point of departure for still another pair of distinctions regarding public relations. Paraphrasing the dictionary definition of public relations, the term may be viewed as: (1) the *relationships* of an enterprise with its publics; (2) the *quality* or *state* of such activities and relationships; and (3) the *art* or *science* of achieving favorable relationships.[10] All are concerned with *relationships,* their existence, how good they are, and how they are achieved. These are the broad concerns of administration generally.

Woolpert's pair relate to (1) and (3) of Webster; the Sherwood and Best pair and the pair of Cutlip and Center relate primarily to Webster's number (3).

There is still a fourth pair of distinctions which may be useful in this context: public relations as *concept* or idea and public relations as *process*. The former symbolizes the notion and trade or specialty of public relations to which many segments of the public, both past and present, react adversely; the latter relates to the function itself as a human process, however labeled, and embraces all three of the facets of the Webster definition.

The Confusion Matrix. The multifaceted activities of the governmental administrator in program and policy formulation and implementation all have public relations implications. This is the essence of the administrative process—a continuous interweaving of policy and program within which public relations is inextricably interwoven. This is why identification of the public relations function in government has been confused and confusing. This is why some writers, as they have advocated professional recognition for public relations, have exalted public relations functions above all else;[11] this accounts for the fact that rebellious others have concluded there is no such thing as public relations as an identifiable, separable, and purposeful activity.[12]

Much of the confusion over definition in the past has been concerned with public relations as concept, with efforts of the tradesmen and writers to dignify it with the aspects of profession and to define it so as to overcome its unsavory connotations. Thus these definitions have moved to a closer identification with

---

[7] Elton D. Woolpert. MUNICIPAL PUBLIC RELATIONS: A SUGGESTED PROGRAM FOR IMPROVING RELATIONS WITH THE PUBLIC (Chicago: International City Managers' Association, 1940), p. 1.

[8] Frank P. Sherwood and Wallace H. Best, SUPERVISORY METHODS IN MUNICIPAL ADMINISTRATION (Chicago: The International City Managers' Association, 1958), p. 272.

[9] *Op. cit.*, p. 6.

[10] WEBSTER'S NEW INTERNATIONAL DICTIONARY, second edition, 1934, 1939, 1945, 1950, 1952, 1954, 1957 (G. and C. Merriam Co.).

[11] See, for example, Eva Aronfreed, "Public Relations as a Function of Local Government in the United States," pp. 74 and 87, in Martinus Nijhoff, editor, LOCAL GOVERNMENT IN THE UNITED STATES OF AMERICA (The Hague, Netherlands: International Union of Local Authorities, 1961), 133pp.

[12] See, for example, Alan Harrington, "The Self-Deceivers," in ESQUIRE September, 1959, pp. 59–65, in which he, a former public relations specialist, describes public relations as ". . . the craft of arranging the truth . . ." and its practitioners as merchants of "images." Too eloquent to be paraphrased, too beguiling to avoid, the entire article should be read in the original.

management itself without adequately distinguishing respective roles.

It is here contended that public relations as *concept* can best be dealt with by concentrating on effective administrative performance, which is public relations as *process*. When substantive performance is repeatedly well done, then public relations as *concept* will rise in public favor through its own gravitational relationships with process. It is, therefore, public relations as *process,* an integral part of the governmental administrative process, with which this book is primarily concerned.

Rational Administrative Model

Any public relations model which purports to explain relationships in a governmental social system must be predicated on (1) the relationship of public relations to the decision process, and (2) the inseparability of public relations from the politics of government. Public relations as an inherent part of the managerial process is fundamentally based in administrative theory. Chester I. Barnard has postulated that the authority of any managerial order lies with the persons to whom it is addressed, and not in those actually issuing the command.[13] Some orders, he believes, never should be issued because they never will be obeyed. Within what he calls a "zone of indifference," orders are unquestionably accepted, while the breadth of the zone depends on the net inducements which the individual finds in this cooperation. Similarly, sociologists who have studied the administrative process have evolved the view that the concepts of control and consent are indivisible, that authority is permissive, being grounded on its acceptability by those over whom the authority is exercised.

These views are not unknown to the practicing administrator who realizes that he must develop consent to his authority. The behavior of President Lyndon B. Johnson in developing broad consensus among various segments of the American electorate as a basis for effective administration is highly illuminating in this respect.

The successful manager knows that he must establish his authority within the organization, that he must build advance consent to the orders he issues as part of routine operations. He knows that development of organizational responsiveness to his directives is one of the more highly important aspects of his job as a manager.

Administrative organizations may be viewed as cooperative systems. Such a system demands legitimation of authority through the voluntary consent which must precede all obedience. The administrative process may be viewed as an overlapping sequence of events involving the formulation and implementation of decisions. Consent to decisions made within the administrative process therefore must be viewed as a condition of their successful and effective execution. This view may be extended with equal logic to those persons external to the formal organization. As Barnard has noted, the boundaries of any organization extend to all those parties involved in the total organizational activity, including the organization's suppliers, customer-clients, employees, and others who may affect or be affected by organizational decisions and actions.

Within this theoretical framework lies the basis for public relations. It is grounded on the view that successful implementation of any decision is a function of the acceptability of that decision to those from whom a response is necessary. These persons may be located either within or outside the formal organization structure. When directed toward persons outside the formal structure, development of consent is considered to be public relations; however, the process and the need for its application is not different in kind from fostering and negotiating internal employee consent.

PUBLIC RELATIONS IN THE
ADMINISTRATIVE PROCESS

While theoretically it may be possible to equate everything with public relations, some operations in the administrative process have

13 Chester I. Barnard, THE FUNCTIONS OF THE EXECUTIVE (Cambridge: Harvard University Press, 1958), pp. 163–71.

more public relations significance than others.[14]

Determination of Purpose and Operations Analysis. Decision-making is predicated on identification of the problem and consideration of means-ends alternatives. Attitudes of people both inside and outside the formal organization comprise variables of significance to the final choice and may assume importance greater than abstract considerations of economy and efficiency. Public relations can be viewed as a significant aspect of this process, involving:

1. Collection and evaluation of data which reveal the character and requirements of the organizational environment. Public opinion and attitude surveys, personal contacts, newspaper clippings, correspondence, and public complaints reaching the organization are sources of such data. The process also includes identification of the critical decision centers, or "thought leaders" and "power centers," in the organizational environment, determination of their requirements, and assessment of how they will react to and affect organizational means-ends alternatives.

2. Evaluation of organizational means-ends alternatives in terms of the organizational environment. Are they appropriate? What will be the effect if implemented?

3. Modification of means-ends alternatives to accommodate them to the organizational environment.

The selection of appropriate means-ends alternatives by administrators is dependent on a broad spectrum of views, information and data, and expertise within the organization. Since public relations is a condition of effective and efficient organizational performance, it follows that public relations skills and the "public relations point of view" must everywhere be present within the organization.

Facilitating Communication. As a general approach to communication within the organization, Litchfield has suggested that:

The effectiveness of a programmed decision will vary with the extent to which it is communicated to those of whom action is required. . . . The administrator must establish the channels, the methods, and the opportunities for communicating with all of those above, below, and around him whose actions he would influence. . . . He must establish channels and provide the opportunity for others to communicate with him. . . . He must assure the existence of channels of communication among all those in the organization who must influence one another if the organization is to achieve its total objectives. . . . Communications is a method by which an individual or group transmits stimuli which modify the behavior of another individual or group.[15]

It should be added that the extent to which individuals are involved in the means-ends determination process often establishes to a considerable degree the extent to which such decisions are acceptable to them and, in turn, the degree to which they support or resist such decisions. An effective communication system facilitates their involvement.

The task of ordering and structuring communications among an organization and significant groups and persons within its environment is a matter of increasing complexity requiring highly developed skills and expertise. Recommended organizational purposes and means must be presented to relevant segments of the environment in a manner that will reveal their compatibility with the value systems, mores, and other means-ends choices of that environment.

Influencing Attitudes. The implementation of agency programs, however legitimate their source and evolution, is dependent on their acceptability to several significant publics within the environment. It requires appropriate cooperation and services from them. If such programs are not fully consonant with prevailing value systems, then only limited choices are open, such as (1) abandonment or substantial modification of the program, or (2) alteration of the prevailing value systems.

Assuming the desirability of the proposed programs, then program advocacy—influenc-

---

[14] Barnard holds that administrative functions involve three central tasks: (1) establishing goals, (2) developing and maintaining a system of communication, and (3) securing cooperation and services from individuals in the organization. *Ibid.*, Chapter XV. These three tasks are here adapted to portray public relations significance.

[15] Edward H. Litchfield, "Notes on a General Theory of Administration," ADMINISTRATIVE SCIENCE QUARTERLY, Spring, 1956.

ing, molding, and altering value systems within the environment—becomes critical to the successful governmental administrator. While program advocacy is thus clearly an administrative function it also has crucial public relations implications.

ADMINISTRATIVE BASE FOR PUBLIC RELATIONS

Although most public relations units in traditional organizations are primarily concerned with sampling attitudes and opinions and with certain facets of communications, herein we assume a broader base. Public relations is both an influence upon and a consequence of program achievement. No one within an organization can be absolved of public relations responsibility. Attitude surveys and opinion sampling performed by the public relations staff have organizational and program significance far more pervasive than the usually conceived public relations needs. Publicity and communications are much more fundamental than "image-building"; they lie at the heart of program achievement. Consequently, as will be observed later in this chapter, it is proposed that the traditional public relations office or function be expanded into an *operational effectiveness unit.*

Urban Ecology as Setting

Public relations as process may be considered in general terms, with variations dependent on particular environments. Since we are here concerned with public relations in the governmental setting, and more specifically with local government public relations, it is appropriate to analyze the special circumstances of the urban environment.

GOVERNMENT AS A SALIENT FEATURE OF CONTEMPORARY AMERICA

An almost overwhelming transformation has occurred with respect to government during the present generation. This transformation is featured by a monumental increase in the role, variety, and significance of government in contemporary life. As Odegard and Baerwald have observed:

A century ago, on the eve of the Civil War, for a population of 31,000,000 the federal government employed some 66,000 persons (civilian 50,000 and military 16,000), had an income of $41.5 million, expenditures exceeding $66.6 million, and a national debt of $90 million. By 1961, the number of employees had grown to more than 5 million, about equally divided between civilian and military, federal revenues to more than $87 billion, expenditures to over $88 billion, and a federal debt was in the neighborhood of $300 billion. It thus appears that between 1861 and 1961, while the population of the United States has multiplied about six times, from 31,000,000 to 180,000,000, the number of civil and military employees of the federal government has increased nearly 80 times, the national debt more than 3,000 times, and federal income and expenditures 1,300 times. Even allowing for changes in the value of the dollar, federal expenditures have increased many times as fast as the population. And if one adds the expenditures of state and local governments, the total is even more impressive. The 11,000,000 civilian and military employees of federal, state, and local governments now represent more than one out of every six persons gainfully employed and a total payroll in excess of 40 billion dollars a year.[16]

MULTIPLYING FUNCTIONS AT THE LOCAL LEVEL

Transformation at the local level has brought new obligations for cities. They facilitate industry and commerce, aid the sick and poor, protect the well, safeguard life and property, and provide uncounted conveniences for householders.

Most cities have a reasonably pure and adequate water supply. Pumping machinery has been improved greatly, and water is used liberally and widely. Before 1909 well-paved streets were usually confined to business and select residential districts while today the unpaved street is encountered only in undeveloped sections. Collection of garbage and rubbish was formerly the personal problem of each householder, but city-wide sanitary collection is now the rule. A few years ago, street cleaning was limited to downtown mainstreets by hand broom, in addition to seasonal cleaning in spring and fall throughout the city. Today streets are cleaned regularly with dustles motor-

---

[16] Peter H. Odegard and Hans H. Baerwald, THE AMERICAN REPUBLIC: ITS GOVERNMENT AND POLITICS (New York: Harper & Row, 1964), p. 4.

ized sweeping machines and flushers. A few years ago, sewers were turned into some river bed or creek while now most cities are completely sewered, and the sewage is treated by scientific methods at treatment plants.

City planning was a dream of a city beautiful less than a generation ago while today it is accepted as a major social responsibility. An accompaniment of the master plan has been the zoning concept which grew from two feeble attempts in 1909 until in 1963 90 per cent of cities over 10,000 population have such laws on the books. Parks date from 1858, but their full use was not realized until recently with such features as picnic grounds, golf courses, outdoor theaters, athletic fields, and often a zoo and a swimming pool.

It is not difficult to recollect the horse-drawn hook and ladder and the steamer of earlier years, but today firefighting equipment is motorized and specialized. Chemicals have replaced water for certain types of fires and fire prevention has become a well-organized activity. It is possible to remember the policemen on horseback, usually hired through political pull. Now police applicants are subjected to aptitude and other psychological tests; police schools are flourishing; scientific laboratories, once a source of mirth to detectives, are operating; accurate records of crimes reported are no longer the graveyards of ambitious chiefs; and radio has demonstrated its utility in apprehending criminals.

Public health formerly meant little more than maintaining contagious disease quarantine. Now public health activities include free serums, free clinics, home nursing service, community mental health centers, instruction in prenatal care, infant welfare, and tuberculosis control. Sanitary control over food, milk, meat, and housing has been strengthened.

Municipalities today are governments of science and invention, of segregated budgets and accrual accounting, of serial bonds and sinking funds, of electrophotometers, rapid sand filters, activated sludge, kilowatts and peak loads, of computers and research programs, and so on through a long list of technical services which the citizen demands but for which he sometimes does not want to pay.

Urban Frenetics[17]

Central to the transformation occurring is the shift from rural to urban populations. In 1864 half of the employed people worked on the farm. A century later only one in 12 is a farm worker. Thus, the principal feature of municipalities today is urbanism, with its accompanying bigness, complexity, variety, vitality, and confusion.

In the burgeoning growth of urbanism in America, both abundance and blight have sprawled uncontrolled across the land. In the wake of each surge have appeared cluttered and butchered landscapes; polluted water and air; tangled and congested transportation and traffic; inadequate schools, housing, and recreational facilities; conflicting and overlapping jurisdictions and governmental patterns; and prolific urban inhabitants whose anxieties are so paradoxical and overwhelming that they find expression in deviant behavior of both youth and adults, a behavior which erodes and destroys human values and physical resources, which curtails and precludes human growth, development, and fulfillment. Man appears bestial, and survival and plunder his jungle trappings.

But cities and urban places also are where man desires to live and where, with accelerating pace, he is congregating. It is in urban places where most of our universities, research centers, museums, and libraries are located and where literacy is high as man finds maximum opportunities for intellectual growth and stimulation. It is in urban places where virtually all of the nation's music centers, art galleries, performing arts studios, and creative workshops are thriving and where man's desires are matched by opportunities for cultural development and expression. It is in the urban places where pluralism prevails, where men of all ethnic and cultural origins congregate, and where man discovers his finest opportunity to learn of the richness and diversity and individuality of his fellowmen.

And it is in urban places—these man-built

---

[17] This section is adapted from Desmond L. Anderson, "Many Influences Contribute to Image of Urban Manager," PUBLIC MANAGEMENT, May, 1965.

centers—where man feels closest to his governmental official and where governmental services are most immediate and direct. In these urban places man's interchange with municipal officials is most diverse and frequent. It is where man perceives that he is fulfilling most of his governmental needs in a relationship which is intimate, friendly, and personal.

CITIZEN INVOLVEMENT THROUGH HOME RULE

Proximity, access, and familiarity seemingly engender greater citizen interest in local government than in other less immediately available levels of government. A majority of basic human needs are met at the local level. A natural consequence of this has been the strengthening of citizen participation in municipal government through the concept of home rule. A concept which varies in strength from state to state, home rule is especially strong in states such as California which permit self-chartering of local government through the initiative of local citizens. Penetrating to the very roots of democratic government, the concept of home rule motivates individual citizens to resort to every device available to influence action or inaction at the municipal level. Increasingly, citizens wish to be consulted before policies and procedures are finally established and implemented.

Human Behavior—the Backdrop

The interests of any citizen or group is interlaced with divergence and conflict. Social scientists increasingly are devoting their attention to such manifestations by studying human behavior in a variety of settings.

BEHAVIORALISM AND PUBLIC RELATIONS

As the study of behavioralism in administration and politics develops, leading to additional insights about relationships among men, it is likely that our traditional approaches to the study and practice of public relations will be modified and that we will develop a more sophisticated understanding of human relationships.

Public relations obviously connotes a concern for people. During the past two decades concern with and for people has variously been denoted as internal public relations, external public relations, human relations, and people-centered management. Each is yielding place as new insights about human behavior are unfolded through behavioral science applications to ". . . social research concerned with a scientific understanding of man in society . . ."[18]

ATTITUDES AND PUBLIC RELATIONS

In human relationships the behavior of individuals and groups reflects prevailing and developing attitudes of such individuals and groups. These attitudes condition human behavior in many ways.

Although the public *en masse* consists of individuals, public audiences consist primarily of interacting and overlapping groups of individuals. Each such group, whether formal or informal, has a system of values and standards which condition the attitudes of individual members. It thus can be seen that public attitudes are primarily a composite of group attitudes.

Attitudes are derived from a variety of influences. They may result quickly from some overwhelming emotional experience or they may develop from exposure to a series of stimuli over an extended period of time. Thus, attitudes are acquired tendencies to react or behave in certain ways. Among different individuals, attitudes vary in both kind and intensity. They may be mild predispositions or deep-seated convictions. The environment of which a man is a part—his total ecology—fashions his attitudes toward elements within the ecological setting.

Since there are elements of both stability and change in human ecology, so too are the attitudes of individuals susceptible to both stability and change. This is of significance to city managers and other administrators as they provide direction in the policy determination and implementation process. Some human atti-

---

[18] David Easton, "The Current Meaning of 'Behavioralism' in Political Science," p. 14, in James C. Charlesworth, editor, THE LIMITS OF BEHAVIORALISM IN POLITICAL SCIENCE (Philadelphia: The American Academy of Political and Social Science, 1962), 123pp.

tudes facilitate organizational stability while the capacity of human beings to change attitudes provides necessary flexibility for innovation and program achievement.

Unfavorable attitudes toward government or toward proposed programs, unless modified, are hazards to both program achievement and public relations. Since attitudes are acquired from personal experience it is possible to change undesirable attitudes by providing new or different information and experience for those whose attitudes we wish to change. In doing so, the discerning city manager will endeavor to influence individuals and modify their attitudes by focusing attention on the identifiable and influential groups within the community from which individuals seek information and guidance.

The influence of attitudes on program achievement may be observed in specific situations. Where respect for the police and for the principles of law and order are high, law enforcement problems are likely to be minimal. However, where the public attitudes are unfavorable and where respect for law and order is low, the total staffing requirement for the police force may be high and the total quality of law enforcement may be substandard.

In such a situation, public attitudes toward the institution—its program, activities, and personnel—may be said to exert an immediate and direct effect on program achievement. Even where such a relationship is not readily apparent, public attitudes and feelings affect the operations of the governmental institution. An agency or institution is a part of the community, drawing its sustenance therefrom and existing to satisfy some system of community needs.

From the foregoing discussion it can be deduced that information substantially affects attitudes. If the city manager is to influence his own attitudes and those of others in a meaningful way, sufficient information must be available to him and he must communicate it appropriately. The mere lack of information may cause distrust and misunderstanding which may be corrected by making appropriate information available. The less information we have, the more we are apt to distort. To influence attitudes and behavior, information must be related to individual, group, and community values.

The first requirement, therefore, is to determine what attitudes and values are, what their causes are, how widely they are held in the community and by which segments thereof, and their relative disparity within the community. If disparity exists among attitudes and values with respect to socially desirable objectives, then appropriate change is necessary.

PERSPECTIVE, PERCEPTION, ROLE, AND IMAGE[19]

As a general premise it was observed above that attitudes are derived from prior experience and information and that attitudes condition human behavior. It is useful, however, in management and public relations to derive another set of concepts related to attitudes and behavior—namely, perspective, perception, role, and image.

Perspective is essentially that frame of reference from which you view a given scene or set of phenomena, whereas *perception* is your particular awareness of that which you see. *Role,* on the other hand, is the responsibility and behavior expectations held for an incumbent of a particular position in a hierarchy, while the resultant *image* of an individual, agency, or institution is a composite of your perceptions.

Perspective, perception, role, and image—plus actual performance or behavior—are interacting influences on one another. They both influence and are influenced by each other. It is clear that because of individual human differences there is no common perspective and hence no common perceptions of reality. Our perceptions of specific acts and roles are different because our perspectives are unique to us as individuals. All of us will see the same role differently, but there is, nevertheless, some coincidence of specific details from one perception to another.

Perspective. Attitudes are the principal influence in shaping one's perspective, but important also are personal temperament, philoso-

---

[19] The following section is adapted from Anderson, *op. cit.*

phy, and background or experience. It is from the totality of these influences that one views a given set of circumstances.

Perception. What a person sees through his frame of reference as he views that given set of phenomena is his perception of reality. A series of such ideas and impressions for any given institution becomes that person's perception of the institutional image. The set of phenomena at which a person looks in formulating his perception usually is either role or actual performance, or a combination of the two.

Role. Defined in terms of expectations, role is an organizational concept and a derivative of the behavior requirements of a particular position within a social system or organizational hierarchy. As a basic influence on human behavior, role expectations are perceived by as many people, including the incumbent, as view a given position, and their perceptions vary accordingly.

Image. Wherein the common elements in the perceptions of a group of people coincide, therein is the foundation for personal, agency, or institutional image.

In a distinctly limited sense, public relations may be viewed as an "image-building" device— *i.e.,* a means of evoking a predictable and uniform public perception of a person, act, organization, or facility. It involves highly purposeful publicity as well as other techniques. It is not a random exposure of a subject to public attention. It is selective, discriminating, and highly purposeful. Its object is to present the desired image of the subject to the world and to produce a popular perception of the subject that conforms to the desired image.

Images depend on total performance. It is clear, therefore, that the variables are many— each individual, thing, and activity—and that many, if not most, of them are uncontrollable. There are, however, many elements which are controllable by management—a wide variety of communications that are planned, conceived, and issued to convey the desired image. These communications are the framework of an image through which periodic "image audits" may reveal how well the image holds. For municipalities, the analysis of the controllable elements and their functioning focuses on mu-

nicipal nomenclature, municipal symbols, and municipal graphics.

Municipal nomenclature is the core of any image program. It includes the name of the city and its consistent use or derivative use in all the departments, activities, and programs. Without consistency the municipal image is likely to be diffused.

Municipal symbols include official seals, slogans, and program symbols which are shorthand messages for asserting the purpose and character of the city. They are continuing reminders for the citizens.

Municipal graphics concerns the form or appearance of all communications. Consistency and quality of ink colors, typography, and paper stock are all pertinent.

The next step is to review the appearance of these three elements through all the controllable message carriers: (1) packaging, (2) advertising and promotion, (3) signs, (4) institutional literature, (5) stationery and forms, (6) transportation vehicles, and (7) buildings and equipment.[20] Appropriate observation, control, and maintenance of this communications network by the municipality will have a noticeable effect on the resulting image.

Relation of Public Opinion and Communication to Government

In a complex urban ecology which generates divergent human behavior and attitudes, no simple formulation of the nature and significance of public opinion and communication is possible. Few subjects have been more extensively analyzed and investigated than public opinion and communication, yet clarity and agreement have not been achieved.

Because public relations is conceived herein as a means of program accomplishment, those views of public opinion and communication which hold promise of contributing to this end

---

[20] For a more extensive discussion of nomenclature, graphics, and symbols and a review of the image audit through the institution's communications network, see J. Gordon Lippincott and Walter P. Margulies, "The Care and Grooming of the Corporate Image," THE MANAGEMENT REVIEW, November, 1960.

are included as reference points in the ensuing discussion.

OPINION CONSIDERATIONS

That governments derive their authority from the consent of the governed is a concept which has evolved slowly over the centuries and which now has almost universal acceptance. But man's historical resentment of arbitrary exercise of governmental authority is matched by his current bewilderment, stimulated by the rising complexity of public issues for which his experience has decreasing relevance.

Despite this apparent shift in man's relative ability to deal with public issues, the power of public opinion provides the psychological environment in which public officials, agencies, and institutions prosper or perish. In democratic and authoritarian societies alike, it puts governments in and out of office, makes or breaks national heroes, and determines the success of public institutions and undertakings. Public opinion is a principal ingredient in social change.

Whether tyrannical or democratic, no government can long survive without the willing support of many of its citizens. Such support derives from public opinion, of which all governments take cognizance. The late V. O. Key, Jr., eloquently set forth this thesis in the opening paragraph of his last book:

Governments must concern themselves with the opinions of their citizens, if only to provide a basis for repression of disaffection. The persistent curiosity, and anxiety, of rulers about what their subjects say of them and of their actions are chronicled in the histories of secret police. Measures to satisfy such curiosity by soundings of opinion are often only an aspect of political persecution; they may also guide policies of persuasion calculated to convert discontent into cheerful acquiescence. And even in the least democratic regime opinion may influence the direction or tempo of substantive policy. Although a government may be erected on tyranny, to endure it needs the ungrudging support of substantial numbers of its people. If that support does not arise spontaneously, measures will be taken to stimulate it by tactical concessions to public opinion, by the management of opinion, or by both.[21]

_____

[21] V. O. Key, Jr., PUBLIC OPINION AND AMERICAN DEMOCRACY (New York: Alfred A. Knopf, 1961), p. 3.

In the American democratic society, this concern for public opinion is an ethical imperative; it springs from the ideology upon which this government is based. While in authoritarian societies the concern for public opinion is a function of maintenance of power, democratic doctrine assumes that a recognition of the wishes of the governed is a condition of governing rightly. Because of the universal political appeal of this concept, modern dictatorships took over much of the symbolism, ritual, and semantics of democratic ideology.[22]

Public opinion is a concert of individual opinion. Man's opinions, not unlike his behavior, are shaped and molded by the culture within which he finds himself. Public opinion thus emerges out of a social situation where human differences are articulated in reference to a particular matter or issue. They may result from an intellectual appraisal of factual data or from emotional reaction.

It was noted above that the process by which opinions are formed and altered has been subjected to considerable study. The variety of conceptualizations resulting therefrom have lacked unanimity. Inasmuch as the public relations model postulated herein assumes a broad base of influence, it is undesirable to narrowly restrict the base of public opinion. Accordingly, Key's conceptualization is paraphrased in the next paragraph.

The public opinions which governments take cognizance of include both live issues and those based on the customs and mores of particular societies. Such opinions may be shared by few or many, may be the veriest whim, or may be settled conviction. It may be contingent opinion, or estimates of probable responses by citizens which condition governmental decisions. Views lightly held and transient opinions both have relevance. Sometimes a small segment of the society may hold a position so tenaciously that it may block or even direct public action. It may be that customs control particular governmental actions, but actions also may seek the modification of existing custom. Governments may find it prudent to heed private opinions by action

_____

[22] _Ibid._, p. 4.

or inaction, by attempts to alter, divert, or pacify. Governments, however, may at times be so sensitive that opinion can be anticipated before action occurs, but opinion commonly gains its influence by being communicated. Such communication may occur directly between citizen and governmental functionary, but frequently it is done through specialized institutions such as political parties and pressure groups which shape, organize, and represent opinion to governments.[23]

THE PUBLICS—WHO ARE THEY?

Throughout the foregoing discussion reference is made to the *publics* of governmental jurisdictions and agencies. It is clear that today we live in a pluralistic society consisting of people of diverse backgrounds and value systems. Each citizen may be affiliated with many and diverse groups in a society in which he develops and maintains multiple loyalties. As we organize ourselves into a variety of groups, there is no single transcendent group affiliation. We divide ourselves on various bases, such as social, recreational, political, religious, fraternal, civic or service, professional, clientele, etc. Consequently, governmental officials and employees find themselves dealing with a multiplicity of publics as well as individuals. The constituency of a municipal park and recreation department, for example, would include an extensive list of different groups who want to use, complain about, praise, and request the elimination, modification, or addition of facilities which are maintained by the department.

These constituency relationships are two-way in that they flow from and to both the jurisdiction and the constituents. Maintaining these relationships effectively requires concern for attitudes and actions of both parties. Not only must favorable public attitudes toward the government be cultivated but also there must be fostered among public officials an attitude of good will and respect. Conversely, it builds the foundation of support upon which democratic government is fabricated.

Through an increasing volume of behavioral research we are becoming more sophisticated in our understanding of both the general and special publics. The general public (1) is essentially passive in nature, (2) has only limited ability to comprehend complex data, and (3) is likely to reject data which is inconsonant with existing values and attitudes.

Accordingly, awareness of the nature of publics is necessary if communication is to be effective. If change in behavior and values is desirable, it should be planned through existing value systems.

Certain distinctions are emerging between the general public and special publics. It appears that on only a few questions does the entire citizenry have an opinion. In reality, one issue may engage the attention of one sector of the population, while another arouses interests of a different sector, and a third question attracts still other special publics. On a particular issue, the operative public may consist of a well-structured identifiable association, while on another question opinions may be diffused throughout the general public which lacks any special organization. When the concern of a small special public prevails, it is presumed that it does so with the tacit consent of the general public.[24]

INFORMATION AND COMMUNICATION

Because hierarchal organizations come into existence to implement social objectives, it follows that communication among the organizational constituency must exist to facilitate program achievement. Opinions and attitudes are influenced substantially by the nature of the communication system and the information available. The extent to which an effective communication system is established and maintained is both a measure of and an influence upon the effectiveness of the institution.

Individual Needs and Governmental Objectives. When the constituency of an institution includes all who live within particular jurisdictional boundaries—as with a municipality, county, or other local government—the communication network must interlace the institution with those groups in the community through which individual citizen contacts are

---

[23] *Ibid.*, pp. 12–18, *passim.*

[24] *Ibid.*, pp. 10 and 15.

made. The increasing mobility of Americans makes communication impossible except when they join groups with a common interest bond. But despite this propensity to join groups, every person is an individual in his own right, and a key to effective communication therefore is identification of the institutional message with the aspirations and purposes of individuals.

The meaningful sublimation of individual aspirations within major social objectives has been a continuous responsibility of democratic government. Success and stability of such governments ultimately are determined by the continuing approval of the citizenry which, in turn, is predicated on their interest and awareness. Paradoxically, citizen interest and awareness require communication from governmental sources, but traditionally citizens have been suspicious of efforts by governmental bodies to publicize themselves and the services available to the public. Accordingly, until recently, administrative officials have been reluctant to inform their publics appropriately about services, activities, and problems.

Informed Citizenry Fundamental to Governmental Goals. The highest conception of providing information to the public is that it enables the citizen to render intelligent judgments regarding the policies and activities of democratic government. American democracy is based on the premise that citizens are capable of self-government. In the formative years, the New England "town meeting" afforded virtually every citizen of the community opportunities to know his town government. When issues arose, facts were available on which to base an opinion.

Today, except in a relatively small number of New England villages where the tradition has persisted, the town meeting has ceased to exist because of the changed nature of our complex society. Yet the governmental and social imperatives of shared information and common participation are greater today than in earlier times.

Always in the forefront of efforts to maintain open communication channels between governments and citizens have been the nation's news reporters and commentators. Their efforts in recent years culminated in the adoption in 1957 by the American Society of Newspaper Editors of the following "Declaration of Principles":

> . . . citizens must be able to gather information at home or abroad, except where military necessity plainly prevents; they must find it possible to publish or relate otherwise the information thus acquired without prior restraint or censorship by government . . . they should have freedom to distribute and disseminate without obstruction by government or by their fellow citizens. . . .

The members of the American Society of Newspaper Editors . . . are doubly-alarmed by measures that threaten the right to know, whether they involve restrictions on the movement of the press to sources of news and information at home or abroad, withholding information at local, state, or federal levels, or proposals to bring within the purview of the criminal statutes those who do not place security of the nation in jeopardy, but whose only offense is to disagree with government officials on what may be safely published.[25]

In accordance with the ASNE statement which emphasizes the public's "right to know" several states have enacted legislation such as California's Brown Act which prohibits executive or "secret" sessions of public legislative bodies except in certain personnel matters. From the point of view of facilitating program achievement perhaps it would be desirable to emphasize the complementary proposition of the public's "need to know." If the citizen is to assume effectively his responsibilities for self-government, the discerning administrator will assure the availability of sufficient and adequate information.

While an informed citizenry is indispensable to democratic government, the critics of government, except for the fanatic fringe, are to be found primarily among people who are partly informed and partly misinformed. It is difficult to eliminate misconceptions once they have been assimilated and encrusted in the form of opinion. The antidote, of course, is systematic communication which provides a continuous flow of information to the public.

Complete, Accurate Information. Candid reporting repeatedly has engendered citizen appreciation and understanding of difficult

---

[25] Robert U. Brown, "ASNE Spells Out Broad Scope of the People's Right to Know," *Editor & Publisher* (90: 9), July 20, 1957.

governmental problems and situations. Often there is temptation to offer alibis, to reveal only partial truths, or to take refuge in the silence of "no comment" when a potentially embarrassing development occurs. Such evasiveness is strategically undesirable because it invites inquiry. There is nothing more challenging to a newspaper reporter than the intimation of a story being suppressed by governmental officials. There is nothing more likely to precipitate a citizen revolt than a discovery that officials have been attempting to "cover up." A simple error, admitted openly and freely, is usually forgotten quickly, whereas the same mistake, subjected to the mystery of the cover-up process, may become a major scandal. To minimize surreptitious rumor, complete information should be released at the earliest feasible moment to encourage formation of opinions based on accurate data from the original source rather than the grapevine.

Ethically, of course, there is no justification for governmental deceit or distortion. The government, after all, is the citizen in an institutionalized sense, which should symbolize his highest aspirations of honor, justice, and fair play. The matter of ethics is detailed more fully later in this chapter.

While citizens and public officials alike require information to make decisions, to explain availability of services, and to evaluate performance, there are specific approaches to handling information. In the routine matter of giving information over the counter, the importance of using speech and hearing faculties simultaneously is indicated by the following:

. . . in answer to a simple inquiry as to how many persons serve on the City Council, the answer "five" may or may not provide the information sought. But if we are to answer the same question by saying, "There are four members of the City Council, plus the Mayor who serves as Chairman, making five altogether," we then invite the questioner to clarify his inquiry and perhaps to obtain the information he really is seeking, such as the method of election of Council members, or the organization of the Council.

. . . even in the simplest procedure by which we direct a visitor to the proper office, we can combine listening and questioning with our answers in such fashion as to prevent embarrassment and confusion. If a caller were to inquire as to where he could obtain a "permit," an adequate answer might be, "That would be in room four." But the additional moment required to answer, "Our *building* permits are issued by Mr. X in room four" could provide the caller with a specific person to seek in a busy office containing several people; furthermore, the additional information supplied in the longer answer could enable the caller to clarify his inquiry by saying that he had been dealing with Mr. A, rather than Mr. X; we in turn could reply that the caller was seeking a *business license* rather than a *building permit,* and that Mr. A could help him in room five.[26]

Regular Reporting. It is apparent that there is need for a continuous flow of information as it develops. In most state, county, and local governments public reporting is a legal requirement, particularly in fiscal matters. Public relations requirements of providing information to the public transcend this legal duty, however; it is an imperative of both common sense and morality. Nor does the provision for making information public through such vehicles as the annual report fulfill the entire obligation of government. Information should be provided on events and activities as they occur.

Both legally required annual reports and public notices continue to be plagued by archaic, legalistic, and confusing specifications. How many public reports are readable and understandable? How many legal notices clearly indicate what the situation is? Requirements for insertion in newspapers of general circulation often are met by publication in weekly or legal papers of limited circulation.

Assessment of available resources and opportunities, coupled with ingenuity and innovation, will overcome what probably continues to be the most negative aspect of governmental public relations—namely, public reporting. Even financial problems associated with an effective public reporting system may be minimized by a little ingenuity.

For example, the head of the North Carolina Department of Employee Security and his secretary, using regional office managers to a great extent, taped 15-, 10-, 5-, and 1-minute radio programs which are used on more than 25 stations across the state. In his special case, he needed equipment costing about $2,000, but his annual budget for the whole project is less than $5,000.

In order to optimize opportunities of this sort, government officials must familiarize themselves with requirements of the information media in their areas and develop programs which will both achieve institutional objectives and effectively utilize available media.

Whatever is undertaken to facilitate information flow and effective communication should be predicated on the prior understanding that communication is a mutual process among senders and receivers whereby information is transferred from its source to its destination where it is given meaning through reception and interpretation.

Administrative Responsibility for Public Relations

The primary purpose of administration is to achieve established organizational purposes and to assist in clarifying and delineating such purposes. Accordingly, all administrative functions should service or facilitate effective operations of the organization.

ADVISORY AND FACILITATIVE ROLE

It is the function of public relations to facilitate the effective rendition of services and to provide the public with adequate information on governmental services. Public relations, thus, is a means of defining and achieving program goals. Anti-litter campaigns which have been administered quite successfully in some cities should be viewed as an administrative alternative to expending much larger sums of money for frequent policing of roadways by city crews. "Smokey, the Bear" campaigns provide information to increase citizen awareness that care by them is a much more desirable alternative than the tremendous costs incurred through depletion of natural resources and by mounting costly fire-fighting campaigns.

Contributing to program or goal achieve-

ment by providing information is itself a facilitative operation, as is the evaluation of programs such as by sampling community opinion regarding a municipal activity. These are however, administrative operations which are commonly identified as public relations. Such operations may be handled entirely by line administrators themselves or they may be shared by the administrators with staff assistants who are often designated as public relations specialists. The extent to which this sharing occurs depends on a host of factors, such as the size and complexity of the jurisdiction, personal predilections of the administrator, availability of public funds, and controversiality of the particular line function. However much these public relations operations are shared by the line administrator, he can never be absolved of responsibility for them.

While the public relations specialist does not have major responsibility for policy determination and administrative competency within an agency, he is concerned in a major way with public knowledge and understanding of city government activities. To the extent that he has special knowledge about public reaction, or is skilled in certain techniques, he has obligations to the line officials in utilizing such knowledge and skills in advisory and facilitative ways which will make administrative performance more effective.

Elton Woolpert wrote that

. . . a government that concerns itself only with basic policies and efficiency falls short of providing the service which the people demand and have a right to expect. Efficiency does not preclude public convenience. Human values are no less real than material values. Competence is not impaired by courtesy. Furthermore, lack of attention to these minor factors may itself distort and prejudice public opinion and attitudes. A government that deserves good public relations on the basis of its policies and operating efficiency may incur public disfavor because it neglects the other factors. In short, there need be no conflict between these several factors. They supplement each other, and all must be brought into balance if the city is to secure, and deserve, good public relations.[27]

It is advisable to express a caveat at this point. Sometimes in this advisory and facilita-

---

[27] Elton Woolpert, *op. cit.*, pp. 3–4.

tive role, public relations staffs overextend their role with the misconception that popular support can be built by a public relations program without much consideration for the substantive conditions involved. It is contrary to human nature, however, to accept information unless it conforms with individual experience, and any institution courts danger when it seeks to create a point of view which differs from realities. High-powered publicity cannot conceal ineptitude in government. Indeed, there are great hazards confronting any governmental administrator who attempts to hide his failures and organizational inabilities behind a façade of publicity. Effective public relations rest upon a foundation of actual needs and effective service. This kind of support-building is a substantive line function in which every member of an organization participates. It is not an isolated staff function.

Accomplishment of objectives, however, is no assurance that the agency will enjoy good public relations. Again the competitive and pluralistic nature of modern democratic society may produce a completely erroneous public image of the agency and its programs. As a competitor on the social market, the governmental institution must maintain community support if its activities are to continue and if its program objectives are to be accomplished. Some programs may not be attainable without publicity and attitude-building efforts. For example, without attempting in any way to alter the public's attitude toward the use of good books, a public librarian will publicize new additions to his stock and will report those branches which have the new books available for public distribution.

Beyond this type of activity, however, the local health officer, for example, may engage in overt public information and attitude molding activities in order to convince people in poorer sections that they should learn about personal health and use of clinics and other health services. He is not accomplishing his mission unless he engages in education of this sort and unless he concerns himself affirmatively with altering prevailing public attitudes and values within his jurisdiction.

In still another way the facilitative and advisory role of public relations must be made clear. From the days of Ivy Lee's prescription of himself as a "physician to corporate bodies," public relations specialists have sought to overcome the stigma associated with the notion of a palliative or cure-all for an agency's ills. While public relations men have complained against this negative connotation they have emphasized that public relations is positive, too, and should be viewed as a preventive as well as a curative. From the task of soothing troubled feelings, they have moved vigorously to remedying the conditions involved which caused the troubled feelings. It should be borne in mind constantly that remedying malconditions is distinctly a management function and as such it obviously has public relations implications, but just as obviously it is not a separate or distinct public relations function.

It may be recalled from the discussion of the definitions of public relations that one of the problems of arriving at appropriate definitions has been the desire of the public relations specialists to remove the unsavory stigma associated with the term. It bears emphasis that public relations will gain increased status and prestige as it becomes interwoven in the performance process of government to such an extent that government: (1) is sensitive to and capable of discernment of needs of society; (2) renders excellent service; and (3) works positively to maintain open channels of influence so that high level morality may always have a chance to flourish—so that reason, the bulwark of justice, may always prevail.

The changed status cannot and should not be accomplished through a deliberate effort to demonstrate the value of public relations *per se*. Although they obviously have public relations implications, techniques for the development and continuance of democratic principles are fundamental to the democratic process itself and are not uniquely public relations contributions to the process. Public relations, as the quality of relationships, is best when government is most effective. When government is ineffective, public relations as process through techniques will not change it; but modifying the governmental process so it becomes democratically effective does change public relations as to the *quality* of relationships. Public relations narrowly construed cannot make bad government good, but public relations broadly construed is inextricably interwoven in the democratic process and is improved when democratic machinery and its operation are improved.

MANAGERIAL LEADERSHIP AND PUBLIC RELATIONS

Both Politics and Administration. Public relations is inevitably bound up with managerial leadership, a responsibility which cannot be delegated. Municipal managers have a dual responsibility to maintain good operating conditions within their jurisdiction and an equal obligation to implement the legislative program adopted through the political process. They must be responsive to the changing objectives of government fashioned by politics. Yet the manager, no longer strait-jacketed by the misconception of the politics-administration dichotomy, himself has a community leadership role to perform. This is the major departure from the original theory of the council-manager plan.[28]

Amplifying upon that community leadership role, Harlan Cleveland asserted that the professional manager no longer can leave to the politicians the arguments over values and that ". . . the administrator's task is not to make peace among the contending experts but to make sure there is enough tension among them to produce out of their vigorous advocacy a solution to each problem that takes into account all the relevant factors. . . ."[29] The administrator's own value system becomes involved and whether he relishes it or not, he is catapulted into a leadership role.[30]

Such a role involves not only the discovery of majority purpose but also development of community consensus. In this latter phase his leadership role is especially noticeable. He may suggest goals and indicate avenues of achievement hitherto unattainable in the minds of local citizenry and wielders of power. He may cater to opinions of clientele groups and other organized interests as well as legislators and the public at large. He will solicit good will everywhere and promote successful relations for the city's and his own welfare. If there is variance of opinion and judgment he has opportunity to teach and enlighten. Thus, his educative function is especially significant. The extent to which, under any particular set of circumstances, he carries out this function, is dependent in considerable measure upon many influences. But with the responsible citizen—the responsible and professional manager—there is an automatic governor arising out of his own value system: his concern for the ethical as determined through wisdom. If he himself cannot yield his point of view and if he cannot, through his teaching efforts, win the consent of the governors, as institutionalized in his city council, then to maintain his integrity, his ethical orientation will cause him to resign rather than to launch a crusade for his point of view.

Both Conservator and Change Agent. The very nature of the role of the city manager is such that he is clothed with responsibility for innovation and change on the one hand and, on the other hand, for conserving that which is desirable in the existing order against the wishes of those who seek change. His role as change agent is brought into stark relief when viewed against public opinion which, once solidified, is stubbornly resistant to change. In the process of focusing or aiding in the focus of opinion on public policy issues, participating in policy formulation, implementing a favorable program, and overcoming resistance to change in each phase of the continuing process, the manager is operating in part as a public relations official. Ability to accept changes to meet progress is an important phase of an effective public relations program.

Defending the organization to a client may be quite noble, but it probably causes an antagonistic client to become more aggressive. In fact, the very thing defended may be wrong. The municipality must stand ready, as a part of

[28] See articles by Hugo Wall, "Changing Concepts of Managerial Leadership," PUBLIC MANAGEMENT, March, 1954, pp. 50–53, and Douglas G. Weiford, "The Changing Role of the City Manager," PUBLIC MANAGEMENT, August, 1954, pp. 170–72.

[29] Harlan Cleveland, "Education for Public Complexity," PUBLIC MANAGEMENT, December, 1959, pp. 281–83.

[30] Desmond L. Anderson, *op. cit.*

effective public relations, to change those procedures which citizen-clients don't like. The
burden on the counter or contact employee
becomes greater than we can realistically expect of him if the municipality stands for good
public relations despite unpopular procedures
which could be changed. Bureaucratic red tape
significantly influences the image of both the
municipality and the manager. His leadership
must be positively exerted to encourage procedural and organizational change where the
organization is inconsonant with human behavior. His role in attitude and behavioral change
is discussed in a previous section. Behavioral
change and organizational change are reciprocal influences.

But to say that these are political considerations begs the question. All public servants, in
proportionately decreasing degrees, from the
chief administrative officer to the humblest and
least discretionary officer, will discover, if they
are not already aware, that at times they must
serve as a change agent and at other times
as the pilloried defender of the status quo. This
role is particularly highlighted at the local
level of government, because of the immediacy
of interest with which governmental functions
are vested at that level.

Primacy of Culture.   Traditions, customs,
mores, folkways, habits, all condition the environment in which these roles are enacted. The
public employee who does not effectively adjust
to the environment in which he plays his role
fails to do so at his peril.[31] Although it may be
only tangential to this point, Paul Muni, like
many other stalwarts of the theater, never
played a role of a particular personality on stage
or screen unless he had first spent several months
through vicarious experiences pretending and
practicing to be the individual whom he was to
portray. This is not to assert that the public
official must become so immersed in the culture
of his jurisdiction that he becomes a captive
thereof, and hence unable to function as a
change agent when it is appropriate to do so.

Change is inevitable. And the public servant
needs to know the community sufficiently well
so that in each particular case he may determine which are the acceptable or least offensive
ways of both innovating *and* defending the
public policy.

Support through Participation.   Working together for common purposes is the basis for
group achievement. Personal involvement in
the processes which lead to such achievement
often develops both understanding and support, which are among the ingredients of effective public relations. Inasmuch as a major
concern of public relations is support-building,
any expression of management leadership in
the public relations context must take into
consideration the leadership techniques for securing support. An important factor seems to
be a sense of some participation in group
decision-making. The problem of participation
has over-all administrative implications, but it
has particular significance in public relations.
Alexander Leighton concluded, as a result of
his observations at the Poston War Relocation
Center for Japanese, that one of the essential
elements of good administration is to "provide
opportunities that will enable people being
administered to develop their constructive tendencies; this not only provides intrinsic satisfaction, but compensates for stresses that cannot be relieved."[32]

Amplifying upon this, as a result of his
findings in another research project, Kurt
Lewin concluded that "If one intends to create
a friendly atmosphere of cooperation rather
than a straight authoritarian system, if one
wants to gain full cooperation, the lowest
group should do the planning for the first step,
since they would regard any other action as an
attempt to make them agree to a procedure set
up by authorities."[33]

It would seem therefore that to serve over-all
administrative purposes, as well as to operate
effectively in a public relations way, the administrator should find ways of involving people in

---

[31] For a comprehensive sociological consideration of
differing organizational environments, plus an interesting analytical model and typology, see Amitai Etzioni,
A COMPARATIVE ANALYSIS OF COMPLEX ORGANIZATIONS
(New York: Free Press of Glencoe, 1961), 366pp.

[32] Alexander H. Leighton, THE GOVERNING OF MEN
(Princeton, New Jersey: Princeton University Press,
1946), p. 285.

[33] Kurt Lewin, RESOLVING SOCIAL CONFLICTS (New
York: Harper and Brothers, 1948), p. 139.

a participative manner in the process of discovering solutions to problems.

EMPLOYEES AS PUBLIC RELATIONS AMBASSADORS

The officials and employees of a municipality are its most effective public relations ambassadors. Like other facets of administrative responsibility, public relations is a cooperative undertaking in which every individual associated with the municipality has a part to play. This is especially true in view of the nature of municipal functions and the direct citizen-employee contacts involved.

All people associated with an enterprise, whether that enterprise be a municipality or the Kiwani-Anns, inescapably are public relations representatives of such an enterprise and have a correlative responsibility. They may be neither good representatives nor willing to accept the responsibility, but this does not alter the reality of the relationship.

Nearly every municipal employee, whether he be fire inspector, city clerk, meter reader, recreation leader, water superintendent, refuse collector, traffic patrolman, or innumerable others, normally has direct and frequent contact with at least some segment of the public. This fact magnifies the problem of control of the public relations image by the administrator because he must rely on all such employees in the composite of their relationships with the public to project an effective view of the city.

Not only are the employees' work-connected relations with people important but also their innumerable indirect and off-the-job contacts. One dissatisfied employee can by his deeds and words do irreparable harm to the public view of the city. If such actions are multiplied by several complainers, the result can be very damaging.

There is, obviously, much that can be done through training programs, but training cannot substitute for a deep-seated loyalty and understanding of the institution among the employees, which will be reflected in all their contacts with other people, private as well as public. Such loyalty cannot be inculcated solely through training programs; it must be inspired by the tone of conduct of the city administration, through the development of a genuine

attitude of support stemming from effective administration. These are differences between form and substance, between desire and behavior, between that which is sham and that which is genuine. Employees who are stimulated to make suggestions and recommendations will enhance the quality of administrative performance and public relations. Through the democratic exchange of information, ideas, motivations, and experiences, public relations may attain maximum effectiveness for local governments.

Preparing for and maintaining effective public relations is really a matter of increasing the social awareness of employees. A municipality's employees should not be taught to "be nice" to the public so that the city will gain a better public image. The training rather should be goal-oriented so that employees understand typical citizen action and reaction and thus can more easily and effectively perform the service for which employed. Their behavior should be such that institutional goals and programs are attained with the least energy output. This means that the employee must learn to be a sort of nondirective clinician.

WHERE IS RESPONSIBILITY LODGED?

Good public relations begins at the top and is a direct line responsibility, an integral and continuous part of management. The city manager has an inescapable obligation for public relations, an obligation that is just as compelling as his responsibilities for sound public finance, effective personnel systems, and other areas of management. He must instigate training for employees in all areas of public relations and see that training programs are properly staffed, equipped, supported, and attended. It is the city manager's job to deal with the press on a knowledgeable basis and to develop good press relations for the entire municipality. It is the city manager's job, using all means available to him, to fashion improvement in the image of the city. He sets the pace for the entire municipality, and if the city's public relations program is lagging, he first should have a rendezvous with his conscience. A matter of attitude is often involved here. Too many officials consider the public relations function of management marginal at best. In this view, public relations is a managerial responsibility to be attended to if there is time or if there are not other more pressing matters at hand. There is a lack of understanding that attention to public relations can make the whole task of governing a great deal easier and more pleasant.

As Wright and Christian have written,

Public relations begins at the top where policy is made. In business and industry public relations is a responsibility of management. In governmental and social organizations it is a function of administration. In military affairs it stems from command. If public relations is to achieve maximum effectiveness it must be directed by the responsible officials at the head of the institution or enterprise, and they must be conscious of its importance and power. . . .

The chief executive must always be the hub of the public relations wheel. From him must radiate the policies and decisions that will govern the institution's relations with the public.[34]

How, then, can public relations be administered systematically or in an orderly fashion?

First, it should be recalled that public relations is fundamental to and nonseparable from the administrative process.

Second, it must be understood clearly that no one in the hierarchy, least of all the top administrator, can abandon responsibility for public relations nor divest himself of the representation function. Public relations, by its nature and relationships, *is nondelegable as to responsibility.*

Third, it should be noted that there are certain tasks and activities which can be separated out and performed by staff assistants. This separation and allocation of tasks, however, should not lead to a lack of continuing identification with the administrative process and organizational goals, irrespective of the size of the jurisdiction.

The community survey used to gather data on citizen reactions has public relations importance. But its importance often transcends the entire administrative spectrum. A "public relations specialist," whether an assistant city manager or a technician, cannot have exclusive jurisdiction over nor interest in such a survey. So it is with many other such activities.

It should be clear from the foregoing that many of the tasks which some writers and practitioners claim should be allocated to a public relations section or staff are of general administrative concern. They should be performed by all means but within the general administrative context, not alone in the specialized setting of public relations.

In the small city, the city manager himself may necessarily perform most such tasks; in most municipalities they can be performed by an administrative assistant so designated, without raising questions of political and social impropriety; in the medium-sized jurisdiction there may be one or more administrative assistants who perform some of the tasks, occupying either part or all of their time; in the metropolis there may be an entire section performing public information tasks, including preparation and distribution of annual and other municipal reports. In such cases, the designation, "public information assistant," may be entirely proper. Such personnel should be organized within the hierarchy, however, under an assistant city manager or similarly designated person who has administrative responsibilities broader than those usually encompassed by the duties of a "public relations specialist."

DIVISION OF OPERATIONAL EFFECTIVENESS

Complexity in the urban milieu—the setting in which most municipal public relations today finds expression—requires sophisticated data gathering and analysis for both policy determination and implementation. During the turmoil of the postwar years we have learned that we cannot resolve critical social issues through traditional patterns and with little effort. The temper and mood of our times—the urgency—require innovation, new approaches, action.

In fabricating the new approaches for the future, it seems appropriate to weave together three strands which connect the past with the present: (1) the municipal research bureau movement; (2) the more recently developed municipal public relations bureaus or units; and (3) the advent of urban complexity.

Municipal Research Bureau Movement. Beginning with the establishment of the New York Bureau of Municipal Research in 1906,

[34] Wright and Christian, *op. cit.,* pp. 42, 43.

an independent citizen agency, the municipal research bureau movement gained impetus by developing concurrently in two principal directions. Through the influence of many civic-minded persons, private citizen research bureaus were established which have evolved into the taxpayers associations of today. Most such taxpayers associations are active in the Governmental Research Association which was established in 1915.

On the other hand, municipal research gradually became an integral feature of city government, especially in the larger municipalities, through the establishment of various bureaus of budget and efficiency which evolved into municipal sections or divisions of administrative research and analysis. Deriving impetus from the spirit of reform which swept the country, these evangelists of scientific management raised economy and efficiency as their credo as they focused on techniques, processes, and organization structure.

Contributing significantly to the improvement of municipal government, these staff units gradually have been transformed to an array of individuals bearing such titles as organization and methods analysts, administrative analysts, systems and procedures analysts. With their focus on system, process, and technique, these skilled professionals were unprepared for the accumulating pressures of the impact of the man on the job. Accordingly, today, both in the classroom and on the job, increasing attention is being given to administrative behavior and its impact on structure and process.

Formalizing the Public Relations Unit. With the realization that no amount of publicity can long conceal ineptitude in government, the public relations practitioners have been searching for legitimation and proper role. The quest has taken them near the central concerns of management. Because of the very nature of public relations, while the practitioners have retained the publicity function, they have demonstrated in practice an increasing interest in the behavior and attitudes of people both inside and outside the formal hierarchy. Increasingly their efforts are devoted to ascertaining public attitudes through opinion polls and attitude surveys. It is on this basis that they have sought legitimation and, in some cases, achieved formal status—as a combined publicity and social survey research bureau. In this appeal for legitimation, many of the advocates of public relations have introduced ideas and notions which are extraneous to the issues involved. Public relations is intrinsically a part of the administrative process, revealing as it does the interaction of the elements as expressed through human behavior and resulting action.

The Advent of Urban Complexity. Earlier in this chapter the vastness of the technological, cultural, and behavioral problems afflicting the urban areas is discussed. Our society has changed from the simplicity of rural independence to the complexity of urban interdependence. Frustrations and anxieties have magnified and multiplied as traditional schemes have failed to respond adequately to the needs of a new, a different, an urgent society.

The Strands Become a Fabric: A New Research Unit. An approach which may hold promise of more effective understanding, control, and resolution of these issues is the establishment of what may be called a *municipal division on operational effectiveness.*[35]

Merging existing administrative analysis and public relations sections, the new staff unit would be manned by assistants trained in the social and behavioral disciplines, including organizational theorists, administrative analysts, and those having social survey, statistical, and journalistic skills. Concerned primarily with applied organizational and behavioral research, including community analysis, to ascertain attitudes and reactions, the resources of the new unit would enhance the totality of management decisions and actions. In addition to the publicity function which would be retained by the new unit, the services available through this research approach obviously have

[35] John M. Pfiffner has suggested expanded use of social scientists in government in his article, "Why Not Make Social Science Operational?" in PUBLIC ADMINISTRATION REVIEW, September, 1962, pp. 109–14. This point of view was foreshadowed 25 years ago by Henry G. Hodges in his book, CITY MANAGEMENT, THEORY AND PRACTICE OF MUNICIPAL ADMINISTRATION (New York: F. S. Crofts & Co., 1939), p. 304.

public relations significance, although by no means limited thereto.

For planning and evaluation purposes, an operations analyst would probe opinions, attitudes, and reactions of those concerned with organizational goals, policies, and procedures. The proposed operational effectiveness division would identify current public issues and problems, derive data, and analyze and propose alternative policy and procedural recommendations regarding the environment in which governmental units operate, the degree and extent of program achievement, and the effectiveness of existing organizational arrangements. While such research, fact-finding, and analysis would be carried on centrally, the information should be made available, with follow-up counsel, to operating level officials where training programs and procedures modification are most effective.

Even if the proposed unit is not established, it seems entirely possible that existing public relations units, except for the publicity function, will disappear from the organizational scene in the more effectively administered agencies as new assistants trained in the behavioral disciplines are added to the administrative staff. Under their direction, social surveys, analyses, and campaigns will be conducted for a variety of administrative purposes, and all such efforts will affect the image of both the manager and the municipality.

Public Relations and Ethics

In American society the democratic ethic, which recognizes the dignity and importance of the individual, has both public relations and management significance for the administrator. In terms of his relationships with all those associated with his jurisdiction or agency, the administrator must regard himself as in the service of all, dealing with each person fairly, honestly, and intelligently, recognizing and respecting the interests of each.

Upon this foundation—recognition of the dignity and importance of the individual—is erected a host of ethical considerations which transcend the public relations process in gov-

ernment. Herein we shall examine briefly two principal aspects—namely, ethical behavior in providing citizen services and ethical considerations in administrative communications.

Noting the mediating role among contending individual desires within a public system, Stephen K. Bailey remarked: "Politics and hierarchy induce the public servant to search imaginatively for a public-will-to-be. In this search, the public servant is often a leader in the creation of a new public will, so he is in part accountable to what he in part creates. But in any case the basic morality of the system is in its forcing of unitary claims into the mill of pluralistic considerations."[36]

Delineating a particular responsibility of the public official in this representative role, however, Edmund Burke observed in 1774 that the citizen's

. . . wishes ought to have great weight with him; their opinions high respect; their business unremitted attention. It is his duty to sacrifice his repose, his pleasures, his satisfactions to theirs—and above all, ever, and in all cases, to prefer their interest to his own.

But his unbiased opinion, his mature judgment, his enlightened conscience, he ought not to sacrifice to you, to any man, or to any set of men living. These he does not derive from your pleasure—nor from the law and the Constitution. They are a trust from Providence, for the abuse of which he is deeply answerable. *Your representative owes you,* not his industry only, but *his judgment; and he betrays,* instead of serving, *you if he sacrifices it to your opinion.*[37]

If Burke's public official owes to his constituents his mature judgment, within a plural system of contending individual desires, then his judgment must be preconditioned by acceptable ethical standards. It is Bailey's contention that

. . . personal ethics in the public service is compounded of mental attitudes and moral qualities. Both ingredients are essential. Virtue without

[36] Stephen K. Bailey. "Ethics and the Public Service," PUBLIC ADMINISTRATION REVIEW, December, 1964, p. 235.

[37] Edmund Burke, WORKS, Vol. II (Boston, 1881); quoted in Glendon A. Schubert, Jr., "The Public Interest in Administrative Decision-Making," THE AMERICAN POLITICAL SCIENCE REVIEW, June, 1957, pp. 346–68. Italics added.

understanding can be quite as disastrous as understanding without virtue.

The three essential mental attitudes are: (1) a recognition of the moral ambiguity of all men and of all public policies; (2) a recognition of the contextual forces which condition moral priorities in the public service; and (3) a recognition of the paradoxes of procedures.

The essential moral qualities of the ethical public servant are: (1) optimism; (2) courage; and (3) fairness tempered by charity.[38]

With respect to the required mental attitudes, Bailey is of the opinion that awareness of the dilemmas and paradoxes inherent in all men and policies, in specific contexts and in general administrative procedures, leads to the development of other personal attributes which increase understanding and facilitate making ethical judgments.[39]

Of the requisite moral qualities, optimism enables men to face ambiguity and paradox without becoming immobilized and to see possibilities for good in the uncertain, the ambiguous, and the inscrutable. Moral courage is not only the willingness to assume responsibility for decisions but more especially the willingness to take purposeful action and to make necessary decisions, the organizational significance of which transcends offense to personal friends. Justice tempered with charity ". . . makes of compromise not a sinister barter but a recognition of the dignity of competing claimants" fortified by persuasive rather than coercive arts.[40]

Morality and ethics thus not only precondition but are constant influences upon administrative performance and behavior. At the municipal level, the behavior of those involved in the "big-city machines" of Tweed, Crump, Shaw, and Tammany contravened acceptable standards of morality. "McCarthyism" and demagoguery, "five-percenters," mink coats, and Billie Sol Estes raised more than eyebrows at the federal level. But these are the spectacular and the flagrant. Unethical conduct is involved in the misuse of public funds, personal favoritism, private gain, and administrative ineptitude. It is spawned in the agency-client relationships of federal and state regulatory agencies. The matter of "conflict of interests" relating to private holdings and public responsibility of the same public official is frequently headlined at all levels and in all branches of government. Where personal behavior of public officials deviates from acceptable standards of morality there is rising public clamor for statutory prohibition. Increasingly, legislators, administrators, and jurists are becoming circumscribed by legal prescription. Although much of the legislation has a negative tone, some legislation is deliberately calculated to put the public official in the "gold fish bowl." This serves as a restraining influence on impropriety while assisting the official to maintain high ethical standards of performance.

Impropriety and misconduct in public office are properly proscribed, but also reprehensible is the sometimes blatant, often clever, use of public relations techniques and communications media to minimize or conceal such offenses. Such abandonment of ethics in the use of public relations techniques can never be condoned. Perhaps an overly dramatic representation is Alan Harrington's caricature of the public relations man who makes

. . . the mistake of all those who don't believe in anything: he thinks that through the artful employment of words and images he can fool the people all the time—*no matter what* the actual, physical state of affairs may be.

Imagine a clever but exceptionally corrupt PR man with a house of prostitution for a client. Why, this will soon turn out to be the noblest profession of them all! Here are those generous girls serving lonely men. Their lives are easier than the lot of the average housewife! He will produce statistics to show that as a group they have six tenths of one per cent less heart trouble than housewives. He will release photos showing them happily playing volleyball in their off hours. He will arrange a press conference for one of the girls who has just returned from a world cruise. He will prove that the girls from his client's house make happier marriages than other women. He will saturate all media with these lying truths. But all the while, off-camera, broods the enduring truth, if you will, that no girl should have to go to bed with men she doesn't know. No matter how our PR man twists and turns and

[38] *Op. cit.*, pp. 235–236. For an effective understanding of the "mental attitudes and moral qualities" essential to personal ethics in the public service, the entire article is recommended.

[39] *Ibid.*, pp. 236–40, *passim*.

[40] *Ibid.*, pp. 240–43, *passim*.

"presents facts," he cannot move out of the shadow of certain enduring truths, whether they be moral or economic.

All PR men are aware of the lurking presence of these truths, and are made nervous by them, doubly so because the majority are educated people with dim or corroded memories of classic principles. . . .[41]

Even if all publicists are not jaded with deceit, the fact remains that arrangement and adjustment of facts to conceal, mislead, misrepresent, or confuse are all contrary to ethical public relations standards. The reprehensible administrator who is guilty of unethical administrative performance and behavior compounds his guilt by resorting to deceitful use of publicity. But the American free press, militant taxpayers associations, and opposing political factions will not allow him peace. Even the less deceitful and those who seek to glorify the insignificant through publicity are vulnerable.

If these instances portray the negative aspects of morality in government and public relations and emphasize the repression of wrong-doing, what, if any, are the positive alternatives to induce ethical standards of behavior?

Legislatures, employee associations, professional societies, and thoughtful individuals have been active for a long time in promoting high standards of conduct by public officials. As early as 1924, the International City Managers' Association adopted a Code of Ethics, amended in 1938 and 1952, which has become the standard of conduct for all municipal administrative officers. In February, 1962, ICMA disseminated widely a proposed "Code of Ethics and Creeds of Municipal Officials and Employees," including a creed for city councilmen. These have been reproduced in Appendix A.

During the decade following 1950 a heightened interest in ethical behavior in government produced several new codes of ethics and new conflict of interest legislation. The Citizens League of Greater Cleveland adopted and promoted "A Code of Ethics for Citizens and Public Officials," which recognized a dual relationship through the responsibility of individual citizens for promoting ethical standards of conduct in government. Revealing their con-

cern for ethical practices the Public Relations Society of America adopted a 16-point "Code of Professional Standards for the Practice of Public Relations" which has been reproduced in Appendix B.

While it should be recognized that desirable behavior cannot be legislated, neither for renegades nor kings, the increasing interest in and visibility of high standards of conduct for public officials augurs well. When coupled with Bailey's mental attitudes and moral qualities our expectations justifiably can be high.

Conclusion

Public relations, good or bad, is a natural phenomenon in nature. Wherever human beings are, whether public official or private citizen, it is with them every day, in every act, in every procedure. Effective public relations does not just happen. It is a positive, continuous activity in which everyone has an interest.

Contrary to popular belief, municipal public relations is not of recent origin but is rooted in antiquity. It is partly because we have tried to impose new and unacceptable names and give it separate organizational status that we consider it recent. These, among other influences, have caused resistance to the concept of public relations. In this very resistance is a clue for gaining acceptance: organize it administratively throughout the hierarchy, utilizing and developing the techniques for *general administrative applicability,* not specifically for public relations alone.

Public relations is one of many important variables which affect the ability of an administrator to accomplish program objectives. It involves reciprocal influences between the agency (its personnel, its decisions, and its programs) and the attitudes and desires of persons and groups in the agency's external environment. It imposes on the administrator the necessity of dealing with public relations as an inherent and continuing element in the managerial process. He must be mindful of public relations considerations at every stage of the administrative process, from making the decision to the final point of its execution.

---

[41] *Op. cit.,* p. 60.

3

Research and the Public
Relations Process

MOST PUBLIC ADMINISTRATORS view the public
relations official as an expert at gathering
intelligence about clientele satisfaction levels.
Later, after management has formulated an
agency action program, the special communication skills of the public relations expert are
employed to influence public opinion through
favorable publicity. This book, however, assumes a larger role—one in which the public
relations staff continues to perform intelligence
and communications functions for agency administrators but in addition provides a specialized research component.

As experts in discovering agency-related trouble spots among outside special interest groups,
the public relations staff holds a unique advantage and could be trained to develop more
systematic information on which decision-makers can build more effective agency programs.
Recent advances in social science research
methods can provide the practitioner with a
variety of tools for conducting research on both
(1) the character of outside interest groups
and their agency relationships, and (2) the
effectiveness of various agency attempts to influence public opinion.

Figure 2 diagrams a proposed municipal
government public relations research cycle and
identifies eight steps: perceiving clientele
needs; clarifying the research problem; formulating the research design; gathering the data;
analysis, interpretation, and reporting to management; planning the agency response; com-

municating the program; and evaluating
agency public relations activities. The balance
of this chapter deals, in the above order, with
these eight steps.

Perceiving Clientele Needs

Regardless of the motivation—reportorial or
administrative—public relations programs are
handicapped by two characteristics of modern
life: increasing specialization among interest
group publics and overexposure to information by competing forms of mass media.
Officials in most organizations, both public and
private, have developed informal ways of listening for trouble signals in their relationships
with special interest publics. Experienced public relations practitioners consult regularly
with such bellweathers as editors, reporters,
ministers, labor leaders, bartenders, civic leaders, bankers, and housewives about their views
on municipal government activities.

Individual written and oral complaints provide further indicators of public opinion about
specific municipal programs. Letter writers, as
most administrators know, tend to be critical
rather than commendatory. Nevertheless, when
systematically classified, properly weighed, and
carefully considered, these written and oral
complaints provide useful storm warnings.

At the customer level, governmental agencies
have many employees dealing with special in-

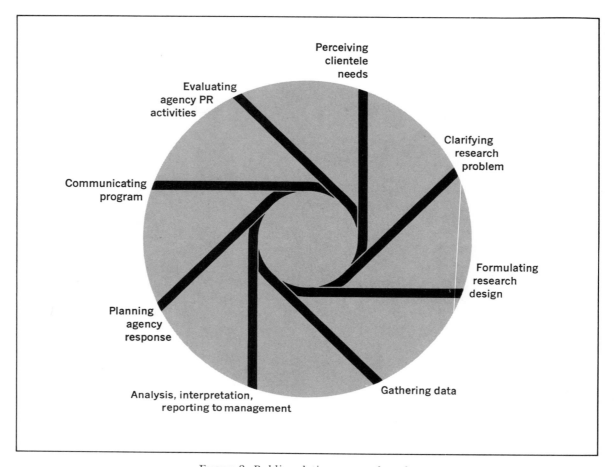

FIGURE 2. *Public relations research cycle*

terest group members on a day-to-day basis. Such first line agents should develop valid information sources and be encouraged to report what they hear. As Thoreau said, "It takes two to speak the truth, one to speak and another to hear." Systematic ways of reporting complaints and commendations can be created by imaginative administrators to offset most usually favorable but—for management—relatively useless periodic agency reports.

Idea panels in the form of advisory committees composed of leading citizens representing major community interests are characteristic of still another approach to listening. Appointment of such advisory committees creates the opportunity for frank interaction where interested and informed members can return to their own circles with new insights and support

for agency activities. Healthy mutual exchanges, however, continue only when officials pay serious attention to critical, as well as complimentary, views.

Regardless of approach, most experienced public relations practitioners take pride in their own political or public relations sensitivity. In one sense, the concept of listening described here goes far beyond our personal "infallible ear tests." Frequently, we fail to realize that regardless of our personal experience, our organizational role tends to make our limited informal sources of information questionable. Only gathering systematic information from a variety of reliable sources can better apprise the public relations practitioner and consequently the administrator of actual clientele needs.

Clarifying the Research Problem

Perhaps the most critical yet least appreciated step in the research process is the proper identification of the research problem.[1] The inexperienced investigator usually jumps immediately from the selection of a topic to the collection of data. Following such a fact-gathering spree, he will be faced with the task of formulating a meaningful problem; even worse, he will likely fail to produce anything meaningful at all.

Summarizing American pragmatist philosophers on the importance of clarifying the problem, Wayne Leys develops three useful questions that will help initiate any inquiry:

1. What is the difficulty that made us think in the first place? What precisely is the problem?

2. What will satisfactorily terminate our inquiry? Is thinking solving a problem?

3. As the result of further experience and reflection, are our ends or objectives changing?[2]

Translating an immediate or potentially troublesome situation into a concrete and explicit research problem of manageable size, then, requires imagination and creative effort. This initial step, however, should not be confused with selecting a methodology with which to study the problem. As Northrup has pointed out, ". . . it is the problem that designates the method, not the method which designates the problem."[3]

One approach to clarification is determining just what objectives are to be accomplished through research. Once again, Northrup cautions the careful investigator:

Clearly, a scientific method appropriate for answering a question concerning what ought to be the case must be different from the method which answers a question concerning what is the case. . . . Thus in the social sciences and the humanities two kinds of problems must be distinguished,

problems which require factual social theories for their adequate answer and problems which require normative social theories.[4]

In clarifying the research problem it becomes critical to determine the type of solution that will satisfy your requirements. For example, where—as a value position—citizens resent governmental operation of a publicly supported utilities company, it becomes difficult if not impossible to impress them with statistics reflecting the low cost of operation. For those who favor a mixed economy and efficiency of operations, however, comparative figures on cost and level of service provide a basis for future political and administrative support. The point is that research is not magic; it answers only those questions that are built into the initial design. Where questions are too vague and far-reaching, research will produce data that are of little value. One approach to research problem formulation is to start with such questions as these:

Precisely what would the decision-maker like to know about clientele group representatives, given the troublesome situation that has arisen?

What can public relations research yield that will enable officials to achieve their objectives?

To illustrate the steps of the research cycle shown in Figure 2, suppose we follow a hypothetical municipal public relations problem in the city of Garden Acres—population 60,000—located 40 miles from a larger metropolitan center. Members of the city council have received, over the past six weeks, "a number of written letters complaining about the low quality of the city-owned bus services." Because the City Transportation Service (CTS) has lost money for two consecutive years, City Manager Jones has been ordered to investigate the troublesome situation and make a report at next month's city council meeting. With only four weeks before the report is due, Manager Jones calls for his public relations director, Green. Together they consider the research task. Following a lengthy discussion, it is agreed that:

1. On the basis of "a number of written

[1] See discussion in Thomas C. McCormick and Roy G. Francis, METHODS OF RESEARCH IN BEHAVIORAL SCIENCES (New York: Harper and Row, 1958), p. 14.

[2] Wayne A. R. Leys, ETHICS FOR POLICY DECISIONS (Englewood Cliffs, New Jersey: Prentice-Hall, 1952), p. 154.

[3] F. S. C. Northrup, THE LOGIC OF THE SCIENCES AND THE HUMANITIES (New York: World Publishing Co. [Meridian Books], 1959), p. 20.

[4] Ibid.

complaints" (actually eight complaints over a six-week period), very little can be inferred about the nature of CTS services.

2. In order to develop sound recommendations for city council action, a more complete picture is required. Research strategy indicates three main approaches, including:

(a) conducting an experience survey of CTS officials responsible for providing the services to ascertain their perceptions of the system;

(b) conducting an opinion survey of citizen clientele group attitudes toward CTS services; and

(c) developing information on alternative methods of providing city-wide transportation such as hiring private carriers or even abandoning all bus service.

After further clarifying discussion, Manager Jones assigns the experience survey and the citizen attitude survey to Public Relations Director Green and his staff; the search for alternative transportation methods and comparative costs—essentially a literature search of city and other written documents—is assigned to another member of the city manager's office staff.

Formulating the Research Proposal

Having identified the need and translated the troublesome situation into a researchable problem, the investigator is then prepared to formulate a careful research proposal. This step, also frequently neglected by inexperienced investigators, might be compared to the drafting of architectural plans. Few builders would begin construction of an expensive building without first creating a detailed blueprint specifying building location, schedule of operations, kind of materials required, and alternative elements of cost.

In much the same way, the research proposal represents a detailed work plan showing the interrelated steps involved in the research process. Such a proposal should include: background information and survey of previous research; statement of the research problem; formulation of hypotheses; clarification and formal definition of the concepts used in the study; specification of indicators and methods to be used and kinds of evidence that would support or reject the hypotheses; and a description of the sampling process.

The role of the hypothesis—a proposition describing an assumed relationship between two or more factors—is to suggest logical explanations and to guide investigators in discovering new relationships. The level of explanation will vary, depending largely on what is known about the research problem through experience or previous research. The attempt to develop research hypotheses forces the investigator to make critical relationships explicit and to develop ways of testing these explanations against factual situations.[5]

This approach to collection of data suggests that answers to problems can be obtained in a variety of ways. Practical limitations of time and money may force officials to restrict the quality or quantity of information to be obtained. Such limitations, however, increase the chances for error. Regardless of the approach, both investigators and administrators should reach a clear agreement on the research objectives to be achieved in a specific study. Such prior agreement reduces the anxieties and conflicting expectations that are associated with most serious research projects.

At this stage, the researcher can also come to grips with the technical requirements of the research task. The topic selected for investigation—be it an evaluation of an action agency program, an administrative analysis, a diag-

---

[5] This process of generating hypotheses in turn leads to clarification and formal definition of the concepts used in the study. For example, public opinion is a concept that most public relations men feel comfortable in using. Yet how can this concept be useful in determining public support for, as an example, collecting refuse in a particular way? Mayor Samuel Yorty was first defeated by the Los Angeles City Council in his attempt to change the method of garbage disposal, but he has more recently succeeded in reversing that decision in favor of a combined pickup. Throughout the controversy, both sides claimed the support of public opinion. The public exchanges produced little factual information on which to judge. How favorable must the public opinion be to claim support for one method over another? Who represents public opinion in such a case? Which questions are administrative and which are political?

nostic survey of a community, or a public opinion survey of attitudes and opinions on specific government services—is usually of such scope that not all aspects of the problem can be investigated simultaneously. The task must be reduced to one that can be handled by the agency's research staff, divided into several smaller studies, or contracted to an outside research organization.

Once the major concepts set forth in the hypotheses have been operationally defined— that is, defined in terms of specific relationships of passengers, bus fares, employee wages, etc.—it is necessary to determine just which method or combination of methods is to be used in gathering data that indicate the presence or absence of certain factors. Depending once again on the research problem, the investigator may elect to study documentary sources indicative of past performance as, for example, in a statistical analysis of the types of major crimes occurring over time in various sections of a city.

By contrast, an intensive descriptive study of administrative procedures in issuing building code licenses may result in suggestions for improving services at several critical points in the process. The development of survey research techniques and systematic structured interview methods also permit the trained investigator to obtain data on attitudes, perceptions, and behavior of both agency officials and clientele group members.

An important objection might be raised at this point by those public relations practitioners who question the necessity of following such formalized research procedures at the day-to-day working level. The choice of research strategy depends on the importance of the problem to be solved and the penalty for failure. Developing an adequate written proposal requires the investigator to clarify his thinking by demonstrating careful analysis and planning. Regardless of the size of the research task, time is saved and administrative support more easily developed when written work plans are prepared in advance of the actual collection of data.

Whatever data collection method is employed—observation, personal or official documents, personal interview, sociometric methods, statistical records, content analysis or mass media, mail survey, survey polling, or some combination—it becomes necessary also to specify the information source—commonly referred to as the sample. Where documentary or statistical methods are employed, references should be identified in advance; where people are to be interviewed, the specific individuals should be determined according to the requirements for probability or purposive sampling.[6]

Returning again, by way of example, to our hypothetical study of transportation services in the city of Garden Acres, we can appreciate the task facing Public Relations Director Green. In order to translate his general assignment into a written research proposal, he must:

1. Divide the research task into two separate research problems: one, interviews with CTS officials to obtain a description of the present status of the city's transportation system together with their perceptions of its strengths and weaknesses; and, two, a survey of attitudes of citizens who actually use or are potential customers for public transportation in the city of Garden Acres.

2. Obtain background information on the CTS that will give ideas for building questions, suggest points that should be investigated further, and indicate terminology, organizational traditions, symbols, and position titles that are critical to any study in public administration.

3. Contact a social science research consultant at the local college who can be of technical help in drafting the final research design which includes sampling procedures and questionnaire construction.

4. Determine likely relationships in hypothesis form that will guide and sharpen questionnaire construction and later analysis. For example, one might expect that complaints can be categorized in such a way as to relate income with cost of transportation—i.e., "the lower a person's income the fewer the complaints about service." In addition, "the lower the income the more objection to raising the transportation fares to improve service." This speculation, in turn, leads to other questions of interest such as: "What percentage of CTS customers can be classified as low income citizens? Is the usage pattern distributed in such a way that property owners should be taxed to support a more

6 Space does not permit a treatment of sampling; for additional references, see Selltiz, et al., RESEARCH METHODS IN SOCIAL RELATIONS (New York: Henry Holt and Company, 1960), McCormick and Francis, op. cit, and William H. Riker, THE STUDY OF LOCAL POLITICS (New York: Random House, 1959), p. 14.

efficient system or should limited groups of CTS customers bear a larger share of the cost? Hypotheses, then, are bridges that help the investigator connect citizen attitudes to larger policy questions that must inevitably be considered by decision-makers.

5. Identify CTS officials to be interviewed by position and name as well as select through a randomized sampling procedure a group of public transportation customers whose attitudes toward services could be determined by an inexpensive poll-type, short-answer interview.

6. Develop questions for each group that are designed in advance to elicit information that can be easily tabulated by percentages and reflected in tabular form.

7. Pretest questionnaires on smaller samples to improve wording, eliminate poor questions, design closed-end questions for alternative type responses, check for timing and clarity, etc.

8. Prepare for data gathering phase by developing copies of final questionnaire schedules, coordinating and training interviewers and obtaining access to CTS officials, and determining exact locations and approaches to CTS customers.

No research design will be complete without a careful description of the time, personnel, and financing required to complete the study. The usual procedure is to subdivide each phase and estimate the resources needed. One promising approach to this critical problem is the introduction of the program evaluation review technique (PERT) as a tool for scheduling research according to the interrelationships of time, cost, and coordinated event analysis.

By indicating through a symbol system each event (O) and its connecting activities—managers can see during any phase of the project the logical sequences of events, their interdependencies, and the relative completeness of a research task. Fully utilized, such a scheduling system also shows over-all job planning, provides a vehicle for project simulation over time, indicates in advance where bottlenecks are likely to occur—thereby giving advance warning for corrective action so as to avoid delay on the critical activity path—allows optimum resource scheduling of personnel and materials, pinpoints responsibility, and allows all participants to visualize interrelationships of activities with the total project.[7]

As a final reference to our hypothetical, 30-day study of the Garden Acres transportation system, Figure 3 illustrates a modified version of PERT as applied to the research assignment about to be undertaken by municipal Public Relations Director Green and his staff.

Gathering the Data

Regardless of the main methodological approach employed—observation, personal or official documents, personal interview, survey polling, sociometric methods, analysis of statistical records, content analysis, or mail survey—a useful initial step to solving any research problem is what has been described as the natural history stage of inquiry.[8] Information obtained at this stage often suggests new relationships for systematic research. Investigators should become familiar with the history, terminology, and general operation of the agency or group to be studied before undertaking field research to gather more specific information.[9]

Organizational access to agency materials is vital to the success of most serious research projects. Where agency personnel must be diverted from routine assignments to assist outside investigators in collecting data on agency operations, research becomes expensive business. When not successfully resolved, accompanying hostility and resistance may so limit the investigator's source of data as to seriously bias his results and make it difficult to justify the high cost of the research.

Advanced planning to obtain official cooperation plus efforts to minimize field work through prior selection of the sample and development and pretesting of a systematic interview schedule or content analysis guides can minimize organizational or interest group resistance to data collection by an outside group of investigators and minimize any bias of the investigator's results.

---

[7] Technical information on PERT application supplied by Ron R. Platt, of Data Perspectives, Inc.

[8] Northrup, *op. cit.*, p. 35.

[9] See Selltiz, *et al.*, *op. cit.*, Chapters 6, 7, 8, and 9 for a review of these frequently used methods of gathering research data.

Analysis, Interpretation, and Reporting to Management

Where a carefully formulated proposal for data gathering has been linked to specific research questions, analysis, interpretation and reporting become relatively simple; such is not the case with research where little time has been invested in anticipating the results of data collection and interpretation.

According to Selltiz, *et al.:* "It is the purpose of analysis to summarize the completed observations in such a manner that they yield answers to the research questions. It is the purpose of interpretation to search for the broader meaning of these answers by linking them to other available knowledge."[10]

Once data gathering has been completed, it is necessary in most empirical research projects to establish categories so that raw data may be coded or classified according to some systematic method. Certain basic rules should be followed when categorizing data: (1) the set of categories should be derived from a single classificatory principle; (2) the set of categories should be mutually exhaustive; and (3) the categories within the set should be mutually exclusive.

Frequently the hypotheses guiding a study will indicate the logical categories to be established. Where responses to questions, for example, are a simple yes or no type of response, the procedures are relatively simple. Coding data from unstructured interviews, by contrast, is much like content analysis in that decisions must be made that may affect the statistical outcome or validity of the study. Questionnaire schedules or other instruments therefore should be examined prior to coding for completeness, legibility, comprehensibility, consistency, uniformity, and inappropriate responses.

Tabulation, part of the technical process in the statistical analysis of data, is simply counting to determine the number of cases that fall into the various categories. The terms "cross-tabulation" and "breakdown" are often em-

ployed to refer to the associations between cases that occur in two or more categories. Tabulation and transfer of data to cards for easier handling may be done entirely by hand or by machine.[11]

The purpose of statistical analysis by transferring raw data to tabular form is (1) to determine what is "typical" in the group through such measures of central tendency as the mean, median, and mode; (2) to indicate how widely individuals in the group vary in terms of range, quartile deviation, and standard deviation; (3) to show the relation of different variables in the data to one another—such as age, education, income, or occupation to attitudes toward government service; and (4) to describe the similarities and differences between two or more groups of individuals.

A critical step in statistical analysis and interpretation is to link the findings of a specific local study with the results of other research in the area. Limited generalizations from samples to similar or larger groups must be carefully considered to prevent the evidence from being misused. Derrel Huff has colorfully pointed to the usual pitfalls in his little book, *How To Lie with Statistics.* The objective of analysis and interpretation is to provide investigators with a rationale by which to test the hypotheses guiding the inquiry.

Having analyzed and interpreted his data, the investigator is faced with the task of reporting his research findings to any one of several audiences. For example, the report to a group of top decision-makers would undoubtedly contain materials and conclusions not published for, say, a public relations type of pamphlet. Since the utility of the research may well depend on his ability to communicate accurately with his readers, the report writer's first step is to clearly identify his audience and determine both what a specific audience needs to know and how the information can best be transmitted.

The next step is to decide just what informa-

---

[10] *Ibid.,* p. 386. Much of the discussion in this section has been taken from the Selltiz volume.

[11] While each method has its advantages and disadvantages, where the number of cards used is below 500, a skilled clerical worker can handle most jobs efficiently. Machine tabulation actually involves more clerical and other specialized operations than hand tabulation does, largely because of the "get-ready" or programming time.

CITY COUNCIL REQUESTS C.M. REPORT ON CTS

MARCH		
1		
2	Start research design construction: problem, hypotheses, questionnaire.	Conference C. M. Jones, M. P. R. Green. Research problem identified; concepts, hypotheses, methods. — Start research design construction: problem, hypotheses, questionnaire.
3		
4		Background information on CTS officials and operators.
5		Select sample CTS officials. / Assignment of sub-project for alternative systems.
6		Pre-test.
7		
8		
9	Select sample of CTS customers. Pre-test questionnaire.	Review complete research design with C. M. / Interviewers trained. Interviews prepared. / Complete search.
10	Interviewers trained. Interviewing starts.	Appointments with CTS officials. / Interviewing starts.
11		
12	Interviewing completed. Prepare schedules.	Interviewing completed.
13	Coding starts. — Secretarial, tabulation.	Coding starts. — Secretarial, tabulation.
14		
15	Coding ends.	Coding ends.
16	Interpretation of results.	Interpretation of results. / First draft.

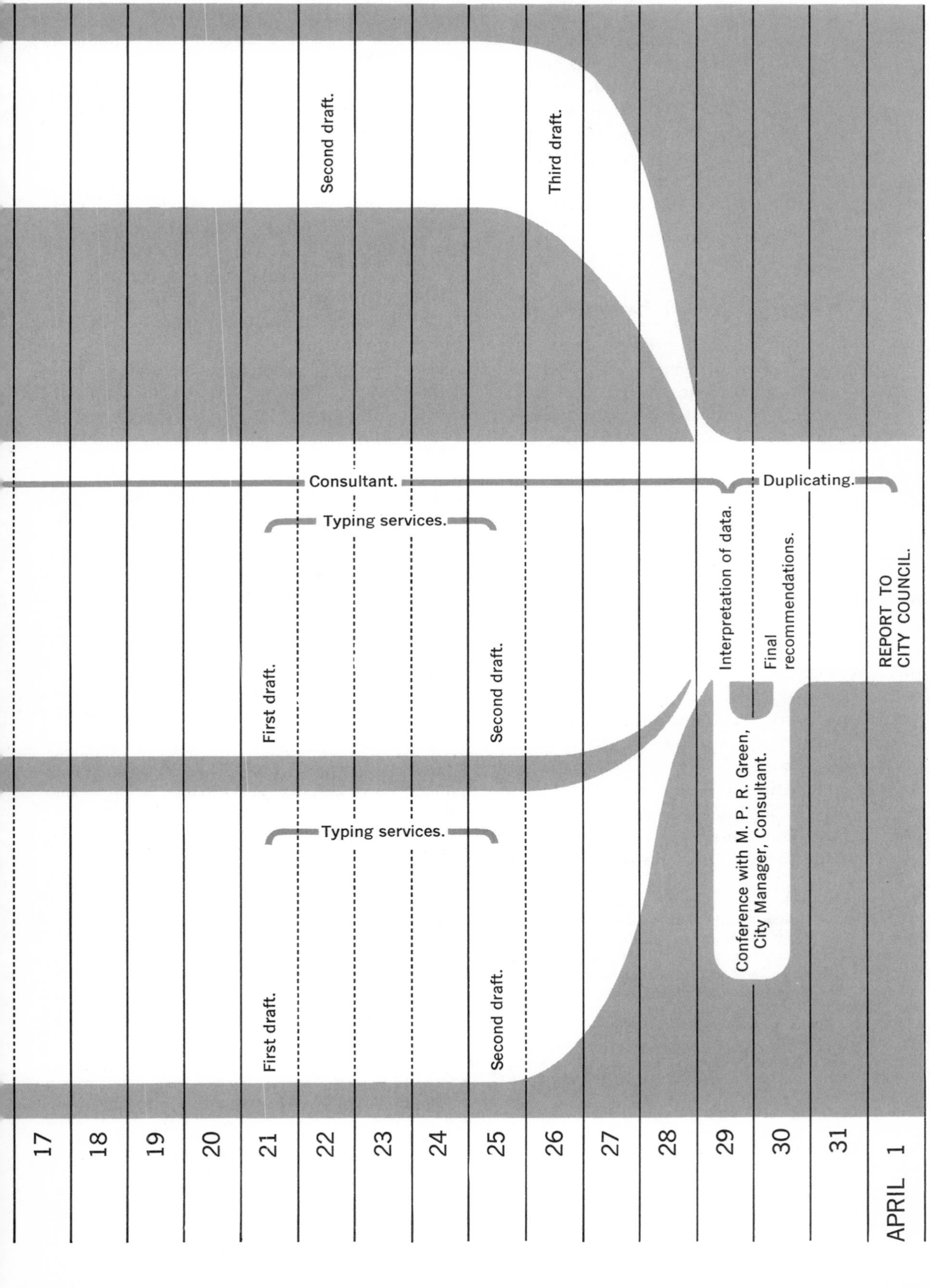

FIGURE 3. *Modified PERT scheduling analysis of 30-day municipal public relations research project on Garden Acres City transportation services*

tion is to be conveyed and how the various points are related to one another. Third, the preparation of a detailed outline allows one to concentrate on what is to be said, without worrying about how to say it.[12] Many authors agree that time is probably saved in the long run by writing the first draft quickly. Once content, form, and length have been determined, attention can be given to style and precision.[13]

Planning the Agency Response

Once the report has been written, clearly describing research results together with interpretations and suggestions for action, the next major step is for administrative policy-makers to plan the agency response. Planning, in contrast to the earlier steps of the research process described here, is "a wholly practical matter, a step-by-step analysis of how objectives are to be made realities. . . . Planning is clarifying one's objectives and then determining what action shall be taken by whom, when, by what methods, and at what costs in order to achieve the desired goal."[14]

Long-range planning relates to broad outlines of strategy, short-term projects to the tactics that make the strategy work. The first step, as with any decision-making situation, is to determine the over-all long-range objectives of the agency and relate them to the specific written statements of policy that have been agreed on by top decision-makers. At this point, it becomes possible to review specific programs and their relation to these long-range objectives in light of research findings. Research and planning thus are integral parts of the total programming process.[15]

The role of the public relations man in this planning process is far from clear. Traditionally the public relations man has been seen largely as a staff director in the publication of programs that are well established. There are, however, two principal reasons why he should not only be closely tied into the research and analysis phase but also should participate actively in the planning stages. First, having completed the research relating to a troublesome situation, the public relations man is best able to interpret the public's needs, desires, and opinions to the policy-makers. Second, by participating in the planning process, he can more fully understand and interpret basic policies.

New York Times staff writer William M. Freeman has stated the situation this way:

How many men with a public relations title actually take part in management? . . . Public relations is an all-inclusive concept, defined as the effort to improve the relationship of a product, a person or a company with the public. Yet, when it comes to a showdown, "public relations" is watered down to publicity, the running of errands between the decision-makers and the media selected to spread the news. If the public relations man is to be worthy of the title he should be a full-scale advisor to management, and he should take part in the mapping of plans for improving the regard in which the management product is held.

. . . It is important to remember that public relations at the highest level uses advertising and publicity as techniques. The PR man is out in the cold because he isn't doing the job he says he is doing. PR people have only themselves to blame for this state of affairs. Instead of practicing public relations, many are merely using the title, and engaging in publicity, or press agentry.[16]

From this observation, then, we see that it becomes critical not only to establish agency objectives but also to meaningfully involve those who are responsible for achieving these objectives. Planning, like problem-solving at all

[12] While there is no set form for a research report, it should contain these points: (1) a statement of the problem the study is concerned with; (2) research procedures, study design, nature of the sample, data collection techniques, and method of statistical analysis; (3) results; (4) implications drawn from the results; and (5) the summary.

[13] See William J. Strunk, THE ELEMENTS OF STYLE (New York: The Macmillan Company, 1959); Rudolph Flesch, A NEW GUIDE TO BETTER WRITING (New York: Harper and Row, 1963); and Margaret Nicholson, A DICTIONARY OF AMERICAN-ENGLISH USAGE (New York: Oxford University Press, 1957).

[14] Marshall Edward Dimock and Gladys Ogden Dimock, PUBLIC ADMINISTRATION (New York: Holt, Rinehart and Winston, 3rd ed., 1964), p. 131.

[15] See PROGRAM DEVELOPMENT AND ADMINISTRATION Chicago: International City Managers' Association, 1965), a monograph dealing with the totality of the programming process.

[16] Quoted in Scott M. Cutlip and Allen H. Center, EFFECTIVE PUBLIC RELATIONS (Englewood Cliffs, New Jersey: Prentice-Hall, 1958), 2nd ed., p. 117.

levels, proceeds one step at a time. The first is to create an atmosphere where creative problem-solving is possible.[17] Such an atmosphere requires top administrators to recognize that time spent in planning is time well spent. Following the initial idea-getting stage, characterized by much talking and discussion, comes the need for a written proposal similar to the outline of research steps described above (see Figure 2) in which agency resources are deployed at critical targets. Organizational resources must be identified and assembled in such a way as to produce the most effective ideas and methods for implementation.

In the effort to link planning with action programs, like many sensitive private organizations, the DuPont Company has developed a program project analysis formula that may be adapted for municipal agency activities.[18]

A most critical factor operating in any municipal public relations situation is a concept of time. Program objectives and agency resources must in the final analysis be circumscribed by the time available for administrative action. *Planning, then, is that encounter where the public relations research man, whose major concern is long-range agency image-building, must compromise with the practicing administrator, whose primary responsibility is immediate effective agency performance.*

A sense of timing is also a critical factor in implementing action programs. Conflicting press releases or other ill-timed news items can all but destroy the attempt to influence public opinion, as when government officials trying to gain public support for fair employment practice policies are embarrassed by officials in a sister agency charged with discriminatory hiring practices.

Communicating the Program

Once planning has been linked with agency objectives and intermediate programs have been created or modified by research evidence, the next step is implementation through communication. It appears that people begin, modify, and end relationships by communicating with each other. Communication then is a channel of influence and, therefore, a mechanism for change. Leavitt defines communication and the advantages of two-way systems this way: "First, to communicate is to shoot information *and* to hit a target with it. Shooting alone is not communicating. Second, to have more than chance probability of hitting a target requires that the sender get feedback from the target about the accuracy of his shots."[19]

Communication can hardly be effective when the audience is not listening. The champion marksman who shoots for a bullseye takes care to adjust his sights to compensate for the nature and distance of his target. In a similar way, identification of those special interest publics affected by municipal government activities represents the initial step in more effective communication.

Identifying special interest publics goes beyond simple enumeration. Members of a given public are continually in motion, shifting their associations, age groupings, economic and political interests, and geographical residence. "In public relations you must communicate with a passing parade, not a standing army."[20]

[17] Norman R. F. Maier and John J. Hayes, CREATIVE MANAGEMENT (New York: John Wiley and Sons, 1962).

[18] Quoted in Cutlip and Center, *op. cit.*, pp. 115–116:
What is the objective this project is designed to gain or approach?
Is the objective sound and desirable?
Are there collateral advantages?
Is the project feasible?
Can it be done with existing personnel?
Does it involve cooperation outside the department?
Is it counter to sound public relations policy?
Is it counter to company policy?
Is the expense too high in relation to possible gain?
Can it embarrass sales, production, research?
Where is the money coming from?
What are the penalties of failure?
Why do it now?
Why do it this way?
Who must approve the project?
Who must be informed?

[19] Harold J. Leavitt, MANAGERIAL PSYCHOLOGY (Chicago: University of Chicago Press, 1958), p. 125.

[20] Cutlip and Center, *op. cit.*, p. 160. Also see Chapter 8, "Communications," SOCIAL SCIENCE IN PUBLIC RELATIONS, by Rex Harlow (New York: Harper and Row, 1957), p. 28.

Having carefully identified the specific characteristics of interest group members and their leaders,[21] the public relations man is prepared to establish a two-way communication channel. Cutlip and Center have summarized several factors associated with effective communication as the 7 C's in the following manner:

1. *Credibility.* Communication starts with a climate of belief. This is built by performance on the part of the source. The performance reflects an earnest desire to serve the receiver. The receiver must have confidence in the sender. He must have a high regard for the source's competence on the subject.

2. *Context.* A communications program must square with the realities of its environment. Mechanical media are only supplementary to the word and deed that take place in daily living. The context must provide for participation and playback.

3. *Content.* The message must have meaning for the receiver. It must have relevance to him. In general, people select those items of information which promise them greatest rewards. The content determines the audience.

4. *Clarity.* The message must be put in simple terms. Words must mean the same thing to the receiver as they do to the sender. Complex issues must be compressed into themes, slogans, stereotypes, which have simplicity, clarity. The farther a message has to travel, the simpler it must be. An institution must speak with one voice, not many.

5. *Continuity and Consistency.* Communication is an unending process. It requires repetition to achieve penetration. Repetition—with variation—contributes to both factual and attitude learning. The story must be consistent.

6. *Channels.* Established channels of communication should be used—channels which the receiver uses and respects. Creating new ones is difficult. Different channels have different effects and serve in different stages of the diffusion process.

7. *Capability of Audience.* Communication must take into account the capability of the audience. Communications are most effective when they require the least effort on the part of the recipient. This includes factors of availability, habit, reading ability, and receiver's knowledge.[22]

The municipal public relations process, then, is a two-way process in which agency performance is communicated to outside clientele groups, members, and agency officials. Figure 4 illustrates this process by identifying external public and private interest groups affecting most municipal agencies. In a superior relationship to agency officials are the policy-making bodies represented by the city council and chief administrative officers.

At a corresponding level with agency officials are other line and staff departments within the municipal government system. These officials form a special interest public through their day-to-day exchange of technical information with agency personnel. Other members of this lateral interest group include professionals from neighboring city, county, state, federal, and—in some cases—certain international jurisdictions.

Most public relations attention, however, is focused on those clientele groups that benefit directly from municipal government services. Such vocal groups as the local chamber of commerce, veterans' organizations, service clubs, PTA groups, property owners, and minority group organizations represent a sampling of special interest publics that demand constant political and administrative attention from city officials.[23]

By following a systematic program for research as described in this chapter clientele groups can be carefully identified as to their membership, the numbers of active members participating, their potential influence, their level of satisfaction with agency programs, and their methods of influence throughout the community. Once program policy has been formulated, research should also be undertaken to determine the relative effectiveness of attempts at mass or special interest communication techniques. How effective, for example, is television compared with newspaper coverage? Under what conditions are smaller clientele group conferences superior to media cover-

---

[21] For systematic and extensive treatment of publics and interest groups, see Chapter 5, "The Multitudinous Publics," and Chapter 8, "Community Group Relationships."

[22] Cutlip and Canter, *op. cit.*, pp. 140–41.

[23] For detailed consideration of the range of interest groups that can be serviced, see Chapter 8, "Community Group Relationships." See also Part II, "Divisions of Public Relations," in Rex Harlow and Marvin Black, PRACTICAL PUBLIC RELATIONS (New York: Harper and Row, rev. ed., 1952), and Section II, "What Public Relations Includes," in PUBLIC RELATIONS HANDBOOK, Philip Lesley, editor (Englewood Cliffs, New Jersey: Prentice-Hall, 1950).

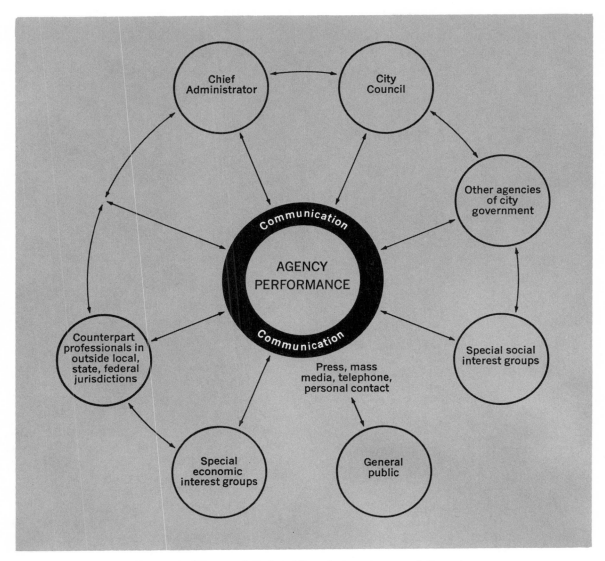

FIGURE 4. *The municipal public relations process: influencing opinion through performance and communication*

age? These are questions that can only be answered through researching the public relations process.

Evaluating Agency Public Relations

The final step in the research process is that point at which hard questions of effective performance can be raised.[24] How effective is a

specific public relations program? What indicators can be used to demonstrate effective performance? What cost factors must be considered in evaluating competing programs? What are the political and administrative consequences of implementing specific programs? Is a stronger public relations program the answer that is required to meet a troublesome situation?

Charles R. Wright points to a common fallacy characteristic of many public relations approaches, the attempt to flood the public with mass media. He states that unread leaflets,

[24] For a review of certain difficulties, see Burns W. Roper, "Can We Measure Results?" PUBLIC RELATIONS JOURNAL, April, 1958, pp. 3–6.

unheard broadcasts, unviewed films—however abundantly and skillfully produced—have no chance of influencing an audience that is not there. Volume of output does not guarantee that an audience is reached.[25]

Wright has suggested four dimensions on which public relations program effectiveness may be judged:

1. *Audience Coverage:* To produce results you must first reach the audience. How large an audience is reached? What are they like? What proportion of the desired audience do they represent?

2. *Audience Response:* How do members of the audience respond? Does the content of the message strike them favorably or unfavorably? Does it arouse their interest? Does it bore them? Do they understand it?

3. *Communications Impact:* After an appraisal of these immediate reactions, you must consider the impact which a message has on its audience. What are the lasting, discernible effects upon people exposed to a message?

4. *Process of Influence:* What is the process by which a communication operates to influence its target audience? Through what channels of influence and mechanisms of persuasion does the message finally affect the individual? How effective is the program in setting into motion the social processes necessary to influence the opinions and behavior of its target audience?[26]

By way of contrast David Cox reports a study of public relations in a local unemployment compensation office which demonstrates that public relations programs beyond the "point of sale" where employee meets customer have limited value to an agency's success where (1) publics are limited and highly specialized, and (2) where an official's action alternatives are constrained.[27]

The following five-point checklist may prove useful in assessing particular municipal public relations programs:

1. Is your target objective realistic, given your ability to commit resources? For example, is the objective to lower the night-time incidence of burglaries in suburban residences? Or to enhance the prestige of the law enforcement agency and to produce a greater concern by the public over law enforcement problems?

2. Has your campaign organizational strategy been realistic? Or has it been merely a token effort to try and demonstrate administrative support of a grand objective, and thus virtually a waste of effort?

3. Have proper resources been allocated to the research, planning, and execution of a given program? What plans have been approved to conduct intensive follow-up research where results have not been satisfactory?

4. Has the activity prescribed been of sufficient duration to justify results? If the problem is a continuing one, has a permanent commitment to the activity been made?

5. After inauguration, is the program evaluated from many perspectives from time to time to determine if it is accomplishing desired results? Are checks made to assure that proper resource allocations have been made to the program? Have the views and opinions of experts been solicited in this evaluation activity? Are proper techniques being used in the program? Are they adequate to the job? Are unnecessarily refined techniques being used?[28]

The new public relations model that is proposed in this book adds to the traditional intelligence and communications skills attributed to public relations experts by building up a research component capable of developing vital decision-making information.

---

[25] Charles R. Wright, "Evaluating Mass Media Campaigns," UNESCO INTERNATIONAL SOCIAL SCIENCE BULLETIN, Vol. VII, No. 3 (1955), p. 425ff. Some government agencies experienced in public education techniques have actually moved away from an emphasis on mass media to programs of community participation by opinion leaders. For an analysis of state civil rights agency public education programs, see Kent M. Lloyd, STATE FEPC PUBLIC EDUCATION PROGRAMS: A COMPARATIVE CIVIL RIGHTS STUDY (Seattle-Olympia: Washington State Research Council, 1957).

[26] *Ibid.*

[27] David M. Cox, "How Much Public Relations in Government?" PUBLIC ADMINISTRATION REVIEW, Summer,

1961, p. 136. For some ideas on training employees, see Douglas Williams, "How Employees Influence a Company's Reputation," PUBLIC RELATIONS JOURNAL, May, 1959, pp. 11–15, 29. Also see Roger D. Bonham, "Ambassadors of Ill Will," PUBLIC RELATIONS JOURNAL, July, 1959, pp. 16–17.

[28] Also see John T. Cunningham, "Evaluating Public Relations' Effectiveness," PUBLIC RELATIONS JOURNAL, January, 1962, pp. 21–23.

4

City Council: Focal Point
of Influences

On being taunted for his lack of social accomplishments, Themistocles, in antiquity, clarified his goal: "I never learned to tune a harp, or to play upon a lute; but I know how to raise a small and obscure city to glory and greatness."

The transition from considering public relations perspectives to discussing program involvement is no less dramatic than Themistocles' transition from harp tuning to city raising. The municipal legislative body—the city council, village board, or town selectmen—is and must be the focal point of a community's public relations. Certainly the councilman, as he is termed in most cities, raised to prominence by the electorate, recognizes the deep personal need for public understanding and acceptance, or he will not be a councilman for long.

From Both Ends of the Telescope—
and More

As the principal instrumentality in municipal government for translating myriad and divergent citizen interests and influences into governmental policy, the city council, both as a body and as indivduals, sets the tone for a municipality's public relations.

It is in the city council where interests converge, both those emanating from within the city hierarchy and from outside among individual citizens and groups. Moreover, the convergence of such influences is given high visibility because, under law and by its nature, the city council transacts its business—makes its decisions—in full view of the public. Therefore, both schisms which exist within the community and differences among municipal employees are often opened to full public view through councilmanic discussion and action.

Furthermore, because individual councilmen's tenure in office is dependent in considerable measure on the public relations of the municipality as well as on their own, the resolution of individual citizen grievances and other problems and needs by each councilman, acting either unilaterally or in concert with one or more other councilmen, heightens the visibility of the city council as the *focal point of interests.*

The electoral process by which councilmen ascend to public office provides the basis for the resolution of community interests, or the synthesizing of diverse points of view into governmental policy and programs. Some actual resolution and synthesis occur during the political campaign. The synthesizing process, however, continues interminably. It occurs both formally and informally. Viewing the city council as the legislative body, it is revealed by continuous legislative-executive (strong mayor or city manager or both) relationships, legislative-employee relationships (ranging from department head to custodian, street-sweeper, and file clerk), legislative-citizen relationships, and relationships of city councilmen with other public officials outside the specific municipality. Some of these relationships in addition to some special variations are highlighted in this chapter.

Citizen Attitudes toward Municipal Government

One of the chief differences between government and private enterprise is that the "patrons"—that is, the citizens—of government are more or less forced to lend at least their financial support to government operations.

While all persons are theoretically able to choose their occupations and places of residence, all are required to pay taxes, regardless of how they earn a living or where they live. And while they theoretically direct the use of their tax money by electing the policy-making officials of government, they obviously do not vote for each item of expense incurred by government.

Perhaps it is because of the attitudes which some people have about government and the special attitudes which councilmen have about the public that public relations is so very important in local government. It is perhaps somewhat easier to list the attitudes of the public than it is to describe the attitudes of city councilmen. We should keep in mind, however, that in describing attitudes of the public, we may also be describing councilmen's attitudes toward government, either as expressed by them prior to becoming councilmen, or even while they serve.

A major concern expressed by the public toward government has to do with money. While taxes are here to stay, public acceptance of taxes is not guaranteed. It is thus not uncommon for a dissatisfied citizen to feel that he is paying the salary of the public official whom he confronts at the moment.

Closely connected with the idea that the dissatisfied citizen pays the salaries of government employees—which is, of course, true to a certain extent—is the belief on the part of some people that a majority of government officials are "political hacks drinking at the public trough," or that they are "politicians for profit." Or, we may look at it this way, taking a specific example: the citizen who notices that a certain councilman is using a city-owned automobile during the evening hours may assume that the official is using the vehicle for private purposes and is thus misusing the taxpayer's money; or the same citizen may admire or pity the official for having to leave his family in order to attend a meeting of importance to the city.

Of course, these different attitudes are rarely stated by citizens. We know that they exist, however, as a result of what we hear privately and what we ourselves may have at one time believed. Unfortunately, the several negative attitudes which the public may have toward government often are the principal basis for municipal government concern with public relations. Fortunately citizens also hold a variety of positive, constructive attitudes about city government.

Few cities provide opportunities for the development and maintenance of a public relations program which incorporates the best known principles of communication and also permits experimentation with some of the less tried but promising techniques in this field.

Where do we find the "public" that cities, counties, school districts, and other local governments are trying to reach? In one sense, the task is simplified by the tendency of people to join with others of similar interests; thus are formed a great number of groups which constitute a portion of what we call our "public." One person may join several groups, and one such group may actually represent a variety of interests and viewpoints.[1]

The city council of course has more than one public; there are great varieties of them. Most people join groups with common interests of one sort or another to promote the group's interest, and many citizens belong to more than one group. The members of the city council, sitting as they do on the board of directors of the municipal corporation, represent not only their particular constituents but also the entire

---

[1] For a more thorough discussion of publics and group participation, see Chapters 5 and 8.

electorate. It is indeed a rude awakening for the new councilman who finds his opinion on the public interest of a particular project violently opposed by major influential persons and groups, some of whom have worked long and hard to place him in his new post of power and prestige.

The councilman must have a high threshold of understanding and patience when the local chamber of commerce insists on lower taxes and at the same time decries competitive bidding and requests city financial support. The point is that there are different publics for different purposes. The taxpaying resident businessman with income property who has children in school, goes to church, and is a member of the leading service club is, in fact, a member of seven publics, several of which consistently bring conflicting pressures to bear on city councilmen.

From Policy to Operations

"The people elect the city council. The council determines the policies of the city government. . . . In determining policy the councilman does his best to represent his constituents. . . ."[2]

The many influences upon a councilman make him acutely aware of the need for understanding and acceptance by the electorate. Nor are these pressures limited to policy determining matters. From Professor William B. Munro's vivid and biting description of the "silent voter," one infers that no problem is too small, too unimportant to be called to the attention of the councilman.

The city dweller whose rubbish is not picked up, the resident who gets a ticket for violating the overnight parking prohibition, the influential businessman whose nephew does not get a city job, the person who lives along the street being rebuilt too slowly—each of these tells his councilman and demands his rights as a taxpayer. The councilman must be ready and able to deal with each problem—be it policy, procedure, personnel, or operating detail—and give

---

[2] HANDBOOK FOR COUNCILMEN IN COUNCIL-MANAGER CITIES (Chicago: International City Managers' Association, 2nd ed., 1964), pp. 1–2.

his constituent the representation for which he was elected.

THE MAYOR RESOLVES THE "ARREST CASE"

Typically, the mayor as the ceremonial head of the city government is confronted with a myriad of problems ranging from minor complaints to major grievances.

This is an actual case that occurred in a small California city. As the mayor recalls, it went something like this.

I am a realtor and many times people with civic problems come into my business office. One day two men came in, one of whom I recognized as a local minister. After sitting down, the other man, whom I did not know, burst out:

"We are good, law abiding citizens! We're respectable—and that Captain Dingle arrested her—like a common criminal. He forced his way into our home and said, 'Let's go, Skinner, I'm taking you in!'"

"Now, now," interposed the minister, "calm down, Mr. Skinner, we're here to get to the bottom of this. Let's not get excited! Please tell the mayor just exactly what happened."

"That's what I'm doing! He came in and started swearing and cursing and ordering her around. He said vile things and I don't have to put up with that! Yes, I went to the chief of police and he didn't help at all—he said I should be glad she wasn't thrown into jail. You can't pick on us just because we live in a trailer park."

"Who is he?" I asked.

"Captain Dingle, that no good badge-happy Captain," he replied. "He's the one who caused all the trouble. He told the trailer park manager that we were wanted by the police in four states—now she always looks at us funny when we come in."

"When did all this happen?" I asked.

"About three or four weeks ago," he replied. "Without any warning he pushed the trailer door open, almost knocked her down—and said, 'Let's go, Mrs. Skinner, I have a warrant for your arrest!'"

"Are you sure that's exactly what the Captain said?" I asked.

He almost shouted, "What difference does it make what he said? He swore, and called her dirty names, and he arrested her——We're good church people—we never had any trouble with the law!—why are they picking on us?—just because we live in a trailer court, that's why."

"What did the Captain say?" I asked quietly.

"He said that she was under arrest—wanted by the police in Los Angeles—why, we've never been in Los Angeles. I'm going to the newspapers and tell them how my wife was treated, just like a common criminal! We don't have to stand for it."

"What else did the Captain say?"

"He said that she was a - - - - - well, I won't repeat it, but he called her dirty names and was very abusive."

"Just exactly what did he call her? What did he say that was abusive?"

"Well—it wasn't exactly what he said, it was the way he said it!"

Then I pursued the point, "He really didn't use any words that were dirty, or vile, or insulting?"

"No," he admitted, "but his manner upset her terribly. She was sobbing when I came home."

"Oh," I said surprised, "then you weren't there when the Captain came?"

"No, but I came home right after he was there, and she was almost hysterical, we are good citizens, we would never do anything wrong." He repeated. "She was treated like a common criminal."

I resisted the temptation to ask how a common criminal is treated. Instead I asked, "In what way was his manner abusive?"

"Well," he replied, "he arrested her, and now her name will be smeared forever."

I was interested in this problem now. With all my restraint, I asked, "How did the Captain arrest her? Did he take her to the station? Did he handcuff her?"

"No," he answered with disgust, "he said she was under arrest and told her the L.A. Police had a warrant for her."

"Then what did he do?" I questioned.

"He went away, and left her, and when I came home, she was so upset she couldn't tell me what happened for a whole hour." He continued, "He had no right to upset her that way—to treat her like a common criminal."

"I see," I said.

"Mr. Skinner," the minister said softly, "let's leave the matter with the mayor and when he has looked into it, he will call us."

"Yes," I said, "I will call you. And thank you for telling me about this."

Later in the day, having finished a discussion with the police chief about vehicle preventive maintenance, I told him of Mr. Skinner and his wife, Margaret Skinner, who allegedly was arrested by Captain Dingle.

"I'll let you know about it," he said.

The following morning, the chief sent over a memo with a teletype attached. The teletype message read as follows:

RE MARGARET SKINNER AKA MADGE SKINNER AKA VIRGINIA SKEEN AKA MARY SKEEN. WE HOLD LA SC B/W NO———CHARGING PERJURY AND VIOLATION OF PROB. SUBJ DESC AS FEM WHITE 26 YRS 5–2 108 LBS BRN AND HAZEL. HAVE INFO SUBJ IS NOW AT SPACE 31 HARVARD TRAILER PARK. PLS PICK UP AND ADVISE.

The memo, typed neatly on police department stationery, said: "Following receipt of attached warrant, Captain Dingle contacted suspect, and after investigation, requested suspect to appear at station for fingerprint check. Captain satisfied suspect is not wanted fugitive, but print verification would be certain. Captain courteous, but firm with suspect."

I put in a call to the minister and together, we talked with the woman's husband. He still insisted that his wife had been arrested and that her good name had been ruined.

Finally, the minister accepted the job of counseling the man and his wife, who never did contact the newspapers, but I have often wondered what impression of police these people now have.

This case only typifies the misunderstandings and communications problems which complicate the legislators' public relations.

Seeking the Public Interest

The councilman, in the last analysis has been elected to represent that nebulous concept—the public interest—as best he can. He is required as the pressure point of community influences to make continuous decisions relating to the public interest and to make complex value judgments on what in fact such an interest constitutes. But the councilman must first and foremost represent the public interest while maintaining a public image acceptable to his constituents.

THE ELUSIVE PUBLIC INTEREST

We should perhaps consider the term "public interest." It is easy enough to describe what the public interest is not. To say, "the public interest is what I say the public interest is," as stated by a certain mayor not long ago, immediately evokes impassioned disagreement. The public interest cannot be described in such a cavalier fashion.

Boss Tweed of New York used to resent it when people would accuse his administration of graft and corruption and of favoring only a few at the expense of the public interest. "It's not so," Tweed would protest. "Everything I have done has been in the public interest." For an example he would cite a park he had just given to the people. The fact that the park was in the area of a swamp that Tweed had purchased and sold to the city for personal gain did not seem to matter.

Early in 1963, President John F. Kennedy and Roger Blough, the president of the U.S. Steel Corporation, had a showdown in the White House. Mr. Blough informed the President he was preparing to raise the unit cost of steel and the President said if he did he would be jeopardizing the national interest. Failing to see it that way, Blough proceeded to raise the cost of steel anyway. Then the President marshaled his powerful forces. He went to the people and convinced a good many of them that the steel company was defying the public interest, and he succeeded in getting the price increase rescinded.

Rather typical at the local level is the citizen pleading to the city council not to align and widen a residential street in front of his house because it would destroy the value of his property. The new alignment was going to consume all but the front 5 feet of his yard, placing his front door right at the foot of heavy vehicular traffic. As he stood speaking against the street project, he was rudely interrupted by an impatient councilman who cried out: "Sir, do you realize that the position you are taking is in defiance of the public interest? You are asking us to protect your own personal interests at the expense of the community's needs!" Looking about him and seeing that all eyes in the assembly room were fixed upon him, the mild mannered man decided to sit down and press his case no further. In this instance, the invocation of the public interest was successful in cutting off debate.

The public interest as a determinant of governmental action is probably the most cherished concept to be found in the annals of American politics. It is also the most vague and abstract.

When any community group announces a policy position, it seeks explicitly or implicitly to associate its stand with the public interest. In fact, nearly every active individual or group claims—sincerely, no doubt—to be acting in the name of the public interest.

Yet in a pluralistic society such as ours, made up of so many conflicting, overlapping, and competing interests, it is virtually impossible for all factions to espouse commonly accepted goals. How can it happen, then, that all the forces can say they are acting in the public interest? Perhaps the confusion rests in the various ways the public interest is defined.

PUBLIC INTEREST AS PUBLIC CONSENSUS

For perhaps the greatest number of its supporters the public interest has come to mean *commonly held* interests or values which, if they are not universally accepted, are at least widely held. A decision is said to be in the public interest if it serves the ends of most of the public rather than just a limited sector of the public. The key to this concept of the public interest, then, is its wide acceptance as a common interest. It qualifies as being public by virtue of its broad acceptance or commonness. As such it is a consciously desired goal which individuals and groups are struggling to achieve.

Yet, how wide must acceptance be for this definition of the public interest to be valid?

If a particular value were embraced by the great majority of the citizens, it would be an accepted interest and almost completely noncontroversial. There would consequently be no need to debate or to secure public support. The public interest in these terms would be identifiable only with those matters with which governmental policy was largely unconcerned.

Some proponents of the public interest, however, argue that a standard of universality or consensus for the public interest is too demanding. We cannot hope to secure this on a realistic scale. But if we abandon the standard of either unanimity or consensus, we are forced to defend the public interest as being an interest that is simply more widely held than other interests.

Frankly stated then, we would determine the public interest through the act of counting noses. But if government were to resort to this on every issue that confronts it, the machinery of government inevitably would come to a halt. Furthermore, in evaluating an interest in terms of the number of people who subscribed to it, such important considerations as the intensity with which an interest is held would regrettably be overlooked.

PUBLIC INTEREST AS SUPERIOR WISDOM

Another concept of the public interest that commands a considerable amount of allegiance is one that sees the public interest as *wise* or *superior* interest. In the day-to-day practice of American politics, the term public interest is most frequently equated with an interest that its supporters feel deserves a special priority among interests because of its superior wisdom or desirability. Its validity as the public interest depends not on the range of its acceptance but on the superiority of its claim to rationality or wisdom.

A danger lurks here, however, for this definition of the public interest fails to qualify as being "public" at all. Once the paternal and knowledgeable men who possess this clairvoyance discover what would be wise for all men, the public interest can become quite paradoxically an interest that is unknown to the public that reputedly holds it. If we concede interests which the possessor neither knows nor recognizes, our understanding of the concept of interests will have to be thoroughly overhauled. Furthermore, the condescension and paternalism implicit in the suggestion that each man is not the best judge of his own interest bodes unhappily for democratic theory in ways fairly self-evident.

PUBLIC INTEREST AS MORAL IMPERATIVE

Perhaps a third definition of the public interest may prove to be more satisfactory. For many people who believe in the natural law or traditional American understanding of natural rights, the public interest as *moral imperative* makes a strong bid for acceptability. Life, liberty, property, equality, and justice are held to be inviolable standards that defy transfer or abridgment. Having their sanction in higher morality they are values that all people are obligated to respect. The public interest then in this sense would be what Walter Lippman said men would choose if they saw clearly, thought rationally, and acted disinterestedly and benevolently.

But there are problems inherent in this concept. For the public interest as moral imperative concludes in being neither public nor interest. Because of its divine origin, the standard would exist even if no one embraced it as an interest. What is more, there is implicit in this concept the peril that the majority will, in the name of a higher morality, attempt to impose the "truth" on all of society. The zealot, confident of having found the "true" public interest, may choose to impose a freedom that is no more than "doing what is right."

PUBLIC INTEREST AND PROJECTION OF PERSONAL VALUES

Another way the public interest is frequently discovered is through the process psychologists call "projection," which is simply a way of equating the public interest with one's own value system. A person will usually do this when he feels that his views are surely held by a large number of persons in the general public without knowing in any precise way how many people, if any, actually do share his attitudes.

While there may be some merit in recognizing this projection as an interest, it is a bit untenable to accept this mirror-gazing as public. For if we are to admit that every man is representative of a public, we might as well discard any further thoughts of catering to the public interest. In view of the fact that no two people are exactly alike, the need to satisfy all of the publics in a community would reduce any effort of government in this direction to futility and defeat.

PUBLIC INTEREST AS SYNTHESIS OF VARIED INTERESTS

Fortunately, this is not a matter for concern. For as it works out, the task of government is not to express an imaginary popular will, but to effect adjustment among the various competing wills which at any given time are attempting to make their claims upon other groups in society by acting through or upon any of the institutions of government. "The public good," V. O. Key has written, "rarely consists in yielding completely to the demands of one class or group in society." It more often consists in the achievement of compromise between conflicting groups. Thus the *public interest as a balance of interests* becomes another way of defining the concept we are analyzing.

To view legislative acts generally as being the product of a common or popular will is little more than a romantic fiction, for it ignores the facts. The individual man does not have opinions on all public affairs. He does not know what is happening, why it is happening, or what ought to happen. It is ludicrous to insist that he should have an intelligent opinion worth expressing on every question that confronts a self-governing community. Unless he perceives an issue to affect his interests directly or indirectly he is simply not motivated to take political action. However, when he is affected crucially by a matter before the legislature, you can expect him to join forces with like-minded persons in bringing pressure to bear.

These pressure groups—or interest groups— will make their preferences heard at some crucial stage in the policy process, provided they are not manipulated into quiescence. They will write their councilmen, lobby before committees, drum up support for their cause among the electorate, and contribute money to advance their goals.

Most decisions on important questions of policy necessarily have to be made by officials— by officials who, while they may be elected by the people, are still independent in the sense that they must make choices of their own without being able to rely at every step for rule and guidance on specific orders formulated by the electorate.

Government by elected representatives ordinarily affords opportunity for practically every interest of importance in the community to find somewhere in the representative council a spokesman to voice its claims. But for the most part the councilman discerns that his greatest responsibility is to produce an outcome that will represent a compromise of competing wills and a harmonization of interests. For only in this way can he maintain a stable political climate and generate loyalty and support for the work he has accomplished.

PUBLIC INTEREST AND "THE MIDDLETON CASE"

A case which shows the benefit of the "public interest" as an effective compromise of competing wills is presented here.

The small city of Middleton, being one of the multitude of incorporated towns which felt the initial impact of the post World War II building boom, found itself during 1954 knee-deep in a maze of earth-moving monsters which threatened to reduce the rolling and hillside terrain of this sleepy community to man-made mounds of fill dirt and cut shelves of sandy clay. This was the new concept of land development which was to engulf a vast portion of the state. Some of the established and larger cities were somewhat prepared to cope with the problem, but little Middleton, anxious to expand its boundaries, welcomed the subdivider and the earth mover, the cat and the sheepsfoot roller in an aura of naivete.

Having no grading ordinance by which the moving earth could be contained, Middleton suddenly found itself facing a dilemma. Established residents awoke to find a mountain of earth sloping toward their rear yards or to gape down unimaginable precipices, the crests of which began at property lines.

City hall phones rang frantically and the routing of all complaints followed a line of referral directly to the mayor. Mayor Atkins, a civil engineer by profession, handled the barrage with the oft repeated explanation that all was legal and followed well-established principles of mechanics and sound engineering practices.

Whether filled slopes were compacted and formed to a maximum slope of one and one-half to one, or whether cut slopes were formed to a maximum of one to one was of no consequence to the irate residents. The sudden appearance of monstrous earth movers was interfering with a way of life. Some residents sold their property and moved away; others entertained law suits but were discouraged in their efforts by well-knowing attorneys. Some harbored feelings of resentment toward the city, but most feelings were assuaged by the healing element of time and the ingenuity of the residents themselves. Many once formidable hillsides were transformed into show places of landscaped beauty.

Mayor Atkins faced the problem repeatedly from one development to the next. As the pace increased, first two, then three, then four tract developments would mushroom into existence at the same time. He concluded that the plunder of the earth in the Middleton Valley must be controlled by other than conservative, minimum engineering standards.

The problem was compounded when in the winter of 1956 the heaviest rains in a decade washed over and under many of the unvegetated and unestablished slopes. New homes stood in lakes of water, or water freely flowed under houses and had to be bailed out or pumped out. The resulting erosion was followed by heated public reaction, pointing out the need for an adequate cut-and-fill ordinance.

Mayor Atkins had foreseen this need and had

already made frequent pleas to the city council for such control. However, past conservative policies in the city of Middleton, fostered by a conservative city manager, slowed down any movement toward such control. The status quo remained through a moderate building period until 1957 when a sample ordinance was finally presented to the city council by the city manager.

In the meantime Mayor Atkins had been successful in persuading the city council to adopt the most recent editions of the widely accepted *Uniform Building Code, Uniform Plumbing Code,* and *National Electrical Code.* However, the need for a basic cut-and-fill ordinance still went unfulfilled. Atkins had carefully studied the ordinances of larger cities which, while not completely adequate, were further advanced and based on more cut-and-fill experience than other codes.

The ordinance first presented by the city manager incorporated big city flavor into a little city's cup. Tentative tract maps prophesying ever increasing building development in 1958 plus continuing public criticism finally convinced the city council that the time had come to seriously consider the adoption of a cut-and-fill ordinance.

The proposal was greeted by real estate and building interests with arched eyebrows and minds unprepared toward complete objectivity. In view of the widespread indignation of the citizenry, it was believed by the mayor that it would be a simple matter to push through his desired grading code. However, from the beginning of his effort until the ultimate adoption of the ordinance, the mayor learned that a subdivider's domain could not be readily controlled by local grading regulations in conservative Middleton—especially since subdivisions already were meeting all requirements of the state subdivision act. Having pierced the line of the city council and then having passed the ball to that line, Atkins then was faced with another delay in the passage of his earthy ordinance.

Late in 1957 during its initial month of consideration, the city council gingerly tossed the proposal up and down, never allowing it to land, and at the same time never dropping the matter. It was then decided to set the first public hearing on the ordinance to more or less feel the pulse of public reaction.

The ordinance was patterned after the provisions of a nearby city's code regulating hillside grading. The general requirements consisted of the usually accepted engineering standards for cutting, filling, compaction, and control by licensed soil engineers. The unique portions of the code, however, would control heights and locations of slopes, would provide for detailed drainage facilities, and specified slope planting requirements. The items which considered drainage and planting regulations were not objectionable although, on the other hand, also were not relished by the land developer and the builder. It was, however, that section of the code which regulated slope heights and slope locations that incited a flood of protests. The council retracted their feelers like an unsuspecting child touching a hot stove.

Reducing the vertical height of a slope from 40 feet to a series of terraced slopes, each not to exceed 10 feet in vertical height separated by 4-foot wide benches or terraces, was an example of what the ordinance would cost the subdivider in terms of usable building site area.

The current ordinance sections on slope locations merely required that property lines be established at the top of slopes. The reasoning behind this regulation stemmed from a series of sour experiences of property owners who had the misfortune of having to view the neglected faces of hillsides which belonged to property owners at the top. The old axiom, "Out of sight, out of mind," never proved truer. The distasteful condition stimulated a rash of complaints by the low-landers, and the city, although not obligated, was caught up in the business of requiring hillside improvements. To set the property line at the top of the hill would leave the slope as a part of the lower property. The bottom-lander would then be responsible for and would have the view of his own slope. This requirement, although not costing the developer in land area, had a slowing down effect in that grading crews would have to be more deliberate and accurate in forming their slopes.

The most violent protest emanated from John James & Son, Inc., Developers, who were putting the finishing touches on their first subdivision in Middleton. The proposed ordinance of course would not affect their current project, but tentative maps were being prepared for two more tracts totaling over two hundred lots. The grading ordinance would deal a death blow to their proposed project.

Lot sales for James & Son were being handled by Joe Mack, a local realtor and president of the Middleton Area Board of Realtors. The association of James and Mack threw the first punch in the name of the Board of Realtors, and the second punch arrived from James & Son's civil engineer who objected on the basis "that state civil engineering practices were sufficient and adequate to satisfy all city grading needs." The city council felt the impact of both punches, not to forget the lighter but tormenting jabs from other interested groups.

The quick decision to table the proposed ordinance and refer it to the realty board and the chamber of commerce for study and comment was probably the only expedient thing to do. Whether by chance or design, this move by council brought forth some constructive suggestions and had the effect of back-firing on the special interest groups who at first visualized the "committees" as the burial ground of the ordinance.

The "chamber" committee, not qualified by experience or knowledge in this area, soon found themselves in abject disagreement. Upon the suggestion of the city manager, this committee quickly agreed to a "catch-all" provision which would allow the building official to exercise judgment or waive requirements in cases of "extreme hardship" or in cases of "small and unimportant work."

Mayor Atkins, in the meantime was requested to discuss the matter with the realty board committee. The realtors, recognizing their community responsibility in this matter, looked at the ordinance objectively and agreed with Atkins' reasoning. Joe Mack, who was not a member of the committee, eventually found himself pitted against the entire remaining realty board, and his argument and appeals were rejected. The realty board committee, wishing to make some contribution to the cause, agreed to the same amendment as the chamber committee.

The ordinance regulating and controlling grading, filling, and excavating in the city of Middleton was adopted on October 7, 1958.

While the Middleton case study concerns itself with increasing the regulatory power of the municipality, it strikingly shows the balancing of interests to arrive at a solution adequately serving the public interest.

This, however, is only a sample of the municipal legislators' responsibility.

Impact of the Public on the Council

We cannot explore the public's influences upon councilmen without at least a short consideration of the public itself.

SENSING WHO THE PUBLIC IS

In 1785, Nicholas Chamfort wrote, "The public, the public—how many fools does it take to make a public."

While Alexander Pope wrote that "The public is a fool," Shakespeare had earlier written that "The public is the world."

A generation ago Professor William B. Munro described his "forgotten man" in municipal politics. "He never appears before committees of the City Council at public hearings telling the councilmen or supervisors what the people want, nor does he write letters to newspapers. He doesn't even read the letters that other people write."

The chamber of commerce, the taxpayers' association, and the good government group do not count him among their members. He has never signed a petition for or against anything. He isn't organized, can't be mobilized, and won't be hypnotized by the politicians. Because he makes no noise, we call him the silent voter; between elections his interests and desires are crowded out by his more vociferous fellow citizens; he is the "forgotten man" of municipal politics. Yet when the polls are open, he is often the most influential factor in the whole electorate. When the ballots are counted, it frequently appears that he has turned the trick. Indeed, when upsets and surprises come on election day, it is usually because somebody has failed to reckon with the potential sovereignty of the "forgotten man." With the ballot in his hand, he has become articulate and as a rule he votes his resentment rather than his appreciation. He resents the fact that no one in the seats of the mighty has regarded his interest or paid heed to his unuttered opinion.

The "forgotten man" does not know much about the principles of political science, he has never heard of Aristotle, Locke, and Montesquieu. He would be stumped if you asked him about segregated budgets or police power condemnations, but somewhere on one of the city streets he owns a little home, or at least an equity in it. This ownership has not failed to teach him something about assessors and tax bills, about water rates and street paving assessments. Consequently, he does not swallow the alibis which flow so freely from some elected officials about inevitably higher public expenditures and uncontrollable outlays. No one needs to tell him that the city administration is flawless, particularly if the garbage collectors come irregularly, if the sewer backs up in his cellar, or if he can't locate a policeman when he needs one.

Moreover, he rides the buses or drives to work and back again at peak hours, which makes him an expert on transportation and traffic congestion. He has as much right as any other man to form opinions on these matters—and he does it!

Professor Munro's forgotten man represents extremely important unuttered influences upon the municipal legislator—influences which cannot be ignored if the councilman is to do his job.

We can be quick to point out that interpreting the needs, desires, and wishes of the silent voter is not a simple task. It requires a sensitivity and perception of the "common interest" of a high order, indeed an uncommon behavior pattern. We have heard this ability to perceive expressed as "an ear to the ground," "sensing what's in the wind," or a "feel of the public pulse." The councilman who fails to recognize the silent voter—the forgotten man—will not for long be unrecognized by the forgotten man.

We might contrast the "forgotten man" with the other persons, groups, and organizations who directly cause the councilman to be the focal point of community influences.

RESTRAINTS ON COUNCIL INDEPENDENCE

The direct and potent influences brought to bear upon councilmen as a part of the decision-making process can be classified as personal, internal, and external.

Personal influences are those attitudes and opinions held by individual councilmen. Hardly a council meeting will pass when at least one item on the agenda is not related to a preconceived idea held by a councilman. The councilman who will not permit his children to sell candy door-to-door is asked to consider a request to allow a worthwhile youth group to do so. The councilman who owns a furniture store is asked to consider bids on office fixtures which he considers to be of inferior quality. The realtor on the council is asked to approve the purchase of property at a price he considers exorbitant. The pious Christian considers pool-room regulations or liquor licenses. The political conservative must act upon urban renewal or a job training program for school dropouts.

Internal influences are described as intracity organizational and include council-manager relations; the influence of department heads, staff, and employees; and the limitations imposed by laws, codes, and ordinances.

The council manager relationship involves the greatest amount of pressure upon a councilman primarily because the manager can marshal the forces of research, logic, and managerial expertise. It is because this type of influ-

ence is so great and at times so overwhelming that we hear the term "rubber stamp council" when it appears that a city council follows the advice or recommendation of the manager to the apparent exclusion of other influences.

The consideration of the effect of the managerial influence upon members of the city council is becoming even more significant in view of the trend to regard a major part of the manager's job as involving policy formulation.[3]

Even if the manager's involvement in policy were not increasing, the legal framework of the executive-legislative relationship creates an atmosphere of broad influence for the manager. Even lacking a legal basis, the psychological impact of the manager's position, his staff knowledge, his professional expertise—all these provide tremendous influence on the council.

The legal limitations upon council members, whether state laws, local codes, or simply policies set by precedent, also exert a restrictive influence upon councilmen which upon occasion may prevent the council member from satisfying his constituents and his own ideas of good government.

Other influences of an internal nature can be classified as the influences of technical staff, with special skills such as personnel, finance, or purchasing; the effect of pressure by employees and employee groups; and the influence of department heads who for one reason or another may have the sympathetic ear of a councilman. (The threats or warnings of doom by the city attorney or the police chief are bound to have an influence upon even the most courageous and stalwart councilman.)

The third general classification upon the councilmanic decision-making is external or "public" influences. City councilman will be pressured by parents and pigeon-fanciers, by lawyers and landowners, by bankers and businessmen, by realtors and residents, by all manner of reasonable and logical persons and groups, and by many who are not. All are members of the councilman's constituency; all are advocating a cause.

---

[3] Clarence E. Ridley's monograph, THE ROLE OF THE CITY MANAGER IN POLICY FORMULATION (Chicago: International City Managers' Association, 1958) gives the essence of a large volume of writing on this subject.

PUBLIC PRESSURES AND THE "CENTER CITY CASE"

Another case involving some of these pressures is a good example of expediency as a guide in making decisions.

Center City, a bedroom city of 11,200 people, was incorporated in 1910. Approximately 25 per cent of the population is Mexican, and the city has a decidedly poor Mexican district. The city covers about five square miles and is located in a large agriculture valley. Center City has the commission form of government with five councilmen elected at large. One of the five is appointed mayor by the other council members.

Center City's former police chief informed the council when he was hired that he could not live in the city. One of his daughters had a respiratory disease and could not tolerate the climate. This was agreeable at the time, but a change in councils brought a change in sentiment. The former chief was given six months to move into the city limits. When he refused to do so he was discharged.

The employees of the police department felt this was an unfair action by the council, and all but three resigned with the chief. Lieutenant Peters, with less than three years of police experience, was appointed chief of an almost nonexistent department. Chief Peters has held this position for two and a half years.

On the afternoon of Sunday, December 6th, the Center City police received a call from Mrs. Pete Rodriquez that her husband was threatening to kill her. One police officer, Charles Bragg, answered Mrs. Rodriquez's call for help.

According to a statement made by Officer Bragg at a later date, the following action took place. Mr. Rodriquez resisted arrest. Officer Bragg struck Mr. Rodriquez five times with a night stick before it broke and then hit him twice with a sap. Mr. Rodriquez then ran into a small neighborhood store and armed himself with a pop bottle. Officer Bragg, not wanting to risk smashing up the store or hurting children close by, returned to his patrol car and radioed for help. Meanwhile Mr. Rodriquez escaped. He was picked up four hours later by a neighboring city's police.

A few days later a petition was brought into the police department signed by 11 witnesses protesting Officer Bragg's brutality in his attempt to arrest Pete Rodriquez.

No obvious effort was made by the police department, the mayor, or the city council to discover whether Officer Bragg's actions were justified. As a result of the petition and the pressure of prominent Mexican citizens, Officer Bragg was forced to resign on December 11 by a majority vote of the city council.

Officer Bragg asked for a hearing to clear his record of the brutality charge. The open hearing before the council on January 6 attracted a crowd of 75 or more people who overflowed the council chambers.

Two Mexican attorneys were seated at the main table. They were there, they stated, without pay to see that witnesses' rights were protected. There was an occasional flare-up over the extent of their participation in the hearing.

Among the witnesses testifying were Mrs. Rodriquez and Pete Rodriquez, brought in from road camp where he was serving 80 days for assault and battery and possession of a deadly weapon. The neighboring city's policeman who had arrested Rodriquez stated that there was a slight cut on his head, but no bruises on his hands or face.

Both Police Chief Peters and Assistant Chief Gomez said they felt Officer Bragg was justified in using the force he did to make an arrest. However, both added that they would have brought Rodriquez in regardless.

The hearing was quiet and orderly. No comments were permitted from the audience during the four hour meeting. The council did not make a decision at this time but called a special meeting the following Saturday to discuss the hearing. The action restoring Officer Bragg to duty was unanimous with Councilman Gonzales absent.

By its action, the council exonerated the patrolman of all charges and, without saying so, indicated its mistake in forcing his resignation.

This case demonstrates some of the external influences on city councilmen. While it appears to deal with a personnel matter only, it includes overtones of other pressures. The councilman is faced with influences which both hinder and help him in representing the needs of his community. He must use these influences in a way that will make him a more effective municipal legislator.

The Role of the Councilman

To most residents and taxpayers, the councilman is city government. He is responsible for its successes and is at fault in its failures. What then is required of the citizen who would venture into the maze of local government as a legislative representative?

No technical skill is required for a citizen to serve on a city council. It may be assumed that in larger communities, professional talents will be supplied by the staff and in smaller communities by the city manager or a consultant.

To be a councilman requires that the candidate have integrity, good judgment, a substantial amount of "horse sense," and a devoted interest in his city and its future. He comes to his position as councilman in many areas without a partisan political label. He is in a position to exercise his very best judgment and foresight and to do so fearlessly, for he is not dependent on this job for a livelihood. He can always look his neighbors, singly or collectively, in the eye and say with conviction, "This is my best judgment on the matter."

It is generally considered desirable that the composition of the city council represent a diversity of interests and occupations. In this manner, the council membership will be in a better position to reflect a cross section of local opinion.

Membership on a city council is a high honor and an unusual opportunity for real public service. Every individual councilman should understand the job as a whole and consistently work and vote in a manner which will contribute toward doing that job right. Each individual councilman, and the council as a whole, are concerned with the general public good. Where some local interest or some business interest is in conflict with the general public welfare, the latter should prevail.

Each councilman should make a conscientious effort to be present at each meeting. Unless he is there he cannot perform his duty. Acceptance of the position includes an obligation to devote the necessary time to its work. In addition to attending council meetings, it is necessary that each councilman do a certain amount of research, study, and inspection of proposals in advance.

Every councilman should shun anything which deviates from the straight and narrow path of plain, old-fashioned honesty. Each member should make it crystal clear that the council treats every citizen the same as every other citizen.

A councilman must recognize that the desirable approach on any given problem is not always the popular choice. Frequently his attitudes or decisions may differ with those of his friends or of important local groups. At such times, he must remain steadfast and coura-geous. He should endeavor to justify his position in an effort to win the support of his critics, but regardless of whether he is successful in such efforts, he must always retain the long-range outlook and insist upon carrying out those programs and policies that will be for the ultimate benefit of the community.

Occasionally a councilman may find himself in a position where he has a personal interest in some matter up for consideration by the city council. Clearly, there are no two ways about this sort of situation. When this occurs, he has but one course of action—namely to call attention to the situation and request that the chairman excuse him from participation while the matter is under consideration and to disqualify himself from voting.

Councilmen serve in a quasi-judicial as well as a legislative capacity and, as such, it is preferable that they not discuss cases in any detail with applicant or protestant prior to consideration by the council as a whole. A councilman can sometimes handle this delicate situation by advising the person contacting him that all relevant matters should be submitted through proper applications and through established hearing procedures for consideration by the council.

Closed sessions of city councils, county boards, and other public agencies, at which the public and press are barred, are contrary to American tradition. They breed suspicion on the part of both press and public. There is no reason why matters relating to the general development and welfare of the city cannot be discussed in public. The city council represents the public just as much as it does the municipal corporation as an abstract entity. In fact, the local citizen generally feels closer to the city council than he does to county and state government. He believes, and rightly so, that he will receive equitable treatment and sympathetic consideration of his problems.

The local citizen is not only a member of several councilmanic publics, he is also an individual with different attitudes, prejudices, and opinions. The successful councilman must understand voter behavioral characteristics if he is to retain his position of prestige and responsibility.

5

The Multitudinous Publics

IN A DEMOCRATIC SOCIETY, government exists to serve the people; hence public employees are servants of the people. In ascertaining and achieving the purposes of government, public administrators must be concerned with what citizens want from their government. This involves the complicated process of translating public opinion into public policy and administrative activity. This process may be conceptualized within a social action continuum of opinion, through policy, to administration.

While much has been written about the opinion-policy-administration continuum, there exists only limited knowledge of the nature of the continuum. What writings are available suggest a much more complicated process than the mere mechanical motion of identifying public opinions, shaping them into policy guides, and then initiating programs.

Little is known about what constitutes a "public" and its underlying influences; only scanty knowledge is available as to how opinions of government personnel and community organization people mutually influence the deliberations of public officials; only a superficial understanding prevails of how public opinions are formed and circulated in the community.

Nevertheless, greater understanding of the opinion-policy-administration continuum will provide more effective comprehension of the process by which governments serve without dominating. The role of public officials is to translate public opinions into administrative action. In this chapter we examine part of this continuum—the segment dealing with the "multitudinous publics"—and suggest a simple working scheme by which municipal officials may analyze the "publics" in their cities and initiate sound and effective opinion and informational programs.

Opinion and the Publics[1]

RELATION OF OPINION TO PUBLIC RELATIONS

The crux of public relations is the opinions of people. Programs are geared to conserve or protect favorable opinions, to crystallize active or latent opinions into favorable reaction, and to change or neutralize hostile opinions. Persons engaged in public relations are constantly striving to initiate, lead, modify, or accelerate the opinions of people. The term public opinion is used to describe all of these and associated social relationships.[2]

OPINION BRIEFLY DEFINED

Opinion may be defined as sets of beliefs, convictions, or views of individuals, groups, or organizations on matters or issues. It is noted that in this definition, groups and organizations are treated as social entities with the capacity to articulate opinions in the same

[1] For a more extensive discussion of public opinion, see section on "Relation of Public Opinion and Communication to Government" in Chapter 2.

[2] The term "social relationships" is used here in the sense of a continuing *process* of interaction between opinion and information in relation to governmental institutions, personalities, physical environment, motivations, needs, and other elements that make up "society" as the sociologist conceives it. It is the interacting, interdependent, and interrelated workings of these and other elements that make governments and other formal institutions possible.

manner as individuals. These forms of social entities operate as "behavior units," and exhibit their own identifiable and peculiar behavioral patterns not unlike that of an individual person. As such, they function as individual behavior units in the democratic processes and, in a real sense, become identifiable elements involved in the discussion processes.[3]

THE FLOWS OF INFLUENCE AND OPINION

Two useful analytical techniques are described as (1) the flow of influence, and (2) the flow of opinion.[4] In the first you examine the cause (that which influences) to ascertain the effect (the opinion), while in the latter you examine the effect to ascertain the cause.

Flow of Influence. Almost every aspect of the opinion-policy-administration continuum can be analyzed in terms of the direction in which influence is being exerted. Researchers are interested in the extent of influence of mass media on their audiences. Students of small group behavior are interested in the extent to which one person influences the opinion of another person. The study of elite groups centers almost exclusively on those who possess influence, why, and how it is exercised. The focus is on the process by which one behavior unit influences the behavior of another unit. The difficulty in analyzing the flow of influence is that influence cannot be directly observed but must be inferred from observable behavior.

Flow of Opinion. This appears to be a more useful concept for public relations work. Earlier it was stated that any set of beliefs, convictions, or views about any issue or matter constitutes opinion. Opinion is communicated directly from one behavior unit to another.

Whatever form the act of communicating these opinions takes, it can be observed, categorized, and measured to some degree. Behavior units can be identified and compared in their roles and performances.

Unless opinion circulates between a government and a public, neither party may be influenced, nor its behavior modified. However, this relationship should not be limited simply to a communication system which links a public to the government and vice versa. A flow of influence is also involved which shapes and molds the behavior of both parties. Both flows are involved, one way or another, in the process of the modification of behavior. We should note, however, that influence cannot be operative without prior transmission of opinion; whereas opinion can act independently of influence. In other words, how can parties involved in the flow of influence modify their behavior unless the influence is conveyed to them in some manner?

In sum, influence (and thus modification of the behavior of the principals) is a result of behavior unit interaction and can be manifested only when it is communicated in some fashion. On the other hand, opinion can and does circulate without corresponding modifications of behavior of a behavior unit. An official who rejects opinion transmitted to him illustrates that influence and opinion do not concurrently flow together. He may cut off influence altogether and at the same time perpetuate the flow of opinion by reintroducing the rejected opinion into the channel of communication by using a speech or writing an article for the press in which he gives his reasons for opposition to the submitted opinion.[5]

---

[3] Kenneth E. Boulding clarifies the meaning of "behavior unit" in Chapter One of his CONFLICT AND DEFENSE, A GENERAL THEORY (New York: Harper Torchbooks, 1963), by indicating that a "behavior unit may be a person, a family, a species of animals or artifacts, a class of ideas, a theory, or a social organization such as a firm, a nation, a trade union or a church." A mere aggregate of people is not a behavior unit because it does not behave as a unit. "The test that decides whether an aggregate is a behavior unit . . . is whether it can be a subject in a sentence with a verb of action." The fundamental point to remember is that opinion arises from the exchange of ideas about living issues—*i.e.*, community matters on which individuals

and groups take stands and express themselves. As American society becomes more and more complex, opinion of individuals *per se* becomes less important and opinion of groups becomes more important. To make oneself heard and felt, it becomes imperative to represent some community group. The term behavior unit is a convenient shorthand way to refer to the numerous varieties of group and individual behavior patterns in community settings.

[4] See James N. Rosenau, PUBLIC OPINION AND FOREIGN POLICY (New York: Random House, 1961), pp. 9–16.

[5] For illustration, certain elements of the community may inform the city manager that they want special services such as street sweeping twice a week instead of

Study of the flow of opinion centers on identification of particular opinions, their communication (by whom and to whom), and the nature and extent of their impact. The flow of opinion—the act of communication—sets the boundaries within which influence operates.[6]

OPINION-POLICY-ADMINISTRATION RELATIONSHIPS

In order to gain understanding of complex social situations it is necessary to generalize patterns of social systems. It is suggested that relation of opinion to policy and administration probably can best be visualized as being composed of several closely related but discrete systems of social interaction.

Concept of Social Systems. Talcott Parsons has formulated a concept of social systems which may be applied usefully to local government. Social action is a starting point,[7] and social systems develop spontaneously whenever the pattern of two or more actors becomes stabilized (patterned mode of interaction) and oriented toward specific goals. The basic element in the social system is role, and the social system is merely a network of roles.[8]

This concept of social systems includes far more than formal organizations—local governments, religious denominations, trade associations, etc. The spontaneous development of social systems is not necessarily related to a legal framework of formal institutions.

A social system is not the same as a "society," at least for purposes of definition in this book. A society is a more formal type of organization in an institutional or organizational sense. Common to any complex political society, such as the United States, is a system of local governments. Each local government is continually working out sets of mutually compatible roles—that is, concrete social systems. These social systems are operating within a complex framework—matrix, to use the sociologist's term—of roles (peoples' expectations of others), values (democracy, religious beliefs, etc.), and goals. This environmental framework—or matrix—can be clarified by further definition.

Role essentially is the expectations that many people, including the incumbent, have as they view a given position.[9]

Normative standards refer to values. Philosophically it is more than attitudes and beliefs because it involves what a person thinks ought

---

once a week. The city manager rejects this attempt to influence his administrative behavior by delivering a speech before a leading civic organization such as the junior chamber of commerce where he discusses in depth the policy and program of street sweeping in the city.

The attempt to influence him failed because he did not consent to having the streets swept twice a week. Channels of communication were used to communicate the rejection of the attempt to influence the city manager's administrative behavior. Thus, the action of the manager represents only communication, not communication and influence.

[6] There is some difference of opinion regarding influence and power structures of American communities. The elite theorists, of which Floyd Hunter is a leading proponent, believe that there is a dominant community elite that governs a community. The pluralist theorists, represented in part by Dahl, Banfield, and Sayre, believe that power is dispersed among groups having narrow interests relating to particular matters. They hold that public policy is an aggregate of decisions reached in a competitive political environment. See Floyd Hunter, COMMUNITY POWER STRUCTURE (Chapel Hill: University of North Carolina Press, 1953); Robert A. Dahl, "The Analysis of Political Influence," in Charles R. Adrian, ed., SOCIAL SCIENCE AND COMMUNITY ACTION (East Lansing: Continuing Education Service, Michigan State University, 1961), and Nelson W. Polsby,

COMMUNITY POWER AND POLITICAL THEORY (New Haven: Yale University Press, 1963).

[7] "Social action" is a rather precise term in Parsonian theory. It involves not only an "actor" (principal person) and a situation but also a psychological context of cause and effect and of standards or values. In psychological terms it is considerably more than a stimulus and an automatic response. It is rather the context—subconscious impulses, moral standards, attitudes, and beliefs—that provides a social setting.

[8] The general properties of any social system, in Parsonian theory, are: (1) two or more actors occupying differentiated statuses or positions and performing differentiated roles; (2) some organized pattern governing the relationships of members and describing their rights and obligations with respect to each other; (3) some set of common norms and values, together with shared cultural objects and symbols; (4) system boundary-maintaining tendencies (i.e., there tends to be more integrated organization among the components of the system while it is operating, than there is between these components and elements outside of the system); and (5) a built-in tendency toward system stability or equilibrium. For more details see Edward C. Devereux, Jr., "Parsons' Sociological Theory," in Max Black, ed., THE SOCIAL THEORIES OF TALCOTT PARSONS (Englewood Cliffs, New Jersey: Prentice-Hall, 1961), pp. 26–27.

[9] See the section on "Human Behavior—The Backdrop" in Chapter 2.

to be. All of us refer at least occasionally to values—our values, his values, their values, society's values, religious values, educational values. Values that are generally accepted in a society or a social system tend to become normative standards.

System goals refer to what we are striving for in both concrete and abstract terms. A city government, for example, has quite specific system goals such as clean streets. A city also may be seeking a higher level goal of paving or repaving all of the streets within the corporate limits within five years. At a level of abstraction, the city is working toward a better urban environment, and this is likely to mean a whole set of system goals relating to housing, education, schools, race relations, and employment.

This then is the sociological framework within which a city, county, or other local government operates. Each local government must work out a set of mutually compatible roles—that is, a concrete social system within its environment of roles, normative standards, and system goals.

Building further upon this line of reasoning, each city or other local government is in itself a complex of "concrete social systems." Thus, while analytically separable, these concrete social systems interpenetrate one another and function within a larger system of interdependence. Concrete social systems are embedded in a larger environmental framework. Each concrete social system represents in part its own unique organization and in part its organization drawn from higher and lower-order systems.

Processes of System Interaction. The social systems involved in the opinion-policy-administration continuum are linked together by numerous forces and processes. For our purposes three significant processes are noted: (1) decision-making process, (2) opinion-submitting process, and (3) opinion-making process. Each of these processes may exist independently of one another, but at the same time they are linked together in some unified whole. Figure 5 depicts what is meant by this statement.

1. The decision-making process integrates public opinion in the formulation and the reformation of policy and its implementation.

Participating behavior units are usually termed "decision-makers" or "policy-makers."

2. The opinion-submitting process occurs whenever opinions are transmitted to decision-makers by the publics or by institutionalized groups. Behavior units so involved are usually termed "opinion-submitters."

3. Opinion-making pertains to the formation and circulation of issues throughout a community or within a public. This process involves the interaction of opinion-holders and opinion-makers.

In Summation. At this point the reader may ask the question, "Why all of this involved discussion of something that is not important to me?" He may add, "I know what public opinion is. I am involved with it all the time."

The purpose of the discussion thus far has been to provide both a warning and an opportunity for urban administrators. The city manager is not aware of public opinion if he talks only to associates at the Rotary Club. The school superintendent may be in for quite a shock if he persuades the school board to adopt a policy on redistricting, and he has not consulted with teachers, school principals, and civil rights groups. He who acts should know the publics and how opinion flows and continually interacts through social systems. The astute administrator knows the community and thus can anticipate problems.

A good understanding of opinion and the publics provides the urban administrator with an opportunity to work both idealistically and realistically. By being as aware as possible of the social setting and the social systems within the city, he can plan what is possible and begin to work for what is desirable. He thus is more than a caretaker and an administrator in the orthodox sense, he also is a leader in the dynamic sense by showing what can be done and persuading people to work toward larger community goals.

The Publics: Forms, Composition, and Structure

It is a common mistake to think of "the public" as one massive, monolithic assemblage which can be molded into some type of "mass opinion." The mass mind concept in our times is faulty and should be divorced from our thinking.[10] In a sense, we may speak of something like a "general public," but efforts to communicate persuasively with the "general public" are, on the whole, inefficient and often ineffective. The total public (general public) is complex and heterogeneous. Within it are found smaller publics which can be identified. The opinions

of smaller publics can be ascertained and, in turn, influenced.

CONCEPT OF A PUBLIC

The number of different publics theoretically is the number of distinct combinations of individuals within a given community. A "public" is only one form of social organization. Sociologists have identified other forms such as crowd, audience, group, and association. Such forms of organization represent a more institutionalized social structure than a public. Not much will be said here of these more institutionalized social entities since they are discussed in Chapter 8.

---

[10] The mass mind concept lies at the base of any totalitarian system. For two light but excellent articles debunking the "mass mind," see Arthur Joyce Cary, "The Mass Mind: Our Favorite Folly," HARPER'S, 204 (March, 1952), 25–27, and Peter Drucker, "The Myth of American Uniformity," HARPER'S, 204 (May, 1952), 70–77.

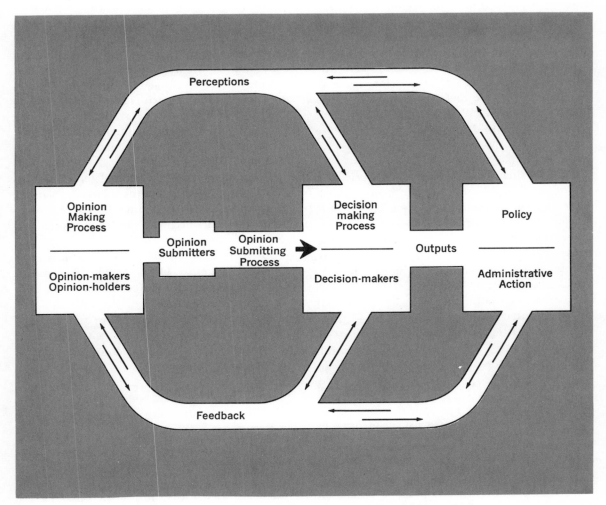

FIGURE 5. *Processes of social system interaction: decision making, opinion-submitting, and opinion-making*

A public may be defined as any loose association of individuals who are held together by common interests and objectives and by various means of communication. "In terms of stability and degree of institutionalization," it is "a transitory, amorphous, and relatively unstructured" grouping of individuals.[11] There is, so it is generally agreed, not one public but rather many "publics." Some of the publics are large in scope and membership while others are narrow in purpose and claim relatively small numbers of people. A public, as a loose association of individuals, lacks any formal institutionalization, and it should not be confused with more formal types of social organization such as a civic association, a fraternal order, or a political party. These, like publics, are opinion groups. Decision-makers also are interested in the attitudes, views, and convictions of these more institutionalized social entities.[12]

In distinguishing between "publics" and the institutionalized forms of association, some illustrations may be helpful. Veterans are a public, but the VFW, American Legion, and Amvets are groups. Physicians and surgeons are a public, but the American Medical Association is a group.

Some further characteristics of a public may be useful. A public is always concerned with achieving or maintaining a specific purpose which, in some manner, is opposed by some other type of opinion entity. The opposing entity may exist as a real or an imagined group, but in either case an issue is born which is sufficient to generate opinion.

Members of a public need not be in personal physical contact with each other. This leads to the characteristic termed by social scientists as "nonspatiability." This characteristic is a product of the development of the wide variety of communication means. Individuals who have never seen one another in person can experience a bond of common interest and unity. Of course many spatial publics, based on person-to-person relationships, also exist.

A person can be simultaneously a member of several publics: a business public, a temperance public, or a jazz music public. He can quickly shift his attention as well as his full participation from the issue of one public to that of another.[13]

Forms and Composition of Publics

Earlier we noted that the concept of a public pertains to a grouping of individuals who, relatively are in tenuous and unstructured relations with each other and are united by a common interest and communication. This concept, in general terms, spells out the composition of a public (interest, objective, and communication). We further noted that publics may be of two general forms: spatial and nonspatial. Here we will elaborate further by (1) illustrating the various types of publics, and (2) pointing out the internal structure of a public—i.e., the opinion-makers and the opinion-holders.

Types of Publics. In general terms, publics may be identified by one of their two primary characteristics: place or interest. Table 1 notes types of publics according to these two characteristics.

Structure of a Public: Opinion-Makers and Opinion-Holders. The structure of a public can be discussed in a variety of ways. We have already referred to some of the structural features, such as spatiality, nonspatiality, and interest. Here, we will deal with the basic structural relationship between opinion-makers and opinion-holders.

The inner circle of a public—the opinion-makers—has been designated in different ways: the elite, the influentials, the opinion leaders,

---

[11] Kimball Young, "Comments on the Nature of 'Public' and 'Public Opinion,'" INTERNATIONAL JOURNAL OF OPINION AND ATTITUDE RESEARCH, 11 (1948), p. 385.

[12] Publics and institutional opinion groups should be regarded as being at the opposite ends of a continuum. As a public becomes more structured and formalized, it becomes an institutional opinion group. Somewhere along this continuum a public ceases to exist, but the exact point is difficult to ascertain. However, some formalization and structuralization does not automatically place a public into a more institutionalized classification.

[13] Nearly all textbooks dealing with public opinion will treat in elaborate terms the characteristics of the public(s) and give illustrative cases. A few suggested works are V. O. Key, *op. cit.,* pp. 8 *et seq.;* Emory S. Bogardus, THE MAKING OF PUBLIC OPINION (New York: Association Press, 1951), particularly pp. 7–10; and Clarence Schettler, PUBLIC OPINION IN AMERICAN SOCIETY (New York: Harper and Bros., 1960), pp. 17–28.

the issue-makers, and so on. An effective public must consist of individuals or groups who successfully articulate and represent (and thereby strongly influence opinion) the beliefs, convictions, or views which hold together the loose association of individuals (the public). These persons to be successful must work within a more institutionalized setting with access to communication channels and contact with decision-makers. Several of these relationships are discussed in the subsequent section.

Opinion-holders, on the other hand, usually make up the vast majority of a public. They cannot circulate views (opinions) to individuals and groups with whom they are not ac-

quainted. They often disseminate opinions on a face-to-face basis, but do not have ready access to channels of communication. Thus, we can distinguish the opinion-makers from opinion-holders of a public by their accessibility to circuits of communication.

The implications in the relationship between the opinion-makers and the opinion-holders are numerous. The relationship is not necessarily static. In one set of circumstances, some persons may be opinion-holders and in another, opinion-makers. Shifts do occur and frequently in a short space of time. Although the opinion-makers frequently capture the limelight, the role of the opinion-holders should

Table 1. TYPES OF PUBLICS BY PLACE AND INTEREST

Place	**National**	**Regional**	**Local**
	Voters	New Englanders	Angelenos
	Citizens	Southerners	Brooklynites
	Adults	Middle Westerners	Texans

Examples of Common-interest Publics	**Race and Nationality**	**Sex**	**Residence**
	Negroes	Male	Urban
	Chinese	Women	Suburban
	Italian	**Income**	Rural
	Age	High	**Class**
	Children	Low	Labor
	Youth	Middle	White-collar
	Middle Age	**Professional**	Blue-collar
	Senior Citizen	Lawyers	Managerial
	Religion	Professors	**Business and Trade**
	Christian	Surgeons	Stockholders
	Protestant	**Economics**	Employees
	Moslem	Consumers	Customers
	Jewish	Distributors	Managers
	Occupational	Producers	**Educational**
	Farmers	High Tariffs	Students
	Truck Drivers	Farm Subsidies	Graduates
	Salesmen	**Social**	Teachers
	Political	Trial Marriage	Educational Administration
	Conservatives	Planned Parenthood	
	Liberals	Social Welfare	
	Moderates		

Source: Adapted from J. Handly Wright and Byron H. Christian, **Public Relations in Management** (New York: McGraw-Hill Book Co., 1949), p. 17.

not be overlooked. It is usually the opinion-holders, or a particular element therein, who internalize the opinion.[14] Thus, they can become as influential as those who introduce opinions into the circulatory system.

Concentric Gradations of a Public. In the previous sections we structured a public by the degree of accessibility that members had to circuits of communication. Here we will introduce another kind of motivation-information which separates the opinion-holders and the opinion-makers. This concept treats a public in the general terms of three gradations: the opinion-makers, the attentive opinion-holders, and the inattentive opinion-holders.[15]

It may be helpful to use an analogy of concentric circles (see Figure 6) to show how members of the internal elements are constantly shifting their roles. If the circles in Figure 6 are visualized as being in constant spirals, it would indicate that a public is in an incessant state of motion, juggling its position of influence in relation to other rival publics and constantly varying in magnitude of influence and number of members.

The outer limits of the concentric circles represent the inattentive opinion-holders. They have neither the opportunity nor a strong inclination to become involved in the opinion-making process. Their accessibility to circuits of communication is limited and their position is rather far removed from the epicenter of action (information-motivation). Thus, their information-motivation circuit is weak and frequently not clear. However, they constitute the great *latent* force of public opinion, one which occasionally can be suddenly sprung into action, playing an important, if

not decisive, role in the influence process. This is why we should visualize a counter-spiral force which could be called feedback-reevaluation-assimilated opinion.[16] This indicates that the flow of opinion and influence is a two-way proposition and that the persons involved in the inner circle cannot avoid or overlook those farther removed, even though it may appear that they are relatively uninterested.

The attentive opinion-holders are found toward the middle of the pattern of influence in a public. They are persons who are inclined to participate but lack accessibility or opportunity. As attentive members they are aware of the issues and informed about the activities in play. Frequently, they are better aware of the totality of the implications than are the opinion-makers.

Located at the epicenter of Figure 6 are the opinion-makers. This element does not necessarily preempt the function of making opinion. However, they are the persons who strongly *influence*, as well as *articulate* and *represent*, the opinion of a public. They are engaged in the critical functions of opinion-circulation, opinion-formation, and opinion-submitting. It is true that these functions are often performed simultaneously by the same person. Nevertheless, we should not forget that the opinion-makers must perform several functions in relation to their role, and in many cases they are more typically opinion assimilators and disseminators rather than opinion-makers. Just the same, they are found at the epicenter of action,

---

[14] Internalizing the opinion is the process in which the public or a group finally feels that the issue is uniquely related to their position, if not solely part of their own collective thinking or efforts.

[15] A wide variety of terms have been employed to describe these relationships. Rosenau, *op. cit.*, uses opinion-makers, attentive public, and mass public. In discussing this matter in broader terms Elmo Roper designates six gradations moving outward from the inner circle: "Great Thinkers," the "Great Disciples," the "Great Disseminators," the "Lesser Disseminators," the "Participating Citizens," and the "Politically Inert." See Elmo Roper, "Who Tells the Story-Teller," SATURDAY REVIEW, 37 (July 31, 1954), pp. 25–26.

[16] It is possible to "communicate about communication." The basic aspects of the feedback process involve: (1) the orderly collection of information about the functioning of a system, (2) the reporting of this information into the system, and (3) the use of the information for taking further social action. The entire operation is not unlike a thermostat in a house. When the temperature drops in the house this information is fed to a mechanism which releases more fuel for the fire in the furnace. Subsequently, the heat in the house reaches the prescribed temperature and again this information is fed to the mechanism which reduces the amount of fuel for the fire. For more information on this subject, see Karl W. Deutsch, THE NERVES OF GOVERNMENT (New York: The Free Press of Glencoe, 1963), and Norbert Wiener, CYBERNETICS: COMMUNICATIONS AND CONTROL IN THE ANIMAL, THE MACHINE AND SOCIETY (Cambridge: M.I.T. Technology Press, and New York: John Wiley, 1948), and THE HUMAN USE OF HUMAN BEINGS (Boston: Houghton Mifflin, 1950).

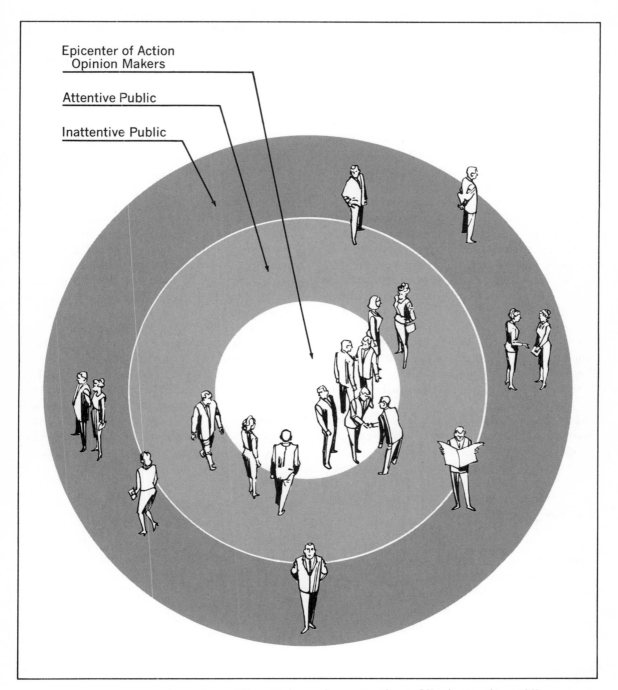

Epicenter of Action
Opinion Makers

Attentive Public

Inattentive Public

FIGURE 6. *Gradations of a public: opinion-makers, attentive public, inattentive public*

and as such direct the input, magnitude, and extent of opinion (and as we have also noted, in some cases, influence) .

Mobilizing the Publics

MOBILIZING DOES NOT MEAN MANIPULATING

Much of public relations centers around the process of mobilizing the publics. This is the essential aspect of public relations to which, unfortunately, has been ascribed so much unfavorable discussion. Public relations people have become known as influence peddlers, pressure boys, and opinion manipulators, all of which have had unfortunate implications for the professional field. How can responsible government occur unless the publics are fully informed of governmental affairs and the public officials and administrators cognizant of public opinions? A municipality has an obligation to keep its citizens well-informed of its policies and activities and to treat them courteously at all times. When the officials of the municipality start to abuse the public relation function, manipulating publics for selfish reasons and advantages, then rightfully they are open to criticism.

The media of public relations have no moral character. They are only instrumentalities which can be used for either bad or good purposes. Public officials should be fully aware of this simple fact and employ full discretion in their planning and implementation of public relations programs.

It is not our purpose to outline a detailed discussion, but rather to sketch out three fundamentals for mobilizing the publics: (1) knowing your publics, (2) linking publics with more institutionalized groupings, and (3) channeling opinion. Note that we mention these three fundamentals in the active and not in the static sense. This is how the entire subject should be viewed: in essence with a mathematical mind, almost employing the techniques and methods of calculus in keeping track of all of the variable factors.

KNOWING YOUR PUBLICS

The first responsibility of public relations work is knowing your public. Who are its members

and what are their interests? What do they think and why? How does a public reach its conclusions? Remember that publics overlap, and hence a person can belong to several publics, depending upon his politics, beliefs, values, vocation, religion, membership in organizations, and so on. For illustration, a man may be a conservative, a Protestant, a farmer, and a veteran.

We earlier noted in Chapter 3 that in recent years some rather sophisticated techniques and devices have been developed to identify a public, measure its size, magnitude, and scope of influence, what it thinks and why, etc. A public servant should not become involved in a public relations program until he has the facts. These may be determined by formal and informal surveys, questionnaires, opinion polls, voting patterns, or by interviews and discussions, by attending meetings, or reading member publications.

Considerable insight may be gained by analyzing opinion leadership in the community, to whom people look for advice, guidance, and support. But facts are not enough. They must be critically examined, evaluated, and reevaluated. Judgments must be made and decisions arrived at. In the final analysis, the public relations worker must resort almost to a sixth sense, but this *sixth sense* is not so much guessing as wisdom based upon practice and experience.

LINKING PUBLICS WITH INSTITUTIONALIZED GROUPINGS

Under our discussions concerning the "concept of a public," we noted that publics and institutional opinion groups should be regarded as being at the opposite ends of a continuum. As a public becomes more structured and formalized, it becomes an institutionalized opinion group. It is now important to note that the more formalized and institutionalized groups dominate the flow of opinion and influence. publics as loosely formed associations of individuals are not effective in action until they are tied up with other groups of a more formal and institutionalized nature. This contingency is one of the most important, yet often overlooked, aspects of a public.

On the other hand, more formal and institutionalized groups need the support of publics. Thus, a political party or an interest group may try to manipulate amorphous publics to a particular end.

In a free and open society such as ours, it is very difficult to design a continuum for a public to the highest form of institutionalization which will be generally accepted. However, a general guide may be useful, with full realization that this is only a superficial treatment of the subject.

Near the base of the continuum is found the elementary grouping of a crowd. A crowd is a transitory and relatively unorganized grouping of individuals. In one case it may be very dynamic, persistent, and somewhat organized and in another situation more passive, such as an audience of some sort. A crowd unlike a public needs a definite locus in space, and its members are in physical contiguity with each other.[17]

Near the top of the continuum are found the primary groups in which the family, the churches, and the schools are frequently placed.[18] Below these primary groups are found a wide variety of institutionalized groups such as political parties, interest groups, trade associations, fraternal organizations, and business concerns which strongly influence the flow of opinion.[19]

While our continuum may be superficial, it is sufficient in detail to indicate that a person concerned with public relations must deal constantly with attitudes, facts, and opinions from a wide number of collective groupings, and in

the struggle to influence peoples' minds think in terms of an almost infinite combination of forces. Back of all of this is the delicate decision of what technique, approach, and circuit of communication should be employed. He has to learn how to work with and not against the elements in play. By skillful analysis of the issues, of the people, of the conditions, and of the effects of the media of communication, he can direct a strong influence upon public opinion.[20]

CHANNELING OPINION

After the facts are in and some evaluations and conclusions reached, then comes the delicate problem of channeling opinion. The circuits of communication in most communities have pretty much been established and developed. The task of the public official is to discern them and to decide ways and forms by which ideas and information will be fed in and circulate.

Channels of communication include personal, organizational, and mass media.

Personal media include those forms of communication used by individuals in direct contact with each other—face to face, over the telephone, or by mail. The notion of direct personal exchange is involved.

Organizational media are those impersonal instruments such as various house organs and memoranda, assemblies, and programs. These are utilized for communication with a differentiated public.

Mass media are those impersonal instruments of communication that are intended for, and made available to, anyone who is able to utilize them within the limits of the media's distribution. These include the various periodical publications, whether daily, weekly, monthly, quarterly, or some other time interval, and the electronic media such as radio, telephone, and television. While mass media often are directed to specific categories of publics, such as geographic, economic, ethnic, racial, or cultural, in contrast with organiza-

[17] For other characteristics see Kimball Young, *op. cit.*, and Rex F. Harlow, SOCIAL SCIENCE IN PUBLIC RELATIONS (New York: Harper and Bros., 1957), pp. 35 *et seq.*

[18] For breakdown of institutions in these terms see Frederick C. Irion, PUBLIC OPINION AND PROPAGANDA (New York: Thomas Y. Crowell Co., 1950), particularly pp. 277 *et seq.*

[19] See Rex F. Harlow and Marvin M. Black, PRACTICAL PUBLIC RELATIONS (New York: Harper and Bros., 1952), particularly pp. 130–50 for a treatment of such groups. For a discussion of the relative importance of such groups within various environmental settings, see William Allieg, MODERN PUBLIC OPINION (New York: McGraw-Hill Book Company, 1956), particularly pp. 276ff.

[20] Chapter 8 discusses in detail various strategies and techniques for articulating publics and community groups with action programs.

tional media, these communications are distributed essentially to undifferentiated audiences.[21]

Summary

In recent years a wealth of knowledge has been developed concerning the "multitudinous publics," their forms, composition, and structure as well as their roles in making and conveying opinion and influence. This has led into more reliable conceptualization of ways and means of mobilizing "publics" for improved public service.

It should be reemphasized that the study of public opinion is vital to success in public relations work. It is particularly important that the public servant recognize that he is dealing not with one but many publics, each of which constitutes a specific problem and requires special study. Success in dealing with these publics requires a thorough knowledge of the "publics," linking them with more institutionalized groupings, and effectively channeling opinion.

---

[21] Communication literature is expansive and almost unmanageable. Rosenau, op. cit., in his Chapter Six, "Channels of Opinion Circulation," does an excellent job of detailing the conceptualizations alluded to here. The following works are also useful: Bernard Berelson and Morris Janowitz, eds., READER IN PUBLIC OPINION AND COMMUNICATION (Glencoe: Free Press, 1953); Wilbur Schramm, ed., THE PROCESS AND EFFECTS OF MASS COMMUNICATION (Urbana: University of Illinois Press, 1954);

Melvin L. DeFleur and Otto N. Larsen, THE FLOW OF INFORMATION: AN EXPERIMENT IN MASS COMMUNICATION (New York: Harper and Bros., 1958); Richard E. Charpin, MASS COMMUNICATIONS: A STATISTICAL ANALYSIS (East Lansing: Michigan State University Press, 1957); and Karl W. Deutsch, THE NERVES OF GOVERNMENT, MODELS OF POLITICAL COMMUNICATION AND CONTROL (New York: The Free Press of Glencoe, 1963).

6

Serving the Public

PROVIDING SERVICES to the public constitutes the basic function and responsibility of municipal governments. Although the nature and scope of the services change somewhat from time to time and vary from city to city, the fundamental objective remains the same. The purpose is to provide on a broad scale those services which help to meet the daily needs of the citizenry but which cannot be performed as efficiently or economically by individual citizens acting in their separate capacities. For example, it generally is economically impractical for individuals to attempt to furnish their own police and fire protection.

This was the basic rationale underlying the establishment of some of the earliest cities in history. The citizens realized that numerous services, particularly of the protective type, could be much more effectively performed by a central body supported by a majority of all the residents in the area.

Citizen Interests and Wants

In the mid-twentieth century, throughout our nation, cities are experiencing an increase in public expectations regarding municipal services. These demands on the part of the public relate not only to the quantity of services provided but to the quality as well.

The reasons for this heightened interest are numerous, but they primarily are the result of major changes in our cultural and institutional patterns. Among the major causal factors have been (1) the demographic transition of our society from one that was traditionally rural to

one that is now predominantly urban;[1] (2) the increase in the complexity of government policies, rules, and practices, and the difficulty which many citizens experience in attempting to comply with and understand such laws and procedures; (3) the tremendous increase in the mobility of the American public and the resulting feeling of "rootlessness" on the part of millions of persons who do not reside in any one city for any great length of time; (4) the widening chasm in communications between the citizen and government and the difficulty in obtaining information or services, or even in making his needs known to public officials; and (5) the increased citizen demands without corresponding understanding of the financial, legal, and political limitations on municipal governments in terms of providing services.

Public Relations and the Concept of Service

All municipal employees from the top administrator on down are responsible for serving the citizens of the community. Although some of the responsibilities may be indirect—in the sense that some personnel do not frequently have face-to-face contact with the public—their obligation to the public is just as important. In one sense, the public service responsibility of supervisors and managers is even greater than

---

[1] The population of American cities doubled between the beginning of the Civil War and 1900. By 1920, over one-half of the nation was living in cities. The percentage in 1960 was around 70 and continues to climb. Charles R. Adrian, GOVERNING URBAN AMERICA (New York: McGraw-Hill Book Company, 1961), p. 22.

that of operating personnel because the former group tends to establish the public service climate of the organization through its own attitudes and actions toward the public.

Over-all public opinion regarding city government is formulated largely on the basis of public satisfaction with the quality and quantity of the services provided by municipal personnel. Moreover, the manner in which the services are performed is often more important than the actual service itself in terms of public reaction.[2] If a citizen feels that he is being given considerate and fair treatment by a municipal employee, he will have a more favorable impression of the city government. This holds true even if he is disappointed in his request. For example, if a person is denied a zoning variance he may go away disappointed, but if he feels he was treated fairly then he will usually be satisfied with the service.

In order to establish good relations with the public, the municipal employees must not only be effective in performing their duties in a technical or professional manner, they must also carry them out in a manner that earns citizen approval and confidence. In order for a city to gain and maintain citizen satisfaction and confidence, the person must not only be served well, but he must *feel* that he is receiving good service.

Service Through Information

As mentioned earlier in this book democracy has a special need for the general public to be informed regarding the activities of government. Unless citizens are aware of and understand public laws and regulations, they will be unable to carry out their civic responsibilities. At the same time if citizens are uninformed about the benefits and services which may be available, they will not be able to use their rights and privileges.

That cities increasingly are recognizing the need to keep the public informed regarding municipal services and activities is apparent

from the surveys regularly carried in the *Municipal Year Book* and from reports appearing from time to time in *Public Management*.

THE MASS MEDIA

The basic problem with providing informational service to the public through the mass media, or even through correspondence, is that the communication is one-way. It is difficult for the receiver of the information to clear up any misunderstanding especially if the information is not clear to him. This can be critical from a public relations standpoint if the members of the public misinterpret the information and perhaps act or fail to act to their personal detriment. Public reaction to such faulty informational services will be anything but favorable. This is why it is so important for municipal personnel to see that informational materials are clear and complete before they are disseminated to the public.

MUNICIPAL GREETINGS AND BROCHURES

Although "Municipal Reports and Events" are described extensively in Chapter 12, some examples cited below illustrate ways of informing the citizenry of the kinds of municipal services available.

A description of city services in Elgin, Illinois, has been prepared in the form of a pamphlet for general distribution to the public. It includes a description of the city's financial activities, organization, boards and commissions, service departments, and a list of phone numbers to obtain services.

Buchanan, Michigan, distributes "request-for-service" cards to the public through city departments and members of the city commission. The citizen fills out the card and sends it to the city manager's office or turns it over to any city employee. The cards are designed to make sure that the request is clearly understood and to avoid mistakes as to what is said.

Plymouth, Michigan, maintains a continuing public relations program to keep citizens informed on what the city is doing. New residents receive a letter from the mayor and city manager welcoming them to the city and outlining briefly the city services that are available. The

---

[2] John M. Pfiffner and Frank P. Sherwood, "The '90%' of Public Relations," PERSONNEL JOURNAL, 17 (1954), pp. 2–7.

letter includes the phone numbers for the city hall and fire department and invites new residents to visit city hall, register for voting, and become acquainted with the administration.

Evanston, Illinois, has prepared postcard "Citizen Request Cards" so that citizens can mail in requests for service or information on any problem relating to city government. The cards have been distributed to city employees so they can give them to citizens who make inquiries concerning other than their own departments.

Alexandria, Virginia, issued a booklet giving historical background for the city together with a description of current city problems and services, including urban renewal, industrial development, highways, education, and public works.

Rockville, Maryland, issued a *Citizens Handbook* to provide information on city government and community services and facilities. It includes city offices, a city map, a street guide, and directories of parks and playgrounds, schools, and churches. Rockville also has issued a four-page folder to new residents to welcome them to the city. Information is shown on governmental organization, elections, city government services, recreation facilities, and a directory of city officials.

Edina, Minnesota, recently issued a five-year progress report on the growth of city services. The report is illustrated with photographs and maps and includes a directory of city officials.

In terms of public relations, such informational projects as these can be invaluable to the citizenry and the city from both a short- and long-range point of view. They immediately benefit citizens by providing specific information about municipal services, organization and location of various departments, and other helpful information. Such activities can help engender and sustain public confidence and appreciation.

Points of Service: Citizen Contacts

Most city employees in their work come in contact with members of the public either directly or indirectly. Many of these contacts

are made daily. Municipal office employees meet citizens daily who come in to request information, apply for permits, or inquire about services. Daily contact with citizens outside of municipal offices is characteristic of policemen, firemen, garbage collectors, meter readers, building inspectors, utility service men, and construction workers.

Although these daily contacts may be routine and "part of the job" to city personnel, they are usually considered very important by members of the public. Most people have some misgivings about going into government offices, and relatively few go there voluntarily. Frequently individuals must contact government agencies to perform tasks which they regard as onerous, such as paying a traffic ticket or appearing in court, filling out involved forms, and being subjected to intensive questioning to obtain permits or licenses.

Persons who contact city officials for such purposes are usually apprehensive and dread going through the "red tape" involved. Because they are not familiar with the procedures involved, they fear that they may not qualify, and they realize that they may be subjected to fines or fees which they feel are unjustified or too high.

Underlying all these anxieties is the uneasy feeling on the part of many persons that governmental officials have the authority to impose controls or restrictions on them such as refusing to issue licenses or to approve building construction, levying high penalties or fines, etc. They are acutely aware that such decisions are made by public officials and that the results may be to greatly restrict their personal activities, to interfere with their plans or schedules, and perhaps to create serious financial hardship. It is little wonder then that many persons go to city offices only when they are required to do so, and then with apprehension.

Service Contacts Mold Opinion

In the long run the profusion of "routine" day-to-day contacts between city employees and citizens adds up to the over-all impression which members of the public have toward the city government. Whether public opinion of city government is good or bad depends basically upon whether citizens have been favorably or unfavorably impressed, satisfied or dissatisfied in their contacts with the municipality through its employees.

The comments regarding day-to-day contacts are not in any way intended to negate the importance of public information programs and the utilization of mass media. The importance and value of the formal public information program has been pointed out elsewhere in this book. However, irrespective of the amount of effort put forth through formal public relations activities, and regardless of the favorable public impression that has been built up as a result of these activities, a single unsatisfactory personal contact by a citizen with the city can change the good impression to a bad one. When individual contacts are multiplied hundreds and even thousands of times daily, it is apparent that the very act of providing daily routine services is critical in achieving and maintaining favorable public opinion.

DIRECT AND INDIRECT CONTACTS

Although contacts between a city and the citizenry can be classified in various ways, a useful way to consider such relationships is whether they are made on a direct or face-to-face basis or in an indirect manner. Examples of direct contacts include all those occasions when city representatives and citizens meet each other face to face, such as when persons come into city hall offices to converse with various personnel or when such contacts are made in the field.

Indirect contacts occur when meetings are on a nonface-to-face basis, such as telephone conversations and through correspondence. Mass media, municipal reports, and photography also are avenues of indirect access to citizenry but are not treated here because they are primarily publicity resources which are considered in detail in other chapters of this book.

From the standpoint of effective communications, the face-to-face contact usually is more advantageous, since there is a better opportunity for achieving understanding between the parties involved. If the information which is offered or requested is not understood by either party, the *opportunity* is immediately available to furnish or secure additional information from the other person. If the matter under consideration is of a technical or detailed nature, the face-to-face situation is especially helpful in achieving better understanding.

In face-to-face meetings there exists, in effect, a system of "two-way" communications which also makes it easier to overcome barriers which may distort or prevent understanding between the parties involved. Although categorized as indirect, it should be noted that telephone contacts provide opportunity for two-way communication, also, even though to a lesser degree than face-to-face.

Even two-way communication is pregnant with potential difficulties which may lead to misunderstanding or, worse, to antagonism. These problems may be based in semantics or emotion or both. For example, the information being conveyed may be technical in nature, such as meteorological data and the chemistry of smog; the client-citizen may be foreign-born and unable to understand easily the indigenous or native language; or the client-citizen may feel uneasy in the governmental office and unable to think clearly or to recall pertinent information when requested to do so. Such problems emphasize the need for great care by the municipal employee in communicating with citizens. The quality of the information service, which is the responsibility of the employee, is determined in part by:

1. The interest shown in the citizen's problem: Do you give him complete attention? Do you listen to him? Do you ask questions to clarify his wants?

2. The quality of information given: Is your communication complete and accurate? Is it clear and concise?

3. The manner of speech: Is your grammar correct? Do you pronounce and enunciate properly? Are your words meaningful and appropriate?

4. The personal attitude: Do you express cordial greetings? Are you polite and friendly?

5. The personal appearance: Is your dress and grooming tasteful and appropriate? Do your facial expressions convey a helpful and courteous demeanor?

Various applications of the above five determinants of information quality are discussed in succeeding paragraphs. It may be appropriate to summarize at this point, however, by quoting from a municipal public relations training manual:

Everyone has a different personality and must be handled or dealt with in a different way. In some regards, a person involved in public contact work must be like a chameleon . . . adapt himself to his environment.

A person who is slow and deliberate by nature might feel his problem isn't being given adequate consideration if it is too speedily handled. He will suspect carelessness and slipshod work.

Do not, of course, mimic any unfavorable characteristics your client or visitor might have, such as unpleasant manner, skeptical attitude or sarcasm. You might sum up the fundamental techniques in handling people in a few short points:

1. Respect the dignity of the individual.
2. Be a good and sincere listener.
3. Try honestly and sincerely to see the other fellow's point of view.
4. Ask questions instead of giving orders.
5. Speak kindly to and of others.
6. Smile—and mean it. Say "no" with a smile.

Remember that there are many different ways, good and bad, in which the visitor to a government office can be greeted and received. Among the factors entering into proper greeting and reception are:

1. A tidy office.
2. Acknowledging the presence of the caller promptly.
3. Adopting a "professional" manner in talking with the caller.
4. Not leaving the caller unattended without explaining where you are going and how long you might be gone.
5. Giving the caller a thorough hearing.

The importance of having the caller leave in a pleasant, satisfied frame of mind cannot be overemphasized. If he entered your office by mistake, adequate directions should be given to set him on his course. We should all bear in mind that these are respectable jobs we hold, but we are public servants. We cannot afford the luxury of a temper, discourteousness, and other forms of poor public relations.[3]

Through Correspondence. Special care should be taken in the composition of letters to be sent to local citizens. This is particularly true if the letter is concerned with technical or detailed matters which may be unfamiliar to the general public. A letter is used as a substitute for a direct or face-to-face contact, but the writer should attempt to create as favorable an impression on the recipient as if he were talking to him personally.

One of the biggest problems in governmental correspondence is the tendency of public officials to use an excessive amount of legalistic or technical terminology. If the recipient is unfamiliar with such language, he may only become frustrated and confused and blame the government for all the "red tape." This type of reaction is the exact opposite of the objective of correspondence—to communicate effectively with specific members of the public and usually to secure a desired response.

Certain basic concepts relative to effective correspondence with the public have been developed through years of experience in both public agencies and private industry. The following is a list of major criteria that may be used as a checklist in the preparation of correspondence.

1. The letter should be friendly in tone and concise, clear, and accurate.
2. Get to the major point or issues early in the letter.
3. Use short sentences and paragraphs; restrict the length to the minimum that is adequate to convey the necessary information.
4. Avoid inexact, stilted, technical, and vague language.
5. Refer to the other person's letter if there was one and if it is related to the letter being prepared.
6. Be sure of the facts and information contained in the letter.
7. Review the letter carefully before it is mailed to see that it meets these standards.

Although form letters or notices are often time-saving devices, care should be taken in their construction and discretion exercised in their use. Frequently, such correspondence may appear to be very impersonal to the recipient, especially if it is of the type where most or all of the body of the letter is preprinted with only the name and address typed in. This is most likely to create the impression in the mind of the individual that government personnel do

[3] City of Beverly Hills, California, PUBLIC RELATIONS TRAINING MANUAL, revised edition, November, 1962.

not want to take time to write a personal letter and that this is just one more example of government red tape.

The decision on using a form letter depends on each case. It should not be used unless the information is completely adequate and sufficiently clear to answer the inquiry.

Telephone Contacts. Proper telephone usage improves communication between government and citizen and at the same time heightens citizen appreciation of governmental functions and personnel. When individual citizens can transact public business satisfactorily by telephone, without making special trips to governmental offices, they usually will consider this as a very helpful and time-saving service. Such contacts with the public are beneficial to municipal personnel in elimination of other more time-consuming personal or mail contacts with the private citizen.

Communicating by telephone is another substitute for face-to-face contacts which involves hazards as well as benefits in terms of public relations. The key to the successful telephone usage is the *manner* in which the employee communicates with the person on the "other end of the line."

Although the other party cannot see the city employee with whom he is conversing, the manner of speech and tone of voice help form a mental picture in the mind of the citizen. As in all such contacts, the employee speaking *is the city* as far as the citizen is concerned.

The use of the telephone is so common in the day-to-day operations of city government that it tends to become routine procedure on the part of many of the municipal personnel. This, in itself, may not present any problem, but if the personnel become careless in their attitude and manner on the telephone, a serious public relations problem may result. Good telephone habits help to promote good will for any organization dealing with the public.

Telephone Technique. A substantial amount of research has been conducted by both private industry and public agencies in the proper use of the telephone. The results of this research indicate that the following points should be recognized and practiced by persons who wish to use the telephone effectively.

1. A telephone should be answered promptly when it rings.

2. When answering a telephone, a person should identify himself and his organization adequately so that the caller knows that he is or is not connected with the office he desires. An example would be, "Planning Department, Mr. Jones speaking." Identification also applies when placing a phone call.

3. Talk directly into the telephone transmitter and speak clearly, distinctly, and naturally.

4. When a call needs to be transferred, this should be indicated to the caller so that he will not become so deeply involved in explaining his problem or request that he will have to repeat much of it over again. This can be very irritating to the caller and can waste the time of both parties. When transferring a call, secure sufficient information from the caller so that he can be transferred to the proper party so that the caller will not feel he is getting the "run-around."

5. Maintain a pleasant tone of voice throughout the conversation and use tact in talking with callers who may be emotionally upset. If the caller has the mental impression that the person to whom he is speaking is not arguing back, he will usually calm down within a short time.

6. Concentrate on what the caller is saying and talk only to him while you are on the telephone.

7. Talk only as long as it is necessary to furnish or to obtain sufficient information, but do not give the impression that an attempt is being made to get the caller off the line before he finishes what he has to say.

8. Keep a pencil, paper, and message pad by the telephone so that pertinent information can be written down immediately.

9. Persons should ordinarily place their own telephone calls, because otherwise it may appear to the person receiving the call that the caller is not sufficiently interested or concerned to place the call himself.

10. Deliver all telephone messages promptly to prevent unnecessary delays in returning calls or embarrassment to the person for whom the call was intended.

11. End a telephone call in the same courteous manner as it began, so that the last as well as the first impression will be a good one.

Reception Area Contacts. Another key contact between the city and the public is the reception areas of public buildings and offices. Persons who come to a municipal office for the first time or who are not familiar with the location of specific offices within buildings may become confused as to which direction to go. It is not uncommon today to see persons wandering around the halls of public buildings obviously unable to locate a specific office. Since they may be somewhat apprehensive anyway about coming in to government offices, their frustration can easily turn into hostility toward the city government unless they are given help.

Numerous devices can be used to guide people to appropriate offices. A directory of room numbers placed in an obvious position, or placards or signs identifying the directions to the most frequently used offices, can assist callers greatly. It is especially helpful to maintain an information desk in the main entry area or lobby of public buildings, with a receptionist in attendance throughout working hours. This person can direct visitors to the proper offices more rapidly than they can locate these offices themselves. Frequently, the receptionist can save time for city employees by providing certain kinds of information directly or by referring the visitors to the appropriate office without delay. If misinformation or an incorrect referral is given to a person, however, he will probably get the impression that the receptionist is incompetent or that he is getting the "run-around." Special care should be taken in the selection of a receptionist, as this person may be the only city employee many citizens come in contact with, and the resulting impression can greatly affect their over-all impressions of the city government.

Service Requests and Complaints. Every request for service or complaint from the public is a potential public relations asset for the city. Whether it becomes an asset or a complaint depends on how the request or complaint is handled.

A complaint is a warning signal which indicates that a problem exists in some aspect of services to the public. When a complaint or a request for service is received by a municipal employee it should be given immediate attention and investigated thoroughly. Even though the matter may be of a minor nature to the city employee, it will be extremely important to the citizen. If the matter is handled promptly and conscientiously, the action will be appreciated by the person making the request; if it is neglected or ignored, the result will be a poor impression of the city's concern.

Four basic steps are involved in processing complaints and service requests: (1) welcome the complaint or request from the citizen; (2) assign specific responsibility for immediate investigation to determine the feasibility of providing the service, or making corrections in the case of a complaint; (3) provide a follow-up procedure to insure that the matter receives proper attention; and (4) in the case of a complaint, notify the person that the correction has been made; or if it involves a service request, be certain that the desired action is performed or if it is not feasible, that the person knows why.

It is not possible, of course, to satisfy all service requests or reconcile all complaints in a completely satisfactory manner. Some complaints are unjustified and some requests are unreasonable. Nevertheless, it is sometimes difficult for those persons making the requests to understand this.

This is why it is so important that the employees who are designated to receive complaints and requests have a good understanding of human nature and be able to meet the public well. Such persons should understand that every person is different in his background, experience, and personality and that each person must be handled as an individual. Even if the request is unreasonable, the employee should "hear the other person out," remain objective and calm in the conversation, and if the request is impossible to grant, strive to make the person understand why.

Many cities have developed special procedures to improve and streamline their handling of complaints and service requests. The following are some examples.

Roanoke, Virginia, uses a postcard form which allows citizens who requested service or filed a complaint to comment on how well the request was carried out. When a complaint is received by the city it is referred to the appropriate department which sends a man to investigate and make whatever improvements he can. This person leaves a card at the home of the complainant. The card provides space for identifying data, the type of complaint, and several lines for comments. The card is stamped and self-addressed to the city manager's office. The response has been very satisfactory in that the returned cards have expressed satisfaction with the work done, and some have made additional suggestions for improvements.

In Ojai, California, when a service request is received from a citizen, the form is prepared in duplicate. The original copy is delivered to the department in which the service is provided. The employee who is designated to receive such requests determines the priority of the request, and schedules a completion date. After the request is performed, the original copy is returned to the central file and the second copy is destroyed. For control purpose, the city manager reviews folders containing the completed requests and those which are pending.

Because it emphasizes the significance of complaints in effective municipal performance, the following is quoted from the public relations training manual for the city of La Habra, California.

We most often associate complaints with anger or irritation, and certainly many complaints which come to our attention are caused by ill feelings. But even the most embittered citizen is presumed to be seeking some sort of positive reaction to his complaint. We thus find it helpful to assume the attitude that complaints are requests for service and/or information. We differentiate these service requests from the more routine inquiries . . . because they represent a request for something which should have been provided in the normal operating pattern of government, or at least because the citizen honestly believes that his complaint is based on the failure of the city to provide some service to which he is entitled.

Thus, our most important attitude toward the complaint is that the complaint is genuine, that to the citizen his complaint is of vital importance. Indeed, our receipt of a complaint is of vital importance to us. Even if the solution to a particular complaint is beyond our responsibility, our willingness to listen and to at least suggest the source of solution can aid us in our job of informing the public. Cities vary as to the types of services they perform, and it is not uncommon for the citizen who feels he has been taken advantage of by some public or private agency to call upon his city government for help, and even to call upon the particular city agency whose title suggests a possible remedy for the problem.

Whether or not we believe that a complaint is valid, we cannot forget that to the complainant his problem is real and vital. While we encounter a variety of methods and types in the presentation of complaints, there are some citizens who find it particularly difficult to present their complaints rationally and in a form which we can readily understand. These people need our special attention and sympathy, as they often are the ones who feel that they have been deliberately mistreated when, in fact, there has been a breakdown in communications.

Our most important task, then, in receiving complaints is to fully understand their nature and specific facts. As in the case of inquiries, careful listening and thought-provoking speech are among our most useful techniques, either for helping to find a solution or another party where the solution can better be found.

Perhaps the only rule we need stress in this approach to public relations, other than those of courtesy and intelligence, is that we must, under all circumstances, listen carefully and completely to all complaints before replying. While we can tactfully prevent callers from inconsequential rambling, we cannot afford to obscure or confuse an honest complaint by argument or denial on our part.[4]

Personal and Physical Appearance. Members of the public judge a city not only by services but also by the appearance of the municipal personnel, equipment, and facilities. As pointed out in a number of previous chapters, good public relations cannot be guaranteed by merely doing a good job; the public must be convinced that the service is good.

The personal appearance of those employees who come in contact with the public is especially important in terms of dress and personal neatness. The city is not expected to set standards of fashion, and the type and style of clothes worn depends somewhat upon the cli-

---

[4] City of La Habra, California, "Training in Public Relations and Communications." January, 1962, mimeographed, pp. 11 and 12. For an example of the procedures used by La Habra in handling such "service requests," see Appendix C, "Use of the Service Request Form."

mate and styles of a particular city. But neatness and cleanliness can be maintained regardless of type and locale.

The behavior and bearing of office personnel is an important factor in the formulation of public opinion. If persons coming into city offices observe employees drinking coffee, reading magazines, or just "fooling around on the job," this will create a bad impression regardless of how they are dressed. In order to prevent this, there should be a special room or area away from public view in which employees may relax on their coffee breaks; many jurisdictions do provide such facilities.

The appearance of uniformed personnel is of particular importance, since the public is more apt to notice these employees. Uniforms which are soiled, unpressed, or in need of mending are quite conspicuous. The appearance of the uniform depends upon the way it is worn as well as its condition. The police officer or other uniformed employee will create a much better impression if he is alert and conscious of his bearing than if he is untidy and careless in appearance.

The appearance of public buildings, equipment, and offices is also significant in the public's opinion of the city government. Regardless of the design or age of a public building, its exterior appearance can remain favorable if it is kept in good condition and the grounds are cared for. The interiors of buildings and offices are also important to the city as far as appearances are concerned. Just as many commercial establishments are judged by their interior conditions, so is a city judged by the inside of its buildings and offices. The public does not ordinarily expect or desire to see government offices as elaborately furnished as business establishments, however, and if the walls, floors and office equipment are maintained in a clean, neat condition, the public will be favorably impressed. These same standards of appearance apply to other types of city equipment, such as motor vehicles, street maintenance equipment, construction machinery, street signs, etc.

Safety as a Factor in Public Relations. Sometimes overlooked is the role of safety measures in municipal public relations, both inside and outside of offices. Thoughtfulness and consideration for others and a disposition to observe and report possible trouble areas or unsafe conditions are basic for safety-conscious employee behavior.

Especially significant are the driving manners of public employees when operating motor vehicles, the source of some of the best and worst impressions on individual citizens. Observation of the normal rules of driving courtesy and of statutory vehicle safety are only minimum standards of safe vehicle operation. Public vehicles have distinctive markings and are easily recognized. Thus, the municipality is judged by the operator behind the wheel, whose basic standard when operating a non-emergency public vehicle should be *always yield the right-of-way*. In this sense courtesy is equated with safety, and behaving in a safe manner engenders favorable attitudes toward those who behave in such a fashion.

PERFORMING THE SERVICES

During the course of a typical day in most cities, there may be hundreds and frequently thousands of contacts between municipal employees and the public. Most of these contacts are the type that might be called "service contacts," since they occur in connection with providing a service to the citizen in one form or another. These types of contacts usually involve a direct relationship between the municipal representative and the citizen, such as occurs in many of the daily activities of police officers, firemen, receptionists and counter clerks, inspectional personnel, and construction workers and their supervisors.

Every department of city government needs to maintain good relationships with the members of its respective "publics," not only for the purpose of being able to achieve its program objectives more effectively but also to maintain public satisfaction with its services. Underlying these immediate departmental objectives, however, is an even broader and more fundamental reason for high quality service contacts with the public. The public relations status of an organization is basically only as high as the amount of public respect attributed to its weakest unit. For example, if all the departments of a city enjoy favorable public relations except the police department, then it is likely that the over-all public respect for the city will not be high.

This example, of course, is not in any sense used to imply that police departments are the major cause of bad municipal public relations, since lack of public respect and support can occur as the result of poor service contacts with any department or unit in the city. If a city is to earn the good will and cooperation of all or even most of the people, these persons must be satisfied generally with the relationships which they have with all the departments or units with which they come in contact.

Law Enforcement Contacts. The importance and variety of responsibilities of law enforcement personnel place them in an unusual position relative to public opinion. The very fact that so many of the police officer's public contacts are restrictive or disciplinary in the minds of the citizens makes his a key responsibility for developing public respect.

Most law enforcement personnel will state that it is not easy to convince most citizens that they are "in the wrong" when they have violated the law. The reasons for this type of reaction can be numerous. It may be a matter of personal pride, or the fear of possible fines, loss of privileges, or even imprisonment. Or it may be that the violator earnestly believes that he is innocent. A fundamental reason for such an attitude is often due to the average American's traditional resistance to governmental rules, regulations, and restrictions.

There is no denying the fact that the public relations responsibilities of law enforcement personnel are difficult. The basic question is how can such personnel carry out their duties in an effective manner and yet satisfy, or at least not offend, the citizens involved. The key to this is the manner in which such enforcement actions are taken. This is discussed in some detail in Chapter 9.

Fire Protection Contacts. Although fire protection personnel may not have as many direct contacts with members of the public as police officers, their presence in all parts of the city and the special nature of their work are significant determinants of public opinion. Their duties consist basically of the protection of life and property of citizens from fires and many other types of emergency. The services offered the public are, in general, highly valued and appreciated.

Aside from the critical effect upon public opinion of the competency demonstrated by fire personnel to cope with fires and other emergency situations, some aspects of the more routine, day-to-day operations may in the long run prove to be more important. A basic responsibility in fire prevention is inspections. The purpose is to guard against the unintentional creation or presence of fire hazards due to accumulation of waste materials, inferior wiring and other electrical and mechanical defects, and improper materials storage.

Two general types of inspections are handled by firemen—inspections of commercial, industrial and public buildings, and inspection of private residences.

In the former category fire personnel are usually authorized by state laws or local ordinances to inspect the interiors of commercial establishments to determine whether the proprietors have complied with the laws and standards relative to fire safety. Even here, however, it is sometimes difficult to obtain the full cooperation of the persons operating such establishments. This is especially so if the person is in doubt that his facilities and building may meet the safety standards. In this situation a tactful, though firm, attitude will usually achieve more cooperation on the part of the building occupants than a forceful approach. A basic purpose of such inspections is to convince the occupants that maintaining high fire safety standards will be to their benefit in the long run. Ordinarily, a sincere, objective approach is much more effective in achieving compliance than an authoritarian approach.

The inspection of private residences frequently is more of a problem than commercial building inspections. Ordinarily fire personnel have no legal authority to enter the premises unless the residents give them permission to do so. Exceptions are where a definite fire hazard is known to exist, and even then a search warrant may be required.

It is common knowledge of fire personnel

that many actual or potential fire hazards such as defective wiring, ventilation, waste materials, etc., exist in private residences and that if the opportunity were available to demonstrate and explain this to the residents in their homes, many costly fires, injuries, and even deaths could be prevented.

The key to effective residential fire inspection is gaining entry by voluntary consent of the residents. If this can be done, then it usually is relatively easy to point out and discuss any fire hazards. A letter to residents often helps (Figure 7). Care should be taken by fire personnel even inside the home not to give the impression that they are "snooping around," and they should indicate by their attitude that they are there only to help the occupants make their home a safer and better place in which to live.

Gaining voluntary entrance is often a problem in the very homes where fire personnel know or suspect that a fire hazard exists. Usually this is because the occupant realizes that he is not maintaining adequate safety standards and fears reprisals or possible repair expenses if he permits "government inspectors" in. This is a difficult problem to overcome, but if the fire personnel use a friendly, helpful approach in their initial encounter with the occupants, and take special care not to inject an authoritative tone in their voice, the person's resistance may be overcome.

Public Works Contacts. Many of the physical facilities and services provided in a modern American city are constructed and maintained through municipal public works operations. The department responsible for public works and related activities has a very special role to play in municipal public relations. This is due to two primary factors. First, the services and facilities which are provided are extremely important for the convenience and comfort of the people. Second, the construction and maintenance of these facilities often create inconveniences and may even become nuisances for the residents, and such conditions can lead to unfavorable public reactions.

Some of the more common activities and responsibilities of such a department which have public relations implications include construction and maintenance of streets and highways; checking plans, issuing permits, and inspecting new building construction; refuse collection and disposal; and maintenance and operation of street lighting systems and traffic signs. (See Figures 8, 9, and 10.)

All of these activities involve direct contacts between city personnel and members of the public at one time or another. Some involve more contacts than others, however, and some are more critical activities from a public relations standpoint since they affect more people directly.

For example, a very substantial amount of time and energy of a department of public works is spent in enforcing building and safety requirements for new buildings and other construction. This means checking building plans, issuing appropriate permits, and inspecting structures as they progress to make sure the specifications are drawn and the construction is performed in accordance with approved plans and building code requirements.

Citizens who are involved in construction which is subject to these regulations usually have established time schedules and may find it not only annoying but expensive if they are unable to maintain their schedules due to delays caused by the city. In the inspection of new construction, the inspection approvals are not limited to structural consideration but also must include plumbing, heating, ventilation, and refrigeration system approvals.

Inspectional services is another area of municipal operations where members of the public are often prone to feel that they are being victimized by bureaucratic "red tape" and inefficiency. This attitude is often the result of public ignorance of the law and also due to a lack of insight as to the need for such standards. In order to prevent such negative attitudes, it is necessary for city officials who are responsible for inspectional services to strive to see that members of the public involved understand the reason for and nature of the regulations and procedures involved.

Another phase of public works which has particular relevance to public relations is construction and maintenance of streets. Such projects can become irritating to the public,

City of Downey

CITY COUNCIL

CARROLL M. DUNNUM
MAYOR

SCOTT E. TEMPLE
MAYOR PRO-TEM

EDWIN W. GIDDINGS

BEN D CORBIN

HOLLIS M. PEAVEY

CITY MANAGER
OREN L. KING

ASSISTANT CITY MANAGER
GLENN KENDALL

CITY HALL
TOPAZ 1-0361

8425 SECOND STREET
DOWNEY, CALIFORNIA

Dear Neighbor·

We are happy to be able to make this personal contact with you.
We know that to visit briefly with each citizen in our community
is a step toward making our city a safer place in which to live.

Public education is a major factor in the control of fire.

To have each person in our city aware of the proper telephone
numbers to call in the event of an emergency would be of great
help in time of need.

Our goal at this time is to visit each home in Downey and to leave
the emergency FIRE and POLICE numbers at every telephone.

It is intended, also, that our visits into your neighborhood may
stimulate a "fire conscious" feeling among your friends and neighbors and thereby help to eliminate many careless fires which are
taking the lives of thousands in residential properties each year.

Please help us to help you make your home, your neighborhood
and Downey a safer place in which to live.

Sincerely yours,

R. W. Gain, Chief Engineer
Downey Fire Department

YOUR LOCATION IS	YOUR LOCATION IS
11435 Downey Ave	
CROSS STREETS ARE	CROSS STREETS ARE
Downey Ave & Phlox St.	
CITY OF DOWNEY	CITY OF DOWNEY

FIGURE 7. *Fire service inspection letter, Downey, California*

FIGURE 8. *Road construction announcement*

especially if the work is performed in residential areas. In view of the inconveniences involved, such as detours, "washboard" roads, accident hazards, and dust and dirt, it is little wonder that members of the public react as they sometimes do.

There are frequent personal contacts between city personnel and citizens in street construction, particularly if done in residential areas. Care should be taken to see that yards are not damaged or littered with dirt and debris, that driveway accesses are maintained, and that construction workers do not use private property or facilities such as water faucets without the consent of the owner.

One way to help prevent problems is to notify beforehand those persons who will be affected. The following examples illustrate some effective methods for doing this.

Before street construction is undertaken in Montgomery County, Maryland, a letter is sent by the county construction engineer to all property owners along the streets that are to be worked on. The letter sets forth the construction schedule, the name of the contractor, the approximate timing for each major stage of development, the name and phone number of county inspector assigned to the project, and related information. The letter concludes with the statement: "As homeowners ourselves, we can appreciate your feelings and will give them every consideration during our work."

FIGURE 9. *Water main construction announcement (Good: shows when project will be completed. Bad: this sign was still in place even though project had not been completed on October 10, 1965.)*

Phoenix, Arizona, has utilized a public informational program for residential street construction. The purpose is to provide the residents with information on the formation of residential street improvement districts to be used for paving residential streets. The procedure includes the distribution of descriptive brochures, the distribution of booklets with detailed information on the formation of street improvement districts, the preparation of radio and television spot announcements, and the use of newspaper releases and advertising.

Some municipal officials now feel that if one group of city employees who have the most effect upon the public's opinion of city services had to be singled out, it would be those employees who are engaged in refuse collection and disposal. The ordinary duties of such personnel include the collection and disposal of garbage, rubbish, tree and garden trimmings, papers, cans, bottles, and ashes. Although these tasks may appear to be menial compared to building construction or other major projects, they are highly significant pub-

lic relations activities. The fact that these employees are observed by residents several times each week in the neighborhood, and that they often enter private yards to obtain the refuse, places them in more frequent contact with and observation by the public than almost any other municipal employee group.

Many cities, aware of the public relations involved in refuse collection, provide uniforms and train employees in proper ways of handling the refuse so as not to damage the containers. These personnel are being given special training in the proper way to deal with the public, with emphasis on courtesy.

A special problem occurs when a change in collection procedures or schedules is needed. Glendale, California, conducted an extensive informational campaign to help make a smooth transition. The new system requires householders to provide uniform, metal rubbish containers with tight-fitting lids; garbage must be wrapped separately. An informational leaflet was first distributed to 60,000 homes by house-to-house delivery service, which was

FIGURE 10. *City landfill announcement (to the left: sign posted on site of a city landfill facing a group of tract houses. This sign is bad public relations because it is too blunt. To the right: this kind of sign will do a better job.)*

cheaper than bulk-rate mail. A special version of the leaflet was printed for one area of the city where the collection day was changed.

Two days after the leaflet was distributed, news releases were run in three local newspapers repeating the information in the leaflet. The principal points in the change-over were also covered in the city hall newsletter which goes to leading civic groups and key citizens in the area. The utility bills for the following month had a special printed insert to emphasize the importance of the change-over to the citizens. The sanitation supervisor and foremen visited numerous restaurants and other establishments to explain the change.

The results were excellent in terms of public cooperation. The key again was the use of effective communications to achieve public understanding and support.

Other Key Contact Points. Many other key points of contact between the city and the public greatly affect public opinion. Examples of such key contact personnel include park and recreation personnel, especially in recent years when members of the public have more leisure time available and spend more of it in public parks and recreational activities. Other examples include city clerks and their staffs and library personnel. Additional city offices which are key contact points include health and welfare offices, personnel recruiting offices, the chief administrator's office, and offices of department heads.

Success of the various public contacts depends ultimately on the ability of the personnel to meet and deal effectively with the many types of individuals who come to the offices seeking information and help.

7

The Employee–Citizen Team

In his relationships with citizens the municipal employee must always remember that he cannot gain public confidence unless he earns that confidence by effective performance.

Achieving Confidence by Cooperation

What are the means of gaining such confidence? This chapter focuses on the cooperative relationships of the municipal employee in working together with the *individual citizen* for the achievement of desirable objectives of the city, and goals which are compatible with the over-all purposes of municipal government.

In other chapters a variety of relationships with individuals and groups and their impact on the public relations of the municipality is discussed. Chapter 5 identifies various publics and outlines working relationships. Chapter 6 analyzes behavior of municipal employees in serving the citizenry. Chapter 8 identifies various types of community groups and the manner in which they influence municipal government. Here we look at the individual as he is asked to participate singly with a municipal official on some problem or to join with other *individual citizens* in meetings, on commissions, in community advisory committees, and in a variety of other cooperative endeavors.

The following discussion reveals the nature of employee-citizen collaboration, ranging from the most informal to the more formal highly structured arrangements for citizen advisory committees and municipal commissions, from the employee-to-citizen to the employee-to-group relationships.

The range of relationships includes the simplest role of the public employee as a citizen neighbor; special purpose committees, such as a citizens' urban renewal advisory committee; *ad hoc* advisory committees for bond elections; and standing advisory committees. It includes permanent departmental commissions, such as planning commissions, personnel commissions, and park and recreation commissions. It encompasses special-purpose "blue ribbon" commissions, such as those for disaster inquiry. Where citizen commissioners take on the role of government official, they may in turn appoint advisory committees, such as a library commission appointing a citizens' advisory committee to advise on the cultural needs of the city.

This work is not concerned with elections, initiatives, and referenda, nor with administrative and judicial remedies, although occasionally reference may be made to them for purposes of illustration.

What are the problems confronted with these types of arrangements and what are alternative ways of overcoming such problems? The theme throughout is working together—the individual citizen and the city employee—on the solution of problems of the citizen and the municipality.

Analogy of the Producer-Consumer

An oversimplification of the employee-citizen relationship is a comparison with the producer-consumer relationship, viewing the public employee as the producer and the citizen as consumer. There are some important differences, however.

Under most circumstances a consumer may take the offered product, or he may leave it. This is not true in government. With government, he may take the offered product if it pleases him; if it doesn't please him he may wish, through the electoral and political processes, to revise the management or to develop a whole new line of products.

The paying process is almost as important. In an ordinary consumer transaction, a consumer knows the price of the commodity under consideration. In purchasing government he cannot be sure, and he is likely to feel, no matter what it is, that the price is too high! But he cannot decline the product for which he has already paid. His tax bill is something he must pay or lose his property.

The producer-consumer relationship in government grows more complex as government grows. This multiplying complexity is one of the most important problems in city life and growth.

In face-to-face communities and groups our friends generally knew us for what we were, and could evaluate motives and activities in the light of this knowledge. Not so the masses who are incessantly peering at us through the magnified, but sometimes distorted, lens of journalists, broadcasters and motion picture producers.[1]

IGNORANCE IS NO EXCUSE

Few have been as painstaking or as comprehensive in their studies of the modern city as Edward Thorndike, who spent a number of years collating statistics of 310 American cities, covering more than 300 items for each city.

The keynote of this study in which more than a million items were treated by statistical method is contained in the first paragraph of the report:

As a matter of local pride and patriotism, each of us may be ready to say with St. Paul, "I am a citizen of no mean city." But as a matter of fact, many of our cities are mean in their provision for health, comfort, education, recreation and other features of a good life.

This is partly because of a lack of resources, but it is partly because their citizens do not know what a city can be and should be, and what some American cities have made themselves, and do not know their own city in comparison with others.

On the other hand some of our cities are at or near the acme of what this world has attained in public and private provision for the good life. Many of the residents of these cities do not realize their good fortune. And people in general do not know which these cities are or how they have succeeded so well in their community life.[2]

"What the citizen doesn't know doesn't hurt him," has been a guideline for some public employees in the past and perhaps even exists in some badly governed cities today. Herein we explore the relationship of citizen and public employee and the way in which the citizen reports and discusses the "mean" aspects of his city with the city employee, who may be expected to correct them and to report back to the citizen what his city has attained in "public provision for the good life."

Nature of the Community

Any effort to explain adequately the influences which produce municipal problems necessarily would be deficient, but certain patterns of trouble seem to recur: problems of the developing community, problems of a stable community, and problems of an aging community.

THE DEVELOPING COMMUNITY

In a new or developing community, problems include zoning, which sets the pattern of the community; the nature and placing of new streets, sewers, street lights, libraries, and parks; and the location of municipal, state, and federal buildings, present and future. Usually community interest in this area and during this early period of growth is not acute. It is probable that a community meeting might be dominated by land developers with land areas to sell—people who are not deeply interested in what happens to the area once its pattern has been set and its growth assured.

THE STABLE COMMUNITY

A second category of citizen-employee problems —of maintenance in a stable community—is

[1] Harwood L. Childs, AN INTRODUCTION TO PUBLIC OPINION (New York: John Wiley & Sons, 1940) , p. 10.

[2] E. L. Thorndike, YOUR CITY (New York: Harcourt, Brace and Company, 1939) , p. 7.

simply one of easing the abrasions of city life. Generally, interest in government among the citizens in an older community is greater, city employees have more funds with which to work, there are more voters per precinct, and the voter's voice is heard more clearly.

Street sweeping, street and sewer repairs, and municipal housekeeping problems are rampant here. Additional parks and expanded libraries are other problem areas. Traffic problems are increasing in importance. More heavily populated areas demand slower traffic in both arterial and secondary highways. School children need better traffic control, and PTA community members are in the vanguard of the groups that assemble on city hall steps. Too frequently home purchasers discover an airport or a dairy in the neighborhood after they have signed the escrow papers.

THE AGING COMMUNITY

Problems of decay in an aging community are in the third and perhaps most difficult category. Older residents predominate. Poverty is a frequent if not omnipresent factor. Absentee landlords contribute to the problems. Lethargy and discouragement are ever-present. Nobody reports a hole in the street or rubbish on vacant lots. Nobody bothers if the rubbish collector skips a collection. The population gradually becomes accustomed to nuisances and unnecessary danger if these problems are not remedied.

Only one of these categories may characterize a particular community, or all three may be found in a metropolitan area. Their manifestations are reviewed below.

Employee as Citizen-Neighbor

The public employee-citizen role is common to all on a civic payroll, from the mayor to the night watchman. Such a role often calls for turning negative citizen attitudes into positive ones, and for generating citizen cooperation where citizen indifference and apathy exist. Literally hundreds of examples may be used to portray this point but the following example is illustrative:

Less than a month ago a teenage youth one morning attempted to snatch the purse of a woman standing at a bus stop on a heavily traveled street in one of Piedmont's handsome residential districts. In the scuffle, the woman holding onto her purse was dragged down the street while the residents of Piedmont sped by. Some honked their horns but like the others continued on their way. It was not until the assistant to the Mayor of Oakland saw the incident and stopped to help, that the delinquent youth ran from the scene.[3]

Unfortunately, there are many examples of the "apathetic American," citizen indifference toward the commission of violent crime like the celebrated (or notorious) "Kitty Genovese" case. Fortunately, however, there are instances of volunteer and instantaneous citizen cooperation with the police as the following account illustrates:

Last July 16 James Stone of Duarte risked his life and damaged his car pursuing a juvenile hit-run driver whose stolen auto killed a 16-year-old girl.

Today a Monrovia businessman is raising a modest fund to pay the $200 repair bill on Stone's small foreign car.

The money comes from citizens, as a token of thanks. Anything over that amount will go to the parents of the young victim, Diana Lee Howard.

Stone, 29-year-old electrician and father of two, gave this account to officers after his wild chase:

He saw a car strike Diana as she stepped off a curbing on Foothill Boulevard in Monrovia. He took after the fugitive car, as did two other drivers.

On a narrow, hilly street Stone overtook the fleeing suspect, a boy 14 with a record as incorrigible. The boy's name was withheld by police.

Repeatedly Stone tried to force the boy's car to the curb. He was sideswiped and sloughed off. But he stayed in the race until one of the other drivers got ahead, blocking the youth's path. The boy abandoned the car, fled into nearby shrubbery and was subsequently apprehended.

After the incident Stone nonchalantly went fishing. When he returned this week he found a stack of letters of goodwill from businessmen and other citizens who had read newspaper accounts of the pursuit. He also received a citation from the Monrovia City Council for "alertness, courage and exceptionally fine citizenship. . . ."

Bud Conner, a businessman who is handling the fund, said: "This is simply a gesture of apprecia-

---

[3] Wayne E. Thompson, "Law Enforcement in the Central City, Everybody's Responsibility," an address delivered before the 7th Annual Institute on Police and Community Relations, University of Southern California, February 6, 1964.

tion. When citizens assume their responsibilities like this, other citizens should pitch in and help them out of their trouble."

He added that "this shows not everyone is like those people in New York" who witnessed but failed to act in the murder of Kitty Genovese weeks ago.

Why did Stone do it? He has two sons, 8 and 4, and his wife expects another child in October. All he said was:

"I saw the girl flying through the air and bouncing on the street. I saw the car speeding away. I just took off."[4]

In this section the emphasis is placed on the responsibility of the employee in responding to the citizen's requests for assistance and generating positive attitudes of cooperation.

EMPLOYEE-TO-CITIZEN COOPERATION

The employee's responsibility is to solve the problem if it comes within the range of his training, experience, and responsibility. For example, almost any employee of the engineering staff of the city would know that the first step toward the development of a public improvement project is to obtain signatures of interested property owners on a petition addressed to the city council describing the desired project. He may not know that this procedure for the "right of petition" dates back to the settlement made by King John and the barons at Runnymede in 1215.

But he will know that this is appropriate procedure. He may even know the approximate cost per householder of the improvement and the length of time needed to process the improvement through the legislative body of the city, and the administrative and engineering department in order to obtain the granting of a contract, the construction, and the property tax assessments.

These elements of procedure and estimate of costs in time and money are important to citizens seeking protection of health, traffic safety, or convenience, through public improvements. The city employee who can answer these questions "off the top of his head" is doing a good job of maintaining public confidence in government.

If the neighbor's problem is more complex,

involving medical care or fire protection, the engineering employee may have to seek help from the health department or the fire department. If the neighbor is equipped by background and has the time to thread his way through the maze that is frequently known as interdepartmental responsibility, the employee may advise him whom he should telephone in the respective departments.

However, if the citizen neighbor is not equipped to carry on the quest for help, it is the responsibility of the public employee to advise the right department of his neighbor's problem and have that department contact the individual and provide appropriate help.

Having advised another department of a problem the good employee will later check with his neighbor to determine if the problem has been solved or if no immediate solution is possible. If there is "no solution" forthcoming from the department involved, it should be the responsibility of the public employee to see that recourse is available through the head of the department. Action by the city council may even be required.

COUNCILMAN COOLS WALL-HEATER PROBLEM

A case in point: a house in a tract of 100 homes caught fire and was destroyed because of the overheating of a wall heater. The heating installation was guaranteed for one year. The fire occurred a few days after the guarantee had expired. Officials of the building and safety department advised the owner of the property that he had no recourse.

When the matter was brought to the attention of the appropriate elected official, however, he made a trip to the tract and satisfied himself, as a former building contractor, that the installed heaters were not safe. The fact that the walls of many other homes in the area were dangerously hot from the same type of heater created a neighborhood fire hazard in nearly a hundred homes.

A quick conference with the principal building inspector brought out the fact that the building contractor for the tract was a man of good reputation and had no record of previous trouble with the department.

In a face-to-face contact the building contractor and the elected official found a solution quickly. New heaters of an improved model were installed at the expense of the contractor in every home where the home-owner wanted one.

FAMILIARITY DEVELOPS UNDERSTANDING

In the larger municipalities and in urban areas the elected representatives, whether full-time city councilmen or county commissioners or supervisors, often maintain field deputies and assistants whose role is to ascertain clientele needs and to provide intercession for the citizen so that he may satisfy certain desires.

Many special opportunities for citizen participation in municipal activities are available, such as the use of school-boy patrols at pedestrian cross-walks, involvement of Boy Scout troops and councils in municipal traffic surveys, distribution of reports, and municipal conservation projects. Citizens may also participate effectively in such things as personnel interviews and real estate appraisals.

The state of Wisconsin promoted public understanding of highway construction within the state by sponsoring tours for citizens to highway construction sites. During the program, the highway construction program and operational details were not only explained to the site visitors but a general citizen information program was conducted which developed general public support and understanding.[5]

Meetings as a Form of Cooperation

Small informal gatherings of neighbors or community leaders may sometimes present themselves at the home of a public employee or invite his presence at a sidewalk conference on some problem. To some employees this is an annoyance. It should be considered an honor; it usually means that the person extending the invitation respects the public employee's knowledge and ability; or it may mean that some of the neighbors have "ganged up" on him to sound off.

In the latter case it must be recognized that our society embraces a few people who find some sort of psychotic reward in castigating those in authority. A dignified appearance by a public employee with the emphasis on listening can do much to ameliorate this situation. Sympathetic listening by public officials often serves a therapeutic function. Possible answers or solutions should be advanced sparingly if at all, but a full treatment of the problem should be reduced to writing and distribution made to those in attendance at the original meeting, and also to anyone in the neighborhood who has an interest in the matter. If the decision is adverse it may be well to include in the answer the proper method for an appeal, or a recommendation for further study of the problem.

The following example is indicative of the positive results which may accrue from neighborhood conferences:

We felt that significant progress was being made when a group of neighborhood leaders came in to see us two weeks ago. Present were a group of merchants and home-owners, both Negro and White, representing a neighborhood which is almost entirely Negro. For several years the delinquent and disrupting behavior of a "gang" of 50 neighborhood youths had plagued the merchants in this area. The latter, however, had consistently refused to aid the police in the apprehension of the guilty youngsters. The police were frustrated. The merchants were at their wits end. At this meeting the merchants had acknowledged their lack of cooperation in the past and were asking for a more strict law enforcement program in the neighborhood, and were now offering their all-out assistance. Upon hearing of this, the Chief said, "This will do it! Now we can quickly resolve the trouble!" All the police needed was genuine citizen cooperation.[6]

Sometimes a municipality may wish deliberately to have members of the city council and members of various boards and commissions sit as a panel at neighborhood meetings on a rotating basis to allow citizens to meet their officials and discuss municipal problems with them. While such meetings are only a variation of the neighborhood or sidewalk conferences, they range from the city council sitting as a body to a public works engineer on a new street-widening project or a hearing with other technical personnel on a freeway routing.

[5] Cliff Hutchison, "A Public Relations Program for Highways," PUBLIC RELATIONS JOURNAL (August, 1959), pp. 20–21.

[6] Wayne E. Thompson, *op. cit.*

SPECIAL PROBLEM MEETINGS

Larger meetings which extend beyond the confines of the neighborhood and embrace an entire community call for a more careful approach. The employee invited to speak should consider it an honor and should try to anticipate the problems which will be presented. He should be prepared with appropriate solutions.

Help Is Available. If he feels he will be unable to meet any situation which might arise, he should enlist help through his department head from other departments, including as many members of the city administrative and legislative groups as may appear advisable. Every precaution should be taken to insure that no question is left unanswered and that the correct answer to a question is given by a person with enough authority to insure that the answer is correct. Representatives of the legal department are very helpful in explaining the logic behind some laws, ordinances, or regulations that may not at first glance appear to be in the public interest.

Meetings Clarify Facts. The primary purpose of most meetings is to determine the facts in a controversy or in cases where the consequences of civic action may not be immediately clear to the citizens.

A warning should be expressed, however, to indicate that citizen meetings are not the best way to gather the facts.[7] Bernard Baruch has given us an excellent axiom for each individual in attendance at any meeting: "Every man has a right to his own opinion but no man has a right to be wrong in his facts."[8]

Fact finding backed up by dispassionate discussion of the facts that can be agreed upon, and an agreement on what facts must be further explored, are fundamentals of good meetings. Once the areas of agreement have been determined, the extent of disagreement appears and the problem may be reduced in size.

Honor Privacy. If meetings include more

than a dozen persons, personal problems of individuals with government employees may be handled more effectively if they are discussed privately with the concerned individual at the end of the general meeting. However, if there is general interest in an individual problem the public employee may find it advisable to discuss the problem before the whole group. No public employee should ever seek to embarass a citizen before a group of his friends and neighbors; this is unforgivable. Not only is it impolite but it is the very worst kind of public relations.

Use Care with Humor. A touch of humor may relieve a tense meeting if the speaker has a flair for it. It is also dangerous. Citizens do not appreciate jokes arising from their problems. A bureaucrat once upset the apple cart completely when he asked a Los Angeles audience to "wait a 'cotton pickin' minute." The audience felt that he had called them cotton pickers and had the situation developed in a cotton field the meeting hall would have been reduced to ashes by the heat of indignation.

Time of Meeting Important. Afternoon meetings are often more desirable than meetings scheduled at other times. This permits a larger attendance of wives and mothers, who, although not always as articulate as their husbands, are much more apt to have definite feelings about what's wrong with the neighborhoods near their homes.

Special Interest Groups May Control Meetings. Problems arise for the public employee when a meeting is "stacked" against him. An individual was in violation of zoning laws, since his horse barn was illegally close to a neighbor's place. When he was told to move his barn he appealed to his horse-owner friends for help.

Horse owners were sympathetic; other neighbors were not. But the offending horse owner gathered a following at the next meeting of the "Trails" groups, and a sensitive public official was greeted by a hundred or more horse owners demanding that the zoning laws be changed for the greater accommodation of horse lovers. From 60 to 70 per cent of the citizens of the area were not represented; in fact they knew nothing of the meeting.

---

[7] See Chapter 3 for discussion of techniques of gathering data.

[8] "Park Bench Philosopher," Bernard Baruch, in an inscription of his photograph sent to the author.

Under these circumstances a public employee may wish to recruit a few non-horse owners, but again this can be dangerous. For the horse owners recruited for this event did not want to hear about the rights of others. They wanted to *change* the law; they were organized and it was their meeting. Anyone protesting against a change in the law probably would have been hooted down.

Respectful attention was paid to the speeches of the horse owners. They were advised that the matter would be taken under consideration. They hired an attorney and drew up legislation that they thought would be effective. It was generous to the horse owners. The legislation was introduced in the city council of Los Angeles and was handed to the city attorney for advice. In his office it was amended to provide that special horse districts could be set up similar to park districts, on the petition of property owners, when 90 per cent of the residents approved.

This meant that the horse owners either had to dominate the areas in numbers or make their peace with the other home owners. This legislation became a city ordinance. It appeased the horse owners and set up a means whereby they could have horses under zoning conditions more liberal than the earlier law.

The fundamental of public relations in this situation is described by Hadley Cantril in his book, *Gauging Public Opinion,* "Once self interest is involved, opinions are not easily changed.[9]

It should be stated here that the opponents of the plan for more liberal zoning had an opportunity to present their side of the case in a fair manner before the planning committee of the city council and that thoughtful deliberation was accorded the plan by the zoning department and the council before the final draft of the city attorney was requested.

WHY RESORT TO MEETINGS?

Most meetings of citizens and public employees are arranged because of one or more of the following:

[9] Hadley Cantril, GAUGING PUBLIC OPINION (Princeton, New Jersey: Princeton University Press, 1947), pp. 220–230.

1. The orderly routine of government has either broken down or has not met the expectations of the governed.

2. The citizens in attendance at the meeting, regardless of its size or intent, want to know facts or they want a decision on already known facts.

3. Meetings can be held as a precaution to insure that government does not break down; they can anticipate a crisis.

4. Meetings may become necessary because of the circulation of erroneous reports stated as facts.

MEETINGS CAN FAIL!

The fact that meetings are held, however, does not guarantee achievement of objectives. Meetings fail for many reasons:

1. The people in attendance are not sufficiently representative of the community. A meeting is "stacked" (devoted to a special interest group seeking special treatment in which other citizens cannot share).

2. The chairman fails to preside effectively, to keep order, to allow divergent views to be presented, and to call on authorities in the field to develop the facts.

3. The chairman may fail to develop and expound the importance of a correct decision or an honest presentation.

4. The time and place of meeting may defeat its purpose of being representative.

5. The meeting may drag on interminably with repetition of one viewpoint until the opponents weary and go home.

6. A strong community individual with an axe to grind may "stack" a meeting with friends to support his viewpoint and harass other speakers. This is particularly true in zoning cases.

In recent years a problem of a new dimension has arisen in the conduct of many public meetings of cities and other local governments. This is the organized appearance of representatives of various extremist groups that specialize in fright and hate. They can be identified rather easily because they never are *for* anything—just opposed. They are opposed to intergovernmental cooperation or any other move that has the slightest taint of metropolitan government, fluoridation of the water supply, city planning, or almost any other proposal that may be considered by a governing body. They specialize in organized chaos, and they can reduce a meeting to shambles by their tactics.[10]

Citizen Committees and Commissions

More formal means of enlisting citizen interest and cooperation are by appointing various types of committees officially recognized and established by the municipality and by responding constructively to citizen-established protest committees. Although there are many kinds and combinations of committees, this review highlights citizen-protest committees, community advisory committees, *ad hoc* committees, "Blue Ribbon" commissions, and unpaid municipal commissions. Legal authorization for such committees may be provided in municipal codes or city charters or by council action.

ORGANIZING CONCEPTS

Much helpful information is available on the establishment and use of committees.[11] "People," wrote Hadley Cantril, "are less reluctant to have critical decisions made by their leaders if they feel that somehow they, the people, are taking some part in the decision."[12]

Opportunity for service on community committees is often appealing to leaders of community thought and opinion. Involvement of such persons in an advisory capacity frequently attracts not only their individual support but also that of their wide circle of friends and associates. All such persons are potentially constructive emissaries for the particular function or project involved. Not only does involvement

of such persons provide a means of support but their ideas assist in clarifying issues and outlining appropriate procedural tactics.

Involvement, or at least the opportunity for involvement, in the municipal decision-making processes is important, and of equal significance is the appropriate recognition of services rendered by such citizens. It may require only a "thank you" letter from the city manager to each member of the committee after its purpose has been accomplished, but adequate appreciation should always be given.

Wiksell suggests the following criteria for selection of committee members:

1. Are they individuals who will study problems with an open mind?
2. Are they punctual and will they come to meetings regularly?
3. Can they listen intelligently?
4. Are they well-informed individuals?
5. Can they avoid temptation to railroad the group?
6. Do they have a spirit of investigation and inquiry?
7. Are they capable of working together?
8. Do they have respect for attitudes of others?
9. Have they a positive attitude?
10. Are they interested in a given project?
11. Do they have a suitable background for the problem?
12. Will they allow others to talk?
13. Do they represent different points of view about a problem?
14. Do they abide by majority decisions?[13]

An elected official sometimes has an advantage over a department official in setting up an advisory committee. While both want opinion leaders "who will carry the story back," the political leaders often are more aware of who these opinion leaders are. Representatives from the business community, from school and religious organizations, from the professions, and particularly from groups of senior citizens are often selected for committee assignments. These people find time, they have maturity of judgment, and they like to work in a quasi-official capacity. Also, they influence votes and

---

[10] For an informative and dispassionate discussion of these groups, and how to handle them at public meetings, see "Here Come the Hate Groups," by Arthur Prager, NATION'S CITIES (November, 1964), pp. 20–24.

[11] See, for example, Milton J. Wiksell, "What's Wrong with Committees," in Appendix D.

[12] Hadley Cantril, GAUGING PUBLIC OPINION (Princeton, New Jersey: Princeton University Press, 1947). See especially Rule 12 in "The Use of Trends," pp. 220–230.

[13] See Milton J. Wiksell, "What's Wrong with Committees," in Appendix D.

vote themselves. They know the power of the ballot box. A committee with community-wide representation will be much more useful than a committee loaded with political leaders.

If the committee has a political tinge some persons may conclude that it is merely political and may not care to be actively identified with it. Under no circumstances should the committee have a partisan tinge. A few politically minded people should be selected to provide a balance.

It is important also to include on the committee persons outside formal organizations. Unless this is done, the committee may be composed only of those people known as "joiners." Perhaps as much as 30 per cent of the membership should be people with no particular affiliation other than a neighborly relationship with people in the community.

It can be safely presumed that except in times of community stress not more than half of the membership of an advisory committee will be present at any one meeting. Since an audience of not more than 30 is about as large as can be included in a participation meeting, the membership can go as high as 60 or even more.

Agenda for meetings should be mailed to reach the committee members 24 hours before the regular meeting time. The subjects of general interest in the agenda will usually determine the size of the crowd. Following the meeting a report should be prepared on what decisions were arrived at, what subjects were discussed, and a brief note on what may be expected at the next meeting, if possible. Monthly meetings are most successful for the long run, with a possible abeyance of meetings during the summer months except for special emergency calls.

CITIZEN-PROTEST COMMITTEES

Sometimes irate citizens, adversely affected by what they consider to be a public problem, or foresighted individuals viewing a desirable long-range objective for their municipality, will organize their own committees to influence municipal officials. In most such instances, hopefully, these problems will have been anticipated by public officers, and official action will

have been taken to preclude their erupting through a citizen-protest committee. When unanticipated problems bring the protest-committee to his office, however, the public official may view such influence as a constructive force to be dealt with positively, thus increasing the number of citizens who understand governmental processes and cooperation with public officials. Occasionally, public officials simply yield to such pressures without adequate consideration, allowing the occurrence of developments which will produce subsequent problems with which future generations of citizens and public officials must deal.

Community on a Shoestring. The original Pacoima, California, development plan was simply an extension of a single boulevard through a rocky wasteland. Once an 80-foot boulevard was assured the next step was street lights, and then Pacoima, which resembled Death Valley in the daytime, looked like Chicago's Michigan Avenue after dark. These improvements inspired residents to draft a $6 million street and sewer program for the area, which was "slightly inhabited."

The program waited seven years at various political levels until the longer-time residents in the area demonstrated their municipal pride by rehabilitating all of the original desert homes, some 40 years old, by improvements that brought them up to the standards of the city building code.

In most instances the improvements cost more than the original structures, but the renovation job won both national acclaim and the support of city officials, who then reactivated the street and sewer program.

After a period of ten years the errors of the original plan are becoming apparent. The great boulevard stretching for two and a half miles must be zoned as a commercial area all the way. Shoestring zoning, the anathema of the city planning departments, appears to be the only answer, because of the mistakes of ten years ago. Some $10,000,000 have been spent in the community to develop a long, narrow, and uneconomic community. The redeeming features are that the people who developed it reaped a reward for their foresight and the people who live there like it. But the city planners are uncomfortable, rewarded only by the thought that here they have a "horrible example," since further growth of the commercial area is extremely unlikely because the bordering areas have been developed for multiple housing and residences.

Community committees here were small but extremely active and effective. Vocal expression by the community committee was used to advantage in the allocation of funds from city hall in bond issues. When bond issues were on the ballot this area was exceedingly helpful in getting voter approval.

Power Underground Produces Accuracy of Estimates. The use of citizen problems committees is well illustrated in a problem of overhead power lines recently solved in the San Fernando Valley. A preliminary and not too exact estimate by the Department of Water and Power on the cost of putting the unsightly lines underground in a residential area amounted to $1,000,000. An angry residential committee, including some cost engineers, estimated the job at $250,000.

A compromise was agreed upon whereby the lines in some nonresidential areas remained above ground but in the residential areas were put underground. The proportionate cost more nearly corresponded to the estimate by the home-owners group than the official cost estimated by the city department. Instances of this type, while isolated, linger in the memory of the taxpayer and add to his desire to participate in city decision-making.

City Land for Little League. Citizen committees are an effective way to break precedent and policy in an old-line department. It is the policy of the Right-of-Way and Land Department of the city of Los Angeles not to rent city-owned land or to permit its use by private citizens and groups. Little League baseball changed this.

Little League parents hammering on councilmanic doors brought a legislative "instruction" to the department in specific cases and the policy has now been changed to encourage usage of idle city lands by sports groups.

"Look of the Future" Generated by Citizen Initiative. In problems of growth in new areas, citizen committees as well as city employees pay too little attention to the "look of the future." One area where citizens not only looked to the future but motivated the city government to do likewise is indicated in the following striking example. The city of San Fernando, oldest of the San Fernando Valley communities, contains some third generation families and many old homes of delightful adobe lines, on family lots of generous size with beautiful trees and tropical flowers. Next door may be a split-level ranch house or a contemporary model gleaming with glass and fancy cement work. A citizens' committee asked the city council for advice on means of maintaining the traditional charm of the community and yet providing the opportunity for growth. First result was a city-wide study and a plan to maintain the Spanish type of architecture in new commercial buildings. Subsequently, the plan was further implemented by another study, firming up the regulations and city code. It may now be anticipated that the buildings in the area will set a trend for architecture expressing the tradition of the first valley mission. This method of up-dating a community is very useful but not immediately spectacular in results achieved.

From Grade-separation to More Effective Procedures. Experience gained through citizen-protest or citizen-collaboration committees sometimes leads to more effective administrative procedures. Such a case was the Laurel Canyon–Sherman Way grade-separation in the San Fernando Valley. Trains between San Francisco and Los Angeles cut diagonally across the San Fernando Valley. Auto traffic came from four directions on the two streets to cross the dangerous tracks in the intersection. Ten people died in railroad and automobile accidents there in a five-year period. Yet the community sentiment in favor of the grade separation was unable to overcome the problem attendant to redesigning the roadways to avoid the intersection exactly at the railroad.

At long last a city council maneuver put the onus on the county board of supervisors, which shortly approved their share of the funds needed; then the improvement was designed. Due to the cramped working area, delays developed. Traffic was stopped in all directions and merchants large and small suffered. As a result, local committees, several by now, invaded city hall, additional engineers and supervisors were put on the job, and the contractors involved were allowed new funds for overtime. Construction time originally estimated in excess of two years was reduced to slightly more than one.

The effect of the speed-up was salutary. The city engineering department learned that time of construction as well as city funds was an important factor and they learned also that they *could* speed up. Now important jobs that affect businessmen are all considered from the new viewpoint, their probable effect on the profit or loss of the taxpaying businesses.

Not all special committees are concerned with problems of engineering and city dollars. Lewd conduct in the parks, penny-ante games at senior citizens centers, home menageries, including ocelots and an abundance of cats, can give rise to indignation and special committee action. The presence of a rabid dog brings quick community action by mothers' groups.

CITIZEN ASSOCIATIONS

Bearing some similarity to the citizen-protest committees are the various citizen associations, by whatever name they are called—citizens' league, citizen-action committee, governmental affairs league—inasmuch as the initiative for organizing and sponsoring such groups comes from individual citizens rather than from public officials. In many municipalities, especially larger ones, such groups are flourishing. Typically they serve as a "watchdog" for effective government in their communities and usually are maintained on a permanent basis. Sometimes, however, because of default of governmental officials, they come into existence for a specific purpose only, such as a citizen-generated charter review committee.[14] Organization and development of such associations may be encouraged, of course, by the public official in circumstances which indicate there may be merit in doing so. Where such groups already are in existence the alert public official will develop relationships for intercommunication and mutual support.

COMMUNITY ADVISORY COMMITTEES

Perhaps the most widely used device for involvement of individual citizens in municipal affairs is the advisory committee which has a variety of uses and forms. Elton Woolpert has described many of the variables involved in the utilization of advisory committees:

In some cases they have regular terms of office, while in other cases they are appointed for indefinite periods of varying length. Sometimes their duties are quite definitely prescribed; sometimes they are not defined at all. This variation in form and practice is paralleled by variations in the results obtained through the use of advisory bodies. Most of the unfortunate results, however, seem to stem from failure to determine in advance what the lay members of the advisory body are supposed to do. The appointment of a citizen to an advisory board can be expected to arouse his interest immediately, and this awakened interest is a valuable public relations asset. If, however, he finds that his appointment carries no duties or responsibilities, he either becomes disillusioned or takes the initiative in finding something to do. In either case the result is unfortunate. An offended or disillusioned citizen may be a permanent public relations liability, and a layman who tries to make a job for himself is likely to be a very disrupting factor.

It is therefore in the interests of public relations and administrative efficiency to have a fairly clear cut job in mind before advisory bodies are appointed. Experience of cities with advisory bodies indicates that, as a rule, best results can be expected from bodies appointed for short terms and only for the consideration of a special problem. Advisory bodies appointed for long terms tend to think of themselves as experts and acquire a sort of vested interest in their positions. If these limitations are kept in mind, advisory boards and commissions can be used to good advantage for public relations purposes. Not only do they offer opportunities for citizens to become interested in and informed about municipal government through participation in the actual work of the city, but they serve as additional media of reporting and information through which other members of the community may become interested and informed.[15]

For a single and current issue, or for a continuing municipal function, advisory committees may be *ad hoc*, permanent, or of

14 See the excellent monograph, THE CITIZEN ASSOCIATION: HOW TO ORGANIZE AND RUN IT (New York: National Municipal League, April, 1958) , 64pp.

15 Elton Woolpert, MUNICIPAL PUBLIC RELATIONS (Chicago: International City Managers' Association, 1940) , pp. 33–34.

indefinite duration. They may be established for community-wide citizen involvement or they may be "blue-ribbon" in nature. They may recommend policy or they may become involved in the actual performance of some service function. For example, in recent years, in Massachusetts, upon recommendation of the Massachusetts Selectmens' Association, various local selectment have appointed committees of citizens for the preparation of municipal or town reports.[16]

Palo Alto, California, recently has used advisory committees on public information, foothills planning, capitol improvements, human relations, and a hospital center.

Indicating a vital concern for broad policy goals, Portland, Maine, has established the Portland Advisory Committee, which, during the next two years, will develop a statement of community objectives.[17]

An example of a permanent advisory committee is the Planning and Parking Committee of Beverly Hills, California, which consists of more than 60 citizens organized into 12 subcommittees. The chairman of each of the subcommittees serves on an executive committee of the Planning and Parking Committee. Other citizen advisory committees are utilized in Beverly Hills for such functions as recreation and youth activities, civic center development, oil development, boulevard planting, gardening and plantings, and public relations.[18]

Night-time Prowlers Frustrated. From time to time, law enforcement agencies throughout the nation have designed programs to encourage merchants and residents to burn lights in their establishments at night as a means of discouraging burglars.

Never before has such a comprehensive campaign been undertaken as that initiated by the Los Angeles County Sheriff's Department in 1961. The idea for the campaign was conceived and planned by the Sheriff's Advisory Commit-

tee, an organization of leading advertising and public relations executives. The plan itself required two months to complete. It was a carefully compiled timetable of talks, motion pictures, press releases, and radio and television programs.

The campaign was launched at a luncheon for key news, radio, and television executives at which the sheriff discussed the problems of combating rising crime rates. He pointed out that a "public conscience" must be aroused, that burglary represented about 40 per cent of major crime, and that he had high hopes that with the help of the news media, the "burn-a-light" campaign would prove a deterrent.

The campaign was started about September 1, 1961, and continued for a year. Mayors, city councils, and many police departments in the county cooperated. Radio, television, and newspapers gave generously of time and space. Burglaries are reported to have dropped 35 per cent. The number of cases of rape and robbery also decreased.

While the campaign continued in full swing for only a year, it had other lasting benefits. Merchants who had never left lights on in their stores are doing so now as a matter of course. Several big supermarkets adopted the policy of putting their safes in public view and floodlighting them.

The campaign was conducted at all levels of law enforcement. Sheriff's deputies made personal contacts and discussed the program with merchants and citizens. These personal contacts achieved a close understanding of law enforcement in the community, a result which justified all of the efforts put forth in the campaign.

Discovering Homes for Children. In Los Angeles County, taxpayers are saved from $18,-000 to $20,000 every time a child being cared for by the county is adopted. When he took office in 1952, the head of the County Bureau of Adoptions sought a solution to a two-fold problem:

1. To find foster parents for the increasing numbers of Mexican and Negro babies in county institutions or foster homes.

2. To erase the public's bad impression of adoption agencies, due largely to the long wait

[16] John Gillespie, "Citizen Committees Tell Town Story," NATIONAL MUNICIPAL REVIEW (November, 1957), pp. 511–512.

[17] International City Managers' Association, NEWSLETTER (May 15, 1964).

[18] City of Beverly Hills, California, PUBLIC RELATIONS TRAINING MANUAL (November, 1962).

by prospective foster parents for a baby, often two or more years.

Believing that the placement of babies of minority races could be accomplished only through a long-range publicity program, he invited the interest of newspapers, radio, and television in the activities of the Bureau and found them receptive. He arranged special promotion programs, one of the most successful of which was "Adopt a Baby Day" held in the Hall of Administration. Scores of Mexican and Negro babies were brought to the auditorium and posed for television and news cameras in the arms of County Supervisors and celebrities in the sports and film world. Pictures appeared in all newspapers and the activity was featured on radio and television news.

Currently all buses are carrying advertising cards showing a picture of a baby with the legend "Your Very Own by Adoption." The card carries the address of the Bureau of Adoptions.

Another promotion program carried on with limited publicity is with the medical associations. This program seeks to encourage doctors to have babies of unwed mothers sent to the Adoption Bureau. Participating in the development of the program have been a part-time public relations expert and the Bureau of Adoptions Advisory Committee. Serving on the committee are a Hollywood actress, a leading publicist, and several distinguished professional and civic leaders.

The success of the program is revealed by a few statistics. In 1951 the county was able to place 225 babies for adoption. In 1962, 1,300 babies were placed for adoption. In 1951 only 20 babies of Mexican or Negro parents were placed for adoption. This number increased to 140 in 1962.

Permanent Advisory Committees. In recent years, as people and blight have sprawled across the metropolis, there has been increasing use of permanent advisory committees. Whatever one's judgment may be about the desirability of such a development, the fact remains that people in urban areas have found in the permanent advisory committee another opportunity to influence the development of policy. In addition to examples indicated above, the urban dweller serves on urban renewal advisory committees of citizens (for the agency as distinguished from project), on councilmanic advisory committees where a local councilman is elected from a particular district rather than at-large, and others.

Ad Hoc Committees. Public officials solicit the counsel of various segments of society and appoint citizens to committees ranging from an ordinary *ad hoc* committee to resolve a golf controversy to "blue-ribbon" commissions of inquiry to advise on restitution for damage caused by flood disaster. In this category are urban renewal advisory committees for individual projects.

Campaigns for passage of bond issues and public works projects often rely upon advisory committees of citizens. A bond issue to provide a new city hall and a service facility for village vehicles in Glencoe, Illinois, was approved after a public information campaign was conducted by a committee of 47 citizens appointed by village officials. In Richmond, California, a 250-member committee of citizens brought victory at the polls for an $8,000,000 sewer system. After $2,000 of private funds had been pledged to finance printing, publicity, and advertising, a host of sub-committees, a speakers' bureau, and block units were organized, which involved nearly 1,000 citizens.

Commercial and industrial development often follows the appointment of *ad hoc* committees to lure industry or a federal facility.

At the time of a sudden increase of house flies at a dairy located within a municipal jurisdiction, neighbors discovered that flies literally were eating paint off their houses. Under the prodding of a joint committee of citizens and municipal employees the offending dairyman launched a clean-up campaign which eliminated the flies, and repainted the damaged houses.

UNPAID MUNICIPAL COMMISSIONS

In some instances a greater degree of formalization has occurred, providing that advisory bodies of citizens are a part of the actual fabric of municipal government. Where this exists, the body is usually designated a commission. One of the more frequently used commissions is a

THE EMPLOYEE-CITIZEN TEAM 105

planning commission which may have functions varying in nature from advisory, through policy-making, to quasi-judicial. Many cities also provide for personnel or civil service commissions, recreation and parks commissions, and traffic commissions. Perhaps no city has gone farther in this direction than Los Angeles, which provides through charter for a commission of lay citizens for essentially all of its municipal departments.[19]

INTERAGENCY COOPERATION

Of a different order but similar in effect is the technique of interagency cooperation. In the areas of welfare and juvenile delinquency the technique is often called a coordinating council. As Elton Woolpert described them:

These councils consist of representatives of the various agencies both public and private, that are operating in the field. For example, the governmental representatives may include an official of the municipal welfare department, a county probation officer, and a police officer from the city's crime prevention bureau. Private agencies represented often include charitable institutions, character building organizations for youths, churches, service clubs, and fraternal organizations. In addition there may be one or more individuals who are not affiliated with any of these organizations. Co-ordinating councils are not merely discussion groups or advisory bodies but take an active part in the planning and execution of welfare services. Their principal public relations value is that, by bringing together public officials and private citizens who are interested in the same problems, these councils help to develop and sustain an attitude of mutual understanding and cooperation.[20]

A variation on this theme is the associated agencies scheme of Oakland, California, and The Community Progress, Inc., approach to comprehensive social planning in New Haven, Connecticut.

INTERGOVERNMENTAL COOPERATION

City and county governments can work not only with private community groups but also with other local governments on a wide range of problems of common concern. Since 1954,

officials in at least seven multi-county metropolitan areas have voluntarily formed area-wide associations to deal with transportation, land-use planning, parks and open space, public safety, air pollution, and other areas of common concern. Associations have been formed—generally known as councils of governments—to encourage local governments to work together in building better metropolitan areas. These councils are functioning under various titles in Detroit, San Francisco, New York City, Philadelphia, Washington, D.C., Seattle, and Salem (Oregon).

Rochester and Monroe County, New York, have developed intergovernmental cooperation through consolidation of functions and contracts for area services. Often municipalities and school districts cooperate through joint operation of recreational facilities.

One manner of formalization of this approach was the passage of a federal law in 1959 which created a permanent Advisory Commission on Intergovernmental Relations to provide advice and assistance to the President and the Congress in all phases of intergovernmental relations, especially federal grant programs. The commission's role is to:

(1) Sponsor meetings of federal, state, and local officials for discussion of common problems; (2) provide a forum for discussion of administration, coordination, and control of federal grant and other programs; (3) provide technical assistance to the President and the Congress on proposed legislation; (4) encourage discussion and research in emerging problems requiring intergovernmental cooperation; and (5) make recommendations on allocation of governmental functions and responsibilities, revenue sources among government, and coordination of tax laws.[21]

In numerous ways private citizens participate in governmental policy determination and implementation through cooperative relationships with municipal officials. A coordinated program of municipal improvement in which all citizens have opportunities to participate is a desirable municipal objective. A conscious awareness and a planned program ultimately will lead to mutual appreciation of community problems and a pooling of efforts and resources in the resolution of such problems.

---

[19] Because of these provisions, which require department heads to be responsible directly to the departmental commissions, many students of public administration have called for a repeal of the present Los Angeles city charter.

[20] Elton Woolpert, *op. cit.*, p. 34.

[21] PUBLIC MANAGEMENT, November, 1959, p. 263.

8

Community Group Relationships

COMMUNITY GROUPS and associations are playing an increasingly important role in municipal government. These groups are initiating and supporting campaigns to stimulate greater citizen participation. They are identifying and presenting community issues. They are contributing to efforts for municipal reform and improvement. Representatives of community groups and associations serve on special citizen planning bodies, advisory committees, and other municipal agencies.

Groups and associations are helping to bridge and close the gap between municipal governments and people in communities. They are effective influences for increased governmental service and economy and for greater political responsibility. They are prime vehicles through which democratic government functions. Well-planned and intelligible community relations programs are essential for responsible democratic government. Administrators of the public's business must thoroughly understand the importance of community groups and associations and devise ways and means by which to incorporate them into the democratic processes of municipal government.

Nature of the Local Community

The local community has become a center of focus for both the practitioner and the scholar of municipal management. However, the use of the term, "local community," is confusing and inconsistent. The common tendency is to think of a community in geographic terms. But because of the rapid means of transportation and communication in the United States, the community becomes for most purposes a functional rather than a geographical concept. The spatial boundaries of communities do not coincide with the legal boundaries of municipal governments. The community, in the minds of both practitioners and citizens, may be larger or smaller than a given municipality. A community differs in size with the purposes people associate with it, such as water supply, services, and public protection. The community signifies direct social relationships and grass-roots government. People have never been so interested in local community life as now because they feel that they have lost much of it in the wave of urbanization.

Although there is danger of overgeneralizing, an operational concept of the term "community" would be useful. A community is a place of interacting social institutions which produce in its residents an attitude and practice of interdependence, cooperation, collaboration, and unification. Some areas in relatively close proximity do not clearly exhibit these chaacteristics; this is especially true in large urban agglomerations. Other areas, even where the residents do not live in close proximity, do exhibit these characteristics; for example, ranching areas located in the arid West.[1]

Involved in the operational concept are such sociological dimensions of a community as value systems, social stratification, interpersonal relationships, power structures, and ecological patterns. The public relations

[1] See Charles Adrian, "The Community Setting," pp. 1–4, in Adrian, SOCIAL SCIENCE AND COMMUNITY ACTION (East Lansing: Michigan State University, 1960).

worker can best center his primary interest upon how people live together and meet their functional needs through community social institutions (included here are groups and associations and perceived patterns of human behavior). The community can be understood best as a web of social structures, all closely interrelated. From these social structures there evolves a complex of positions (statuses) which in turn prescribes various roles for individuals. Through performance of these roles the various institutions in their complex relationships meet the functional needs and demands of the community.[2]

Social Context of American Communities

American communities, broadly interpreted, have adopted "technical abundance" as a way of life. Under such a framework of purpose, the values, moralities and basic patterns of human and institutional relationships become subject to constant and progressive reinterpretation. Effects of scientific progress and technological ingenuity are reflected in a wide variety of social aspects such as the virtual elimination by machines of hand labor; ability to plan, to some predictable degree, economic and social growth; increase in life span; broader and increased mobility of people, things, and ideas; wider educational opportunities; added leisure for vast new segments of the society; a lessening of the competitive struggle for simple survival, and shifts in foundations of prestige and status.

What does this mean for community life? This abundance, when translated into higher living standards and general security, enables a community to discover and release its human resources in increased numbers and higher quality. A community literally unhobbles itself and becomes more important as a means of achieving the "good life."

This does not mean that social problems end with technical abundance. All that is meant is that the goal of technical abundance is a distinguishing and a driving force of American local community life. Unlike the situation elsewhere, achievement of this goal throughout the United States is either in sight for most communities or has been met by many. Growing technical abundance is a meaningful consideration that profoundly shapes and influences the whole social context that municipal public servants work and live and if any single word so exemplifies this social condition it is "progress."[3]

This progress takes place within a pluralistic society. Every community has a large number of competing influences that are usually organizationally based. Their alignment depends more upon the problem at hand than upon other factors. Thus, the total society is open and constantly adapting and changing itself to new conditions.[4]

Principal Building Blocks of the Community

Groups and associations are the principal building blocks of the American community. They come into existence because men of the community share common values and interests. When individuals and groups wish to accomplish something they form an organization. In some cases the organization is rather simple in structure and purpose, while in others it is a complex, multi-purpose affair involving institutional groupings of various sorts such as churches, governments, and business concerns.

Groups and associations on the local community level are effective means employed time after time to accomplish either short- or long-range objectives. Sometimes they become an integral part of more formalized institutions. Sometimes they evolve as institutional entities in their own right. Because of their critical position, they may be regarded as the principal building blocks of the community. These blocks are reinforced and tied together into a working social whole, a community, by prevailing social forces and institutions. In this sense,

[2] For an excellent short treatise on this subject in simple terms, see Donald W. Olmstead, SOCIAL GROUPS, ROLES, AND LEADERSHIP (East Lansing: Michigan State University, 1961), 54pp.

[3] For a good treatment of American life and culture as it relates to state and local government, see Charles R. Adrian, STATE AND LOCAL GOVERNMENT (New York: McGraw-Hill Book Co., 1950), especially Chapters 2 and 3.

[4] For an excellent treatise on the community examined in pluralistic terms, see Nelson W. Polsby, COMMUNITY POWER AND POLITICAL THEORY (New Haven: Yale University Press, 1963), 144pp.

groups and associations are viewed in static structural terms, whereas prevalent social forces represent the dynamics of community life. This dichotomy is satisfactory only for analytical purposes. Both ingredients partake of structural as well as dynamic qualities.

INDICATIONS OF MAGNITUDE AND COMPLEXITY

A comprehensive determination of the extent of social groups and associations in the local community would reach astronomical terms. Only a few indications are possible.

Community Associations. Studies reveal that American community life is highly organized. During World War II, the Office of Civil Defense "could communicate any message of importance to every citizen of the country." This was accomplished through the use of 1,000 national organizations which were selected from some 10,000 national associations.[5]

The extent to which Americans are organized in associational terms is further shown in a study by Professor Robin Williams, Jr. His investigations show that:

. . . the major fraternal orders . . . claim a total membership of about 20,000,000 persons. As of the late 1930's there were over 1,500 chapters of national college fraternities and 600 sorority chapters. The distinctive "service clubs" (Rotary, Kiwanis, Lions, Civitans, Optimists, etc.) cover the nation with some unit in practically every urban center.

Among special women's organizations, the National Federation of Women's Clubs includes 14,000 member organizations claiming 3 million individual members. There are giant veterans' organizations— the American Legion, Veterans of Foreign Wars, the American Veterans Committee. In rural areas, there are about 11,000 agricultural co-operatives with well over 3 million members; the American Farm Bureau (about 1½ million members) has state bureaus in 47 states; the National Grange lists approximately 800,000 dues paying members; the 4H Clubs enrolled in 1935 about 2 million youth.

As of 1945, there were 123 national organizations devoted in whole or in part to work on problems of inter-racial and inter-cultural relations.

As long ago as 1940, the CIO was composed of 42 national and international unions and organizing committees with 225 state, county and local union councils and 419 local industrial unions.

There are 1,500 national trade associations, 4,000 chambers of commerce, 70,000 labor unions—and 100,000 women's organizations. At the time of the AFL-CIO merger in 1955 it was estimated that more than 40,000,000 persons belonged to unions.

And so it goes. These, note, are in addition to the elaborate formal organizations represented by business enterprises, foundations, and many other forms of private associations.

There is an enormous proliferation of formally organized special interest associations of the most diverse kinds. Specialized associations have multiplied, whereas the parts played by traditional groupings based on proximity, diffused common values, and direct and inclusive personal relations have all diminished.[6]

The study of a "Yankee City" by Professors Warner and Lunt provides additional insights. In a city with a population of 17,000 they were able to identify 900 associations. These associations included almost 13,000 memberships held by fewer than 7,000 persons. It can be generalized that nearly every adult member of the city belonged to one or more associations.[7]

Community Social Groups. Community associations are easily recognizable forms of social collectivities. Besides these, there are various types of social groups which frequently are not so recognizable. Nevertheless, one cannot study community relations without becoming aware of the pervasiveness of the social groups functioning in the community. To understand community relations one must have knowledge about the social groups found in the community, their individual nature, and the ways in which they are embedded within broader social constructs.

We all belong to and participate in several kinds of social groups: families, friendship circles, political clubs and work, educational, religious, neighborhood and recreational groups. As is the case with many other aspects of human social behavior, this everyday sort of experience is difficult to define or describe in meaningful terms. Although a great deal of mental effort has gone into defining the charac-

---

[5] Floyd Hunter, "Studying Associations and Organization Structures," in Roland Young (ed.), APPROACHES TO THE STUDY OF POLITICS (Evanston, Illinois: Northwestern University Press, 1958), p. 351.

[6] *Ibid.,* pp. 348–49. Cited from original compilation by Robin M. Williams, Jr., AMERICAN SOCIETY, A SOCIOLOGICAL INTERPRETATION (New York: Alfred A. Knopf, 1951), pp. 468–69.

[7] Lloyd Warner and Paul S. Lunt, THE SOCIAL LIFE OF A MODERN COMMUNITY (New Haven: Yale University Press, 1941), p. 303 *et seq.*

teristics of a social group, this may not be a very profitable activity. As one writer is reputed to have said of elephants—he could not define one but nonetheless would have no trouble in recognizing one. Similarly, we all know roughly what we mean by a social group. Beyond this point, however, we often encounter difficulty.

The difficulty of developing an understandable working concept of a social group is not sufficient grounds for avoiding the problem. Social groups, elusive as they may be in conceptual terms, exist and play critical roles in community life. No person engaged in community relations work can afford to overlook the possibilities of a useful social construct to incorporate social groups into a public relations program. This construct probably can best be considered within a framework of questions: What are the features of social groups? What should be the level of analysis? What are the functions of a social group?

All social groups have certain common features which the sociological literature generally agrees are: (1) the relations among the members are interdependent—each member's behavior influences the behavior of others; (2) the members share an ideology—a set of values, beliefs, and attitudes—which regulates their mutual conduct; (3) social groups provide functions—internal in the sense of psychological satisfaction for members and external in the sense of relationships with broader social units; (4) social groups are usually functionally related to other groups, and, taken together, form social organizations and institutions.[8]

These common features may be analyzed in several ways. In community relations work is it more profitable to study the behavior of the individuals in groups or the behavior of groups? Any publicity program must consider the question. No neat answer is forthcoming. But, since this chapter deals with social groups, prime concern is group behavior and not indi-

vidual behavior. The essential thing for the community relations person to remember is that there is a significant difference in these two types of behavior. In short, the social group is a behavior unit. It has its own unique characteristics and behavioral patterns, and operates within a set of norms prescribed by the group and by society.[9] Social group behavior and not individual behavior is typical, particularly in urban societies marked by the three big emerging bureaucracies of corporate enterprise, government, and private social associations.[10]

The previously given set of common features notes what are the general functions of a social group: (1) psychological satisfaction for individual members and (2) functional involvement with larger social organizations and institutions. The goals (motives, aims, purposes) provide a way to differentiate social groups.

Social groups conform to a set of norms which guide individual behavior—actions, thoughts, feelings—in social relationships. The main problem here is to distinguish between norms associated with a particular group and those which are a product of the socio-cultural environment. In stable communities the norms of social groups are generally compatible with those of the larger social setting; but some social groups have norms incompatible with those of society at large. Witness those norms of a juvenile gang, for instance!

In developing a community relations program it is important to study "group awareness." How does a group of persons perceive of itself as a social unit? This is a formidable

---

[8] The literature on social groups is almost overwhelming. Two suggested references useful for public relations workers are Olmstead, *op. cit.*, and Heinz Eulau, THE BEHAVIORAL PERSUASION IN POLITICS (New York: Random House, 1963), particularly Chapters 1 and 2.

[9] For a further discussion as to what is meant by a behavior unit, see Kenneth E. Boulding, CONFLICT AND DEFENSE, A GENERAL THEORY (New York: Harper Torchbooks, 1962), particularly pp. 7–18.

[10] The community relations man of the future is going to function more and more within the environment of big social organization. What may be the nature and consequence of this emerging social order we can only speculate. Progressive community relations demand that the public relations people keep abreast of the findings of research and developments in this area. A few suggested references are: Robert A. Dahl, WHO GOVERNS, DEMOCRACY AND POWER IN AN AMERICAN CITY (New Haven: Yale University Press, 1961); Nelson Polsby, COMMUNITY POWER AND POLITICAL THEORY (New Haven: Yale University Press, 1963), and Webb S. Fiser. MASTERY OF THE METROPOLIS (Englewood Cliffs, New Jersey: Prentice-Hall, 1962).

undertaking, but research methodology is available to provide some insights.[11]

In sum, the evasiveness of social groups should not lead one to underestimate their roles and influences in community affairs. Social scientists have devoted much attention in recent years to social groups in all types of human organizational settings. The task of the public relations person is to be fully aware of these research findings, and evolve means by which to incorporate them within improved programs of community relations.

GROWING COMPLEX OF COMMUNITY GROUPS AND ASSOCIATIONS

Our growing industrial and urban society has already formulated the organizational way of life. Organizations of all kinds—government, industrial, and service—have evolved (and are still evolving highly complex forms for attaining political, economic, and social goals. They are found on national, regional, state, and local levels. However, their interests converge primarily on the community level. The large national and regional as well as the smaller community organizations are devoted to the "grassroots" approach, and they employ a host of techniques and coordinating devices to reach deeply into local community life.

What are the social implications of this highly organizational way of life on the local community?

How are community social groups built into the more highly organized and institutional forms of associations?

What are the methods and ways by which the various groups and associations relate themselves to the local community?

Professor Williams puts the answers to these and related questions in the following terms:

Local communities are highly open chains of interaction initiated at far removed centers. . . .

Multiplication of specialized associations, especially of the centralized, hierarchical types, leads to the development of numerous mediating, co-ordinating, or tangential organizations.

Items: co-ordinating committees; clearinghouse organizations; councils; multiplication of offices and associations charged with mediating and co-ordinating tasks; federated associations.

Both the total structure and the internal structures of large formal organizations are highly complex: in the latter numerous specialized statuses are arranged in intricate systems within systems; in the former, varied groups, communities, and associations are interrelated in extended networks, chains, and subsidiary social systems.[12]

One authority in public relations, Louis B. Lundborg, has viewed the complex of organized groups and associations with some alarm. He observed that while conflicts and differences exist in the community, the community in itself is a blending of divergent interests and within it are found interlocking and overlapping groups and associations. A resident of a community is typically a member of several social groups and associations. Through such individual relationships the social groups and associations become interlocked.

Lundborg sums up his observation in these words: "The interlocking directorates of big corporations that have been viewed with alarm by social and economic observers are nothing compared with the interlocking areas of influence within a community, and from one community to another."[13]

Successful municipal management requires a thorough understanding of the nature of the community. The general characteristics of the American local community have been sketched out. Some reference pegs have been planted to help municipal public servants understand better the nature of their own communities. More such pegs are now necessary to bring into sharper focus the subject of working with community groups and associations. Attention will now be given to community relations projects and programs which typically fit within the domain of municipal government. For convenience of treatment, ideas relating to community relations have been arbitrarily grouped into types. These types can easily be viewed as focal points of community interests and are so termed here.

---

[11] Research methodology in public relations is discussed in Chapter 3, "The Public Relations Process," and therefore will not be elaborated upon here.

[12] Williams, *op. cit.,* p. 463.

[13] PUBLIC RELATIONS IN THE LOCAL COMMUNITY (New York: Harper and Bros., 1950) , p. 36.

Focal Points of Community Interests

The first view will be a wide-angled focus of community interests, a view that will encompass the elements of the ideal community.

Elements of the Ideal Community

In 1921 Eduard C. Lindeman sketched out nine elements which the ideal community should provide its residents. These are applicable today and represent an excellent wide-angled focus for a progressive community.

1. *Order,* or security of life and property through the medium of efficient government.
2. *Economic well-being,* or security of income through an efficient system of productive industry.
3. *Physical well-being,* or health and sanitation through public health agencies.
4. *Constructive use of leisure time,* or recreation through organized and directed play.
5. *Ethical standards,* or a system of morality supported by the organized community.
6. *Intellectual diffusion,* or free education and public institutions within the reach of all.
7. *Free avenues of expression,* or means by which all the elements of the community may freely express themselves; free newspapers and public forums.
8. *Democratic forms of organization,* or community-wide organization through which the entire community may express its thoughts and see that its will is done.
9. *Spiritual motivation,* or religious association which may diffuse all forms of community organization, the religious or spiritual motive.[14]

Community Organizational Mazemanship. Municipal government performs the significant role in incorporating these elements into the community. To work effectively toward the goal of the ideal community, municipal administrators need to become experts in what might be termed community organizational mazemanship—i.e., the skill of achieving the objectives of the ideal community through a maze of organizational (social groups and associations) complexities. They must be sensitive to the city as a politico-socio-economic organism and a complex community of human beings. Profes-

[14] Eduard C. Lindeman, THE COMMUNITY, AN INTRODUCTION TO THE STUDY OF COMMUNITY LEADERSHIP AND ORGANIZATION (New York: Association Press, 1921), pp. 7–9. This quotation is also found in Ernest B. Harper and Arthur Dunham (eds.), COMMUNITY ORGANIZATION IN ACTION (New York: Association Press, 1959), pp. 21–22.

sor Lindeman's nine elements of the ideal community certainly suggest a wide-angled focus and thereby give good perspective within which more narrowly focused community action programs can constructively take place.

An Informed Citizenry

Good municipal government in the democratic sense requires an informed citizenry. Municipal leaders have a responsibility to report faithfully and fully to citizens of their municipalities about the policies that have been adopted and why; about accomplishments, problems, difficulties and failures; and about future plans. To aid them in the task of reporting, there are a number of community groups and associations with programs in governmental affairs. These community organizations recognize that citizen action cannot be effective if their members and the public do not understand the organization and function of municipal government, and specific community problems and issues.

Some of these community organizations have as their main purpose the education of their members for leadership and participation in governmental affairs through lectures, discussions, conferences, and related educational techniques. Other organizations sponsor similar educational programs for the community. Some organizations have as the major objective the presentation of information necessary for citizens to vote intelligently at special or general elections. Still others try to stimulate citizens to exercise their voting rights without any special or general elections. Others try to stimulate citizens to exercise their voting rights without any special reference to problems or issues. Some organizations restrict their activities to matters of particular concern such as education, health, and welfare.

Community relations programs for an informed citizenry certainly are one of the primary concerns of progressive municipal government. On the other hand, no subject is probably as sensitive. Municipal officials can easily be attacked as "propagandizers" using the facilities of the city to maintain their own positions! To avoid such an accusation, it becomes imperative to develop close working relations with responsible community groups and associations.

The bases for such relations will be well-conceived educational programs that serve to educate the youth as well as the adult population of the community concerning municipal programs and problems. Throughout this book are suggested projects and means that may accomplish sound public relations programs. The task of community relations is to use these and others so as to achieve a more-informed citizenry.

Two major aspects of a community relations information program are: (1) general information on municipal government affairs, and (2) information concerning special municipal problems and issues. Usually there are many groups and associations which are interested in community relations projects which fit into either or both categories. The following examples are illustrative.

General Information on Municipal Affairs. Every community has several community organizations that are interested in informing the public on general municipal affairs. To maintain good community relations, public officials must learn how to work effectively with all of them, and keep the leadership of these organizations fully informed.

Since many of the leading community groups and associations have close working relationships with chambers of commerce, it is a common practice for the cities to enter into contractual agreements with the local "Chamber" for certain types of informational, promotional, and related activities.

The program of the city of Inglewood, California, is typical and has been in operation for many years. In the fiscal year 1963–64, the city granted $12,000 for support of the local chamber of commerce, which has an annual budget of $75,000. In return the chamber of commerce performs a number of services such as preparation of monthly business reports, responsibility for retail and commercial promotions, dissemination of publications and information, general assistance to community groups and associations interested in municipal affairs, etc.[15]

Inglewood surveyed the extent to which other cities support chambers of commerce. Their findings are as follows:

In our survey of sixteen California cities, we found that all but one provide financial support to the Chamber of Commerce. On page 113 is a tabulation of the data received from these cities.

Of the ten cities contacted outside California, six supported their Chambers of Commerce. The amounts of contributions were substantially less than in California. In the cities outside California, seven indicated that industrial and commercial promotion was the responsibility of the city, but they cooperated with their Chamber of Commerce and other community groups.

The Inglewood Chamber of Commerce is divided into various sections based on common interest and geography: Imperial-Crenshaw, North Inglewood, and Morningside Park. It is also organized by functional committees, such as Governmental Affairs, City Beautification, etc. Special committees also exist and are formed for specific purposes.

Many of these committees, particularly the Governmental Affairs, Industrial, and City Beautification committees, have been of great assistance in legislative matters; area improvements, such as tree planting; traffic problems; and annexations, particularly in the industrial area where "county islands" exist. In the field of industrial and commercial promotion the Chamber of Commerce has been somewhat limited in its activities primarily due to the scarcity of industrial land available for development.

The Chamber of Commerce has assisted the City Council in many specific projects; some examples are the East-West Freeway route, Court site, establishment of the Municipal Library, and South Bay College site. Several of these activities were actually organized by the Chamber or were in response to Council request for assistance.[16]

An example of how chambers of commerce seek to influence municipalities is the following extract from the Pasadena, California, newspaper:

The Pasadena Chamber of Commerce has requested the City of Pasadena to establish a standard operational procedure for informing the public about the scheduling of street maintenance.

* * * *

The Chamber suggested a simple six-point program by the city to achieve this goal.

1. Publication by the Pasadena Street Department of an advance schedule of street repairs and resurfacing for six months to one year.

2. Routing of this information to interested city

---

[15] For more details, see "Public Relations and Information," Administrative Report No. 1 (City of Inglewood, California, July, 1963), processed, p. 7.

[16] *Ibid.*, pp. 8–9.

Table 2. CITY GOVERNMENT FINANCIAL SUPPORT FOR CHAMBER OF COMMERCE ACTIVITIES

City	Population	Amount	Activities
Berkeley	111,268	$21,000	Commercial and retail promotional activities, reports, legislative assistance, etc.
Burbank	93,000	$11,675	Civic improvement, industrial development, retail promotion, visitor promotion, committees, etc.
Downey	90,700	$19,800	Community promotion.
Hawthorne	45,000	$ 7,500	Commercial and retail promotional activities.
Lakewood	70,400	$10,000	Retail and community promotion, city brochures, printing, special events.
Newport Beach	32,000	NONE	NONE
Norwalk	92,000	$12,000	Retail promotion, bond issues, annexation, civic development.
Palo Alto	54,000	$10,500	Christmas decorations, printings, retail promotions, civic development.
Pico Rivera	50,000	$ 5,000	Matter under review by City Council.
Riverside	103,000	$24,000	Advertising, industrial promotion, convention bureau, city maps, civic development, etc.
Redondo Beach	51,000	$19,500 (Chamber) $10,000 (Small Craft Harbor)	Commercial and industrial promotion, advertising for city, handles small harbor promotion, etc.
San Jose	288,000	$78,500	Industrial promotion, convention bureau, retail activities, parades, legislation, etc.
Santa Fe Springs	16.000	$11,000	Floats, county fair projects and specific projects for city.
Santa Monica	86,000	$50,000 (also funds) from L.A. County)	Advertising for city, industrial and commercial promotion, tourist bureau, conventions, civic development, retail activities.
Merced	20,950	$ 5,000	Advertising, holidays, retail activities.
Stockton	99,000	$24,000	Industrial and commercial promotion, retail convention, harbor development.

departments and city-owned and franchise-operated agencies.

3. Notices and maps furnished to the press in advance of work to be done and suggested alternate routes to alleviate traffic congestion.

4. Areas to be worked on posted with warning signs at least three days prior to actual work.

5. Utilization of "Sigalert" radio to warn motorists of street repairs being carried out.

6. Scheduling of repairs on major streets so that they will not be blocked at critical times of the year.[17]

Information Concerning Special Municipal Problems and Issues. Research increasingly has become a more important part of organizational life. Leaders of today realize that the contemporary problems and issues cannot adequately be dealt with unless reliable facts and proven solutions are available.

Although much more research on municipal problems is necessary, the immediate job ahead seems to be more in the area of making the present research findings "operational," rather than developing more research. Too many excellent research reports, at large costs in time and money, have ended upon the dusty shelves of libraries and agency archives. Too often administrative memories are short, and investigation is undertaken upon a matter that has already been adequately researched.

In summary, research has already provided a large body of possible solutions to municipal problems. Municipal leaders must learn how to find and put into use the available research findings as well as undertaking or cooperating with others in further research investigations. Research is expensive. Municipal leaders must learn how to economize on this matter. The best way is, first, to learn what community groups and associations have already done in research on municipal problems and, second, to develop cooperative working relations with these organizations.

Municipal administrators must not only be

---

[17] Pasadena, California, STAR-NEWS, October, 1963.

community-relations-minded, but also library-minded. In regards to the latter item, every administrator should have on his desk several reference books. One such book that is highly recommended is by Paul Wasserman (*Information for Administrators,* a Guide to Publications and Services for Management in Business and Government [Ithaca, N.Y.: Cornell University Press, 1956]). Chapters 8 to 10 particularly are valuable concerning community organizations that have active research programs relating to municipal affairs and problems.

GREATER EFFICIENCY AND ECONOMY IN MUNICIPAL AFFAIRS

Many community groups and associations have as their sole objective greater efficiency and economy in municipal government, and nearly all of them have this objective as part of their total program.

Despite their constructive efforts, there is frequently a tendency for such groups to assume a negative attitude toward government spending, and municipal leadership must guard against efforts that jeopardize long-run efficiency and economy.[18]

There are a number of ways by which a community relations program can build a balanced and constructive approach to efficiency and economy in municipal government. A common approach is to work with community organizations in making a study of the efficiency of all municipal departments. Another is to cooperate with "watch dog committees" in the evaluation of fiscal policy, interpretation of budget documents, and related matters.

Municipal services have been expanded in a number of communities by securing the support of volunteer associations in areas where there is inadequate financing. In other cases, the city has found it more economical to contribute to volunteer organizations than to undertake the responsibility for certain functions itself.

In many communities, the morale and performance of municipal employees have been greatly enhanced by public acknowledgment, by community organizations, of distinguished service of public employees. By the same token, community organizations have increased their civic contributions because municipal leaders have publicly acknowledged their services to the community.

CITIZEN PARTICIPATION IN MUNICIPAL GOVERNMENT

Community groups and associations are vital social instrumentalities to assure greater citizen participation in municipal affairs, and more responsible municipal government. As American society grows more urban and more complex, it becomes increasingly difficult for the citizen to participate in government unless he becomes associated with a significant community organization.[19]

The trend of greater citizen participation through the role of community organizations is clearly discernible. The central problem is to assure that the participation is "citizen participation" and not "interest group" politics. This requires the most skillful type of community relations.

LEGISLATIVE RELATIONS IN THE PUBLIC INTEREST

Some undesirable situations in municipalities can only be corrected by legislation. Community groups and associations can be effective means by which legislation is enacted in the public interest. In working with these community organizations, municipal personnel must carefully follow a nonpartisan approach and avoid any accusation of favoritism.

In some municipalities it is the practice to request the service committees of leading community organizations to prepare a program of legislative needs. Proposed legislation (ordinances and codes) on particular functional areas of municipal government is reviewed with the interested community organizations and their opinions and assistance are solicited.

The aid of the local bar association is fre-

---

[18] What constitutes the short- and the long-run public interest is a question open to debate. One thing is certain. Most people are not too interested in the long-run public interest. Who can be excited about the long-run when the chances are that he will not be around!

---

[19] See Chapter 7, "The Employee-Citizen Team," for an elaboration of citizen participation in local government.

quently sought in many communities for assistance ranging from the review of the present legal base to the drafting of ordinances.

COMMUNITY RELATIONS IN LOCAL DEVELOPMENT

With American communities dedicated to "technical abundance" as a way of life based upon a free and open economic and social system (pluralistic society), community organizations become particularly important in local development. Programs for development depend upon the needs of the community and are generally of two types: (1) community planning and (2) economic development.

Community Planning. Planning is a continuous process for guiding and implementing the future development of the community. It is a process in which citizens, in cooperation with municipal and other local government officials, determine the kind of community they want— including both immediate and long-range goals —in the context of resources and capabilities. In many respects the most important part of community planning is the achievement of consensus on community objectives—be they better schools, industrial development, parks and open spaces, revitalization of the central business district, or development housing.

The city government, through its professional staff, is continually developing and revising plans in line with community goals through capital improvement programs, operating and service programs, the operating budget, and the capital budget. Often such work is done in close cooperation with the superintendent of schools, county government administrators, state highway department administrators, and others.

In recent years increasing attention has been given to social and economic planning in cooperation with the local chamber of commerce, the local health and welfare council, and other significant local groups concerned with public health, education, youth employment, juvenile delinquency, and related areas. Community organizations can work with the city government and other organizations in planning and development in several ways. First, such organizations can be very helpful in outlining community objectives. They can be useful in surveying needs and resources as well as evaluating information.

Second, community organizations can work with other groups, both official and private, in delineating specific steps to be taken. Such steps could include the revision of a zoning ordinance, the drafting of subdivision regulations, the development of a housing code, special educational programs for preschoolers, and parking surveys of the business district.

Third, community organizations can undertake important, if not critical, roles in educating citizens on the content of planning programs and their effects on the community. They can help in running workshops and clinics for people to study community problems and to inform the public at large.

Economic Development. Although most communities devote considerable attention to problems of economic development, only a few have been able to meet this matter in a positive manner. Effective community relations appears to be one of the prime vehicles for successful economic development. Some communities with limited resources and markets have been able to build flourishing local economies, while others in more fortunate resource situations have had slow economic development.

Community organizations primarily concerned with economic development usually have such general objectives as: (1) improvement of physical facilities in order to attract business; (2) promotion of retail trade; (3) development of tourist trade; and (4) establishment of a sound and balanced industry. To achieve these objectives they employ a wide variety of approaches, consisting of publicly financed programs, privately financed programs or a combination.[20]

The role of community chambers of commerce, discussed earlier in this chapter, is especially significant in economic development. It is this role which appears to be the primary justification for municipal subventions to chambers of commerce.

---

[20] For a comprehensive survey of local economic development, see Donald R. Gilmore, DEVELOPING THE LITTLE ECONOMIES (New York: Committee for Economic Development, 1959), 200pp.

Articulating Community Groups and Associations

In recent years there has been an increasing concern with the general state of community life, and this concern has been world-wide. In the United States, prime concern has been directed toward the urban center, its inadequacies in cohesion, its ineffectiveness as a political or social unit, and its shortcomings in human development. In many urban communities, there is little sense of belonging, or feeling of identification, or intimate association. The current popularity of such words as "disorganization," "disintegration," "decline," "insecurity," "breakdown," and "instability" indicate the growing concern with community life in urban and industrial settings.

The problems of contemporary community life, however, are not limited to the urban centers. Of equal concern are the numerous small communities, many in rural settings, that have experienced, over the last 30 years, sizable losses in population. Losses in opportunities for individuals with intelligence and initiative tend to weaken or even destroy patterns of community life.

The dynamism in American life is too strong, and the confidence in local action and progress too great, for community leaders to accept complacently the present state of community affairs and life. Fresh concern recently has been manifested in a great variety of ways to reconstruct and incorporate social innovations within the community so that it can better fulfill its purposes. Municipal officials have critical roles to perform in the process of preserving and rejuvenating the community. How municipal officials can articulate community groups and associations with action constitutes our next concern.

STAGES OF COMMUNITY ACTION

Community action may be viewed as progressing through several stages: (1) the initiating stage, (2) the mobilizing stage, and (3) the executing stage. Within this total process there are numerous steps that do not necessarily group themselves into neat sequential or chronological order as portrayed by these three major stages. However, it is useful to generalize the total efforts within these three major stages because they provide convenient reference points in an over-all action program.

The initiating stage is characterized by the recognition of a community problem or a number of problems. A community problem is nonexistent until it is recognized and articulated by someone. Community action cannot take place unless the organized interests feel that there is a common problem. Once the problem has been articulated within the framework of values, beliefs, and attitudes shared by those who recognize it, the second stage, the mobilization of effort, takes place.

The executing stage occurs when organizational involvement takes place for the solution of the community problem. The nature of the involvement will be conditioned by the culture of the community.

Each of these three stages will now be examined in fuller detail.

INITIATING SOCIAL ACTION IN THE COMMUNITY

Probably the most difficult part of community relations is initiating social action. Social inertia, like physical inertia, is a strong barrier against any kind of movement (change). Once the inertia has been displaced and change is under way, it takes only a small amount of energy to continue the process.

In the previous section on the "Focal Points of Community Interests," a number of action projects were suggested as means to influence people (change their attitudes and awaken their interests) in order to achieve social action. When community life is not working the way certain people think that it should, they do something about it. They talk to their friends, hold meetings, organize groups, and stir associations into action. They try to arouse public interests (and indignation), channel efforts of action-oriented community elements, and win support of the community publics.

Social change involves many elements and facets of the community and any action group soon finds itself within a medley of contending voices. How to work in a constructive fashion with this medley constitutes the next concern of this chapter.

MOBILIZING THE SOCIAL GROUPS AND ASSOCIATIONS

From the beginning, any action group should learn who is in favor of the program and who is against it—the kinds of opposition anticipated and from what quarters. The action group must organize support for its program and overcome opposition or inertia. This should be done in a highly constructive and systematic manner.

Survey of Community Organization Influence Potentials. Early in the process of initiating social action, a survey should be prepared of probable community organizational support and opposition. The information needed to make such a survey can be secured from several places and by several means. Printed records are one source. Newspaper stories and releases, annual reports and special reports, statements of purposes, and community studies or surveys, all may give indications of an organization's potential for social action.

Often current and specific information is directly available from the organizations, or from friends or acquaintances of the members of the organizations. Frequently, information is acquired by sending an observer to meetings of the organizations or by inviting representatives of the organizations to meet with the initiating action group. The information secured should be mapped out in an accurate manner. Table 3 gives an example of how to chart organizational potentials.

Community life is not static. Support and opposition will change as the program develops. The "survey" should be corrected from time to time with the changed conditions of organizational potential.

MOBILIZING THE PUBLICS

An action group cannot reach the people of the community by depending only upon the more formal types of community social groups and associations. Some people do not belong to any organization, and others may belong to an organization which is not vitally concerned. However, all members of a community, in varying degrees of intensity, belong to publics in a community.[21] These publics are joined together through communication networks and thus are frequently in strong positions to influence the final outcome of community action projects.

Survey of the Publics' Influence Potentials. This is usually a more difficult job than making a comparable survey for community

[21] For more details, see Chapter 5, "The Multitudinous Publics."

Table 3. SURVEY OF COMMUNITY ORGANIZATION INFLUENCE POTENTIALS

Names of Organizations	Estimated No. of Members	Probable Relation to Project	Support Activities
	200 active 400 inactive	Active cooperation in project, including financial and moral support	Provide workers to distribute literature, interview, and fund raising.
	200 estimate	Limited financial support	Furnish funds for publicity. Certain printing facilities available.
	400 active, inactive, no figure	Moral support	Could use organization's name as a co-sponsor.
	600 active	Neutral-positive bias	Will inform its members of the project and permit distribution of information.
	400 active	Neutral-negative bias	Probably difficult to have item placed upon meeting agenda.
	400-500 active	Opposed	Will take a strong position against the project.

organizational potentials. Publics are tenuous and unstructured social entities, and lack any formal institutionalization. Their amorphous and transitory nature makes it difficult to determine accurately an individual public's influence potential.

Over the years there has evolved a variety of sophisticated techniques by which to ascertain and measure the influence potentials of publics.[22] The findings of such surveys should be mapped out in a manner not unlike that suggested for community social groups and associations.

GRAND SCHEME OF COMMUNITY MOBILIZATION

One of the most difficult jobs of the action group is to mobilize the community groups and associations and the publics into a well-planned and comprehensive unit. Below is presented a "Grand Scheme of Community Mobilization" (Figure 11) in which the significant elements pertaining to effective community relations are brought together in a systematic fashion.

The scheme includes the major facets involved in mobilizing both the social groups and associations and the publics in a total plan of community action. First is an evaluation of the various types of fact-finding techniques to be employed. The techniques checked will provide immediately some indications of the financial cost of the action program as well as other considerations. The next concern is a plan for publicity. How can the publics and the social groups and associations best be reached? Both of these aspects must be carried out by some organizational form. These forms are noted in Figure 11.

And last, based upon reliable information and findings, an evaluation of the influence potential of each public, and social group and association is necessary in order to plan strategies and action approaches.

EXECUTING SOCIAL ACTION IN THE COMMUNITY

At this stage the action program appears almost to gravitate into orbit. Too much has been invested for the program to suddenly cease.

Influential parties in the community have taken their stands, important community decisions have been made, and organizational resources have been pledged. The task ahead is to keep the action target clearly in mind and to utilize the available resources in a skillful and economical manner toward achieving the goal.

It is not uncommon for the community groups involved to find themselves under attack. In a democratic society anyone may question the policies and actions of all parties. A major source of strength in a free society is freedom to dissent, disagree, question, agree or discuss.

The job of the public relations officer is now particularly critical to the success of the action program. Vicious rumors, half-truths, screaming headlines, or just plain misunderstandings can destroy a sorely needed new action program, force retrenchment in an old one, spoil the accumulated work of months or years, crucify respected citizens, and crush well-established community associations.

Community leaders and organizations, whether they like it or not, must learn to endure such conditions and perform effectively under them. This is the price of democracy. Public opinion plays a dominant role in our society. Any enterprise must develop competence in dealing with the public.

Disagreement and controversy are unavoidable. The object is to use these differences in a constructive fashion to unite the people of the community behind a program. Opposition can be used in many ways to test and expedite an action program. Objections may point up weaknesses in a program. Probing questions may reveal undesirable consequences which the initiating group and its friends were unable to see. Responsible opposition can serve the function of more clearly defining a problem.

Controversy in a constructive framework is essential for a free and a viable society. Community relations programs should recognize and learn to accept this fundamental.

Finally, a community relations program's best defense against attack will always be a reservoir of good will. Any group must acknowledge this fact and spend considerable time deciding how to build a positive position

---

[22] Chapter 3, "The Public Relations Process," covers this aspect.

Grand Scheme of Community Mobilization

	Groups and Associations				Publics								
	Chamber of Commerce	AFL	PTA		Commun. Pop.	Labor	Religion P	Religion C	Adults	Busines	Educ.	Civic Organ.	Profes-sional
Est. population members	400	800	800		30,000	1,200	7,000	6,500	6,500	300	8,000	2,400	200
Fact-finding techniques													
Door-to-door canvass									√				
Interviews	√		√				√			√	√	√	√
Opinion polls			√					√			√		
Field trips										√			
Community surveys	√	√	√			√	√		√			√	
Diag. of commun. forces		√	√			√	√	√			√		√
Publicity techniques													
Press	√		√				√		√	√	√	√	√
Radio	√								√		√	√	√
Television	√												
House organs											√		
Newsletters		√				√		√	√				
Posters		√				√			√				
Displays		√				√			√				
Movies		√				√							
Announcements													
Public speeches								√	√				√
Pamphlets									√				
Mass meetings									√		√		
Commun. workshops													
Leadership train. inst.		√				√			√				
Door-to-door canvass													
Deleg. to pub. officials			√				√	√					
Deleg. to other organiz.			√				√						√
Letter-writing campaign										√			
Sponsorship & endorse.								√					√
Telephone campaigns								√					
Informal personal con.	√	√	√			√	√				√	√	√
Resolutions													
Circulating petitions								√					
Picketting		√				√							
Boycotting													
Arbitration													
Come-and-see tours										√		√	
Meeting-discuss.-meet.											√		
Problem census	√												
Organization techniques													
Face-to-face groups	√	√	√			√	√		√	√	√	√	√
Committees	√						√		√	√			
Block organizations			√				√		√				
Community councils			√				√	√	√	√		√	√
Mass meetings													
Influence potentials													
Active support	√												
Moral support		√				√			√				
Neutral-positive bias							√	√					√
Neutral-negative bias		√									√	√	
Opposed										√			

*Adapted in part from **Taking Action in the Community** (Washington, D.C.; Adult Education Association of the U.S.A., 1955) pp. 14-15.

FIGURE 11.

in a community. Every community group and association or combination of these has a responsibility for bringing regularly before the public its purposes, its backing, and its work and accomplishments.

General Conclusions

Any community relations program must have as its end product the building of a more desirable place to work and live. Municipal government has the major responsibility in this area. Fortunately, the American society is highly organized into numerous social groups and associations with strong civic inclinations. Through constructive programs and leadership, the energies and resources of these community organizations can be directed into channels for building a more desirable community. However, any program must be a two-way proposition. Municipal officials and employees themselves must participate in community life. They must join clubs, lodges, associations, and other private concerns in the community; they must be willing to provide sponsorship or leadership for youth groups and similar organizations, and initiate and organize community betterment programs. In short, they must live as responsible citizens of the community.

On the other hand, all community groups and associations should be encouraged to participate and assume constructive roles in the affairs of the city. This will require that municipal officials and employees exercise ingenuity in devising techniques whereby such organizations can become involved, directly or indirectly, in municipal affairs. Some may be concerned that if too much group participation is permitted or encouraged selfish interests may gain influence too conveniently within the municipal government. This is always a danger under any circumstances. However, our system of government rests upon a belief in responsible citizenship and not bureaucratic expertise. If faith is placed in this ideal and community efforts are spent in building responsible citizenship toward the ends previously noted for the "ideal community," then this danger is considerably minimized, if not negated. In any event, our democratic ideals have served us well over the years and in no area of public relations is this more evident than in community relations. Community organizations largely articulate the various desires of the community and are in positions to assist in vital ways in carrying out community programs.

The job of the public official is to learn what their desires may be and integrate them in a constructive fashion within the community's resources. A coordinated and integrated program of civic improvement in which every individual and organization has an opportunity to participate should be the goal of every community.

9

Municipal Police
and Public Relations

AN AMERICAN PRESIDENT is assassinated and a world rises up in indignation and grief. His apparent assassin is killed by a self-appointed executioner and the world demands an explanation from the police.

A thousand miles north of Dallas, four years earlier (in 1959), an outraged citizenry demanded reorganization of the Chicago Police Department to eliminate collusion between police and the underworld.

Not long after the Chicago reorganization the nation was shocked by the wholesale conversion of the Denver Police Department into a crime syndicate operated within the ranks of police officers themselves.

In Redlands, California, the entire community was rocked by the deposition of a police chief because traffic citations were issued to community stalwarts.

Today, as in decades past, positions in various municipal police departments are bought and sold through political ward bosses. And in a thousand cities all over America—in Rochester and Birmingham, in Grosse Point Park and Jersey City—alleged police brutality, bias in reporting statistics, and prejudice in race relations are raised as challenging questions which police officers and municipal officials must grapple with.

Throughout the United States and in other nations of the world, wire-tapping and search-and-seizure raise the age-old questions of individual democratic freedom and the privacy and sanctity of the home.

Contemporary Issues

Since World War II, a progressive revolution against constituted authority has shaken the stability of the entire world. In country after country, riots and revolutions have occurred. An increasing loss of respect for authority is evident. The police as the physical symbol of authority meet the full shock of these assaults.[1]

Not as spectacular as the anti-American riots in many cities of the world, the confused situation in the Congo, or the revolutions of Cuba or the Dominican Republic, are the Los Angeles teen-age gang wars, the riots such as those in Alhambra and Washington, D.C., following football games, and the frequent riots by teen-age party crashers—not as spectacular, but just as devastating to the peace and order of our communities.

The police are reasonably prepared to meet the assault upon authority arising out of these incidents, but they are finding it extremely difficult to adjust to the assaults from uninvolved bystanders and ordinary citizens who suddenly and without provocation become a mob bent on thwarting the processes of law and order.

The lack of interest in this problem by large segments of the population and the tacit approval by some of the community of such

[1] Noel A. McQuown, Deputy Chief, Los Angeles Police Department, "The Police Role in the Community." Address at the Institute on Police and the Public, Los Angeles State College (March 29, 1962).

unlawful mob action are extremely difficult for the police to understand.

Another problem is that of the reduction of police authority. There is always a delicate balance to be maintained between the rights of society and the rights of the individual. The police feel that there is today, however, as the Honorable Justice Burger of the United States Court of Appeals for the District of Columbia has stated, far too much "straining and stretching to give the guilty, not the same but vastly more protection than the law-abiding citizen."[2]

To law enforcement officers the discouraging feature of the limitations being placed on law enforcement by court decisions and new legislation has been the tendency of the creators to disown any responsibility for the current increase in crime. Policemen feel that these people have time after time distorted the effects of their actions by proclaiming that the police can adjust to these new regulations without any debilitation of the public welfare.[3]

Still another problem is that of a confused attitude toward law enforcement. Society apparently does not want all of its laws enforced, but only enough of them to maintain a "reasonable" balance. Policemen are convinced that we have developed in this country a "tongue-in-cheek" attitude toward the enforcement of law.

The public demands on one hand, in situations in which they are directly concerned, that the law be strictly enforced; that the police do their job as required to the fullest extent, violating the law themselves if necessary to accomplish the desired results, in order that the prosecution of the offenders be swift and punishment dealt out to the fullest extent of the law.

Existing at the same time is a fairly well-accepted subculture of lawlessness approved by the general public—a feeling that the law was made for the other fellow.

Tensions are apparent in our communities. There are evidences of tensions between our older more established residents and our newer residents. These tensions are complicated by antagonisms based on differences in race, color, religion, and national origin. Thus, the stage is set for serious community disorder.[4]

The right of the people to be kept informed through the mass media constantly conflicts with the efficient performance of police duties. Witness the Dallas fiasco where Oswald, the alleged assassin of President Kennedy, was himself shot and killed as he was being transferred, contrary to good police practice, in broad daylight through a room crowded with representatives of the mass communications media.

Throughout America chiefs of police struggle to build good relationships with chief administrators and city councils and to convince their policemen that public relations is good business and their business.

These public relations issues, and many more, daily face police administrators. Their number, identity, and importance are not confined to the police function, but probably nowhere else in the municipal service do they stand out so clearly.

Citizen relations with police are of great significance. No other group of municipal employees, with the possible exception of clerks dealing with the public in city hall, is so influential in setting the tone for municipal government as perceived by the average citizen. Certainly none touches the lives of individual citizens with greater drama and emotion. Accordingly, this chapter deals with the police as a functional application of public relations in municipal management.

The Police Role

The Oxford historian, Charles Reith, in his book *The Blind Eye of History*, states that "If world history is approached and viewed as the history of human communities, it shows man clearly as being unable to live alone."[5] In this

---

[2] Quoted in McQuown, *ibid*.

[3] *Ibid*. See also the highly significant U.S. Supreme Court decision, *Mallory* v. *United States*, 354 U.S. 449, 456 (1957).

[4] Mel Ravitz, "Contra-Cultural Conflict in the Metropolitan Community, "PAPERS PRESENTED AT THE NINTH ANNUAL NATIONAL INSTITUTE ON POLICE AND COMMUNITY RELATIONS, Michigan State University (May 19–24, 1963), p. D–3, 4.

[5] Charles Reith, THE BLIND EYE OF HISTORY (London: Faber and Faber, Ltd., 1952), p. 14.

basic process of our living together in communities, he outlines four basic stages:

First: a coming together for the satisfying of mutual needs.

Second: a discovery or recognition for the need of rules for smooth and cooperative action and living.

Third: always and inevitably the discovery that some will not keep some or all of the rules; and to insure the life of the community, means must be found for compelling observance of these rules.

Fourth: in one form or another, the means are found and established. Their effectiveness is the keystone of community existence.

Even earliest man had rules to insure smooth cooperative action and living. These rules, of necessity, became more complex and formal as the community to which he belonged became more complex.

Reith has stated that to insure the life of the community, means must be found for compelling observance of rules. In every age this has been so, as every group has found that some will not keep some or all of the rules. In the common interest there have always been those who enforce the will of the community on those who will not voluntarily abide by the rules.

In modern society, it is the police who perform this task. Upon the police, in the community's behalf, rests the responsibility for peace, tranquility, order, and the very existence of the community. For, as Reith has stated, *"More communities have perished by their inability to enforce laws than have been destroyed by nature or hostile aggression."*[6]

SHARED RESPONSIBILITY

Under the Anglo-Saxon form of policing, in high contrast with totalitarian forms, law enforcement is the responsibility of the entire community. Citizens cannot discard their responsibility to maintain order merely by retaining professional police to perform the daily tasks for which citizens have neither the time, the capacity, nor the inclination. Hence the importance of public support in the enforcement of law and maintenance of order cannot be overemphasized. Police represent only a small fraction of the public they serve and can

never adequately discharge their obligations to protect life and property unless they are reinforced by the good will and cooperation of the public.[7]

It is highly important that the citizen and the policeman understand and appreciate each other's problems and viewpoints. The citizen has definite obligations too. His security and welfare, in large measure, depend on the maintenance of an orderly society, which, in turn, depends on the efficiency and prestige of the police.

The policeman, on his part, must always remember that law enforcement is not an end in itself but is rather a means to an end. That end is the maintenance of an orderly society that enjoys the support of law-abiding citizens.

Nature of Police Public Relations

No matter how well a police department is organized or how efficient and honest is its administration, it is judged by individual citizens by the nature of its public contacts. Good public relations involve far more than saying—they involve doing. It is the policeman out on his beat, the police officer in a radio car or on a motorcycle, and the desk officer or jailer in the station who make friends or enemies for the department. Though there are other influences involved, the police themselves are the most important factor in determining attitudes of the public.

Building proper relations between the police and the public will result in a high degree of popular acceptance. Media affecting public relations—press, radio, motion pictures, and fiction writers—will both reflect and strengthen this underlying influence. The policies of these media are determined by what the public wants and consequently by beliefs and attitudes of the public itself.

UNFAVORABLE ATTITUDES TOWARD POLICE

In building good public relations, many handicaps must be overcome. Not only do the police

---

[6] *Ibid.,* italics added.

[7] G. Douglas Gourley, "Police Public Relations," THE ANNALS OF THE AMERICAN ACADEMY OF POLITICAL AND SOCIAL SCIENCE (January, 1954), p. 135.

have a product to sell (law enforcement) which often meets with strong sales resistance, but some of their predecessors have been responsible for unfavorable attitudes which make the job more difficult today.

Among these are the widely held beliefs that policemen are uneducated and of low mentality; that they are selected for physical strength and courage alone; that they are of doubtful honesty and integrity; that they are engaged in a continuous offensive against society; that they are often rude and domineering; that they get angry easily, and assume a "smart-alecky" attitude even more easily; that they resort to the illegal "third degree"; and that the only way to be safe from this tyranny is to have either wealth or "pull."

Not all of these indictments can be fairly charged to any one police department, but unfortunately, at various times and places, many such charges have been proved. Despite the fact that many police organizations have made rapid strides and are on the verge of professionalism, current standards in others leave much to be desired.

PUBLIC RELATIONS HAZARDS

In the early days of police departments, the "good" citizens in the community felt a sincere alliance with the police against thieves and outlaws who preyed upon them. Today, in an urban community, citizens too often have no such feeling of alliance. Police work is no longer concerned primarily with a small outlaw group. Modern police departments have become large, complex organizations whose many new duties require intimate day-to-day contacts with all citizens. The greatest number of police contacts today is not with the criminal element of society, but rather with the "good" citizens of a community. It has been estimated that at least 90 per cent of all police business is not strictly concerned with criminals.

Extensive use of the automobile has made necessary an increasing number of restrictions upon the driving public, and the old division of the community into lawbreakers and law observers has thus been destroyed.

As long as policemen confined their activities to repression, detection, and investigation of offenses which were common-law crimes, they won a great measure of popular support. However, as the police have become overburdened with duties outside the sphere of what people usually consider enforcement of criminal law, public support has weakened. These additional duties are often of a minor regulatory nature, rarely produce impressive social benefits, and often prove irritating to people who believe they have a right to do as they please.

Defiance of law and authority is not entirely an individual phenomenon. It is practiced by groups as well. The individual whose activities the policeman may be required to restrict is often a symbol of a well-defined racial, social, religious, or economic group. To become involved with such an individual is to invite the resentment of the entire group, and it is extremely easy to become involved, for most members of minority groups are sensitive and defensive.

It is almost a necessary consequence that any efforts of the police to control actions of citizens meet with resistance. The American citizen in many respects is a rugged individualist and strongly resists efforts to control his personal freedom.

No other form of public service is more likely to cause ill feeling among the public it serves than is the enforcement of laws that restrict the citizen and control his conduct. It is of course the *government* which restricts the activities of its citizens; but as far as the individual is concerned, the government is an abstraction. He regards its symbol—the policeman—as the cause of his troubles; his resentment is usually reserved for the police officer rather than for anyone else.

RESULTS OF PUBLIC RELATIONS

Distinct advantages are to be gained from maintaining a spirit of free cooperation with the public. When such cooperation exists, police morale is improved; this is turn leads to increased police effort and improved police service. Difficult programs, which would otherwise be impossible to undertake, then become possible. A general increase in police efficiency results in still greater appreciation of police, creating a desire on the part of citizens to observe laws, comply with regulations, and assist the police in the performance of their functions.

Without the public's assistance, arrests become difficult and convictions almost impossible. Without it, the police are held up to ridicule, criticism, and censure at every move. Under such circumstances, the public overlooks no opportunity to make the task of the policeman more difficult and his working conditions more disagreeable. Legislatures are nothing more or less than segments of the public and thus reflect public attitudes and beliefs. In the courtroom the most carefully prepared cases may fail because the testimony of policemen is ignored or greatly discounted by jurymen who are, after all, only small parts of the public at large and who naturally reflect current attitudes and prejudices.

NEED FOR GOOD LAW ENFORCEMENT

A good public relations program by the police department cannot substitute for poor, inconsistent law enforcement. The police can have the finest organization along with a poor public relations program or a good public relations program along with a poor police department, and neither will be effective.[8]

The police must convince the public that they not only have the finest men and training but are willing to offer their services to the public in a sincere, friendly, and capable manner.

PUBLIC RELATIONS ROLE OF THE POLICE

Too often policemen think that public relations is a job for the chief. He has his public relations responsibilities, but so do they. To the public, each policeman is the chief. He *is* the police department. He is the man most citizens contact and use as a measure of the police service. The policeman does not make top policy decisions, but he decides to a large extent what the people in his city think about the police department and the entire city administration.

The chief and other administrative officers have certain public relations functions, as do

the person or persons in a larger department who may be assigned specifically to public relations duties. Their jobs are important, but not as important or as essential as the policeman's. If all members of the department do not carry their share of the public relations load, administrators and public relations men cannot do very much. Unless the individual officer's relations with the public are good, smooth, and friendly, the work of the others will not be effective.

Police administrators must, therefore, develop procedures and techniques to insure favorable contacts between individual policemen and citizens. It cannot be assumed that policemen, of their own volition and on their own initiative, will develop favorable public relations techniques.

The Issues Re-examined

Having examined the need for development and maintenance of a satisfactory relationship between the police and the public, let us consider some of the issues raised at the beginning of this chapter.

HONEST AND IMPARTIAL POLICE SERVICE

Bad public relations arising out of the Dallas Kennedy-Oswald fiasco, the Chicago police scandal, the Denver police crimes, and charges of police brutality and prejudice in race relations illustrate the fact that honest, impartial, and efficient police service is the first peg upon which all good public relations must hang.

There is no magic formula by which the factors underlying destructive criticism of the police can be overcome. Good public relations can be built only upon sound management and efficient job performance. To bring about a harmonious relationship between the police and the public there is need for professionally trained personnel, humane enforcement of laws, continuous and intelligent supervision, and positive, dynamic leadership.

Police departments must "keep their own houses clean." From a public relations standpoint it is much better for a police department to uncover derelictions and take punitive and corrective action against its own officers who

[8] G. Douglas Gourley and Allen P. Bristow, PATROL ADMINISTRATION (Springfield, Illinois: Charles C. Thomas, 1961), p. 283.

"go bad" rather than to attempt to cover up or "whitewash" the derelictions and outright law violations on the theory that public knowledge of the facts will create bad public relations. When derelictions of individual officers occur, the resulting public relations will be much better if the local police department uncovers and acknowledges the facts than they will be if another agency is forced to do the job. A police department's reputation for swift and open discipline of nonconforming officers can be a real public relations asset.

CIVIL RIGHTS

Police derive their perspective on civil rights from the Preamble to the United States Constitution, as interpreted in the following passage from Professor Fred E. Inbau of the Law College, Northwestern University:

> We can't have domestic tranquility and promote the general welfare as prescribed in the Preamble to the Constitution when all the concern is upon individual civil liberties.
> Individual rights and liberties cannot exist in a vacuum. Alongside of them we must have a stable society, a safe society; otherwise, there will be no medium in which to exercise such rights and liberties. To have rights without safety of life, limb, and property is a meaningless thing. Individual civil liberties, considered apart from their relationship to public safety and security, are like labels on empty bottles.
> This truism that we can't have unbridled individual liberties and at the same time have a safe, stable society is the first message that we must get across to the public.[9]

The police agree that the individual rights of each person should be protected, but they are convinced that individual rights do not include individual *license* and that when the individual rights of one person conflict with the individual rights of all persons in the community then the rights of all persons must prevail. It is their sworn duty to see that this is so.

Police are seeking a balance between freedom and order and this quest is not easy. The United States of America was the first nation in the history of the world to assert that it was possible to merge the two principles of individual freedom and order as complementary—not opposing—forces. Even today many nations reject the idea that a merger of these two ideas of freedom and order is possible.

In recent years the growing complexity of laws and their interpretation has sharpened the conflict between the protection of personal rights and the freedom which officers feel they need to perform their duty. People are at work today who are attempting to develop the concept that the greatest threat to civil liberties is the police, thus placing the public and the police in separate camps. Realistically, police and the community are inseparable. The police are the agents of the people they serve.

REVOLT AGAINST AUTHORITY

The progressive revolution against constituted authority which is shaking the stability of the entire world has produced innumerable examples in this country. The police see themselves as one of the last defenders of order and morality. It is all too common for an officer to be knocked down and beaten as he attempts to defend the law while able-bodied citizens stand by and watch, or, less understandably still, take part in the assault.

On April 27, 1963, a young police officer in New York at great risk to his own life engaged in a gun fight with two hold-up men who had shot and killed an elderly shopkeeper. After a running gun battle the officer captured both of the criminals. One would have expected hearty approval from persons whose neighborhood had been invaded by hold-up men who killed a neighbor while he was defending his meager possessions. But observe this quotation from a newspaper account of the incident:

> An ugly crowd gathered and as squad cars responded to the shooting a rain of bottles and rocks hailed down from roofs on the officers in the street below. However, the police soon got the throng under control and dispersed a crowd of about 100 that was yelling and pushing them about.

This kind of incident is happening much too frequently, not only in New York City, but in many cities across the nation. This is not a

---

[9] Fred E. Inbau, "Public Safety vs. Individual Liberties," THE POLICE CHIEF (January, 1962), pp. 29–33.

typical reaction, but it is occurring with such frequency as to cause great concern.[10]

The police must take the lead in convincing all citizens that they must never lose sight of their identity with the community and its agents, the police. The community and its agencies of justice and security are inseparable. So also are their triumphs and defeats.

POLICE-COMMUNITY RELATIONS

The vital nature of community relations, and more specifically race relations, is being recognized increasingly by police officials. Progressive police administrators are well aware of the vital interdependence between law enforcement and the community, but they insist on being met half way in this relationship.

The Law and Social Order. Social order is the ultimate concern of those interested in community relations. Individuals are free to select their own views on social questions. They are free to organize in an effort to bring about what they consider desirable social change, or to defend the *status quo*. Ultimately, however, peace must be maintained through social controls. The alternatives are chaos and anarchy. The law is clearly one of our most important social controls.

The law and social controls cannot effectively preserve order unless under the law, in practice as well as in letter, there is justice and freedom for all, a single standard in the administration of justice and a respect for the fundamental rights of each and every citizen regardless of race, color, creed, or ethnic origin.

The police methods of 25 years ago are not adequate for today's job. New functions are not suggested for the already overburdened police, but rather more proficient law enforcement based on knowledge and understanding of the community—its people and its problems.

Community Sociological Data. Community sociological data should be of vital concern to the police. Each year one in five persons in the

United States changes his residence. There are only 11 states today with a population that is predominantly rural. Almost 75 per cent of our citizens live in urban communities. These rapidly moving people are of great diversity in ethnic and cultural background, educational level, occupation, race, religion, social class, and many other characteristics. This is the highly complex community relations situation in which the police officer is trying to maintain social order, with justice and freedom for all.[11]

More Than Just Race Relations. Race relations constitute only one aspect of community relations. There are many other aspects which badly need attention. A survey of the attitudes of Los Angeles citizens toward their police department conducted by G. Douglas Gourley in 1952 brought to light many interesting facts, one of which was that of all the occupational groups represented among the 3,100 respondents the one most critical of the police was female school teachers.[12]

Even within the "family" of agencies dealing with various facets of the administration of criminal justice there exist serious problems of communication and mutual understanding. John M. Pfiffner points out that people dealing vocationally with violators of the law fall into two opposing belief systems.

In one category he places the police and custody-minded prison personnel. In the other he includes those engaged in rehabilitation, such as probation and parole, social workers, and therapy-oriented workers in general. For convenience he labels this last group "rehabs."

Pfiffner suggests that law enforcement officials subscribe in general to the classical theory of criminology which holds that the violator is a wrongdoer morally responsible for his acts, and should take the consequence for breaking the law. They feel that the fear of punishment

[10] Lawrence W. Pierce, Deputy Commissioner, New York Police Department, "The Administration of Justice as a Community Responsibility," PAPERS PRESENTED AT THE NINTH ANNUAL INSTITUTE ON POLICE AND COMMUNITY RELATIONS, Michigan State University (May 19, 1963), p. B-7.

[11] Louis A. Radelet, "An Institute With a History," PAPERS PRESENTED AT THE NINTH ANNUAL NATIONAL INSTITUTE ON POLICE AND COMMUNITY RELATIONS, Michigan State University (May 19–24, 1963), pp. C 1–3.

[12] G. Douglas Gourley, PUBLIC RELATIONS AND THE POLICE (Springfield, Illinois: Charles C. Thomas, 1953), p. 90. Since 1958 an effort has been made, with remarkably successful results, to change the attitudes of local school teachers through a workshop in Law Enforcement, Public Schools, and the Community, conducted at California State College at Los Angeles.

is the greatest single factor in deterring people from breaking the law.

The "rehab" stereotype is common to people with humanistic predilections, a value system which is tolerant of man's weaknesses. They are committed to the efficacy of a therapeutic approach based on counseling, supervision, and guidance. The "rehabs" admit that their techniques have not been highly developed and that their effectiveness is uncertain. They are convinced that great effort should be made to rehabilitate criminals and that in the absence of something better, what they are doing is the best procedure available. The police and the "rehab" stereotypes are forever in a state of latent conflict which occasionally breaks out into open hostilities.[13]

Favorable Reaction Amid Tension. Recent years have been a period of tense community relations. It has been evident through mass media reporting that some police agencies conducted themselves better than others in these situations. We can no doubt accept at face value the public tributes paid by leaders of nonviolent demonstrations to the police for exemplary professional behavior in Washington, D.C., St. Louis, Detroit, and several other cities.[14] Even in Selma and Montgomery the strained relations were marked by mutual efforts to maintain order.

The Role of the N.C.C.J. An agency that has taken the lead in developing better police-community relations is the National Conference of Christians and Jews (N.C.C.J.). Starting in 1955 the N.C.C.J. organized and largely financed a national conference of law enforcement personnel and community leaders held at Michigan State University. At this and subsequent national, sectional, regional, state, and local conferences, co-sponsored by educational institutions and law enforcement groups, the role of the N.C.C.J. has been that of convener and coordinator. The N.C.C.J. has organized conferences of law enforcement personnel and other community leaders in which diverse views might be civilly expressed and defended, and in which misunderstanding is reconciled through direct, personal exchange.[15]

Human Relations Training. Realizing that human relations training for police officers is a necessary ingredient in the development of good community relations, the Los Angeles Police Department and the Los Angeles County Sheriff's Department have for many years incorporated this kind of training in their recruit and in-service training programs.

Other major urban jurisdictions which have developed effective human relations training are Dade County (Florida), St. Petersburg, Atlanta, New Orleans, Houston, Dallas, Washington, Baltimore, Wilmington, Philadelphia, Newark, Trenton, New York, Boston, New Haven, Detroit, Chicago, Milwaukee, Minneapolis, St. Louis, Kansas City (Missouri), Louisville, Lexington, Cincinnati, Knoxville, Omaha, Tucson, and San Francisco.

The Policeman as a Person

As Americans we are noted for our reaction to symbols. Among these symbols is the American flag. The police uniform, too, is a symbol of law and order—a symbol of life in a free country. It is true that the police uniform has many negative meanings, but it has many positive aspects as well.

As Americans we set standards for our symbols. We insist that our flag must be clean and never touch the ground. It must be treated with respect. As a symbol of law and order in a free nation, high standards have been set for policemen and the uniform they wear. A higher standard is demanded of them than is expected from the rest of the public. This applies to their appearance, dress, attitude, and conduct. It applies not only when they are on duty but also when they are off duty. Policemen are like fish in a fish bowl—always in view of the public.

Appearance. One of the most important points for policemen to remember is their appearance in public. After they have been on the job for a while, they tend to forget how

---

[13] John M. Pfiffner, THE FUNCTION OF THE POLICE IN A DEMOCRATIC SOCIETY (unpublished paper, 1964), pp. 5–7.

[14] "As Race Tensions Rise," U.S. NEWS AND WORLD REPORT (June 24, 1963), pp. 33–36.

[15] Radelet, *op. cit.*

much attention the public actually pays to a police officer. Almost every minute they are on duty someone is looking at them. Though a man may be the best police officer in the city, the public will not think so if his appearance is poor.

His uniform should fit and be clean at all times. Policemen's uniforms will take a beating, but they cannot be allowed to run down. It will take only a few minutes a day for officers to see that their uniforms are clean, that their brass is well polished, and that their shoes are shined.

Policemen should always be clean-shaven and their hair should be neat. Their hands and fingernails should, of course, be clean.

Bearing. When in public view a policeman should stand erect. He is in a semimilitary organization and should have a military bearing. He should avoid looking like some of the characters he so often has to arrest. He should walk erectly and as if he had a purpose. If he is on patrol he should take time to observe but should not window shop or loaf.

A policeman should avoid unnecessary conversation. The public should never be given the impression that he is just "shooting the breeze." Such conversations may be improperly interpreted, particularly if the other party to the conversation is a good-looking female.

A policeman should not lean on anything or assume awkward positions. He should not spit or smoke on the street. Each department will have regulations concerning smoking in buildings and in automobiles. Policemen should not chew, and this includes gum. Certainly they should avoid eating on the street.

Attitudes. The police, like all governmental employees, must appreciate the fact that the taxpayer's dollar is paying their salaries and that they have to deliver at least a dollar's worth of service for the tax dollar. Police departments, and in fact all public agencies, realize more and more now that it is not enough merely to do the major job of the department or agency. They must do more.

There is seldom criticism of a police department because its members have inadequate knowledge of police procedures, do not make complete investigations, or fail to solve enough

FIGURE 12. *"The police uniform . . . is a symbol of law and order. . . ."*

crimes. Criticisms are most likely to be based on charges of discourtesy or arbitrary treatment of citizens, indiscretion in a police officer's private life, or dishonesty.

It would greatly assist an officer to exercise good judgment if he would occasionally ask himself, "How does this look to others?" or, "How will this affect others?" or "What will be the citizens' reaction to this?" Often *what* police work is done is not nearly as important, from a public relations standpoint, as *how* it is done.

Some policemen have the idea that they should look and act tough. This apparently is for the purpose of scaring people into compliance. Usually it does not have this effect and only serves to make them angry at all policemen. It is a defense mechanism on the part of an officer who is not sure of himself and therefore puts on an "act." Most persons are able to see through the false front and see the officer for what he is. A really tough, competent officer can be relaxed and easily approached by the public.

Policemen as a group are friendly; but being friendly is like being honest. A man must not only be honest; he must look honest. Policemen's friendliness is not measured by what they say it is or even what they think it is. It is measured by what other people think it is. A smile is a good public relations weapon.

Criticism. Policemen must learn to give

criticism sparingly and constructively. They must learn also to accept criticism in the proper spirit. If criticism appears necessary they should criticize the *acts* of individuals, not the individuals themselves. Policemen must also reconcile themselves to criticism. The public as employers of the police has a right to criticize the police constructively.

It is impossible to do an aggressive job of police work without getting some criticism. A policeman who gets no criticism is probably not doing very much police work. So when a citizen wants to complain, let him complain. His complaint may have to be discounted, but he is trying to tell the police something. He may get it all fouled up. He may be a little rude and rough. But, if the police maintain self-control, they can get from him the message he is trying to give. He is trying to tell them something about their service. They should listen to him and not argue. They may learn how their service can be improved. In any event, they will have eased the tension between that citizen and the police.

Pride. Policemen cannot do a good job of selling their service unless they are proud of it themselves. This pride in one's organization is known as *esprit de corps.* They should not of course display superiority or conceit, but unless they are proud of the police job they are doing —and show it—they will have great difficulty in convincing the public that they are doing a good job.

Prejudice. This is one problem that must be solved by every police administrator. Prejudice is derived from the Latin "prejudicium" meaning to prejudge. Webster defines prejudice as "Preconceived judgment or opinion; an opinion or leaning adverse to anything without just grounds or before sufficient knowledge."[16]

While there may be many harmless prejudices, such as those concerning food, colors, clothing, furniture, or makes of automobiles, there are also many of a harmful nature. In the latter category are prejudices against groups of people based on fixed ideas held by one group against another. Such is prejudice against races, religions, nationalities, or occupations.

All people have prejudices of one kind or another. Police officers are human and have as many prejudices as the societies or communities from which they come. The only position which will serve to implement an effective public relations program is to insist that officers be firm with persons involved in an incident according to the degree of their involvement— not according to who they are. They must judge all persons as individuals and not as members of a minority or other special group.

Discrimination is not limited to minority groups. Some officers may dislike a person because of his occupation; school teachers, car salesmen, bus drivers, and others may be discriminated against by some officers. For instance, an officer may have had an unfortunate experience with a top sergeant in the Army and now as a police officer he will retaliate against every sergeant with whom he deals. Other officers may enjoy writing citations to the drivers of certain vehicles such as Cadillacs, hot-rods, or taxis. Police administrators must encourage policemen to make every effort to rid themselves of prejudices, but if they are unsuccessful in this, to at least *conceal these prejudices and not allow them to affect their* official actions.

Setting a Good Example. Police motor vehicle equipment is easily identified by the public and is visible evidence of protection. There is considerable public relations value in clean, attractive automobiles. Of greater importance, however, is the manner and method of operating police vehicles.

Unfortunately, there is an attitude on the part of some officers that they have an inherent right to misuse city-owned equipment and to drive with a reckless disregard for the public. Police officers do not have extralegal privileges in the operation of motor vehicles. Police vehicles should be operated in a manner that is exemplary in courtesy, safety, and obedience to motor vehicle laws.

A survey of the attitudes of local junior college students toward police indicated that generally they were very well thought of. One criticism, however, stood out clearly. This frequently appearing criticism concerned driving habits of police. Complaints were to the effect

---

[16] Gourley and Bristow, *op. cit.,* pp. 273–274.

that police frequently violate unnecessarily the traffic laws which they are enforcing and that they abuse their equipment. As one teen-aged boy said, "What rodders!"[17]

The violation of parking regulations is another frequently observed situation. It is realized that emergencies may require illegal parking, but too frequently some policemen seem to think that a curb painted red (or some other distinctive color) means "reserved for police cars." This is particularly obvious in front of restaurants.

It goes without saying that a policeman will not drink on duty or report for duty with alcohol on his breath. Not only will department regulations prohibit this but the bad public relations effect will be obvious. Off duty they cannot drink to excess, and it probably would be advisable to do any public drinking in another town.

FORMAL EDUCATION

Officers should be encouraged to continue their formal education. A well-rounded education will best prepare the officer to deal effectively with situations which will arise. Citizens cannot help but be impressed by the officers' added effectiveness.

More and more municipalities are encouraging the higher education of their policemen and other employees through various devices.[18]

THE POLICEMAN AS A CITIZEN

A policeman should not only lead an exemplary life, but he should also take an active part in community affairs. He and his wife should be active in local school, church, and other civic activities. Policemen should make every effort to cultivate friends and acquaintances in other walks of life. Only by letting other citizens become personally acquainted with them can policemen expect others to understand them and the problems faced by all policemen.

---

[17] Survey and report by a police science student, California State College at Los Angeles.

[18] G. Douglas Gourley, "Police Educational Incentive Programs," THE POLICE CHIEF (December, 1961), pp. 14–18.

Relationships of the Police

The work of policemen ranges from catching and interrogating hardened criminals to regulating the conduct of and giving information to the best of our citizens. Here is where the trouble lies. Some policemen are not flexible enough to fluctuate between these two extremes. Too often they treat both the few criminals and the many good citizens alike.

WITH THE PUBLIC

Through training and experience, a policeman will find that each situation demands a different attitude on his part. A lost child will require a calm, soothing attitude possibly climaxed by the purchase of an ice cream cone; later, a criminal may require a stern, commanding voice. This may be followed by attempting to direct a lost motorist and later settling a domestic quarrel. In each situation the officer must adapt himself as needed.

The officer will learn that he often becomes involved in tragedies and that people appreciate a kind, sympathetic attitude. Officers must not become emotionally involved in various situations, yet they must offer sincere sympathy to the people involved and render all assistance possible.

An area which is important to good police public relations is notifications, particularly death notices. The manner in which the police notify a survivor of the death of a loved one will linger in a citizen's memory for years. A story illustrating how such notifications should *not* be made is told about a rookie policeman who was instructed to make a notification of the death of a Mr. Murphy in a traffic accident. He was cautioned to break the news as gently as possible. This he promised to do. He rang Mrs. Murphy's door bell; as she came to the door he said, "Does the Widow Murphy live here?"

Assistance to a citizen, even a small courtesy, can sometimes result in large dividends. A highway patrol officer once observed a stalled vehicle about 20 miles from the nearest service station. There was much snow and ice in the area, and another storm was about to start. The officer arranged for transportation to the highway patrol office for the women and children. He then called a tow for the disabled vehicle. The driver of the car was unable to contact anyone at her home. Since the officer was going off duty he transported the women and their children home, going out of his way, on his own time, and using his own vehicle.

One of the women in the vehicle turned out to be the wife of a state legislator who wrote the officer an excellent letter of commendation which was placed in his file. This legislator has since been one of the highway patrol's staunchest supporters and has sponsored pay and fringe benefit legislation for all state employees.

We can sum up the proper method of dealing with the public in a few words. Policemen should be pleasant and courteous and keep in mind at all times that it is their responsibility to do everything they can to solve citizens' problems.

Every police operation has its public relations aspects. Often these public relations overtones are as important to the continued maintenance of public support for the police as are the actual police tasks performed or the technical efficiency of the procedures employed.

Few citizens know the burglary clearance rate in their community, for instance, or how proficient local police are at writing reports. What they do know and remember is the quality of the interpersonal relations that develop between themselves and the officers. They will remember forever the attitude and demeanor of the officers. They will remember whether the officers were courteous or discourteous, sympathetic or unconcerned, interested or indifferent, prejudiced or tolerant.

Special Role of Detectives

The duties of a detective are many and varied. One duty that has not been sufficiently stressed is public relations. This is especially true when there is very little that can be done to solve a particular crime after the officer has finished taking the original report. Victims expect action from their police department and this is what the police department would like to give them, but, unfortunately, many crimes are committed which the police cannot solve.

The detectives can, however, utilize public relations techniques. By contacting the victim periodically and finding out if any additional information may have developed, the detective is in a position to impress the citizen that the police are interested in his case and are doing everything they can to solve it. The crime that is solved quickly has an obvious public relations value.

Good public relations can result also from those cases in which little action can be taken. Regardless of how routine the case is to the detectives, the crime is important to the victim. If he is left with the impression that the police are not doing anything, public relations will suffer. Not only may the victim have an unfavorable opinion of the police, but the friends and relatives to whom he relates the story will also receive an unfavorable impression.

A Los Angeles County Sheriff's Training Bulletin on Preliminary Burglary Investigations recognizes the public relations aspects of criminal investigation. It states:

Deputies responding to a burglary report call should show a noticeable interest in the victim's loss, and by their actions during the preliminary investigation should indicate that they, as well as the entire sheriff's department, will make every effort to recover victim's property and apprehend the suspect. A deputy, upon recognizing a certain "MO," should not inform the victim that the suspect is "running wild" in a certain neighborhood. The victim should be advised, however, that, if he later discovers additional property to be missing, or learns anything regarding a possible suspect, he should contact the station detectives, instead of calling back the uniformed deputies.[19]

A citizen may need to make only one call to the police department during his entire lifetime, but the impression made at this time will be lasting. Some policemen develop an attitude of indifference and boredom toward routine crimes. To a citizen who has had his automobile hub caps stolen, even though he may not be certain where his car was parked, the crime is important.

Good police techniques go hand in hand with good public relations. When detectives at

---

[19] Los Angeles County Sheriff's Department, Norwalk Station, Training Bulletin No. 2 (January 21, 1957).

crime scenes take pictures and check for latent fingerprints the victim will be impressed with good police procedure. The things a detective can utilize to support good public relations are numerous and varied. Basically, however, they all have the same purpose. The victim must be left with the feeling that everything possible is being done, regardless of the seriousness of the crime.

WITH THE CHIEF ADMINISTRATIVE OFFICER

Conflicts or misunderstandings occasionally arise between a chief of police and the city manager or other chief administrative officer. Needless to say such conflicts are harmful to the police department's public relations and should be avoided whenever possible. The most common causes for these conflicts are: (1) the question of who should establish policies for the police department; (2) an alleged isolation complex of the police chief.[20]

Chief administrators have an obligation to establish policies for the entire municipal operation, and chiefs of police have an obligation to conform with federal, state, and local laws and to pursue sound law enforcement techniques. The chief alone is responsible for the internal administration of his department. Misunderstandings arise, however, over differences as to where over-all city policy ends and internal police administration begins.

A chief of police occasionally resents comments which the chief administrator means only as suggestions but which the chief interprets as directives. This interpretation by the police chief is understandable since he often holds office at the will of the chief administrator. Unfortunately, many suggestions made in this way to a chief of police are resented even when he knows they are excellent ones, merely because he feels the administrator is "trying to run his department."

Resentment is sometimes generated even where the chief of police and chief adminis-

trator have established policy by mutual agreement. This may happen when the administrative officer "bends" a policy—that is, makes exceptions to a policy—or asks the police chief to make exceptions in order to take care of ever-pressing problems.

It would seem obvious that good police policy should be set by the combined efforts of the chief administrator and the chief of police, with their mutual understanding and consent. Exceptions to policies should then be made only when absolutely necessary and with the approval of both parties.

A definite understanding should be had between the administrator and the police chief as to what are merely suggestions and what are orders.

Concerning the police chief's alleged isolation complex, administrative officers point out that there is a need for the police chief to see himself as a part of the management team, not as the highest paid policeman working only in his own bailiwick. He should understand the role of the police department in relation to other departments and to the city as a whole. He also needs to understand the mission, nature, organization, importance, and problems of all city departments.

He should cultivate the generalist approach and learn to sense and appreciate the total mission of local government and the police department's relation thereto. He should work closely with the administrative officer and the mayor. He should also work closely with the city personnel officer and be familiar with civil service ordinances, rules, and regulations.

The way the chief handles his financial responsibilities also affects his relations with the city manager and other elective and appointive officers. He must conscientiously follow budgeting, purchasing, and maintenance procedures.

Finally, in order to broaden his administrative outlook, a chief of police should make every effort to improve his knowledge of public and business administration.[21]

[20] Orval Davis, "Relationships between a Chief of Police or Sheriff and His Chief Administrative Officer as seen by a Chief of Police." Address delivered before the Administrative Institute of the Peace Officers Association of the State of California, Los Angeles (March 14, 1962).

[21] John B. Wentz, "The Police Chief or Sheriff as an Administrator." Address delivered before the Administrative Institute of the Peace Officers Association of the State of California, Los Angeles (March 15, 1962).

WITH OTHER MUNICIPAL DEPARTMENTS

One of the police department's many publics with which it must be concerned consists of members of other city departments. There is a tendency on the part of too many policemen to divide city employees into two categories—policemen and other city employees, and to ignore the latter.

One city manager reported that numerous complaints had been received from city employees working at public windows and counters in the city hall which were passed daily, year after year, by policemen without so much as a smile or nod of acknowledgment. Every effort should be made to bring all city employees together on a common ground within the city structure, preferably on a social level.

The opportunities for cooperation with other city departments are numerous. The reporting of broken or extinguished street lights, damaged pavement, and unsanitary health conditions are but a few examples.

WITH OTHER JURISDICTIONS

Some system of mutual cooperation and assistance should always be established. Bad public relations result from disputes over boundaries. In a southern California community an officer was called to the scene of an accident involving an injury and upon arrival was greeted by an antagonistic crowd. The story was too common.

An accident had occurred at an intersection where three jurisdictions come together. Police from a local municipality were first called. Upon their arrival it was decided that the accident had occurred in a second city, the policing of which was contracted for by a county sheriff's department. The sheriff's deputies, in turn, contacted a third jurisdiction, since the deputies were convinced that the accident had not occurred in their jurisdiction. Upon the arrival of officers from this third jurisdiction it was discovered that the injured had remained unattended and that the investigation had not started. At the scene now were officers from three jurisdictions, and nothing had been accomplished. Needless to say, the public relations of all three governments suffered severely.

A system might well be established by interdepartmental agreement whereby under these circumstances the investigation would be made by the first officers to arrive at the scene. If the incident ultimately turned out to be out of the investigating agency's jurisdiction, the reports could be transferred to the responsible agency.

WITH REPORTERS AND MASS MEDIA

Policemen are constantly coming into contact with newspaper reporters. This is not strange, since more news, particularly local news, comes from the police than from any other source.[22]

The feeling of resentment that some policemen develop toward newspaper reporters need not exist. Policemen should learn to understand the job of the reporter. A free press is the foundation of our democratic form of government. One of the outstanding differences between our country and dictator-ruled countries is that the press has the right to print all of the news. Reporters have both a right and an obligation to print all of the news.

It is not meant that all the news of a police nature must be printed. Most reporters realize that circumstances sometimes exist which make the release of information undesirable. When the matter is properly explained, they will withhold or delay the release of this information. Most newsmen will be willing to "sit on" information that would warn suspects not yet in custody. Reporters usually will voluntarily avoid giving details on specific methods of criminal operations.

Policemen should never, however, expect a reporter to withhold facts merely because they, or someone else, want the facts withheld. There must be a good and sufficient reason such as possible harm to the investigation or the existence of a policy of not printing names of juvenile offenders or victims of sexual attacks.

If policemen keep in mind the two major principles of newspaper business they will have very little trouble with reporters. These two principles are (1) that reporters want all of the

---

[22] Richard L. Holcomb, THE POLICE AND THE PUBLIC (Springfield, Illinois: Charles C. Thomas, 1957), pp. 35–36.

news they legitimately can get, and (2) they want it in a hurry. Unless policemen have good reason to believe that a certain reporter cannot be trusted, it will be better for them to let him know the entire story and ask him to withhold information that would be harmful to the case. If they find a reporter who cannot be trusted, the police need usually only go to his boss and they will find that the newspaper will take whatever steps necessary to restore cooperation.

An excellent way to build good relations with the press is for policemen to go out of their way to call attention to situations which may be newsworthy. All policemen in the course of their work observe interesting happenings that would make good news stories. Cooperation will be increased if reporters are notified of these occurrences.

Newspapers and other mass media such as the radio and television help to mold public opinion. If these media are sympathetic to law enforcement officers they will furnish good publicity whenever possible. On the other hand, police should never jeopardize honest and efficient police service in order to curry favor with the press and other mass media, as apparently was done in the Kennedy-Oswald incident.[23]

Special Police Techniques

Police administrators should insure the most favorable contacts between the public and the police by developing workable techniques and implementing them through training. Generally such techniques divide themselves into administrative and field procedures.[24]

ADMINISTRATIVE PROCEDURES

Telephone Contacts. Probably the most important procedure involves police station telephone techniques. A citizen's first and sometimes only contact with the police department often is a telephone conversation with a police-

How are your telephone manners?

1. Answer your telephone promptly.
2. Speak directly into the transmitter.
3. Establish your identity.
4. Listen intently.
5. Avoid transferring calls unnecessarily.
6. Explain delay in obtaining information.
7. Offer to take message.
8. Ask questions tactfully.
9. Apologize for mistakes.
10. Replace receiver gently.

FIGURE 13. *Telephone manners*

man. The citizen's opinion of the entire department may be based on this one conversation. Over the telephone the voice alone must convey an attitude of cooperation and willingness to be of service. (See Figure 13.)

It should be decided just how the complaint telephones will be answered, when and how calls will be referred, and how special callers, such as prowlers and psychopaths, will be treated. Desk officers must then be trained in the desired techniques and their performance periodically inspected.

Although one can understand the urge to give stupid answers to ridiculous questions, one can easily evaluate the public relations effect of the following incident. On one particularly busy night in one of California's beach cities, the desk officer had been deluged by calls, complaints, and irate citizens. The grand finale came when a feminine voice called and stated, "Officer, there is a dead sea gull on my lawn." Before he could control himself the officer replied, "Keep it for thirty days, lady, and if no one claims it, it's all yours."

---

[23] For a more extensive discussion of media relationships, see Chapter 10, "Roles of Reporters and Mass Media," and Chapter 11, "Reporting through the Media."

[24] Gourley and Bristow, *op. cit.,* p. 276.

Follow-up. Another administrative procedure which must be established to prevent a public relations breakdown is a follow-up system. No citizen should ever be required to call a police station twice for service. When a resident calls to report a hazard, and policemen on that shift are too busy to inspect it, the task must be passed on to the following shift. Some method of clearance of calls and follow-up must be formalized and periodically inspected.

A capital example of the critical incidents that may be created by failure to follow up is illustrated by a police department which was requested to inspect an abandoned cistern. The harassed desk officer, due to a lack of system, failed to insure that the following shift would inspect the hazard. Two days later, a child fell into the cistern. Imagine the unfavorable public relations which resulted when the citizen's tale was related to others and spawned rumors!

Vehicle and Station Maintenance. Maintenance of the police station and vehicles also plays an important role in public relations. Stations which reek of tobacco, sweat, and unwashed prisoners scarcely create favorable impressions on the public. Dark hallways, cuspidors, loiterers, comic books, "coke" bottles in public view, and disarranged surroundings are creators of disrespect.

No administrator can afford to disregard property management and the maintenance of a proper working environment. A little pine oil and disinfectant can work a public relations miracle in some stations. Unwashed or damaged, dented police cars also create an undesirable effect on the public.

Some of the results of poor management are an undesirable effect on visitors, promotion of disorderly habits, excessive use of working space, waste of money and materials, disrespect for superiors, lowered morale, and poor *esprit de corps.*

Satisfactory housekeeping and property management require careful planning. Some of the important factors to be considered are:

1. A good housekeeping plan.
2. Definite procedure for making inspections and maintaining property controls.
3. Training employees to keep their desks and office areas clean and orderly.
4. Developing employee pride in the police department.
5. Supplying essential equipment to maintain clean quarters.
6. Improving departmental storage facilities to save space and improve orderliness.
7. Providing adequate natural light and electric lighting facilities.
8. Providing adequate ventilation, humidity, and temperature control.
9. Controlling internal noise by using proper floor covering and sound-absorbing materials on walls and ceiling.
10. Maintaining clean public rest rooms.
11. Providing service facilities for employees.
12. Adoption of a scientific office layout.
13. Painting offices a light color.
14. Establishing a recreation room for use by officers when not on duty.
15. Allowing no loiterers in police quarters.
16. Numbering rooms and installing a conveniently located directory board.
17. Placing names of clerks and officers on desks.
18. Avoiding the appearance of idleness. Officers should not be permitted to loaf or horseplay in corridors or offices.

FIELD PROCEDURES

Almost every act performed by the policeman in the field affects public relations. Limited space requires that we list only a few of the many areas in which procedures should be developed.

Information Guide. Every policeman should be provided with an information guide to better enable him to direct citizens. The police administrator should not blandly assume that officers will, of their own volition, learn the location of points of interest. Attention should also be devoted to methods of giving directions.

Residential Patrol. When a citizen has been on vacation and has requested that police check his residence, a particularly good opportunity occurs to establish favorable public relations. The beat officer, noting the resident's return, should call on him and comment on some detail of the residence involved in the vacation check and, perhaps, make suggestions involving security precautions.

FIGURE 14. *Every act performed by the policeman affects public relations.*

Another favorable opportunity occurs when a new resident is observed moving into the area. Many departments require policemen to call on new residents, explain available police-fire services, and leave handout material on bicycle safety, home poison antidotes, burglary protection, etc.

Traffic Citations. Issuing a traffic citation probably endangers public relations more than any other routine act. Several procedures have been developed by major police agencies, and each has many factors in its favor. Regardless of the techniques available, the most important element is for the police administrator to realize that policemen will not develop these techniques by themselves. The techniques must be adopted by the department, reduced to orders, and implemented by training.

Babies and Flat Tires. Many departments do not give officers credit at all for ordinary public contacts. They only ask their officers to account for arrests, citations, and other traditional measures of police efficiency. This does not present a true picture of the role of the police officer, who is called upon, in exceptional circumstances, to do everything from delivering babies to changing flat tires.

The Rest of the Field. The California Highway Patrol, which is primarily a traffic agency, has developed a form for the purpose of providing a uniform method of recording services rendered to the public when the orders

of the department do not require the use of another specific form.[25]

The form has various squares to check which apply to a given situation; for example, there are squares marked for "oral warnings," "removed traffic hazard," "information," "assisted other agency," and others, with an explanation section. The items are totaled at the end of the work day along with all other activities. This procedure has increased favorable contacts with the public because the officer now gets credit for contacts which are not of a punitive nature.

Other areas in which procedures should be developed to insure favorable public relations are, among others, appearance, posture, driving, smoking, loitering, administering first aid, eating on duty, directing traffic, searching for missing children, making arrests, conduct in the courtroom, and the officer's private life.

An excellent public relations policy statement is contained in the *Manual* of the Los Angeles Police Department. This policy statement appears as Appendix E.

Communication and the Police Image

It was noted earlier in this chapter that efficient police performance is the peg on which all good public relations must hang; but it is not enough. The performance must be communicated, understood, and appreciated. In this respect a police department is very little different from any other organization. The effective performance of its primary function of law enforcement and related problems and needs must be supported by effective reporting.

This obligation to report as well as to perform must be accepted and enthusiastically supported by top administrators. Adequate manpower, authority, and budget must be provided. Effective means of telling the police department story must be marshaled, recognized, and placed in action. Restated, this means that a police department must recognize that it needs an effective reporting vehicle and

[25] Department of California Highway Patrol, "Headquarters General Order," C.H.P. (November 1, 1959), Sacramento, California 51.2.H.G.O.

that it should create and support one adequate for the task and then see that it works out a suitable communications program with the department's many publics. The responsibility of creating and developing information on the department's achievements and needs should be defined and assigned.[26]

NEED FOR MUTUAL INFORMATION

Since police public relations contacts are made under such difficult circumstances and are so important to successful operations, it seems logical that procedures should be devised to measure the status of public relations at any particular time and to determine which police techniques, actions, and attitudes are approved and which are not.[27]

We must not think of the public, however, as one vast body labeled "The Average American." Every police agency deals with many publics of divergent interests and attitudes. The very first thing that should be done in any public relations program is to determine what these many publics think of the police and their service. Only after this has been done will the police be in a position to evaluate their publics' attitudes and, in turn, their own policies, procedures, and services. Only after this evaluation, and any corrective action which may be indicated, will they be in a position to report to their publics and to correct popular misconceptions.

Unfortunately this first important step in police public relations has too often been ignored. Public relations too often has been thought of only as a way for the department to tell citizens those things it feels they should know. Public relations should be mutual. Law enforcement officers and administrators need to keep informed as to what their publics want and to determine which publics are in need of information.

Application of the principle of selectivity to police public relations means that available time, energy, and money will be most effectively applied. There exists a dual mission of informing citizens who most need information about police activities and instructing policemen regarding modes of conduct which bring about the greatest acceptance of their activities.

DETERMINING PUBLIC ATTITUDES

Attitudes, beliefs, and desires can´ be determined in many ways, some of which are rather informal. Determining attitudes in a small city or town may be a fairly simple task, for police officials may be personally acquainted with most of the residents. In larger places the problem is not so simple; but even here, in their day-to-day personal contacts, policemen can learn much of the feeling toward their department and its policies. Advisory bodies made up of representatives of important interest groups provide a good sounding board for public opinion. A very valuable device is to keep track of complaints, commendations, and requests for information.

Probably the most reliable method of appraising attitudes is the public opinion poll. The conduct of such polls or surveys naturally requires special skills. In 1952 an intensive study of citizens' attitudes toward the police was conducted in Los Angeles.[28] Among the outstanding lessons to be learned from this survey are the following:

1. There is an appalling lack of information on the part of the public concerning the caliber of their police and the conditions under which they operate.

2. Women, especially, are lacking in information about their police.

3. Current relations between the police and minority groups leave much to be desired.

(a) recruit and in-service training in race relations should be intensified.

(b) actual performance of police in dealing with members of minority groups must be critically scrutinized, and improved if indicated.

(c) the police should cooperate publicly whenever possible in movements to advance understanding and harmony among persons of all races and creeds.

---

[26] Los Angeles Public Relations Committee, "Report on Study of Police Public Relations for Mayor Samuel Wm. Yorty" (July 2, 1962).

[27] G. Douglas Gourley, "Research in Police Public Relations." Address delivered before the Institute on Police and the Public, Los Angeles State College (March 19, 1962).

[28] Gourley, PUBLIC RELATIONS AND THE POLICE, op. cit., pp. 105–108.

4. Public attitudes (both good and bad) toward the police are primarily the result of personal contacts between individual citizens and individual policemen.

5. In order to obtain the greatest possible approval for the police, the following things must be discouraged by effective selection, training, and supervision:

   (a) attitudes of discourtesy, prejudice, superiority, and indifference; and

   (b) actions of unjustified arrests or citations, rough treatment, and inconsistency of traffic law enforcement.

6. The following things must be encouraged:

   (a) attitudes of courtesy, cooperation, sympathy, helpfulness, and tolerance; and

   (b) actions of honesty, competency, promptness, and assistance of all kinds.

7. The things of which the public most needs convincing are that their policemen:

   (a) have a high professional interest in their work,

   (b) are selected for personal merit,

   (c) operate under excellent discipline,

   (d) apprehend criminals indiscriminately, without regard for pressure brought by influential persons,

   (e) operate independent of press publicity,

   (f) usually apprehend criminals in difficult cases,

   (g) respect the constitutional rights of suspected criminals,

   (h) are usually fair in dealing with minority groups,

   (i) are careful not to arrest innocent persons, and

   (j) are directed by competent supervisors and top administrators.

10

Roles of Reporters and Mass Media

Democratic government is, in essence, government by consent. A police state relies outwardly on repressive measures to secure compliance, but is heavily dependent on inertia and apathy among its subjects to maintain internal order. In a free society most public officials realize tacitly that legislation which imposes obligations or restricts rights can best be implemented by gaining public understanding of the necessity for such legislation and acceptance of its ultimate purpose. It is a maxim in the United States that an unpopular law is an unenforceable law. The widespread publicity given to anti-litter legislation illustrates this point. There simply are not enough police to enforce such legislation. Harsh and punitive treatment of offenders would lead to resentment of the law and, ultimately, outright resistance to its enforcement. When an occasional offender is cited and punished, it is in the interest of government that maximum publicity be given the case for the purpose of dramatizing the need for anti-litter laws.

Anti-narcotics legislation is another case in which experts, legislators, and administrators alike prefer education to enforcement as a means of securing compliance. Public health laws constitute still another example. A public information program urging citizens to take polio vaccine is considered more effective than legislation requiring them to do so.

This important truth is frequently overlooked, however, in the day-to-day, routinized operations of government. To further complicate the problem, administrators too often lack the basic motivation necessary to induce them to promote voluntary compliance. A new ordinance requiring dogs to be on a leash while on the streets will bring a strong chorus of protest from dog owners and lovers if rigidly enforced at the outset by a humane department which has neglected to enlist and guide support from the press and the public in an informational campaign.

A matter of attitude is also involved. Too many officials consider the public relations function of management marginal at best. In this view, public relations is a managerial responsibility to be attended to if there is time or if there are not other, more pressing matters at hand. There is a lack of understanding that attention to public relations can make the whole task of governing a great deal easier and more pleasant for the official.

Not only is public relations a help to the public administrator who is trying to get his job done, but the avenues of communication with the public are open to him in a manner that makes the commercial public relations man envious. The public official does not have to buy, wheedle, or beg his way into print. The media of mass communication come to him. While this is not true in every community, it is generally correct to say that local government is considered by the news media to be a primary source of news and comment. The press recognizes that citizens expect it to monitor government and to keep them informed, not simply of setbacks and mistakes but of progress and of plans for the future.

The Role of the Press

The First Amendment to the United States Constitution contains the historic guarantee of freedom of the press. Under this guarantee it has been both the privilege and the responsibility of the press—including television, radio, and periodicals as well as newspapers—to concern itself with government. News—defined as anything which is timely, important, and interesting—about government is reported not only to sell papers and advertising but to keep the electorate informed, which the press feels is its special responsibility. If newsmen seem to the public officials to be more prying and curious about governmental affairs than about the affairs of other social institutions, the official must bear in mind this special obligation which the press traditionally has felt it must meet.

As James MacDonald has put it:

In part that responsibility of the press is (1) to report, explain, and make understandable to the people their government wherever possible; (2) to protect the general public against shenanigans either by special interest groups or by public officials; (3) to support by explanation and news coverage such officials, programs, and causes as—in the best judgment of the reporter and his editors—are necessary for the general public; and (4) to give the citizen the information he needs to decide if his government is working satisfactorily, on the theory that our type of government is best for the individual.

But in a more basic sense, that responsibility is twofold: (1) to help government officials make a public accounting of their administration and (2) to make certain that government at all levels operates in the public eye.[1]

There have been, and always will be, differences of opinion between the press and the government as to the extent of the obligation of public officials to make information freely available to the press. Administrators, acting in what they sincerely consider to be the public interest, object to premature or partial disclosure of proposed policies and plans, and of

operations of a developmental nature. The press is accused, or at least suspected, of selecting only the controversial or sensational items for coverage, rather than presenting a balanced picture of government. On the other hand, spokesmen for the press emphasize the need for the fullest possible coverage so that the electorate will not be denied information about incompetence, wrong-doing, or illegality in government. Somewhere between the two points of view lies an as yet undefined middle ground, the essence of which must rest upon a mutually accepted formula for responsible reporting of public affairs.

The Nature of News

Since the press has not one but several major components, the concept of news is a difficult one to define. It is important for the public official to have a working knowledge of the journalist's concept of news, since he himself is a source of news and on occasion is a figure in the news. The manner in which his and his agency's work is reported in the news has a significant bearing on its effectiveness. Some agencies are more often in the news limelight than others. The activities supervised by the director of public welfare are apt to be reported more fully than those of the county clerk. It is particularly important that administrators who work in what might be termed sensitive areas of government be aware of both the advantages and the problems of their position vis-à-vis the press.

The press cannot attain complete coverage of a community. The newspaperman is not a social historian seeking to record all of the pertinent details in the life of a city or metropolitan area. Space and time are scarce, and competition for a place in the paper or time on the newscast is an essential element of journalism. The reading, listening, or viewing public has only a vague idea as to what it wants to read or hear in the limited amount of time it can devote to current affairs. The editor and the reporter, however, must have general guidelines to follow to inform the public about pertinent news of local government.

---

[1] James C. MacDonald, PRESS RELATIONS FOR LOCAL OFFICIALS (Ann Arbor: Institute of Public Administration, University of Michigan, 1956), p. 3.

A standard text on reporting gives this definition of news:

News is a report of an event containing timely (or at least hitherto unknown) information which has been gathered and written by trained reporters for the purpose of serving the reader, listener or viewer.[2]

Timeliness, accuracy, and reader interest are the essential qualities of news. The consumer of news is served when he is furnished with information which affects or potentially affects his thinking or his behavior. He receives information which affects, or may affect, his life or well-being. Reports of a wave of hoodlumism on the city streets may make him more cautious in his coming and going at night, and may move him to complain vigorously to his councilman or city manager.

The emphasis placed by the press on timeliness may seem exaggerated to many a public official who is accustomed to the deliberate, often cautious pace of events in government. It is wise, however, to accept journalism's point of view that news is a perishable commodity that should be delivered to the consumer with all possible speed. In those cities in which there are competing newspapers it is the aim of each paper to beat the opposition. Newspapers, television, and radio all strive to be the first with the news, though newspapers have become reconciled to the ability of their competitors to report spot news first. Even where there is no competition, the reporter and news editor attach great importance to timeliness. By tomorrow, today's news, in their eyes, will have lost some of its impact. Editors of morning papers may tolerate the use of the word "yesterday" in the lead paragraph of a story, but there are afternoon papers which will not permit its use if there is any way to avoid it. Television and radio stations work at even a faster pace. The public official should keep in mind that the extent of coverage of his agency's activities depends heavily on this element of timeliness.

There is a notable exception, in news about government, to the strict definition of timeliness emphasized above. Features and human

interest stories can be developed over a period of time for release in a special supplement or a program on a "dry" news day. The following excerpt from a news story illustrates feature treatment of a series of developments over a period of time. It was printed during the news lull between Christmas and New Year's Day:

Two separate plans for preserving and enhancing the natural beauty of Skyline Blvd. on the ridges of the coast mountain range overlooking the mid-peninsula are spinning in governmental hoppers.

One of the plans, a state proposal to include the winding mountain road and its immediate environs in a new scenic highway system, definitely appears headed for adoption early next year, officials indicated today.

The other concept, less certain at this point, involves inclusion of Skyline in a proposed West Coast Skyline National Parkway under jurisdiction of the National Park Service.[3]

Accuracy is as much a matter of primary concern to the public official as to the press. The official should devote special care to insuring that the reporter has the fullest possible information and understanding of the matter to be reported. The first few pages of Chapter 11 are devoted to suggestions on how to help the newsman get the information and background he needs and to report them accurately. Finally, what is reported must be left to the judgment of the editorial staff; this aspect of journalism is discussed below.

The Nature of the Newsman

Newsmen differ from one another just as much as lawyers, teachers, or public officials. It is dangerous to attempt to attribute common characteristics to members of an occupational group. But since administrators must deal with newsmen, it may be helpful to provide some broad perspective within the limits of which many, but not all, newsmen will fall. Hopefully this, together with a description of the reporter's job, will lay the groundwork for a better understanding of the official's role in municipal public relations. Even more important, it may help to dispel some stereotypes about newsmen

[2] Phillip H. Ault and Edwin Emery, REPORTING THE NEWS (New York: Dodd, Mead & Co., 1959), p. 16.

[3] PALO ALTO TIMES, December 28, 1962.

which can lead to misunderstanding and conflicts between officials and newsmen.

Let us take a look at a hypothetical newsman who has a set of characteristics which a majority of editors would agree are desirable ones. The editor would hope to find some if not all of these characteristics in the people on his staff. The public official must learn for himself which of the several newsmen with whom he comes into contact have the characteristics listed below and therefore can be considered competent professionals:

1. Motivation: Typically, motivation toward a career in journalism is high, having originated in college or even in high school. There is an interest in creative use of the English language which finds fulfillment in the daily routine. There is a desire to get the facts and report them accurately. However, the newsman is definitely not a research worker, searching out all that is to be known. He must contend with deadlines. Motivation based on interest must be fairly strong because the material rewards of journalism are not high, working conditions are not as pleasant as in many other fields, and certainly there is relatively little glamour in the typical newsman's work.

2. Pride in Work: As a corollary of motivation the newsman has a proprietary interest in his work. Journalism is a field in which creative, imaginative people have opportunities for self-expression. Therefore there is a sense of pride in being able to get a story and to get it into print, especially if it has special elements of timeliness and exclusiveness.

The reporter

is a professional.

He is . . .

1. motivated to do a hard job well

2. proud of his work

3. well educated

4. curious about the world around him

5. deserving of your trust

FIGURE 15.

The newsman is sensitive about his judgment with regard to the news value of an event. He will do a technically competent job in writing a story which has more public relations than news value, but prefers to cover truly newsworthy events. An example would be a story in support of a municipal bond issue (public relations) as contrasted with the hiring or firing of a city manager (news).

3. Intellectual Curiosity: The newsman wants to know what is going on in the world about him. The more experienced he becomes, the more apt he is to want to look beyond the obvious, often superficial, explanation for a deed or event. He develops cynicism about people and their motives, causing him to probe for answers. He dislikes pretense and is particularly resentful of a patronizing attitude on the part of those to whom he goes for news. This does not mean that he dislikes people, for typically he is an intensely social being.

4. Education: The newsmen of today are recruited from the ranks of college graduates. Some of the courses the reporter has taken may well have been in journalism, but the bulk of his work will have been in the social sciences and humanities. He is not a scholar, but he has a framework of understanding about society and the forces which affect human events. He is better prepared than his predecessors of a generation ago to explain and interpret the news insofar as he is permitted to do so by the editorial policy of his media. More will be said of the interpretive function of the newsmen in the concluding section of this chapter.

A few more characteristics deserve brief mention. The newsmen with whom public officials deal face-to-face tend to be relatively young. Most men and women enter the field of mass communications as reporters and later move to editorial, executive, or other specialized positions which tie them to a desk. Also there is a relatively high turnover caused by people moving to other fields of work. Public officials should be aware that there is a growing sense of professionalism in journalism, creating more and more interest in and discussion of standards and ethics.

The technological revolution through which our society is moving is affecting journalism as it is other occupations. As a result of this revolution, minimum standards of competence are rising and the poorly- or badly-prepared will lose out to the more competent. This is a trend to be welcomed by public officials, for it will help them in the difficult job of transmitting information on public affairs to citizens of their communities.

The majority of newsmen will respect off-the-record background information provided by public officials in briefing sessions because it helps them deal with the complexities of their job. Also, they will protect their sources of information except when ordered by a court, under penalty of punishment for contempt, to reveal them. It should be noted that newsmen lack a firm legal basis for protection of news sources, except in the dozen states which have enacted statutes specifically providing such protection. Some reporters, however, do not subscribe to the idea that off-the-record information is a sacred trust. The public official must be cautious until he knows his newsmen.

Quest for Reader Interest

Extensive studies of reader interest have been conducted in recent years in an attempt to learn what the consumer wants and expects from the news media. It has been found that reader interest is affected by three important concepts: significance, proximity, and prominence.[4] Significance is attached to news when the reader clearly sees its consequences for himself.

President Kennedy's announcement of the blockade of Cuba in late 1962 had enormous significance for most Americans because they realized that such a move might lead, as the President warned, to retaliation by the U.S.S.R. The use of nuclear weapons on American cities could not be ruled out. News that a city's sewer plant must be replaced has significance because it is immediately clear that a new plant must be paid for out of tax revenues. Much news stemming from local government is significant because it reports actions that will have an immediate effect on numbers of citizens.

If local officials desire full news coverage of the activities of their agencies, they should be encouraged by the importance of the factor of proximity. Local news has great pulling power on readers. A story about local government will normally win more readers than one about state government. But the term "local news" is a slippery one to define. As population has spread over great metropolitan areas with their numerous suburbs, community or suburban newspapers or radio stations have appeared, augmenting the mass circulation and mass audience media which typically have their seat of operations in the central city. While the percentage of total newspaper circulation commanded by the great metropolitan newspapers has declined, the circulation of suburban papers has increased.

People still are greatly interested in what is going on close to home, and the smaller papers focus on this concern. For example, the location of a proposed branch of city hall or a new fire or police station may earn little or no coverage in a metropolitan daily, but will be given full coverage in a regional or suburban paper.

The factor of prominence is a source of both benefit and trouble to local officials. The mayor, councilmen, city manager, and department heads typically can command news coverage for an announcement of a proposed new policy or program. Pronouncements on tax rates, city services, or relationships with the state or national governments will be considered news. Conversely, a public official who criticizes or attacks another official or an action or program of local government gains publicity easily. An off-hand remark or inadvertent comment by a prominent public official may make news in a way he did not anticipate. Reporters quickly find news in disagreements, which may be more apparent than real, between public officials. What prominent people in government do or say is always potential news.

Human Interest Approach

Wherever there are people, there is potentially a human interest story. If human interest is present, other factors are less important. Government is often placed in the position of being an arbiter in situations of conflict, and conflict is a major source of news. Government is also responsible for a good deal of innovation and progress, another source of interesting news.

---

[4] This material is drawn from Ault and Emery, *op. cit.*, pp. 19–25.

Government officials who are alert to human interest stories are in a position to advance public understanding and sympathy for the endless contributions which government makes to the welfare of the community. The unfortunate image of government as a large impersonal bureaucracy whose employees are unconcerned with the trials and tribulations of "John Citizen" can be offset to some degree by inviting the attention of reporters to potential human interest stories.

In some communities the public official faces the problem of stimulating the interest of the news media in covering news of local government. In such communities it would appear that the press is not carrying out its democratic responsibility to keep the electorate informed. The reasons for this situation are legion. The solution, if there is any at all, depends on patient, unyielding efforts on the part of local officials to improve coverage.

In general, however, the press carries more coverage of local government than can be justified solely by the criteria of what makes news. Newspapers have contributed space generously to help achieve civic goals desired by municipal government. The television commentator's report on a youth-in-government program sponsored by the city manager has some human interest value but the story otherwise has little to commend it as news in competition with other more dramatic or topical events. It is covered as news because the commentator feels it is the type of incident the viewing public should know about.

Generally speaking, however, the local public official must compete for reader interest with news of national and international significance and with crime news, the comics, and the sports and society sections. In this situation, whenever possible, he should attempt to find a means to appeal to the potential reader's or viewer's self-interest by identifying his stake in the subject.

Even if the local public official succeeds in getting a news item into the paper, there is no certainty, according to reader interest studies, that it will be read or, if read, remembered. Continuing coverage of a story is important. A single item may be missed by a large percentage of readers, listeners, or viewers; a series of stories will reach a much larger audience than one-time coverage. New developments, new angles, and new comments are grist for the news mill. The development of a new master plan, construction of a new civic center, mall, or convention hall, or the installation of automatic data processing equipment is good for continuing coverage for a period of weeks, months, or even longer, if the officials in charge are aware of the nature of news and alert reporters to fresh material.

For example, the utilization of automatic data processing equipment is so novel that new applications of ADP to the study of governmental problems will probably be newsworthy. An imaginative approach to the release of periodic progress reports on a community survey or study will help to develop public involvement in the project.

Crusade for Clarity

To the concepts of significance, proximity, and prominence discussed above should be added another, that of clarity. The public official and newsman share responsibility for making the news clear and understandable to the public. Clarity is particularly important when the electorate is called upon, as it so often is, to cope with public issues involving technical or abstract concepts. The intricacies of issues of public policy in the fields of planning and zoning, industrial development, race relations, and public health, for example, bring forth debate and disagreement even among experts. Are the pros and cons presented clearly and accurately by the press when such issues are debated in election campaigns or in discussion of proposed ordinances or charter revisions? Scott Greer, director of the Center for Metropolitan Studies, Northwestern University, has forcefully stated his view of the problem to newsmen in these words:

You are becoming so complicated you are forgetting how to be good journalists. You are trying to be educators, social scientists, psychiatrists, experts on medicine, city planners and all the rest. So you are becoming partisans and second-guessers. You know so much about everything else you just don't know how to get out good newspapers.[5]

The point of Dr. Greer's remarks is that the voters cannot make informed decisions on such issues as planning or metropolitan consolidation unless the debate in the press is carried on in language they can understand, and they are given concepts they can grasp and appreciate. Technical people in government tend to use technical language which reporters incorporate into their stories without adequate interpretation

Speaking in the same context, Samuel Lubell, the well-known opinion analyst, made a number of suggestions to newsmen on handling technical material. Government officials can apply these hints to their own public relations efforts. Lubell's concern stemmed from interviews with citizens in communities in which various plans for establishing metropolitan government were under discussion. He found that citizens in these communities had learned almost nothing from newspaper campaigns about these plans. This experience led Lubell to make the following suggestions:

1. Avoid technical language.
2. Think and write in terms of people rather than abstract issues. People like to read about other people but often pass by stories presenting ideas.
3. Controversy is important; show there are two or more sides and give the different sides clearly.
4. Use visual aids.
5. Running stories, full of statements on technical subjects, lose their audience. Newspapermen must be as creative as city planners in thinking up ways to revive the running story, to give it fresh starts periodically.

Public officials should not conclude from this list that Lubell thinks that voters are so simple-minded that ideas can or should be downgraded as news. Rather, it is the manner in which ideas are presented that concerns him. The gist of his argument is that issues must be dramatized to the degree that readers will pay attention to the ideas inherent in the issues.

Reducing the complexity of the potentially newsworthy materials about government is a task falling squarely on the shoulders of administrators. Government is increasingly staffed by experts and the amount of jargon grows apace. Despite the added emphasis placed on teaching about civic affairs in our schools, citizens are simply not well enough informed on the technical aspects of the public service to permit the use of specialized terminology without explanation. This is the time to remind the public official of the politician's maxim: Never overestimate the public's fund of information, but never underestimate its intelligence.

The crusade for use of simple direct language has had some beneficial effects in governmental circles but communication is still badly impeded by the tendency to use technical jargon and "bureaucratese" which lacks meaning even for the knowledgeable reporter. If the administrator insists on making it hard work for the reader or viewer to comprehend his policy or plan, he has no one to blame but himself. It is no crime to "popularize" a story so long as no violence is done to its basic facts or implications. It has become standard practice to keep the public informed of the latest developments in science and medicine by the writer or commentators specially skilled in translating highly technical materials into understandable concepts. Government is badly in need of "popularizers."

In a well-governed community virtually every act of government is performed for the benefit either of the citizenry at large, or of some particular group of citizens. Unfortunately, news about government seldom is reported in such a way as to make the benefits immediately apparent. Every expenditure tends to be presented as a burden to the taxpayer rather than as the purchase of a good or a service related to a function that has been prescribed by law as a result of the democratic process.

Of course a traditional antigovernment bias is at work in the reporting of governmental affairs, and it is not suggested that manipulation of the news is the way to overcome this bias. Administrators, however, should make every effort to report the activities of their agencies in a positive manner in terms of the goal sought and the results achieved.

---

[5] Comments made at the Opinion Reporting Workshop held at Columbia University in June, 1963, as reported in EDITOR AND PUBLISHER, Vol. 96 No. 26 (June 29, 1963), p. 50.

The argument for performance budgeting might be applied to reporting about public affairs on the ground that the reading public is interested in, but seldom reminded of, the goals and ends of government. Taxpayers are told at length about the means—the dollars involved —but seldom are told of the uses to which the dollars will be put in terms of programs. It would be refreshing to see a headline which reads "Defense Budget to Buy 2-Million-Man Nuclear Force" rather than "President Sets Defense Budget at Record $40 Billion." To obtain compliance and cooperation from the citizen, it would be a wise move on the part of the administrator to stress constantly the benefits which the citizen may expect to gain from his program.

Clientele-Oriented News

It is apparent that a number of governmental programs are designed for particular clienteles. A playground recreation program is of particular interest to young children and their parents; a community senior citizens program is of primary interest to retired persons; library service is of particular concern to those who regularly patronize the public library. These clientele groups are sizable, and can provide support to administration when support is needed. Feature and human interest stories can be found in the activities of these clientele-oriented programs if one looks at them with imagination and an eye for news.

Television stations are particularly interested in dramatic incidents which show briefly the work of an agency or institution. A report on a civic luncheon held on the top floor of an unfinished government building, with prominent citizens dining amid the skeleton of steel girders, emphasizes progress and growth, both of which rank high in the American scale of values.

To sum up, it should be emphasized that there is not one audience but a number of different audiences for the drama of government. There is a great variety of news in almost every activity of government for one or more of these audiences. Reporters lack the time and

often the knowledge to dig out stories of special activities for specialized clienteles; they need the help of administrative personnel familiar with the activities and aware of their news potential.

The media differ in their interests in the news. A newspaper may present a detailed analysis of the annual budget, but statistical details are not suited for lengthy treatment on television or radio. The latter media, however, can stage interesting and informative interviews with public officials. A radio or television interview presents the full give and take of the question-and-answer format, while a newspaper would decline to print any more than a brief summary of the remarks made. The large metropolitan dailies and major television and radio stations tend to present only the highlights of local government news, exercising extreme selectivity and leaning toward brevity. Suburban and smaller city media tend to be selective in material judged to be of interest to their respective audiences, but are inclined to give more comprehensive coverage to stories they do decide to use.

In this age of high mobility of the population and rapid urban growth, people tend to lack community roots and have no familiarity with the background of news. Spot news about local government does not permit the public to gain an awareness of relationships, of cause-and-effect sequences, or the background to community problems. A report of rising governmental expenditures or a tax increase does not contribute to the citizen's understanding of his government unless reasons for the rise are explained and the relationship of this increase to past and future trends is given.

It is the administrator's responsibility to provide the reporter with a maximum of background information organized so that it is readily useful. The extra effort required is not simply a favor to the reporter—it is a contribution to citizen understanding. In rapidly growing communities, background information is necessary for virtually every news development because many citizens lack knowledge of what has gone before. If supplementary explanatory and interpretive material is not used in the main story, it may well be utilized in "sidebars" or accompanying stories or in follow-up feature stories.

Key People in the Mass Media

To maintain good working relations with reporters, it is essential to know something about the internal organization of a newspaper. As the result of tradition and the speed which characterizes the publication of a newspaper, responsibilities are carefully defined and delegated to a number of subordinate executives. It is essential for the outsider to go through channels, much as in a military organization. The reporter is by no means a free agent, a fact he understands and accepts. The news side or desk, generally presided over by the managing editor, has supervision over the news content of the paper. All news copy, with certain exceptions, flows to the news desk and its components for processing.

The city side or desk, whose chief is the city editor, is responsible for knowing what is going on in the community and for covering the local news through assignments to reporters and photographers, the writing of the stories, and the length and placement of the resulting news items. The city editor is responsible to the managing editor or editor-in-chief, who in turn reports to the publisher, who is the newspaper's chief executive. As in a military organization, responsibility for what is printed rests on this top executive. He too is subject to limitations, but of a different nature. Restrictions imposed by the law of libel and postal regulations are obvious. Additional limiting factors include the basic editorial policies of the owner, the fact that the paper is a business enterprise which must make money to survive, the financial resources of the paper, the amount and kind of news available on a given day, and the nature of the community in which the paper is published.

The news organization of the typical television or radio station is more simple than that of a newspaper. A news director, responsible to the station's over-all program director, has general supervision of the gathering and processing of the news. Under the news director is a news editor who gives specific assignments to the news staff, controls the content of newscasts, and often covers stories himself.

Despite the newspaper's elaborate managerial hierarchy, it is upon the reporter that the city official is largely dependent for news coverage. Rarely will the city editor interfere with the prerogative of the reporter to gather the news, except to assign him to obtain particular stories or to look into potentially news-worthy situations. The competent reporter knows where and how to get the news, and maintaining good relations with him is important for good news coverage.

The reporter has a real advantage over the official if a spirit of antagonism arises between them. Giving the news or voicing a complaint directly to the reporter is the best course of action. Going over his head in either case will arouse resentment. A reporter is essentially a craftsman, albeit a well-educated one, and has pride in the personal creativity involved in his work. He likes to be treated with the respect due a competent craftsman, not as an employee of a large business firm. Like other craftsmen, he recognizes that he is human, that he makes mistakes, and that his work can be improved.

"I was misquoted" is the most common reaction of the news source when he feels that his views have not been reflected fairly in the press. Often, however, the criticism of distortion is based on the headline rather than the story itself. The criticism may be perfectly justified. Headlines are written by copyreaders on the desk and not by reporters. If there is distortion, the reporter and the news source both may feel offended and both may complain to the desk, where the responsibility lies.

There is one circumstance in which the blame for an inaccurate headline may be placed on the reporter. This is when he did not make his principal point clear in the story, with the result that misinterpretation on the part of the copyreader is understandable. It should be mentioned, too, that copy desks edit and cut stories. If a pertinent sentence or paragraph is cut out or modified, changing the meaning of the story, it is not the reporter who is at fault. Officials should realize, however, that a reporter may try to pin the blame for his own failings on mistakes or incompetence of the copy desk.

In any matter requiring a policy decision in his relations with the press, the public official must go directly to the managing editor, station manager, or other top executive. For example, press cooperation in a campaign for a proposed bond issue or clean-street drive would require top management endorsement.

Covering City Hall

The highly organized process of newsgathering centers around the "beat." This may be defined as a predetermined and continuing assignment of potential news sources to a reporter. Some beats are assigned on the basis of subject, some on the basis of geography and some on a combination of the two factors. News of finance, science and education may be covered on large dailies by full-time specialists. Similarly, a large paper may have a political writer who covers major stories in the area of politics and government, writes features, and handles special assignments.

All dailies, large and small, have reporters who are assigned to cover news of local government on a routine basis. On smaller papers the local government beat usually goes to a young reporter; conversely, on large dailies the city hall man is usually experienced and knowledgeable. The beat reporter pays daily visits to key offices and departments—the mayor, city manager, the planning, police, fire, and other major service departments, and to those county, state, and federal offices that are apt to produce news regularly.

Some offices are checked by phone every day, and these calls are followed up by a personal visit if warranted. Offices which are major sources of news are checked regularly by phone between visits. For example, the coroner's or medical examiner's office is a key source of news tips about deaths by violence. Beat reporters typically cover meetings of the city council, county board, and local commissions.

Considering the extent of the coverage and the curiosity of newsmen, it is surprising that there is not more news of local government in our daily papers. Perhaps part of the fault lies in the failure of public officials to use the media to full advantage.

Since there are not enough working hours in the day to cover all potential sources of news about government, beat reporters depend heavily on tips on potential stories from a wide variety of people in government. These include switchboard operators, secretaries, counter clerks, and various deputies and assistants. News informants are usually subofficial employees—people in the know but not high enough in the hierarchy to be quoted as sources. Every journalism text advises the potential reporter to establish rapport with people who can provide leads.

Reporters also look for help from people whose expert knowledge they respect. The budget officer, principal planner, traffic engineer, and specialist in communicable diseases typify subject matter experts whose assistance will be sought for background and amplification. While an expert cannot often expect credit in print, he can obtain satisfaction from the opportunity to enlighten the public.

Routine news gathered by beat reporters goes to the copy desk in the form of stories written at the reporter's own desk or telephoned from a pressroom in a government building. At the copy desk the process of editing, cutting, and sometimes rewriting takes place.

On a major story—say a recommendation for new taxes—a general or special assignment reporter may be sent by the city editor to take over from the beat man. Similarly, the city editor may direct a general assignment man to do a feature story. Although the general assignment man is an experienced reporter, he probably will lack any real familiarity with the subject matter. In dealing with him, the public official should take special care to provide background and explain technical aspects of the story. (See Figure 16.)

To illustrate, assume that a nationally known consultant on airport construction is in town to start a survey for a new airport. The local airport manager should be prepared to provide a full briefing for the general assignment reporter who is assigned to interview the

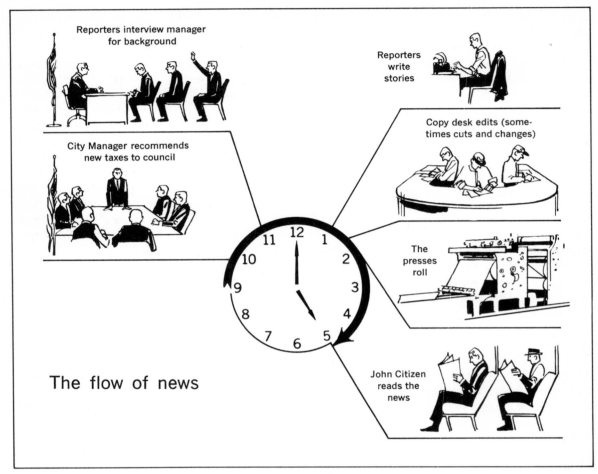

The flow of news

FIGURE 16.

visitor. Without a briefing, the reporter is apt to make errors of fact and incorporate mistaken conclusions in his story.

Frequently an official will be contacted by a reporter who asks for reactions to a story from the state or national capital. Invariably the query is how the development reported in the story will affect the local government. An "I don't know" or evasive answer will, if it appears in print, suggest to the public that the official lacks competence or is not keeping up with events.

In this fast-moving and interrelated world, the official must keep abreast of what is happening in his field in Sacramento, Albany, Springfield, or Washington, D.C., and must anticipate questions as to how the events will affect his own jurisdiction. This is particularly true during a session of the state legislature or when a matter of special concern to the local government is under active consideration in Washington.

There naturally are differences in the mechanics of news coverage between the large metropolitan paper and the suburban daily. The latter will be concerned only in special cases of local interest with what is going on in the government of the central city or the county. The suburban city editor certainly would cover developments in a regional project involving the suburb in negotiations with a larger government. He deserves cooperation, since the friendship and good will of the suburbs are vital to the programs of the central city, county, or other large governmental authority. The metropolitan paper will cover governmental news of the suburbs in fairly abbreviated fashion. Its staff will rely on telephone calls to suburban officials or on part-time "stringers." The stringer usually is a reporter on a suburban or small city daily or weekly paper.

The mechanics of radio and television news coverage are taken up in Chapter 12.

Keeping the Facts Straight

Accuracy is one of the prime requisites of the press; readers and news sources alike are quick to let the media know about mistakes. The factor of speed and the imposition of rigid news deadlines, as well as human frailties, lead inevitably to mistakes. Such mechanical devices as teletype machines and Linotypes are sources of error also.

In the light of the importance of maintaining good relations with reporters there arises a nice question as to whether it is worth while to ask that minor errors be corrected. When the story is subject to continuous coverage, minor errors may not be important. Every effort should be made, of course, to obtain the correction of a serious error as, for example, in the cost of a major capital outlay project or the projected tax rate for next year.

If the correction or retraction does not satisfy the official—especially if a question of interpretation is involved—a carefully considered letter to the editor is an appropriate course of action. Surveys have shown that letters to the editor have high reader interest. The letter should not be argumentative or inflammatory. It should be brief and should set forth the facts as the official sees them. The tone of the letter is important for it is one of the facts of life that no matter how seriously the paper or station seems to offend, the press always has the last word if it wishes to.

An occasion may arise in which the official cannot arrive at a satisfactory solution to a problem—let us say of what he feels is consistent misinterpretation of his point of view by an unfriendly or uncooperative newspaper. In this situation MacDonald suggests three major avenues of recourse:

First and best, of course, would be a frank conference with the editor or publisher of the paper to try to straighten out the difficulties. If that fails to improve matters, pressure could be applied through tactics designed to make the newspaper see that government news coverage is a two-sided proposition. . . .

Most officials are probably familiar with tactics they may employ to harass the press: making records difficult to obtain; sitting on developments until they become old stuff; refusing to explain developments in detail. These devices may or may not work, depending upon the circumstances.

In any event it is important to remember that newspapers are not the only sources of news distribution. So a third possibility is extra effort to get a local government's story across through some other means. . . . Some cities distribute newsletters through taxbills or by other means. The speaker circuit is a very important outlet which should not be neglected. Groups and organizations often have more direct influence on key citizens than does the information casually consumed through the press.[6]

The Question of Secrecy

Governmental secrecy is a problem that has been dealt with at length in the law, commentaries on the law, court decisions, speeches, and writings since absolute monarchy began giving way to the concepts and processes of constitutional government. The inclination of a free press has been to deny that government has the privilege of secrecy, with a few common-sense exceptions.

On the other hand, many public officials contend for the right to withhold some types of information, particularly the discussions and decisions that precede overt action. The basic argument used to support this viewpoint is that the public interest demands such action.

The question boils down to: what should be withheld and for how long? A good deal of interesting philosophic discussion has been going on in recent years, stimulated by a widely held suspicion that too much information is being withheld by public officials. The press, quite naturally, has been the primary source of the criticism leveled at government. By and

---

[6] MacDonald, *op. cit.*, pp. 12–22.

large, the public has seemed uninterested in the issue, except in isolated instances of flagrant and arbitrary official denial of the public's right to know. The concern of the press, however, has been reflected among legislators, and an increasing amount of legislation has been passed restricting governmental secrecy.

Sigma Delta Chi, the professional journalism fraternity, assisted by state publishers' associations, has campaigned actively for adoption by state legislatures of its model laws for open records and open meetings. The former states flatly that all public records are to be open for inspection by any citizen and provides for criminal penalties for any violation. The latter requires that all meetings of government bodies, boards, commissions, and similar bodies, except grand juries, be public meetings, and establishes criminal penalties for violations. These provisions represent the thinking of the working press. While public officials generally agree with such legislation in principle, they argue that it oversimplifies a complex problem and fails to take certain exceptional situations into consideration.

By 1962, 35 states had open records laws on their books, while 26 had open meetings laws in effect. These statutes vary considerably from state to state. California's Brown Act has often been cited as a model anti-secrecy-in-government statute. Passed in 1953, it requires all local legislative and advisory boards, as well as state commissions, to hold their meetings open to the press and to the public. The 1961 legislature reinforced the earlier law by (1) making violations subject to criminal penalties; (2) authorizing the commencement of mandamus or injunction proceedings to halt violations or threatened violations; (3) clarifying the legislature's intent to extend provisions of the Brown Act to such advisory boards as planning commissions and library boards; and (4) prohibiting the taking of action at a closed meeting and defining "action" as any collective decision, promise, commitment, or vote by a majority of members. Language which would have prohibited any closed sessions for discussion or action, was amended out of the bill before it was passed. The major unresolved issues remaining in the Brown Act as amended,

so far as the press is concerned, involve the definition of a meeting, and the question of whether a discussion or briefing session of a governing or advisory body can be closed to the public.[7]

In a recent survey of alleged abridgment of freedom of access to news information in Nebraska, 143 cases of abridgment were reported by 41 newspapers across the state. The survey concluded that:

1. The problem of closed government records and closed meeting of governmental agencies exists in varying degrees, and in many instances accessibility is solely at the discretion of the elected official.

2. A far greater number have done nothing about it, by remonstrance with the officials concerned, by editorial action, or by publicity of the suppression efforts.[8]

The proper source of guidance for public officials is, of course, the law and judicial interpretations of existing statutes. Unfortunately, the guidelines are seldom clear or specific. Typically, there is a good deal of flexibility for both press and government, with local public attitudes constituting the final determinant. A governing body which attempts to operate in what a majority of the electorate deems to be excessive secrecy may find itself and its policy repudiated at the polls.

Administrators customarily operate in "secrecy" in the sense that their day-to-day routine is not a matter of interest to the press and hence goes unreported. Meetings of department heads, or conferences between the city manager and his immediate subordinates, are not normally considered news sources and hence are not covered by newsmen.

Certain administrative matters are handled in confidence because of the harm that would

---

[7] Robert E. Holmes, "California's 'Model' Law on Secrecy Has Its Gaps," EDITOR AND PUBLISHER, Nov. 25, 1961, p. 14. See also, Peter MacDougall, "Open Meeting Statutes: The Press Fights for the Right To Know," PUBLIC MANAGEMENT, February, 1963, pp. 33–37. This article includes a "Proposed Open Meeting Statute" which attempts to resolve these questions by defining the limits and operation of the open meeting principle.

[8] Jack Pollack and Mack Lundstrom, A SURVEY OF FREEDOM OF PRESS TO NEWS IN NEBRASKA, Studies in Nebraska Journalism No. 2, School of Journalism, University of Nebraska, Lincoln (undated), p. 12.

stem from premature disclosure. Examples include: (1) plans and negotiations for the purchase of rights-of-way, building sites, or buildings where publicity might result in raising of prices; and (2) a wide range of personnel matters, including personnel records, investigation of alleged misconduct, and results of examination.

The work of administrators goes on without detailed review by persons outside of government and seldom do their decisions, except on matters of considerable policy significance, find their way to print. When a department head makes a recommendation to the council on a proposed traffic-flow pattern or a progress report on developments at the municipal airport, he naturally expects to find his statement treated as news. Also, a controversy involving an administrator will normally make news.

Ordinarily the administrator finds this atmosphere of anonymity quite comfortable. One city manager experienced a very different and probably unique situation in a midwestern city several years ago. Two competing newspapers representing rival factions kept reporters sitting all day every day outside the manager's office. In the name of freedom of the press they read his official mail, interviewed departing visitors and on occasion insisted on sitting in, without invitation, on conferences conducted in his private office. Unable to resolve this invasion of his managerial prerogatives in any reasonable way, he finally ejected the reporters bodily. He soon moved on to another job.

Members of governing bodies find themselves in a situation quite different from that of administrators. Empowered to make policy on matters of great concern to the community, they find that their discussions and their final decisions are typically matters of public record. To avoid airing all of the pro-and-con debate (and often the acrimony and shifting of positions) which precedes the reaching of a decision, many governing bodies hold informal sessions prior to their public meetings.

In San Diego, California, for example, the council meets in conference for an hour or more before convening for regular meetings on Tuesday and Thursday mornings. The public is not barred, but the conference is held in a small room which can accommodate only a handful of visitors. The press is present on what might be called a watch-dog basis but does not report details of the proceedings. Efforts are made in the conference to resolve disagreements on major issues. Official action is taken at a subsequent council meeting. Similar practices are followed in numerous other local governments, but not always with the same safeguards for the public interest.

It is always possible that abuses may creep in to efforts to conduct public business without full public scrutiny. If all debate and controversy are kept hidden and the formal session is used only to record unanimous "yes" or "no" votes, public knowledge and interest in civic affairs can hardly be expected to be high, and democratic government will be the loser. Secrecy on the part of public bodies tends to breed suspicion of the motives of public officials and to give rise to rumor and unfounded speculation on controversial issues.

Informal discussion sessions or conferences do have value. It is not necessary that every honest difference of opinion between policymakers be reported for reader entertainment or partisan advantage. Administrators need the opportunity to brief and advise governing bodies in all candor and honesty without having to fear that their statements will involve them in local political debate. Since it is almost impossible for the administrator, in the context of American government, to defend himself against partisan attack, he should not be exposed to such attack on the basis of his professional or technical findings and views. Responsibility for meeting such attacks rests with the governing body which accepts or rejects his advice. If his advice is consistently bad, he should be replaced.

In balance, maintenance of good relations with the press in general and with reporters in particular argues for the fullest possible disclosure on the part of public officials. Much of this disclosure may be, by mutual agreement, primarily for background and informational purposes. The very presence of representatives of the press works for fidelity to established procedures and standards of honesty and fair play. The San Diego practice of having reporters sit in on council conference sessions is utilized in order to insure against wrong-doing.

In government, secrets are hard to keep, especially if they concern bad news about official mistakes or incompetence. In the absence of formal disclosure, bad news comes out in the form of gossip—which often finds its way into print. When the truth finally does come out in the press, the attempt at suppression makes public reaction more emphatically negative than it would have been otherwise.

Suppression of any sort—of names, public records, or minutes of public meetings—by open or devious methods is, in general, poor public policy. If information in public records is to be kept confidential for compelling reasons—as, for example, the names of juvenile offenders—this should be done on the basis of agreement between press and government. Many newspapers and radio and television stations have fair and constructive policies regarding the handling of news in which the revelation of identities would do more harm to the individuals involved than good to the public. The press, as well as government, has a sense of public interest.

A Responsible Press and Responsive Government

Public officials can expect criticism, no matter how competently they perform their duties or how sincere they are in their dedication to the public good. A great deal of criticism is irresponsible and based on mistaken information or beliefs. For example, a member of a minority group who does poorly on a civil service examination may allege official discrimination against his group. A citizen arrested for drunken driving may complain about police brutality when he sobers up and begins to consider the consequences of his arrest.

Every complaint should be completely and honestly investigated lest the greater complaint of whitewashing or indifference to the public be lodged. Americans generally have a strong sense of fair play; they may suspect the motivation behind individual complaints, but blanket denials and official complaisance create suspi-

cion and arouse resentment in the community at large.

The intention to investigate the citizen's complaint and the subsequent action taken should be fully reported to the press whether or not there is any likelihood it will appear in print. As a rule a "no comment" answer is worse than silence for it appears to be a willful attempt to suppress information. Timing is important. The more prompt the explanation or answer the better.

Sometimes questions addressed to a public official by a reporter seem to be nothing more than a form of harassment. The same questions may be asked day after day, the same request for information repeated, despite a clear public policy that it is not to be made available. This approach stems most often from a policy position of the newspaper. For example, repeated demands for the names of welfare recipients may be made to the county welfare director because of an antiwelfare orientation of the newspaper publisher. All the welfare director can do is to deny access to the information and cite the law or policy in support of his position. The thing he should not do—from a public relations point of view—is to get angry and issue a denunciation of the paper or its staff. There is no point in getting angry at the reporter, for he is in a position to retaliate if he is so inclined.

One journalistic technique which the press uses to carry out what it considers to be its responsibility to the community is the so-called "crusade." While the term "crusade" is no longer used by the press, the technique of preparing a series of articles or reports to advance some aspect of the public interest continues to be utilized. Editors, writers, and reporters join in the effort, which is based on a policy decision to pursue a particular investigation for the purpose of achieving a specific reform. Many a crusade has begun quite by accident.

A reader walked into the office of the *Chicago Daily News* and remarked that Illinois State Auditor, Orville Hodge, would bear watching. This statement touched off a campaign that ended with his imprisonment. An editor so judiciously phrased a Page 1 appeal in the *New York Journal-American* that George Metesky, the "mad bomber," gave up his campaign of terror in New York City and eventually was caught because he entered into correspondence with the newspaper. A photographer in Buffalo happened to take a picture of a city truck unloading supplies at a private contracting job, and touched off a major municipal scandal. A penciled notation on a card, found by a reporter for the *Seattle Times,* resulted in clearing a University of Washington professor of charges of Communist activity.[9]

In view of the role of the press as guardian of the public good, it is understandable that government agencies and public officials are frequent objects of press campaigns and particularly of editorial criticism. Both of these journalistic techniques are concerned more with arousing readers than with attempting to inform them objectively. Although the reaction of public officials may be quoted, the campaign or editorial comment is a far cry from a debate in which both sides have equal time. In such a situation, the public official is well advised to state briefly and clearly the facts as he sees them and to avoid being drawn into an argument in which his opponent will necessarily have the advantage.

Attempts to conceal information from reporters during a press campaign are seldom successful because of the prestige and investigative facilities of the press. If the criticism is clearly an attempt to smear the official he should avoid, at all costs, being dragged down to the level of his attackers. Attacks of an extreme or "crackpot" nature have a way of being discounted by the reading public, especially that segment of it which attempts to keep reasonably well-informed on community affairs. A cool, factual response to extreme or irresponsible criticism will typically attract support from responsible and respected elements who see the harm which can result to the community as a whole from such criticism. The best defense government can build against crackpot criticism is to keep the community well informed. Trouble comes when a small minority is able to mislead the responsible but uninformed majority.

The sensational press is still with us and will continue to be with us for some time to come. There has been, over a period of years, however, a discernible trend toward a more responsible press. The idea that shock and sensation are the surest way to build circulation is gradually on the wane, particularly in the more thoughtful circles of the press. The reading public is becoming more aware of the necessity of being well informed in an increasingly complex and shrinking world. Journalists are better educated, more sophisticated, and increasingly oriented toward the concept of journalism as a public service.

It continues to be a business, of course, but a business that is slowly adopting a new approach toward the sale of its wares. In the case of newspapers, this trend toward responsibility has emerged from within, for they are subject to the barest minimum of governmental controls. Mounting criticism of the orientation of radio and television toward entertainment that offers the widest possible mass appeal has prompted the Federal Communications Commission to remind these media of their responsibilities in the area of public information and education, resulting in some hopeful improvements in coverage of public affairs.

If this trend continues, government will become increasingly the source of interest and attention on the part of the media of mass communication. If this means fuller and more detailed news coverage, the trend should be welcomed by public officials, for it will mean a better opportunity to create public understanding and support. This is not to say that the press should protect local government—there is too much of an inclination in this direction already, particularly in one-newspaper cities. An interesting example of journalistic indifference to excesses of boss rule is to be found in the history of Hudson County, New Jersey, newspapers during the period when Frank Hague was mayor of Jersey City. In describing the era, Dayton McKean said ". . . there is no newspaper criticism of public officials or public policy in Hudson County, but constant defense of what seems indefensible."[10] Too often the press will refrain from honest criticism for fear

[9] John Hohenberg, THE PROFESSIONAL JOURNALIST (New York: Henry Holt and Company, 1960), p. 391.

[10] Dayton D. McKean, THE BOSS (Boston: Houghton Mifflin Company, 1940), p. 242.

of damaging the "image" of the community in the eyes of the outside world. If, in this situation, illegal or dishonest acts come to light, the press and the democratic process itself as well as the local government, suffer loss of faith in the eyes of the public.

The concept of responsibility of the press, then, is not an obligation to report news about government to the satisfaction of public officials, but to report it in such a way as to insure that the public is as completely informed as possible. Officials who are disturbed by press criticism of their actions or policies have failed, in MacDonald's words, ". . . to see the need for a community well-enough informed to be resilient in times of crises and to maintain a hard core of various publics interested enough in particular phases of government activity to be actively sympathetic with community needs."[11]

Straight News Is Not Enough

A frequent complaint against the press is that it does not report events "objectively." Standards of objectivity vary from individual to individual, but the complaint is based on the widely held belief, shared by public officials, in a standard of impersonal, absolute objectivity for news reporting. Actually, this standard has been breaking down in journalistic circles, for two principal reasons:[12] first, there is a growing belief that a responsible press must provide an understanding of the immense complexities of politics, science, and technology which confront the twentieth century layman; second, the press is expected to supply the missing facts when half-truths are presented as basic truths by unscrupulous persons who expect to turn this manipulation of information to their own advantage.

Because of the necessity for speed and meeting competition, the press still presents great quantities of bare facts to the public, which is expected to have the necessary background to interpret them and comprehend their significance. At the same time many thoughtful journalists agree that the news also must be presented in perspective. The viewpoint is reflected in these comments by John Cowles, a publisher of status and experience:

People will want far more interpretive news from their papers so that they can understand what is happening. People will want more background information. People will want not only the bare facts of what did happen yesterday, but will want from their newspapers information on what is probably going to happen tomorrow or next week or next month.

The relative importance of editorial writers will greatly increase. It will not be tub-thumping, violent, partisan editorial assertions that the readers will want, but understandable analyses of the complicated problems that trouble them.

This means that we will need better reporters and better editors and must give them more latitude than most papers now do.[13]

In radio and television, the commentary and the special feature are designed to provide background and interpretation to important news stories. Frequently these deal with major personalities who influence events. To understand modern India, one must know something about Nehru and his leadership of the Indian people. In newspapers, this obligation to explain is fulfilled largely through special background features, columnists, interpretive articles, and editorial comments. Even in the reporting of daily events the reporter's interpretation of the news can be injected readily into his story, as is shown by the following portion of the *New York Times* coverage of "Boss" Frank Hague's retirement from the office of Mayor of Jersey City, New Jersey, in 1947.

Mayor Frank Hague formally abdicated in William L. Dickinson High School here tonight after thirty years on the Mayoral throne.

Then he graciously draped the Mayoral mantle on the shoulders of Frank Hague Eggers, with royal avuncular gesture, while the Democratic faithful screamed and applauded in almost hysterical loyalty.

The extraordinary ceremony had all the trappings, though in somewhat shoddy imitation, of a royal coronation. The twilit hill where the high

[11] MacDonald, *op. cit.,* p. 50.

[12] This point of view is expressed in Hillier Krieghbaum, FACTS IN PERSPECTIVE (Englewood Cliffs, N.J., Prentice Hall, Inc., 1956) , Chapter 1.

[13] *Ibid.,* p. 3.

school stands was shattered by deafening royal salutes. Aerial bombs burst at regular intervals.[14]

It is quite clear from the story that the *New York Times* disliked Mayor Hague almost as much as he hated the *Times* because it published a number of his ill-considered remarks. Adherence to literal objectivity in news reporting has tended to break down as journalists have increased in sophistication. They recognize the difference between the literal and the essential truth, and feel it is their obligation to inform the reader about what is not obvious or apparent.

The late Elmer Davis, a well-known correspondent and commentator and director of the Office of War Information during World War II, deals with the breakdown of objectivity in these words:

> This striving for objectivity was in its beginnings a good thing; but it went a little too far. From holding that newspapers ought to present both sides it went on to the position that it was all right to present only one side, if nobody happened to be talking on the other; and it was not the business of the newspaper to tell the reader if that one argument happened to be phony. . . .
>
> This kind of dead-pan reporting—So-and-so said it, and if he's lying in his teeth it isn't my business to say so—may salve the conscience of the reporter (or of the editor, who has the ultimate responsibility) as to his loyalty to some obscure ideal of objectivity. But what about his loyalty to the reader? The reader lays down his nickel, or whatever, for the paper, in the belief that he is going to find out what is going on in the world; and it does not seem to me that the newspaper is giving him his nickel's worth if it only gives him what somebody says is going on in the world, with no hint as to whether what that somebody says is right or wrong.[15]

This discussion is included here to suggest to public officials that the news they originate will probably not be treated by the press in the way they may expect. If the press is doing its job

properly, there will be probing and perhaps impertinent questions from newsmen; when the story is reported, it may well contain explanatory or interpretive sentences or paragraphs not based directly on material from the original source. It may be written in a tone not anticipated by the source. In addition to the resources furnished by government officials, the newsman will draw on his own background to supply the explanatory material or to determine the orientation or tone of the story. He may draw on reference materials in the city hall or the newspaper's library for background data forgotten or overlooked by the source. Or he may get in touch with a specialist or expert in the field. The official must hope, of course, that the newsman will make an honest effort at interpretation and not simply reflect his own bias. Bias or prejudice, however, will be apparent to the reader as well as to the news source and will be discounted accordingly except by those who share the bias.

In addition to explanatory material in straight news stories, the press frequently uses interpretive and background features. These may take the form of short stories accompanying the main stories, stories reporting the reactions of informed persons, stories containing historical background, personality stories, surveys or stories dealing in prediction. All of these are designed to help the reader understand the facts in the main account.

It should be clear that the release of news or the raw material that makes news, will not necessarily be reported in such a manner as to reflect credit on government or on any public official. This is not the function of the press, nor should public officials want it to be. The function of both government and the press is to report as fully and honestly as possible on the affairs of government—both its successes and its shortcomings—so that the electorate may be well enough informed to carry on the task placed upon it in a democratic state: the task of responsible self-government.

---

[14] NEW YORK TIMES, June 18, 1947.

[15] Krieghbaum, *op. cit.*, p. 8.

11

Reporting through the Media

ANYONE WHO KNOWS a competent public official realizes he is a busy person, usually burdened with more work than he can take care of in a normal day. Nevertheless, it must be pointed out that it is in the interest of even the busiest official to take an active part in the process of getting out the news. News is perishable. There is a great deal of competition for space in the paper or time on the newscast. Tomorrow may be too late for a story to be newsworthy.

Officials can help the press, the public, and their own programs by surveying the requirements of the news media serving their communities and then doing what they can to help meet these needs. For example, knowledge of such details as morning and afternoon deadlines, whom to call at a radio or television station, and the special interests and needs of the several papers and stations can be obtained and utilized by the official who is interested in building good press relations.

Ways To Help the Newsman

The trained, conscientious reporter tries to get all of the information he needs to write a complete and comprehensive story. If there are gaps, a discerning editor will raise questions. Yet one of the most frustrating aspects of the reporter's job is to convince his news source or sources to take the time and make the effort to get additional information. There is a tendency to "let George do it," George in this case being the reporter, who, with a deadline facing him, must try to dig out all the pertinent facts. If he cannot find them, he must write his story without them.

Advance Notice. There are numerous ways in which a public official can help the reporter do an honest job of reporting. If the occasion is a public meeting of the city council, planning commission, or school board, a copy of the agenda should be made available in advance as a matter of course. If a particularly controversial or dramatic issue may come up unannounced, a tip to newsmen is of great help to them and will earn their gratitude.

Designating a spokesman for the group who will brief the reporter beforehand and be on hand to answer questions after the session is one way to insure something more than a superficial recording of action taken. Better yet, all or most of the members should remain for a few minutes after the meeting to enable the reporter to check on statements, get background information, or ask for interpretation of a decision that has been made, or one postponed to a later session. If the reporter cannot get answers from authoritative sources, the best he can do is to guess or speculate; everyone in public life would agree that this is not a desirable alternative and frequently results in an inaccurate or incomplete story.

The point about making information available to newsmen in advance of deadlines deserves elaboration. The public official can expedite timely and accurate treatment of the news by preparing the press for events or announcements to come. We know that much of the business of government is transacted on paper

How to help
a newsman

1.	Get to know the reporter
2.	Brief him in advance
3.	Provide him with documents pertinent to the story
4.	Direct him to the proper sources

FIGURE 17.

in the form of administrative reports, directives, recommendations, and memoranda. The publication dates of such newsworthy documents as budgets, annual reports, and reports of special study groups, consultants, and citizens' committees are typically known well ahead of time.

For example, it would be a wise procedure for the mayor or city manager to give to reporters a semifinal draft of the budget document, together with a statement of explanation and commentary. The reporter must understand, naturally, that the material is given to him in order that he may prepare himself for a story to be published on the day the budget goes to the council.

This procedure offers several advantages over last-minute preparation of the story. First, it enables reporters to do a better job of analyzing and interpreting the financial and economic data contained in the budget. Second, the greater care used in writing the story—assuming it is prepared in advance of the release date—should prevent errors caused by lack of time to verify with the mayor or manager the reporter's interpretations of budget figures, or errors in the figures themselves. Third, it gives copyreaders and headline writers the time to do a careful job.

Copies of government reports may be sent, as a potential safeguard for the public official, to newspaper, television and radio news editors, and to newspaper libraries. If this is done, the newsman's stories are not the sole avenue of communication between the official and the editor. The editor has at hand a means of checking on the thoroughness and competence of the newsman's work.

Spokesmen. Reporters will be helped by the identification of a spokesman for a council, board, or commission. The spokesman typically would be the chairman of the group. If he does not make himself available to the press, reporters naturally will turn to another member who in turn would be quoted in the news stories. In this situation, the public understandably gains the impression that someone other than the chairman is playing the leading role. It is interesting that businessmen will spend thousands of dollars on public relations programs to get their views before the public, while many public officials shun the opportunity to speak out for their agencies, even when the opportunity is offered to them by newspapers, radio, and television.

Any official who wants his role and activities known publicly must take the time to be a news source and spokesman. He should volunteer to provide supplementary information which will make a story more meaningful. It was stated in Chapter 10 that at a budget session the development of statistics on trends and projections represents an important contribution to the press and hence to public understanding and approval of any increased spending the budget may present.

Know the Reporter. The public official should be careful to size up the reporter, to know his strong points, and to help out if he lacks knowledge or experience. Smaller papers and radio stations in particular tend to have a rather high personnel turnover. The official may have to assume the role of patient tutor time after time in the course of a governmental career. On the other hand, some reporters are veterans on the city hall beat and are well acquainted with local affairs. Dealing with this type of reporter has both advantages and disadvantages, as MacDonald points out.

The official who deals with such a veteran is both fortunate and on the spot because of the reporter's intimate knowledge of local government. He is fortunate in being able to work with someone who already understands such complexities as property tax limitations and equalized property valuations. That same fund of information and experience, however, also makes the veteran reporter capable of looking beyond surface developments and of asking questions which may prod into touchy matters. And

Some do's and don'ts
in working with
reporters

DO Brief reporters on background information.
Take your gripes directly to the reporter.
Go straight to the editor on policy matters.
Take advantage of TV and radio.
Use clear, straight-forward language.
Treat the reporter as a professional.

DON'T Be afraid of publicity
Get into a feud with the press.
Go over the reporter's head (except as a last resort).
Use jargon and technical lingo.
Hide mistakes behind secrecy.
Say "no comment" or be evasive (unless you have no alternative).
Worry about minor errors in the news.
Get angry at reporters over headlines.

FIGURE 18.

the chances are he will not be satisfied with evasive, incomplete answers.[1]

The experienced newsman is the one who will lean toward interpretive reporting. After extensive questioning, he will use explanatory writing to put the spot news he has obtained from the official into perspective, both historical and technical. This may often include interviews with other officials and citizens to supplement information provided by the city official.

Much of the discussion so far applies to governmental agencies regularly covered by newsmen. There are numerous smaller units, for example, townships or special districts, which seldom receive coverage of their day-to-day doings. Regularly scheduled meetings of their governing bodies will be known to the

press, and the meetings will normally be covered by a reporter in person or over the phone. For other news, an official may volunteer to keep the paper or station informed. To perform properly he should do two things: first, find out what is wanted so that he won't waste his time and that of the press on matters which will not be reported; and second, resolve, once he has made his commitment, that he will volunteer *all* of the news. No good can come of holding information back once the arrangement has been made.

The Function of Press Relations

Government at all levels is a large-scale practitioner of the art of press relations. This valuable technique is not used effectively by public officials who mistakenly seek to gain personal publicity rather than to disseminate information. Press relations is like a brokerage business in that it facilitates the transfer of a valuable commodity—in this case news—from a vendor to a customer. The press or public relations man—typically called a public information officer in government—should assume the role of an "honest broker" or middleman who has three principal functions: first, to advise the official or agency on press relations policies; second, to represent the official or agency in the dissemination of news; and third, to serve the press and public by giving the fastest and fullest possible news coverage.

Smaller cities do not feel they can afford to hire information officers, who typically are former newsmen. Medium-sized and larger cities are increasingly aware of the help a competent public information officer can give in developing accurate and responsible reporting of governmental affairs. His basic policy is that truthful reporting is the soundest policy. Having been a newsman himself, he knows what is wanted and he aids and supplements the reporters' efforts. It is not his job to do the reporters' work for them. His experience enables him to see a news story in events or developments which appear completely routine to the public official.

Much more is involved in governmental

[1] James C. MacDonald, PRESS RELATIONS FOR LOCAL OFFICIALS (Ann Arbor: Bureau of Government, Institute of Public Administration, University of Michigan, 1956), p. 12.

How the
public information
officer can help you

He Can	1.	advise you on press relations policy
	2.	represent you in dealing with the press
	3.	help you get fast and full news coverage

He Cannot	1.	cover up your mistakes
	2.	fabricate news for you
	3.	advertise your agency

FIGURE 19.

press relations than grinding out a release. If the story is a minor one, the chances are that a press release mailed or delivered to the media will do the job; it can be supplemented by a telephone call if necessary. If the story is important, the press relations job involves at least the following: notifying newsmen of the impending story and when it will break; arranging an interview or a press conference if the news stems from an individual; arranging for records to be available, if these are pertinent; developing background materials, such as statistical data or lists of names; furnishing or arranging for pictures and answering questions in person or on the phone.

It is poor practice to involve the press relations officer in use of the trial balloon technique. If the official wants to test the political atmosphere by advancing an idea he can later back away from he should do so in a public speech or in a news contact he himself has arranged. Reporters resent efforts to plant stories and will avoid a press relations officer who does anything more than release straight, factual news.

THE NEWS RELEASE

The news release or handout is a useful device for government providing it is used in moderation and with proper regard for the sensibilities of the media. Typically a story given directly to a reporter will be given better coverage than if it is released in a handout.

An advance announcement of a public ceremony, a biography of a prominent appointee to an administrative committee, the text or an abstract of a speech, or a fact sheet about a new assessment procedure are examples of appropriate subject matter for press releases. The treatment of news releases by the media varies widely. Some sources want to use them almost verbatim, in which case they must be put into the usual journalistic format. This, of course, means more work for the government agency if it wants to achieve maximum coverage. More often, the press release provides the raw material for a story or newscast. In this case, the agency should concentrate on providing the facts for presentation in whatever style the paper or station chooses to use. The release should bear the name of the source to be contacted if further information is needed.

The official releasing news should not be surprised if he is subsequently contacted by reporters. An enterprising newsman may find in the release a new angle or the potential for an even better story. The real story, from the reporter's standpoint, may be in what the release does *not* say. The handout quite naturally tells the story in the way the issuing agency wants it told. The newsman's responsibility is to his employer and the public, with the result that the news subsequently may be handled in a way that displeases the official who originated it. This is a calculated risk every official must take. His best protection is to develop, through experience, a sensitivity to

Some uses of the
news release

1.	Advance announcement of a public ceremony
2.	Text or abstract of a speech
3.	Fact sheets
4.	Biographical sketch of a public official

FIGURE 20.

the attitudes of the media in his community toward press releases and to supply the information the press needs, either through the initial release or by answering any questions reporters may have after the release is prepared.

Amateur press relations officers frequently specify a release date and time on a handout. With few exceptions this practice is unwise and unnecessary—unwise because it irritates the media and unnecessary because it tends to delay publication. Delay may mean it never will be used.

NEWS SOURCES

To a good newsman, any government employee is a news source. The switchboard operator in the public works department and the clerk of the planning commission may be key people to the city hall reporter. This is not to say that he gets the bulk of his information from such employees. They are news sources in the sense that they alert him to potential spot news or features and provide a personal link between the reporter and the official who can supply the story.

Most governments have multiple news sources, all of which are cultivated by the newsmen. Seldom is a single individual *the* spokesman for government except that in a very small unit the chief administrator may by process of elimination serve in that capacity. In a small school district, for example, the superintendent would be expected to be the authoritative source on all school affairs, including business as well as curricular matters.

In any unit of local government, the chief spokesman will, of course, be the chief executive or administrative officer: the mayor, manager, superintendent, director, or board chairman. Newsmen will want to establish direct contact with these officials and will go to them periodically. On policy questions and controversial issues they will be sought out speedily. Other major news sources will be the chief fiscal officer, director of finance, controller, business manager or treasurer, and the heads of such major departments as police, fire, public works, planning and zoning, and health, to mention only a few, and the directors of such institutions as hospitals, clinics, and sanato-

riums. Newsmen will go regularly to the public records kept by clerks of such agencies as the city council, or board of county supervisors, or commissioners, and the city and county clerks. Periodically such officials as the tax assessor and collector, the recorder, and the auditor have newsworthy reports to disseminate.

Few local governments have developed a public information policy in any formal fashion. Reporters prefer it this way because they retain a maximum freedom of action. However, a policy will mitigate confusion among employees about who has authority to speak on what subject and eliminate buck-passing when newsmen raise questions. A public information policy should not be designed to force newsmen to follow rigid channels of inquiry, or to go to only one or a few official spokesmen. Such a policy would be self-defeating, for it would be circumvented by reporters, and in the end challenged as unduly restrictive and undemocratic. Whatever its merits, this kind of policy would appear to the outside world to be an effort by government to choke off access to legitimate news.

A Public Information Policy

The public information policy should allocate responsibilities and make it as easy as possible for newsmen to obtain prompt coverage. The elements of such a policy are set forth in the following suggestions.

1. Make it the responsibility of the official clerk of a government unit, e.g. county clerk, city clerk, clerk of the board of education, to provide assistance in obtaining routine information from records under his control.

2. Define as specifically as possible the latitude allowed subordinate employees in releasing information. They should know which types of inquiry to answer directly and which to refer to higher authority. This is not as difficult as it sounds if the functional organization of a department is used as the basic pattern for defining responsibilities for public information.

3. Develop among all employees, preferably through in-service training, an awareness of the importance of maintaining good relations with the press. Public relations training for all employees, particularly those who come into regular contact with the public, can be of value to the governmental unit.

4. Encourage administrators to maintain an open door policy toward the press. The open door is pointless, however, if officials insist on being close-mouthed. A policy of full and frank disclosure within reasonable limits agreed upon by top administration is best. Regardless of appointments and schedules, the official should be available to reporters. He will be wise to try to get the story straight in the first place rather than to catch up with mistakes or misinterpretations later.[2]

Generally, subordinates will be guilty of saying too little rather than too much to newsmen. The natural tendency is to refrain from talking for fear of getting into trouble and to refer inquiries to a superior. The subordinate who talks too much can be controlled through regular administrative procedures. In general, the best policy with regard to public information is to allow the greatest possible freedom within a framework that allocates responsibilities to specific individuals or groups of individuals for the dissemination of news. The function of the subordinate is to make the reporter aware of news or an impending story. For confirmation and the full account, the reporter will normally seek out someone in a supervisory or managerial position.

The Importance of "Quotes"

In writing a news story, the newsman is first confronted with selecting the aspect of the story to emphasize in the lead or opening paragraph. By instinct and training he looks over his material and makes his decision on the basis of the factor of importance. The inverted pyramid structure, customarily used for factual news, calls upon the writer to identify the facts in declining order of importance, placing the most important at the top. The writer always keeps reader interest in mind when he selects the lead. In preparing a story on a meeting of the city council or planning commission he may select what he considers the two or three most important facts and summarize them in a lead. In writing up a speech or interview, he decides either to summarize the whole thing in the lead or to select one facet for emphasis in the opening paragraph.

A neatly turned phrase or an unintended

---

[2] This material is drawn from MacDonald, *Ibid.*

emphasis on a single phase of a complex problem on the part of the news source may lead to what is in effect a distortion of what the news source thought he said. In short, an official who makes news must realize how the newsman constructs his story and should make every effort to differentiate between the vital, the important, and the less significant material he presents.

Time and time again businessmen, public officials, scientists and other technically and professionally trained people claim sincerely that they have been misquoted or quoted out of context. Frequently this allegation stems from a difference of view between the newsman and the news source on matters of emphasis. What appears to the source as an obscure detail may be emphasized prominently by the newsman, who sees in it potential reader interest. Claiming to have been misquoted is an over-used and often abused practice, not designed to promote harmony between the official and the reporter. All too often, the news source tends to overestimate the reporter's background in and familiarity with the subject matter. What the director of health takes for granted may be new to the reporter unless he has been covering the health department for some time. A frank, open and unhurried approach to the reporters, with a painstaking effort to indicate the relative importance of each phase of the story, is best. A relationship based on confidence that the newsman will handle stories honestly and in fairness to the source is warranted until that confidence has been proved to be misplaced.

A Word about News Manipulation

The use of news as a weapon of government in the cold war has been the subject of a great deal of discussion among newspaper editors since the beginning of the crisis over Cuba in 1961. Editors have argued that selective release of news has been used by government officials as one of the tactics of international relations. Deliberate withholding of part of the news in time of peace, it is said, amounts to unwarranted censorship and manipulation of opinion. This is not the first time that this type of criticism has been made against government—federal, state, and local—by the press. The use of the "trial balloon" is a related technique; it is a deliberately planted story designed to test opinion; if it is unfavorably received, the planted proposal can be abandoned.

An attempt to turn a reporter into a spokesman or publicity agent for an official or a governmental agency is still another technique for manipulation of the news. Officials try to cultivate "tame" reporters and editors by emphasizing the need for constructive treatment of the news or even, on occasion, by threats and intimidation.

In American experience, some attempts by government to manipulate the news have had short-run success, but in the end all have failed. Eventually such attempts come to light, and the tradition of a press free of government control reasserts itself in such a way as to lead to repudiation of objectionable practices.

DEADLINES AND FAIR PLAY

Deadlines are as inevitable to a newsman as are death and taxes to all mankind. Time is a dimension of supreme importance in his working career. He writes by the clock, with an hour to turn out his story if he is lucky; he may have only five minutes. The public official must share this awareness of timing with the newsman if a good working relationship is to develop. The factor of competition between newsmen means that the official must bear in mind their varying needs and attempt to be fair in the release of news. Even though both newspapers in a community, or the newspaper and a television or radio station, are under the same ownership, the factor of competition normally prevails, stemming from the newsman's pride of craftsmanship.

The influence of time on news values was discussed in Chapter 10, but other aspects of timing should be borne in mind. One, mentioned previously, was the value of developing new angles and fresh material that will keep a story before the public, thus increasing its impact. Trained newsmen have an acute sense of fresh approaches to a continuing story. It is good press relations policy to keep funneling new developments to the press in the hope that more coverage will follow. The reporter will typically follow through on a good story, asking if anything new has developed. A good news source will try to take advantage of this opportunity. On some stories it is the policy of the paper or station to keep trying to develop new leads. This is particularly true if the story concerns a major civic improvement or development program; for example, a drive for new industry.

A fast-breaking story, such as a fire or epidemic, must be covered and written under pressure. In the case of many stories, however, extra time can literally be created so that the newsman will have the opportunity to cover it in greater depth and with more attention to the accuracy of details. Consideration of deadlines and background briefing of reporters on what the future may bring in the way of new developments permit the official to help the newsman obtain more lead time.

Unless there is a compelling need to keep the lid on an impending news story, the official should keep the media, and hence the public, informed. Discussion in the press of the major outlines of a forthcoming master plan for the city may alert potential opponents, but it may also build a broad base of public support. If a water shortage is approaching, and rationing to homes and industry seems imminent, full public disclosure and a discussion of the nature of conservation measures provide a foundation for cooperation by the public in meeting the crisis. After all, democratic local government assumes the fullest possible citizen participation in meeting problems as well as deriving benefits.

Timing in a broad sense suggests that the official take into account those factors which will help him get the fullest possible coverage of his news. Sunday is a good day for features; Mondays tend to be "dry" news days, and a story may rate more space on a Monday than on a Friday. Thursday may be a poor day for a release because the papers are crowded with grocery advertising.

If a sewer main breaks, the survey of the sewer system's inadequacies suddenly becomes news and the public works director should make every effort to get information from the survey to the media. Water pollution in a bay, river, lake, or stream may not be news in the winter, but when the hot weather comes and the "no swimming" signs are posted, an anti-pollution campaign has the best chance of getting attention from the press.

Considerations of fair play dictate that the news source give all of the media a fair proportion of news breaks. Obviously, news should not be released so that it always appears first in the morning paper and only in warmed-over fashion in the evening paper. This holds true even though both are under common ownership. Similarly the interest of the suburban papers in local news should not be forgotten just because they do not have reporters on hand at the civic center, while the great metropolitan dailies do. There is often keen competition among newspapers, television, and radio. If speed is of utmost importance in getting news to the public, radio and television can move more quickly than newspapers.

It is most important for the public official to know the needs, sensitivities, and prejudices of the local media. For example, in a one-newspaper city, the paper during the early days of television imposed a virtual boycott on local news which had been carried first by local TV stations. This created a very difficult situation for city and county officials until the paper became reconciled to the new medium and dropped the boycott.

Story Treatment

Public officials should not become discouraged if stories they originate are not played up as prominently or written in as much detail as they had hoped. For one thing, most papers carry local news on one particular page or section day in and day out. The reader who is interested in local news knows where to find it and reads it avidly. Readership studies show that the subject matter and writing of the news do more to determine reader interest than bold headlines and a prominent position on page one. If there is reader interest in the story on local government it will be read by a high percentage of those who get the paper. Nor does the official need to be particularly concerned if his notions as to news values do not seem to jibe with those of the press generally. He may think that the more favorable the

treatment given his story in terms of placement, length, and support for his position, the better the public reaction will be. This is not necessarily so. MacDonald suggests several factors about the public relations value of news to be taken into account.

1. *Perfection is suspect.* An official, a government, or an institution which never makes a mistake is too good to be true. An honest mistake or an honest difference can be good publicity in so far as it shows that whoever is responsible is humanly fallible. . . .

2. *Sensationalism loses punch.* The newspaper with a reputation for sensationalizing tends to be discounted by many readers, even the less discerning ones, because a bias becomes apparent before too long.

3. *One story is not decisive.* Most persons form their impressions about public institutions and officials as the result of many factors over a fairly long-range period. The sum total of, say, a whole year's output of news is far more important, therefore, than a single story or one aspect of public administration.[3]

The public official or governmental press relations officer may be placed in an awkward position when a reporter comes to him for confirmation of an exclusive story or a facet of such a story. On the one hand, the news source should not play favorites; any information he has should be made available to all newsmen. On the other, to betray the reporter's confidence by informing other reporters of the story, or making it generally available to all media is to violate an unwritten rule of the working press. The official should respect the reporter's right to develop an exclusive story and the confidential nature of his inquiry.

The Press Conference

The electronic age has brought with it some notable changes in the press or news conference. Once a rough-and-tumble affair with pointed questions and blunt answers, it tends to be a formal, staged device for projecting an "image" to the viewing and listening as well as the reading public. After the first Nixon-Kennedy debate during the 1960 presidential campaign, the critiques centered as much on how

[3] *Ibid.,* pp. 31–32.

Nixon looked as on what he said. Nixon himself commented on the negative impression created in viewers' minds by his appearance and was careful to see to it that the contributing factors were remedied before the second debate.

Newsmen complain that with the use of radio, television, and tape recorders, public officials speak directly to the audience rather than to the newsmen. When officials are speaking for the record, with a verbatim transcript being made, they depend heavily on prepared material and weigh their extemporaneous remarks carefully. Both official and reporter tend to become actors in a drama in which the script to some extent has been prepared in advance.

This point of view may be more applicable to national than to state and local officials. The effects of electronic journalism, however, are apparent on the local scene. The tape recorder, the videotape, the TV camera, and the microphone are facts of life, and the official should learn how to use but not to abuse them. He would be wise to ask for pointers on making the best possible appearance in front of a TV camera.

For example, minor mannerisms which do not bother one's personal acquaintances may be annoying or even laughable on the television screen. A halting or uncertain manner of speech or a speech peculiarity can lead viewers to form a totally mistaken opinion of a public official. An official who shows up badly making a solo statement may do very well when being interviewed. A course in public speaking or a membership in the Toastmasters' Club may pay important dividends in terms of one's public image.

The press conference has several purposes. For one thing, it is a time-saver for the busy official. He sees all the reporters together rather than one at a time. Also, he avoids the chance of favoritism, because all media are invited to be present. All get the same news at the same time, and he is able to reach a maximum audience. There is no guarantee of publication of the news he generates, but a newspaper will hardly play down or ignore a story which will get good coverage on TV or radio; the same thing is true in reverse. The news source who

has kept faith with the press will find his press conferences well attended.

SUGGESTIONS FOR THE PRESS CONFERENCE

The suggestions for the press conference set forth below are based on experience, common sense, and some knowledge of the psychology of newsmen. Though generally applicable, they are not designed to cover every news conference situation.

1. The news to be announced should be worth the extra time and effort devoted by the newsmen to attending the conference. Use the press conference sparingly; if the official overdoes it, the news source will be put in the category of the boy who cried "wolf" too often. It is a waste of time to call reporters together to relay news which could be distributed just as well in a press release or by telephone.

2. Arrangements for the press conference should be made carefully, with attention to details. The setting should be appropriate and comfortable. An overcrowded private office with insufficient seating is not an appropriate site. There should be a stenographer or tape recorder to transcribe a verbatim record. Proper facilities for radio and television should be available if representatives of these media are to be present. Accommodate the conference to the differing needs of newspaper, TV, and radio newsmen. For example, it is not wise to delay newspaper reporters while displaying a bit of showmanship at the request of the TV representatives. It is a common practice to perform for the cameras at the close of the conference. The time and location of a conference should never be changed without notification to the media, unless the public official is anxious to incur ill will.

3. If the ground rules for the conference have not been established by tradition or usage, they should be discussed and clearly understood by the newsmen. If everything to be said is for the record there is no problem. If not, it should be possible for reporters to clearly identify statements which are not made for the record. Off-the-record statements should be used sparingly if used at all.

4. The news source should be brief and concise, particularly if he uses a prepared statement before answering questions. Such statements should be available in written form for the press. If the news source is too long-winded, the chances are the conference will be terminated with a "thank you" from one of the reporters and a rush for the exit.

5. It is wise to have an assistant or subordinate present to backstop the news source and to fill in the gaps, if necessary. No one expects the person being interviewed to have all the answers at his fingertips. Records and papers should be available if

the need can be anticipated, and copies should be available if they are important to the story. If questions can be answered only on the basis of information not immediately available, the best practice is to assure the newsmen it will be made available as soon as the necessary leg work is done.

6. The news source should anticipate the questions and the interests of the newsmen as best he can. For example, he should ask himself what aspect or aspects of his story are most newsworthy. Then he should concentrate on informing himself on these points and perhaps cover these points in an opening statement to be read and distributed at the start of the conference.

7. It is not a wise practice to ask that written questions be submitted in advance. To do so is guaranteed to arouse suspicion that the news source is trying to protect himself or his agency from the release of unfavorable news.

8. The news source should be as courteous and informative as possible in answering all questions, even those designed to needle or offend. If he considers it best, for policy reasons, not to answer a question, he should attempt to explain why no answer can be given. The response may not satisfy the one who made the inquiry, but the explanation will be more satisfactory to the press generally than a curt "no comment."

9. All questions should be recognized, providing they are asked by legitimate newsmen. Refusal to recognize a reporter because he or his paper or

Ten hints for a successful press conference

1.	Use it only for important announcements of general interest.
2.	Provide facilities for comfort and convenience of the press.
3.	Make special provisions for TV and radio.
4.	Be on time.
5.	Speak for the record.
6.	Be brief and concise.
7.	Have someone present to backstop you.
8.	Anticipate and prepare for questions.
9.	Answer all legitimate questions.
10.	Be courteous and informative.

FIGURE 21.

station has been critical in the past will make a bad impression on other reporters. Everyone present will ask himself: "Am I next?" Reporters can easily transmit their negative reaction to the public. This simple statement: "The Director of Health refused to answer a question on a County Medical Society complaint about 'uncooperative conduct' by Health Department personnel" raises a damaging question in the reader's mind: "Why didn't he answer?" It is most unwise to run the risk of becoming the target of a "bad press."

Selecting the Media

All of the media are interested in all of the news. However, an understanding of the differing treatment of news by radio, TV, and newspapers will help the public official to get the best possible coverage on every story.

Radio, for example, now makes extensive use of five-minute newscasts which treat a variety of stories in extremely brief form. A variation on this pattern is the morning and evening broadcasts, which may be as long as 15 minutes, devoted to regional and local news. Even here, coverage is very brief. Radio is primarily interested in up-to-the-minute, fast-breaking news, and presents it in very short stories. It uses very little background material and relatively little in the way of special feature stories. It does employ brief, tape-recorded or telephonic interviews on major local stories. Analytical or interpretive presentations are rare, except in the form of panels or interviews in which outsiders present their views directly to the audience, with a newsman as moderator.

Television tends more toward greater flexibility and variety than does radio. Being a new medium it is willing to experiment and to take chances on fresh and unusual formats. Local newscasts, which are typically 10 to 15 minutes in length, provide the opportunity for several stories on local government unless there has been an unusual rush of other types of news. TV thrives on the dramatic, and excels in the stark realism and emotional impact it can bring to the news.

For the benefit of television, the official should use initiative and imagination in presenting his story. Surely some day an imaginative public official will be able to improve upon

---

Special characteristics
of the news media

Radio	Brief treatment
	Spot news
	Frequent newscasts
	Speed—speed—speed

Television	Dramatic, flexible treatment
	Live interviews
	Human interest
	Selective coverage

Newspapers	Comprehensive coverage
	Treatment in depth
	Large news-gathering staff
	Special interest in public affairs

FIGURE 22.

the hackneyed ribbon-cutting and ground-breaking ceremonies which were developed for the still camera in the nineteenth century.

TV can make excellent use of interviews and conversations conducted on the spot where the news occurs, be it in the council chamber or the city sewage plant. Newsworthy human interest stories are ideal for television coverage. Better than any other media, TV permits the official to project his own words and personality directly to the public. Explanation and analysis of local government operations by public officials are well suited to TV.

There is no substitute for the newspapers in getting the full, complex, and sometimes tedious story of government to the public. There is much the public ought to know about government that is not as timely as the radio bulletin or as dramatic as the TV film sequence. In addition to the timely and the dramatic, the newspaper carries the major burden of keeping the public informed in depth about government and alert to the possibilities of wrongdoing or incompetence. While television may put the spotlight on one phase of government with an occasional special feature,

the newspaper concerns itself day in and day out with the news that involves and shapes basic public policies. It will seek to create news interest in an issue if it feels that continuing coverage is important. The newspaper is the least selective of the media about government in the sense that it typically will carry anything about government that is worthy of being called news. This is an asset to the agency which is in a relatively weak competitive position in terms of creative news.

The Public Affairs Program

Numerous local governments go directly to the public through the medium of a periodic television or radio program. Stations provide time without charge in compliance with a Federal Communications Commission requirement that a portion of their broadcasting schedule be devoted to public service programming. A weekly program of 15 to 30 minutes is typical.

Formats differ, depending in part on the amount of expert guidance available in producing the program. A variety of patterns may be used, including the talk or report-to-the-people, the interview or question-and-answer format, a panel, or a more elaborate pattern involving pre-taped material, remote control broadcasts from field operations, newsfilm or even dramatic productions.

A typical program has the mayor or a member of the city council as its principal participant discussing the forthcoming budget, the tax problem, and the need for street improvements or reporting on new developments in one of the operations of local government.

The governmental unit which employs a public information officer can put responsibility for production on him. Otherwise, reliance will have to be placed on whatever professional assistance can be obtained from the station. If there is no public information officer, someone close to the mayor or city manager should be assigned responsibility for working with the station to develop programs well in advance.

An advantage of the municipal public affairs program is that its subject matter does not have to meet the criteria of news. It can include anything that its producer considers to be informative and instructive and in some cases entertaining. It can be planned so that programs will coincide with such events as civic celebrations, the issuance of tax bills or an increase in utility rates.

On such a program the point of view of the official can be advanced without argument or challenge (at least at the moment). It can and should set forth the government's side on any community issue; differing views have ample opportunity to be heard through the news columns and programs, editorials, and letters to the editor. Too often, government's voice is drowned in the partisan clamor. It is the obligation of government to tell its story on its own program in a factual, interpretive way.

Unfortunately municipal public affairs programs do not command prime time on the air and hence do not reach mass audiences. They have small (compared to the entertainment programs) but faithful followings. Produced on a shoestring, they do not win awards in competition with the glamorous network public service shows. This is not said in criticism. These programs meet a need and deserve greater effort to diversify and improve their content. Many local governments do not recognize the public relations potential in 15 to 30 minutes of free air time, and fail to take full advantage of it—usually for budgetary reasons. Public relations does not have the priority it should have in the management or legislative scale of values.

If broadcasting experience is any guide, the better the program, the larger the audience will be; and as the audience grows, the time assigned the program will be lengthened. Some governmental public information programs are very bad, but this does not mean they *have* to be bad, or are bad because of their subject matter. Educational broadcasting has shown that informative programs can be entertaining as well as instructive. With the outlay of more effort and money, governmental programming can be greatly improved. If a university is located in the community, it may be a fruitful source of cooperation and assistance through its broadcasting and public affairs programs.

Broadcast Journalism: A Special Case

Differences between newspapers on the one hand, and television and radio on the other in their approach to and handling of news of local government has been cited from time to time in the preceding pages. The basic difference is one of degree: covering the news is the central function of a newspaper, but it has a peripheral role in television and radio. At this point it is appropriate to suggest some ways in which public officials can take the fullest advantage of broadcast journalism to inform the public.

Local government is in a position to benefit from broader television and radio coverage. If it is to do so, local officials must show initiative and imagination, since the broadcasting industry at present devotes a relatively small share of its great financial resources to newsgathering. Officials might consider themselves volunteer "stringers" or part-time correspondents for their community stations. There is little prospect that the broadcast media will come to them in an attempt to provide extensive coverage of local government.

RADIO IS BRIEF

Radio news editors skim the cream, exercising great selectivity, emphasizing up-to-the-minute bulletins and spot coverage and omitting details. Only a really major story can claim as much as one minute of a radio newscast. They can process a story rapidly and in the event of an emergency affecting the public safety can alert the listening audience on very short notice. This is the reason radio plays a vital role in civil defense. Radio stations do not normally have staff members who cover beats the way newspaper reporters do. The station with at least one working newsman (as distinguished from an announcer who reads the news) will maintain frequent radio contacts with the principal news sources in a community. The radio newsmen, armed with a tape recorder or a mobile transmitting unit, will be assigned to cover major stories in person.

TELEVISION: NEW TOOLS

Television adds a visual dimension to broadcast news and therefore introduces a new range of tools and techniques to news coverage. The basic tools are the still or motion picture cameras, with or without sound. Production of television news is much more complex than in the case of radio, but it has the great advantage of enabling the viewer to be on the spot where the news is made. The use of newsfilm gives television news its unique character; it also creates problems because of the requirements of processing, editing, and writing an appropriate script. The use of newsfilm means that each story takes longer to tell than on radio; most film stories will run at least 30 seconds and can easily go to 45 seconds or a minute.

A still picture with an announcer in the studio telling the accompanying story is the simplest way of using film. Newsfilm on which the story is recorded in the field by a cameraman on motion picture film and then projected in the studio during the newscast comes in two forms: silent and sound on film. In the latter type, called videotape, picture and sound are recorded simultaneously. The television newsman with his small, unobtrusive motion picture camera is a familiar figure at meetings, conferences, and other major public events. Sound on film equipment is much bulkier and less mobile and thus limited in its usefulness.

Considering the progress that has been made in the past few years, it seems likely that the process of miniaturization will lead to development of a videotape kit that can be transported readily by one man. When that occurs, it will be possible to cover any phase of government on the spot, with sound as well as pictures of the event. This should make it possible to bring directly to public view many interesting but unfamiliar operations.

While the presentation of the news in newspapers and on radio tends to be stereotyped by the limitations of each medium, not to mention tradition, television has an almost unlimited scope for creativity. Television news editors strive for new and different ways of telling a story. The limiting factor, other than money, is the shortage of imaginative and creative human beings. This need for creativity presents a challenge to public officials. The story is told of a television news editor in a city with a large Naval base. He became frustrated by the highly stylized handshake-and-salute routine at the frequent change of command ceremonies. As long as the Navy stood firm, there was nothing he could do but cut coverage to the bone. It is the government official who must come up with a fresh, unique approach. The news editor cannot do it for him.

The Case of Common Ownership

If a radio or television station is linked through common ownership with a newspaper, it benefits from the latter's comprehensive local coverage. In the case of a radio station, news of local government will be based largely on a rewrite of the newspaper stories, plus brief bulletin news and such special features as interviews and panels. The television station will use still photographs taken by newspaper camera men but it will also send out its own camera men for special coverage. If a radio and television station are under the same ownership, the two may have a combined news room. If this is the case, the task of the public official in relaying the news will be simplified. In some cases each station operates its own news room, and the official must deal with each separately.

Taking Advantage of Competition

The element of competition can be significant in expanding news coverage of local government on radio and television. Unfortunately, in smaller communities with only one station there is a tendency on the part of the press to rely on news from a wire service and to neglect local coverage. The explanation is, of course, financial. The smaller the staff, the less outlay there is for salaries. In the community with two or more stations, both of which skimp on local news, one approach would be to persuade one of the stations to provide fuller coverage of local government.

This might be done by arranging to have stories telephoned to the interested station. Incidentally, the same service should be offered to all stations, whether they agree to take advantage of it or not. If the one station begins emphasizing local coverage, and thus offers a richer, more interesting news fare to its listeners, the rest will probably follow suit because of the element of competition in obtaining sponsors for news programs.

COOPERATION IS WELCOME

Generally, the radio or television news director will welcome the fullest cooperation of public officials in covering news of local governments. Some of the ways in which help can be given are listed below:

1. Advance notice of events suitable for on-the-spot coverage is particularly important in the case of television and radio because of limited news personnel and the necessity for special arrangements for their equipment.

2. If television or radio coverage is to be provided, someone in government must be responsible for seeing that the news sources are on hand at the designated time, that necessary props are available, and that special equipment can be accommodated. If sound on film is to be used, the setting is especially important, and someone in government should be familiar with its peculiar requirements—for example, absence of background noise that distracts attention from the story. Since television camera men and crews work on split-second timing, moving rapidly from one story to the next, everything should be in readiness when they arrive.

3. Through the intelligent use of a 16-mm. camera, a government employee can provide a television station with newsworthy film around which a story can be built by the news staff. Essential facts must be provided with the film, but there is no point in writing them in news form, for the story would only have to be rewritten to fit television needs. The tape recorder can be used to perform a similar service for radio stations. If the material is not immediately newsworthy, it can be held for a later broadcast.

4. It is impossible for television newsmen to develop the visual aids which can greatly increase the significance of a story on government for the viewing audience. This is a form of assistance which only government itself can provide. Charts and graphs which explain and clarify news of taxes and budgets are examples. Organization and functional charts can be used to illustrate changes in the assignment of authority and functions. Maps are useful for pinpointing locations.

5. The official can suggest ways to inject color into stories about government. Get the news source to move from behind his desk to the locale of the story. If it is the fire chief who is making a statement, put him beside a piece of equipment. Have the street commissioner out on the job, or at least have him point to a model or display while he is talking.

6. The series of special programs can be of real benefit to local government, but it is pretty much a do-it-yourself operation. The station feels it has gone far enough when it provides its facilities. Responsibility for production of the programs rests with a government employee, ordinarily the public information officer, if there is one. It can hardly be a success unless it has the solid endorsement of top management.

This is by no means a complete list of suggestions. It is intended only to indicate that there are many ways in which local government can stimulate television and radio coverage of its affairs. The essential ingredients in achieving adequate coverage are a desire to let the public know, some basic knowledge of the media, and a willingness to make the extra effort to get the news to the media.

12

Municipal Reports
and Events

A MAJOR ASPECT of the over-all municipal public relations program is the presentation of informational reports to the people. The importance of this municipal responsibility cannot be overemphasized, because the entire American system of representative government is predicated on an informed public. A public which is uninformed—or poorly informed—cannot be expected to vote intelligently on the selection of councilmen, bond issues, charter amendments, or any other matters of basic public policy. The local government therefore has a critical responsibility not only to provide public services efficiently but also to keep the public well informed as to past accomplishments, present programs, and future plans.

This chapter discusses some of the more useful specific techniques of municipal public information and public relations as they have been tested in the crucible of experience and found to be effective. Specific attention is given to reports, press relations, and special events.

General Considerations

"Public sentiment," said Abraham Lincoln, "is everything; with public sentiment nothing can fail, without it nothing can succeed." What are the elements then of a sound, well-balanced and reasonable program for informing the public? This chapter does not purport to be exhaustive but rather suggestive of some of the most effective methods of both informing the

public and gaining its favorable "sentiment" for the city and its programs for progress.

WHO IS THE AUDIENCE?

One of the basic decisions to be made is for what segment of the population (or "public," since there are many different publics) the report is intended. An annual report presumably would be designed for every citizen of the city, while a special announcement regarding utility service in one area of the city, for example, logically would be limited in scope and approach to the problem at hand. Similarly, special problems, such as those related to snow removal, fire hazards, or sweeping automobile-congested apartment house area streets, require the "rifle" rather than a "shotgun" approach.

Closely related to the selection of the proper type of report for the particular "public" is the matter of approach and language. The report *must* be couched in the language of the audience, not the city government. Furthermore, it must be prepared from the *viewpoint* of the audience for whom it is intended. An otherwise well conceived and executed report can fail miserably to achieve its goal if it stresses the city government's area of concern in the problem rather than the reader's.

Specifically, most people are less concerned about which department is doing a job, and how difficult it is to recruit qualified workers for the job, than such factors as how long the job will take, how long they will have to suffer

SANTA FE SPRINGS PROGRESS REPORT 1958-1959

FIGURE 23. *Annual report cover* (*Typical of professional quality reports was that issued in 1959 by Santa Fe Springs, California, with a full-color photo on the cover.*)

the inconvenience of torn up streets, and what it will cost the individual property owner.

THE SPECTRUM OF MEDIA

Selection of the proper medium, or media, for the particular report or event is of paramount importance.

Disregarding for the moment the vast total spectrum of media available to the municipal reporter, discussed in greater detail elsewhere in this book, a wide range of possible media for the municipal report still remains.

Not all are equally effective in all circumstances. For example, a newspaper supplement report would be of much less value and effectiveness in the suburb of a great metropolitan area than in an isolated city, simply because

circulation of the "home town" newspaper in a metropolitan area is likely to be much more limited than a comparable newspaper in the more isolated city. These factors are developed in greater detail later in this chapter.

SERVICE, NOT "GIMMICKS"

Like the over-all public relations program, the individual report must be based on the sound foundation of good municipal services. No amount of salesmanship can take the place of the high quality of municipal services that must form the basis for any meaningful report or program. In the same vein, frankness is essential. No one will believe a "rose colored glasses" approach if services are not of a high caliber in the first place.

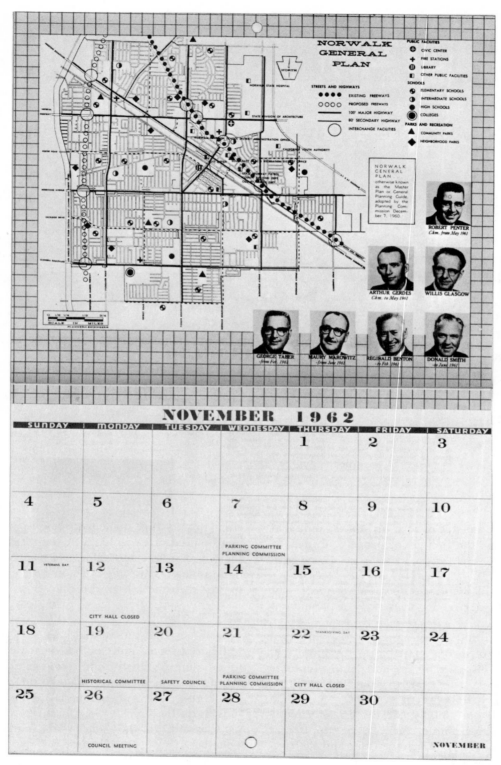

FIGURE 24. *Calendar report* *(Norwalk, California, produced an imaginative calendar-type annual report showing special dates, accomplishments, and goals.)*

In fact, the city that glosses over defects in its reporting is failing to utilize one of the most effective tools for solving municipal problems. If the people see and hear only the "good" side of the question to the exclusion of a frank description of problems, how can broad public support for any program of improvement be expected?

Reports must therefore cover not only those aspects of the matter that place the administration in a favorable light but also a frank discussion of existing problems. Thus the groundwork for future solutions to such problems is laid, and the needs do not come as a surprise to the people who must ultimately make the decisions.

One respected and highly successful "professional" in the public relations field put it this way:

A city council will receive maximum public support if the people believe its actions are (1) necessary, (2) conducted in an efficient and courteous manner, and (3) conceived with an abiding comprehension that the people who pay the bills are entitled to value received.

In trying to prove that a city council is doing a necessary job, and doing it well, it is important to remember that people will pay no more attention to a poorly executed public relations program than they will to a poorly produced play or a dull prize fight. The English language is chock full of colorful, concise, dramatic and informative words. Take advantage of [this] fact or your public relations program will suffer a fate identical to that facing any badly written play when it reaches Broadway.[1]

THE UGLY DUCKLING

Historically, municipal reports have been less than inspiring documents of great interest to the public which is paying for them. Jammed with figures and seemingly endless tedious trivia, they have, in some cases, served as occasionally useful reference sources. If their avowed aim as a report was to inform the public, however, failure was guaranteed by the entire approach to reporting, from general format to the selection of paper and inks.

Recent years, however, have seen a metamor-

---

[1] From "Public Apathy and Public Relations," an address by Clem Whitaker, Jr., presented at the annual conference of the League of California Cities, October 24, 1961.

phosis in the municipal report, and a highly attractive, readable, and effective report has emerged. The former report which resembled an accounting document (and indeed in many cases was exactly that) has given way in many progressive cities to professional quality reports that invite the citizen's attention. Liberal use of photographs, charts, multicolored inks, high quality paper, modern typography, and other factors discussed later in this chapter have transformed the municipal report into something that can and is competing successfully with other reading matter for the attention of the citizen.

USE OF CONSULTANTS

One of the decisions which must be made early in the process of report planning is the question of whether a consultant will be retained to

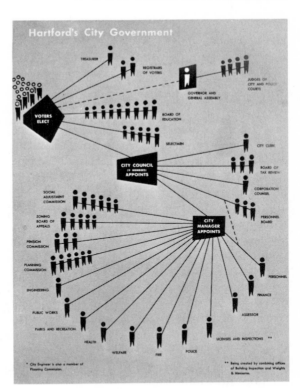

FIGURE 25. *Organization chart (Organization charts, generally of interest to municipal administrators but a bore to the lay reader, have been revised and simplified in some cities to increase readability. An annual report for Hartford, Connecticut, shows this approach.)*

Want to Change Something?

Why Not Help Run Your City?

Your public servants at the City Hall and in all departments of your city government want you to say what you think should be done about this, that, or the other. The services in all different departments are supposed to provide what you want, and here is a chance to let us know.

Tear off the attached card and tell us frankly what you think about it. Don't sign your name unless you want to.

(Detach card here before mailing)

To the Mayor and City Council:

Here's what I'd do to make El Paso a better place for all of us to live:..

....

....

....

....

Name..

Address...

(You don't have to sign the card if you prefer not to)

FIGURE 26. *Use of the double postcard (Feedback from the people is valuable to administrators. El Paso, Texas, is among those cities that include perforated double postcards with their annual reports to solicit views and criticisms from citizens.)*

perform all or part of the report preparation. The primary advantage of retaining a consultant for this purpose lies in the fact that the competent consultant, an expert in the field of mass media communications, can bring a fresh approach to the reporting effort. His tool kit will generally contain techniques, methods, and ideas which may not occur to the busy municipal executive.

The consultant may even be able to save substantial amounts of money which might otherwise be spent on ineffective public reports. Many cities, large and small, have full-time, part-time, or contract-basis public relations consultants who assist in the preparation of reports as well as performing other public relations functions.

The principal deterrent to bringing such expert assistance to many cities is the cost, both in terms of actual dollars and also in terms of what the city council and public *thinks* the cost is or may be. Perhaps, as suggested above, the consultant may save considerable sums of money which would otherwise be spent ineffectively. He may even save the full amount of his fee (or more) through his knowledge and approach to the problem. On the other hand, there may be a local bias against bringing in "outside" help of this type, on the basis that "we don't need any outsiders to tell us about our city." As a matter of fact, many of the most effective reports have been prepared by city employees, without resort to "outside" help.

The various advantages and disadvantages of hiring a consultant to assist in report preparation should be considered carefully, however, before active work on the report is begun, so that the city does not end up with the "same old report" year after year by default.

The Annual Report

The mainstay of municipal reporting continues to be the annual report. This is logical and appropriate, since many private corporations have led the way in this area, and in many cities an annual report is required by law. In other cities, the annual report constitutes both the minimum and maximum effort possible under individual circumstances of available funds, staff time, and other factors.

THE METAMORPHOSIS

As is true of municipal reports in general, the annual municipal report in progressive cities has undergone a drastic and much-needed change. Gone are the endless tables of figures. Gone is the detailed financial data which by no stretch of the imagination could the average citizen be expected to read, let alone comprehend. And gone are the other features which made yesterday's annual report virtually worthless as a true public information document.

Not all cities have made the change. Far too many still cling to the "old reliable" which is simple to prepare in the same format that has been used for many decades.

Those cities that have made the change find that the "new look" is worth many times the additional cost in dollars and manpower which some of the new type reports require. Careful attention is given to such matters as size, for example, as well as paper stock, inks, and type of binding. Full color annual reports are not

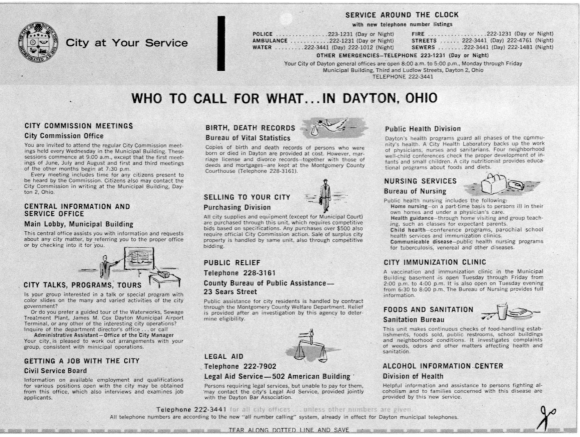

FIGURE 27. *Daily reminder (This useful "tear-out" page was included with the 1960 annual report from Dayton, Ohio. Printed front and back (the front is shown) on card stock, perforated for easy removal, and punched for hanging on the wall.)*

the rarity they once were, and extensive use of photographs, charts, and cartoons drive home points that the old style report either missed entirely or buried in the dark recesses of the interminable text and tables. White space is used skillfully, rather than being filled completely with data.

The new-type report is written from the taxpayers' point of view, rather than the city's. Departmental classifications, with data of interest only to the most avid follower of municipal affairs, have given way to a *service* oriented document. A central theme of some type generally pervades the new-type report, connecting all aspects of the report into a concise, coherent whole, rather than a disjointed collection of individual reports. "INSIDE DAYTON, 1961

. . . taking stock of our city gains . . . needs . . . future" is typical of this approach. Municipal directories of services, complete with telephone numbers and other information, are provided as part of many reports. A professional touch is given by skillful use of photo cropping and emphasis. In brief, cities are recognizing that before the city's story can be told, the attention of the audience must be obtained, and then the quality of the contents and the manner of treatment must be such as to compete successfully with newspapers, magazines, television programs, and a multitude of other stimuli.

THE IMPORTANCE OF APPROACH

Once the decision has been made to issue an annual report, the question of approach is

FIGURE 28. *Annual report cover* (*For many years Santa Monica, California, has presented full-color annual reports of high professional quality, readability, and factual content.*)

next. The straight booklet type report has many advantages and is extremely popular. It might be considered the most natural or basic type of report. It is handier and has a wider range of possible formats than some other types of reports.

The newspaper supplement type has at least one distinct advantage, and that is the absence of a distribution problem: the supplement will be delivered with the newspaper. In general, however, newspaper supplements, by virtue of their very nature, impose a maximum ceiling on quality and are delivered only to subscribers. As a rule, of course, additional copies are obtained by the city for distribution by other means. Many cities, including Norfolk and Los Angeles, have published effective newspaper supplement reports.

A few cities have experimented with a calendar-type annual report, which not only shows important dates and related information on the calendar but also includes some municipal progress information on each page, in the expectation that over the period of a year's use of the calendar, citizens will pick up information about the city and its progress.

In addition to these and other approaches to the annual report is the very important area of audio-visual reporting. Motion pictures, filmstrips, slide programs, and even phonograph recordings have been used with apparent success. This type of report has the advantage of a "captive audience" as well as the tremendous impact of lasting pictorial impressions. The principal disadvantage is the large amount of staff time required to *present* the film or other medium to the public as a unified program. The amount of staff time required to *prepare* the report is in general about the same as for other types of reports, quality and other factors

Key to an All-American City's Progress...

Dayton's Income Tax Program

Dayton's greatest period of progress and its national recognition as an All-American City Award winner are bound up together in the same program.

Since early 1949 Dayton has been moving forward with services and public improvements that meet the needs of a growing, progressive community. The key ... the City Income Tax Program.

When the tax was abruptly halted in court, the people immediately petitioned and then voted to get it restored. This action to preserve their key to progress led to the 1951 All-American City Award.

Here are some of the outstanding results of the City Income Tax Program—

STREET LIGHTING
Street light additions 134% greater than Dayton's 1948 total, and lighting intensity increased even more. Lighting improved on residential and secondary streets and main thoroughfares. Dayton's present 10,449 street lights include 1,864 modern fluorescent lamps on thoroughfares and new expressways.

PARKS AND PLAYGROUNDS
Recreation areas now have 1,800 acres, up 50% or 600 acres over 1948 total. The 54 playgrounds with supervised summertime programs represent increase of 18. New parks include Belmont, Princeton, Nordale, Mallory, McNary-Kammer, Hickorydale, College Hill.

FIRE PROTECTION
Manpower increased to average of four fire-fighters instead of only three on each apparatus. Active fire-fighting apparatus increased from 22 to 25. New special duty rescue vehicle also added. Fire loss per resident cut sharply. New fire stations on Smithville Road, Kings Highway and Monument and Main Streets. Two-way radio and special life-saving equipment on all fire-fighting vehicles. Emergency ambulance service inaugurated with four ambulances operating from fire stations.

HEALTH SERVICES
Health services generally improved, including Grade A Milk controls and immunization program against disease. Evening hours for Central Public Health Clinic and special neighborhood immunization clinics bring services closer to people needing them. Expanded public health nursing program includes physical therapy and occupational therapy. Alcoholism Information Center was established. Special day camps for children with mental and physical disabilities inaugurated.

URBAN RENEWAL
Dayton now clearing blighted areas and encouraging neighborhood improvement. Blighted Haymarket area completely cleared, with some land already sold for redevelopment. Other East Dayton property being improved and renovated. Central Business District Project getting under way. Dunbar-Wogaman Project will improve new Dunbar High School area. Steps under way for citywide program to protect older neighborhoods.

14

FIGURE 29. *Layout and drawings (Otherwise detailed and "dry" facts can be brought to life with a planned layout and interesting drawings, similar to this example from an annual report issued by Dayton, Ohio.)*

being equal. Cost can range from less than $100 to many thousands, depending on a number of factors.

There are many other variables in the matter of report preparation, and many decisions which must be made if available resources are to be used to the fullest. Specific and detailed explanations and guidelines for preparing the annual municipal report are contained in *Municipal Reporting to the Public*.[2] The *Municipal Year Book* contains an annual review of municipal reports and other public relations activities.[3]

[2] Published in 1963 by the International City Managers' Association.

[3] Published annually by the International City Managers' Association.

THE PROBLEM OF DISTRIBUTION

After deciding on the type of report, the critical question of distribution arises. Will the report be mailed to every residence? If so, will it go first class or bulk rate? Large sums of money may be involved in this question, with bulk rate being the less expensive but unfortunately earmarking the report with "junk mail" appearance. There is, therefore, some argument in favor of paying the premium for first class postage to lend a larger measure of dignity and significance to this important message from the city government.

Or will the U.S. mail be used at all? Boy Scouts may wish to take on distribution as a civic project. This involves considerable organization, to insure that delivery is complete, but

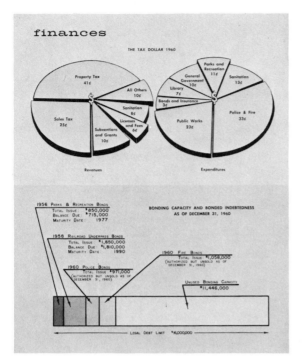

FIGURE 30. *Data presentation (A limited amount of statistical and financial data can enhance the municipal report if done well, as in this example from Pomona, California.)*

it avoids a large measure of cost. In many cities there are companies which specialize in house-to-house distribution, and, interestingly, their fees for large quantity deliveries are in general lower than the U.S. mail.

Several other possible methods of distribution exist, such as newspaper supplements, utility bill mail-outs, and others, and all methods should be considered. Secondary distribution also is important. A good supply of copies should be on hand in every city office which deals directly with the public. Copies should also be available at the library and each of its branches. Barber shops and beauty shops are another excellent secondary distribution point. Close cooperation with the schools can result in reports being distributed in civics classes. There is a wide range of other possibilities for distribution, some of which may be peculiar to a particular city. The important fact is that unless the report is properly distributed, it might as well never have been prepared.

An interesting offshoot of annual reports is the technique of issuing a major report covering a longer span of time. Examples of this type of report are the motion picture, *Decade of Progress,* issued by the city of Glendale, California; *Five Years of Municipal Progress in Beverly Hills;* and the booklet type report, entitled *Pomona, 1950–1970,* issued by the city of Pomona, California, which of course was geared not only to the progress of the past but the prognosis for the future.

Special Reports

The epitome of the "rifle-rather-than-shotgun" approach is the special report. While the term "special reports" covers quite a range of possibilities, the characteristics and advantages that all have is that they are prepared along very specific lines for very specific audiences. They run the gamut from periodic newsletters to leaflets welcoming new residents to the city. Distribution is often via the utility bill, or door-to-door distribution by Boy Scouts or other persons, as suggested above.

In many cities the "Welcome to Your City Council Meeting" leaflet is popular, describing council procedures for the information of visitors who may be unfamiliar with the routine of council meetings.

Several cities have issued comprehensive booklets (some running to 30 and 40 pages) describing the city government in some detail for use in high school and junior high school civics classes.[4]

Distribution of the budget message each year to selected community leaders is also an effective way of bringing important information to the attention of the opinion leaders who make their views known on public policy.

Whenever there is a major change in any municipal service, adequate advance notice is highly desirable. In some cities such notice can be given with the utility billing; in others the notice must be distributed on some other basis. Commercial house-to-house delivery is appropriate if the change is of sufficient magnitude

---

[4] For example, see GLENDALE'S GOVERNMENT, City of Glendale, California, 1960.

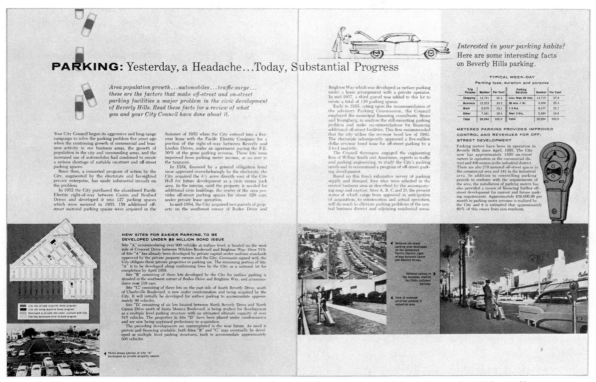

FIGURE 31. *Maps and illustrations* (*This five-year progress report from Beverly Hills, California, makes effective use of drawings, maps, and photographs.*)

to justify the cost. Mailed postcards also afford a reasonably low cost method for reporting such information.

Financial reports of special signifcance may be of sufficient interest to the city's "stockholders" to justify preparing a simplified version for general (or special) distribution. Similarly, reports on special assessment data, urban renewal projects, annexations, fire prevention, conservation, and many other subjects may be found worthy of distribution in simplified form for general or special distribution.

CITY HALL NEWSLETTERS

Newsletters are in a class by themselves. They furnish information which is more current than an annual report and, by virtue of their periodic distribution, permit multiple contacts during the year rather than one concentrated summary at year's end.

Subject matter can be directed more precisely at specific problems and can be more timely. For example, an issue of "Cincinnati Progress," one of the finest of the newsletters,

contains articles on Cincinnati's canine police unit, street repair techniques, a new swimming pool, a new fire building, expansion of health clinics, and a dozen other subjects of real significance in terms of total progress, but possibly not of sufficient magnitude to warrant mention in an annual report.

Budget and finance are also popular newsletter subjects that are approached in a variety of ways, ranging from very detailed descriptions of individual programs to attempts at comprehensive articles for popular consumption. Specific public works projects can also be treated rather elaborately in newsletters, and unspectacular but important cost-cutting and methods improvement programs can be discussed in a manner that would be inappropriate in an annual report.

Newsletters also are often used to chart current trends in building activity, crime, profit and loss on public transportation, library statistics, and similar matters of rather mundane interest which might never find their way into the public press or annual report. Fort

Lauderdale, Florida, has reduced its semi-monthly "Progress Report" to several pages of text accompanied by a series of 21 charts. Each chart (covering sewage treatment, refuse collection, sewer connections, fire calls, auditorium attendance, and other municipal functions) graphically shows statistics covering the last complete fiscal year, with an overlay trend line showing current data in comparison. This type of newsletter is somewhat unusual, and may be less than eyecatching for popular consumption, but it provides timely, accurate, and interesting information on city operations to the serious citizen who will take time to read the charts.

Newsletter format varies greatly. Regardless of size, newsletters are typically less polished than most other municipal public information efforts. Many are mimeographed, concentrating on text. Others are printed and include photos and charts. Some are intended for insertion in utility bills. Some are very simple, for limited distribution to a selected mailing list, while others are mailed to all residents and therefore justify more work and expense in layout, typography, and other features. Several examples of varying newsletters are shown in accompanying illustrations.

Frequency of issue ranges from weekly to semiannually, with monthly and quarterly publication being the most popular. Such regular and reasonably frequent publication permits rather detailed description of behind-the-scenes municipal functions (such as sewage treatment, garbage collection and disposal, and city employee training programs) which might not be brought to the public's attention.

The periodic newsletter also may provide a vehicle for discussing matters of broad public concern which might resemble propaganda if issued as a single white paper but which, if published routinely as part of a continuing program of municipal public information, is generally more acceptable to the reading public. Such subjects might include discussion of proposals for new tax measures, housing codes, capital improvement programs, and other matters which could be considered controversial at the time they are under consideration. It should hardly be necessary to mention that coverage of such subjects in city newsletters must be in harmony with the policies and wishes of the city council and not blatantly campaigning for one side of an issue. Impartial, factual reports on the status of major public issues, however, are in the best tradition of American government. They are essential to intelligent public decisions and as such constitute what is probably the most vital purpose for which the city newsletter may be utilized.

In evaluating the newsletter as a medium for public information, it might well be argued that brief mention of specific, tangible evidences of progress several times a year is more effective in the public mind than "dumping the whole load" at year's end in the annual report. Ideally of course the newsletter and the annual report should be used as a team, with the newsletter carrying the month-to-month details of public programs, and the annual report dealing in generalized results of the over-all program and what this means to the individual citizen.

OTHER REPORTS

Another type of report which is overlooked by many cities is the collateral use of one type of report for another purpose. For example, a very complete bond prospectus may be prepared to sell a certain issue of bonds. Only a few copies are needed, and yet they must be of the highest quality. It costs very few extra dollars to have an extra quantity printed for distribution to the chamber of commerce or other agencies which come in contact with potential industries considering locating in the city.

Official reports from the chief administrator to the city council can also be used as highly effective public information tools. Adequate copies can be prepared so that press representatives may each have a copy. Exercise of considerable care in the preparation of such reports pays big dividends, because the report furnishes a complete and accurate account of the proposal or action. From the newspaper reporter's standpoint, such reports provide an excellent basis for news stories, since they are authoritative and complete, as contrasted with sketchy notes. The report, properly written with the essence of the matter in the first

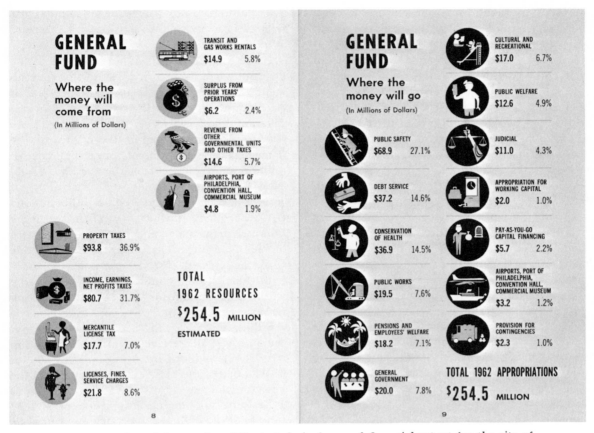

FIGURE 32. *Financial reporting (The popularized annual financial report for the city of Philadelphia shows how complex data can be made more readable by use of charts, graphs, drawings, and illustrations.)*

sentence and certainly the first paragraph, will suggest the headlines and lead sentences that can be either constructive or destructive from the city's standpoint.

In the twilight zone are several "quasi reports" which may not ordinarily even be considered reports. The letters which emanate from the many city offices constitute a very special type of report; the letter is designed for one specific person or group, and the "report" is tailored to fit the circumstances. Such reports can be harmful to the city government, just as they can be highly beneficial, depending on how the letter is written. Some cities, aware of this, have held report and letter writing classes for employees who have occasion to represent the city or one of its departments via letter. The personal aspect of letters makes them a potentially highly effective type of "report."

Paralleling the letter as a "quasi report" is the telephone contacts which daily flow through the city's switchboard. Each call is potentially a favorable or unfavorable contact with the public and should be treated as such. Requests for information must be promptly and courteously handled, and a follow-up call to the complainant (in the case of complaints) gives the citizen double satisfaction: not only is the condition remedied, but the complainant also knows that the city government cares enough to follow up.

A somewhat more formalized version of this same type of report is the use of "special service reports." Several cities have used this technique with great success. It involves little more than a form, coupled with alert city employees and officials. On the form are listed the various types of common defects (cracked pavement, stop sign obscured by tree, etc.) , and referral to the proper department is made, with a control copy going to the office of the city manager for follow-up if necessary. Department heads, policemen, and others whose duties involve field work carry booklets of forms in their vehicles. Again, a follow-up report may be in order if the condition was brought to the attention of a city employee by a citizen.

Another type of "quasi report" is the installation of explanatory signs at the site of major city construction jobs. Such signs inform the people regarding the nature of the project and demonstrate to the public that the city government *does* care about the inconvenience to the public and is doing its best to minimize it.

In brief, the field is virtually wide open in the area of special reports to convey specific types of information. The special report can be more incisive than any annual report, thereby insuring a higher degree of saturation of the information being disseminated.

Press Relations

A special kind of public reporting is that done through the press. It can take a number of forms, ranging from full-scale press conferences, which are rare in all but the largest cities, to simply providing the press with the same materials sent to the city council. Another area is in cooperating with the press on matters of editorial importance, in which factual data to support an editorial stand is needed.

More subtle, but nonetheless worth the time and effort, is the preparation of "fillers," which many newspapers need to fill the blank spaces which would otherwise appear at the end of some columns. If the fillers are on hand, the newspaper is likely to use them. In this manner simple factual matters on a wide range of municipal subjects can be placed before the people on a daily basis.

Coordinating news releases is one of the most important considerations in fostering good press relations. No employee, for example, should release news directly to the press without prior policy clearance from his department head. Similarly, department heads should clear releases of a nonroutine nature with the chief administrator.

It must be stressed that *coordination* of news does not mean *management* of news or concealment of facts. It simply means avoidance of poor timing, or conflicting statements from two different offices, which can be damaging to the city government's program, even though the damage may result from an honest difference of opinion or a failure to recognize the significance of a particular event.

Overlapping areas of responsibility among city departments, such as may exist between the building department and the fire department, or the planning department and the public works department, breed these potential problems. Ideally, such conflicts should be resolved within the organization and then the resulting news released to the press and public on a coordinated basis. This not only insures that the public will receive accurate information free from provincial nuances, but it also helps build a better and more consistent image of the city government.

Building and maintaining good press relations is of the highest importance in the public information program. The press need not *agree* with any particular municipal policy, but if there is confidence in the city official, and a knowledge that "leaks" and "off the record" information is not being made available to favorite reporters, the city government can expect fair play from the press. Obviously, since every citizen cannot observe the workings of the city government, the press becomes his eyes, ears, and conscience, a role of great importance in any representative government.

Press relations—*good* press relations—are of sufficient importance to justify careful cultivation by every public official, as the filter through which information often reaches the public. Inasmuch as this important subject is treated in depth in other chapters, no further detail is necessary here.

Special Events

Another form of municipal reporting is the special civic celebration, open house, or other

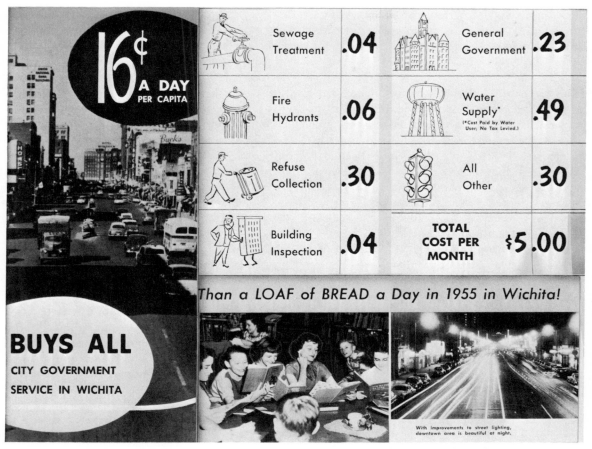

FIGURE 33. *16¢ a day* (*A folder issued in 1955 in Wichita, Kansas, brought municipal costs down to understandable, everyday terms.*)

type of special event. These occasions present an ideal situation for distribution of considerable factual information about the city government. Three dimensional displays may be developed which will tell the city's story more effectively than any pamphlet. Future plans can be shown as well as reports of past progress and current programs.

Similarly, the dedication of new buildings offers a ready-made occasion and a "captive audience" for reporting information. A "Press Night" designed to bring press and news sources into close informal contact has great potential for building good press relations. Use of a "Junior Fire Department" is another technique that has many possibilities. Virtually every child in school becomes an "inspector" in his own home, seeking out fire hazards, reporting them to his parents, and winning recogni-

tion for fire hazards discovered and eliminated. This type of program, involving both public reporting and action, has great potential which has been exploited by relatively few cities.

CITY GOVERNMENT DAYS

"Boy Scouts in City Government Day" has similar possibilities. It allows for dissemination of city information both to the boy at an impressionable age and, through the boy, to the parents at home. Many cities report the use of this technique as well as other "student city government" days during which tours may be conducted, students "substitute" for members of the city council and administration, and they become exposed to some of the facets of city government. These events are generally several hours in length, but some cities have conducted programs lasting several days or even weeks. Such programs can of course do as much harm as good if improperly organized and conducted.

Tours of the City

Bus tours of civic facilities are also being utilized by an increasing number of cities. Typically the tour is conducted by the chief administrator and his staff and includes major points of civic interest, such as city hall, library, police and fire buildings, and public works facilities. A question-and-answer period often follows the tour. Audio-visual presentations, luncheons, and prepared talks by city officials are optional features.

Tours are arranged several days in advance so that exact number of participants is known and detailed preparations may be made. Often such arrangements are offered to service clubs and other civic organizations. Although this technique obviously has a high unit cost, cities utilizing it report high public acceptance and believe that it is successful in telling the city's story.

Town Meetings

Nor have town meetings gone out of style. Increasing numbers of cities are taking the city government's story directly to the people through the medium of neighborhood forums. These programs are often conducted as a series, with one session for each of the major neighborhoods. The meetings are held in school buildings or other public facilities. Members of the city council and professional staff are on hand to speak and to answer questions. In many cases, motion pictures, slides, and other visual aids are used to liven up the presentation. Sometimes the program is televised or broadcasted for wider audiences.

The program must be well organized and well conducted, or the audience will be lost, along with a good opportunity to tell the city's story. And the program must be well publicized, or there will be no audience to address. This is an ideal opportunity to distribute printed information on city affairs, for the audience is preselected and probably expecting and desiring printed information to take home.

One rather specialized version of this type of event is the workshop on local government, which has been employed to good advantage by several cities. Participants are rather carefully selected; teachers and school administrators are the most likely candidates. Speeches, panels, and discussions can be conducted, perhaps preceded by a luncheon or dinner. Top city officials should present carefully organized talks designed to relate to each other and convey the over-all impression desired by the city. With a reasonably small group, participation by all can be maximized and most effective use can be made of visual aids and printed materials.

Other Kinds of Recognition

Special recognition of the city government (such as All-America City recognition and similar awards) can be used to good advantage in focusing public attention on the city government. Rather than accept national recognition only with a two-column story in the local newspaper, many cities have used the occasion for civic banquets, festivals, and assemblies, which can be made as elaborate and inspiring as available resources and imagination permit. Major awards come infrequently enough to any city, and such an event is a "natural" for a civic gathering, a review of the past, a look to the future, and a little added boost for community pride. Even the city's birthday might be used for this purpose.

Sometimes a city problem can be turned into a civic asset. Need a new city seal? Looking for the answer to some knotty problem? Want to involve the general public in some kind of deliberation on a matter of public policy? Hold a contest. The newspapers will be delighted to cooperate, and civic-minded merchants can probably be persuaded to donate prizes. Whatever the contest, whatever the prizes, and whatever the merit of the solutions offered, people will become interested, and they will become involved directly in something that might have otherwise been resolved as a staff study.

Not all problems can be dealt with on this basis of course, and any such program should be instigated only after careful study and with the concurrence of the city council. Properly handled, however, such a technique not only can provide an otherwise elusive answer to a problem but may have the valuable collateral result of uniting the people on a common civic problem. Public relations is a two-way street: people like to feel that they are *part* of the city government, not just the recipients of a one-way stream of brochures and news releases.

Distinguished visitors to the community can also provide the impetus for some sort of special event that will spotlight the city government. In recognizing the visitor, the community is also in a sense recognizing its own significance, for the visitor must have come to this community for some reason. The nature of the event that seems appropriate will of course vary widely, depending upon the visitor and the occasion, but the visitor will be impressed by the city's hospitality, and the citizens will be impressed with the fact that such an important person visited their community.

Departmental Reporting

To this point, the discussion has implied that public reports are generally issued for the entire city government on a centralized basis. This is in fact the approach used in many cities, but such a practice should not eclipse the important role which can be played by the departmental report. Of course it must be assumed at the outset that the departmental report is in harmony with organization-wide policies.

In some cities, charters, ordinances, or state law require filing a departmental annual report. Even in cities which do not require the issuance of an annual report, consideration should be given to doing so, for the purpose of bringing news of the department's good work before the public.

On the other hand, the departmental report need not be issued on an *annual* basis. Special reports may do the job more effectively. Fire prevention is a case in point. An annual or special report from the fire department can both inform the public regarding fire hazards and at the same time generate enthusiasm for eliminating fire hazards, thus assisting the fire department and building a liaison between the

department and the citizens. Civil defense reports can help achieve the same objective, while the police department can issue reports on a multiplicity of subjects, ranging from narcotics to bicycle safety, thus enlisting the good will and cooperation of citizens.

Both the parks and recreation department and the library have similar needs for special reports to inform the public as to services available. And of course any proprietary services (water, electric power, gas, cemetery, harbor, airport, etc.) should be the subject of departmental reports. The examples of this type of reporting are endless; the principal criterion to be used in determining whether to issue a departmental report is whether it will serve the public by informing them as to services available and at the same time serve as a "report to the stockholders" concerning past performance.

Measuring Report Effectiveness

Once the report has been conceived, designed, refined, printed, and distributed, the job appears to be done. It is assumed that a certain proportion of the people will read the report and will thereby become better informed about municipal activities and possibly even (if the report was so intended) motivated to some type of action, whether it be purchasing new refuse containers or joining in the recreation department's ceramics class.

But of those who receive the report (possibly the entire citizenry), how many take the trouble to open it in this age of "junk mail"? Of those who open the report, how many read it, wholly or in part? And of those who read it, how many retain any part of what they read? Unfortunately there has been virtually no scientific research in this field to determine the degree of effectiveness of any particular type of report.

It is this fact, in part, which has caused cities to turn to audio-visual reports, which in general have greater impact than the average (and possibly even the good) printed reports. This does not solve the fundamental problem under discussion, however, because the question of effectiveness must be raised in connection with audio-visual reports just as it is with the traditional printed report.

Crude indicators of report effectiveness are available, of course. Citizen comment, face-to-face or by letter, can give a general idea of report effectiveness. So can evaluation by experts in the field, who know from experience what type of approach, phraseology, and art treatment help elicit the desired response or action. The basis for this type of evaluation lies in the market research which is constantly being carried on by private companies. The criterion of effectiveness is simple: sales. If the sale of a certain brand of cookies takes a sharp upturn after introduction of a new label, for example, and other factors are held constant, it can be concluded that the new label had some quality which sold the cookies, whether it be a cellophane window, an enticing photograph, or special art work. Any number of other types of merchandise, from automobiles to zithers, are sold in large part by the public relations efforts employed.

This type of evaluation, unfortunately, is not open to municipal organizations. Occasional opportunities present themselves, however, such as was the case in which one city offered, in a small article in its newsletter, to haul away backyard incinerators which had been banned for air pollution reasons. The number of old incinerators lining the curbs for collection suggested heavy readership of the newsletter. Another city got the same type of response when pieces of pavement from a street undergoing rebuilding were made available to the public at no cost and an inconspicuous announcement was made in the newsletter. Demand far outstripped supply, giving a general indication of readership of the newsletter.

Opportunities such as these give only isolated evidence on which to base conclusions as to the effectiveness of any particular approach to municipal reporting.

The real job in researching the question of the effectiveness of municipal reports remains to be done. More definitive study must be made than that attempted in the past, and it must be conducted on a sophisticated basis with scientific controls. Above all it must bring in the unknown quantity in this problem: the report reading (or ignoring) citizen.

While this chapter cannot answer the many questions which are inherent in this problem, it is intended to identify the problem and caution the municipal administrator who may assume that because *he* feels a certain report is an effective one, it therefore has had a profound impact on public opinion. Actually its public information value may be nil; even worse, it may actually have an *adverse* effect on the reader's concept of the city government and the subject matter being discussed.

Conclusion

This chapter has suggested the great importance of factual reports in the over-all municipal public relations program. It has stressed the need for building the public information program on the sound foundation of high level municipal services. It has discussed the trend toward the more "polished" municipal report, both annual and special. It has described a number of approaches to municipal reporting and discussed the problems of measuring the effectiveness of municipal reports.

These and other subjects can form the skeleton for an effective program of municipal public relations, but the city itself has to add the "meat" to the skeleton by its own process of selection and adaptation of ideas. In developing its own program of public information, each city should search for the novel, the fresh, and the unique to give the report life, while at the same time realizing that truly new ideas are rare. The approach that may seem hackneyed to the professional who sees municipal reports frequently is probably entirely new and vigorous to the public.

The problem of bridging the gap between a city government and its public is challenging and vital, since the basis of our governmental system is public opinion and consent. In this knowledge, more and more cities are acting to insure that the public's opinion will be an informed one. As city government increases in complexity, this necessity becomes all the more urgent.

13

Reporting in Person

AMONG THE TECHNIQUES of informational reporting, that of reporting in person is without doubt the oldest and perhaps the most extensive. Speech, the primary means of communication, is manifest in all facets of the administrative process. Indeed, speech and face-to-face communication are the principal means of program involvement. As distinguished from those discussions, our focus in this chapter is the public address, presentation, and forum.

Merits of Personal Reporting

Reliance upon reporting in person has many advantages over written reporting and these advantages have positive meaning, particularly for municipal officials.

REDUCES THE ABSTRACTION OF THE CITY

In the *first* place, local government—or any government, for that matter—is an abstraction for many people. Frequently, local government will be referred to in quite abstract terms such as "the city," "the administration," or simply "it." For example, it is not uncommon to hear a comment such as, "The city is planning to build a new library."

Reporting in person reduces the abstraction of government and makes it understandable in terms of the dynamics of people operating the government. Local officials reporting in person to the citizens of a community are the flesh-and-blood embodiment of the government of that community. To the extent that they become known in the community, and respected for the jobs which they are trying to do, the govern-

ment takes on meaning as a real force in people's lives.

PROVIDES THE PERSONAL TOUCH

In the *second* place, oral reporting provides the "personal touch." Even the most brilliantly edited and illustrated written report cannot convey to the average citizen very much about the kind of people who make up his city government. The citizen wants to know "what kind of guy" his municipal official is and "what makes him tick." Personal appearances and reporting in person provide better opportunity for the citizen to discover this than do typescript and photographs. When done effectively, reporting in person conveys warmth and humanity and develops a strong personal appeal created by the speaker's personality.[1]

ADAPTS TO SPECIFIC AUDIENCES

A *third* major advantage of oral reporting is the opportunity of adapting the presentation to the needs and desires of the particular audience involved. Written communications and communications on radio and television are usually and necessarily aimed at general audiences. An oral presentation can fill the needs of audiences who have special interests in particular aspects of the local government's program.

Numerous examples could be given. A local chapter of an engineering society may want to

---

[1] These first two advantages of oral reporting over written reporting will accrue in relatively equal proportions whether the presentation is made literally in person or on television (and to a lesser extent on radio).

hear of the city's plans for future public works construction. A property owners' association may be greatly interested in hearing a report on the local financial picture, probably with emphasis on plans for raising revenue. A parent-teachers association council may desire to hear of plans being made to meet present and future educational requirements of the city.

Reporting in person makes it possible for local public officials to get their messages across to those groups most directly concerned and intimately involved in particular governmental activities. At the same time that the substantive message is conveyed, another more subtle message also is being conveyed—that the people who operate the local government are interested in such groups and their views.

FACILITATES FEEDBACK

A *fourth* major advantage to reporting in person, in distinct contrast to written reporting, is the high degree of "give and take" possible. A written report makes statements for the record. Citizens who find in such reports something which upsets them or with which they disagree must resort to a telephone call, a personal visit, or a letter to city hall if they wish to respond. Many people will not go to such lengths unless they are aroused or feel their interests are threatened. Similarly, statements made by public officials on radio or television allow minimum feedback.[2] On the other hand, the report presented orally allows listeners to make their points—whether in praise or in challenge—directly and immediately.

Further, the "give and take" feature of reporting in person makes it possible for a listener who has failed to understand a point made by the speaker to seek clarification or expansion, which is not possible with the media communications. More effective and immediate feedback is possible through oral reporting. The speaker knows as soon as his presentation and discussion have been finished—the

perceptive speaker knows long before they have been finished—what the reaction is to his presentation. This fact is vital, for it makes possible the launching of "trial balloons" by city officials and thus enables them much more quickly to gauge likely public reaction to a proposed governmental program. An oral statement by a public official is much less likely to commit the local government to a particular policy or program than a written report on such a policy or program.

OTHER ADVANTAGES

As a medium of considerable flexibility, the spoken word has greater capacity than other means of communication to arouse hearers to action, to stimulate their emotions and their thought processes. The responsiveness of hearers is also stimulated by the presence of others in the audience. As a medium of direct communication, the spoken word can convey its meaning more forcefully through intonation, emphasis, and physical mannerisms. An additional virtue of oral reporting is that many people who will listen to a speech will be neither disposed nor willing to invest the time and effort to read a written communication.

Reporting in Person and Program Achievement

As discussed in Chapter 2 the substance of effective public relations is effective program achievement. Though it is true that to a considerable degree good government provides by example its own good public relations, many people are not likely to see or to sense the immediate connections. To these people, governments must explain their programs, their problems, and their intentions. It must be borne in mind, however, that these explanations do not by themselves create effective governmental programs. Although this problem is basic to all communications there seems to be one dimension particularly related to oral reporting. Persons are much more likely to be "taken in" by an effective oral presentation than by a written one. The potential for perversion of "truth" through sheer force of

---

[2] Excepted here are those cases where a public official, typically a mayor or manager, makes a radio or television appearance and offers to answer questions telephoned directly to the broadcasting station.

personality is an ever-present hazard of public life.

Thus, communication, whether written or oral, will have meaning only in a context of reality and performance. Reporting in person, as with other reporting, rests squarely on a foundation of effective government.

A Basis for Citizen Involvement

The accelerating complexity and vastness of government functions and problems has far outstripped the development of communication techniques that will enable the citizen to deal meaningfully with the issues and problems involved.

The extent to which pressures and complexity overwhelm the individual in his ability to give attention to and comprehend the intricacies of government is revealed in the following two examples. In one case, citizens bombarded their local city hall with the telephone inquiry, "Where's my water bill?" after they had thrown away the contents of a mailing from city hall in which had been included, for economy, both a municipal report and the *water bill*.

The second example is revealed in a recent community-attitude survey conducted in a southern California municipality. In response to the request for suggestions to provide funds for financing the rising costs of municipal services, one citizen replied, "The way to finance city services is to stop foreign aid." Although these responses may constitute provocative caricature of citizen understanding, they nevertheless suggest the need for more effective communication.

Perhaps the most effective way to create the positive attitudinal framework through which official and citizen interact most productively is by direct and personal confrontation, with the public official reporting to citizens of the community in person. Although all means of communication should be refined and utilized, particular attention should be devoted to improving the effectiveness and the extent of municipal reporting in person.

An outstanding example of the need for reporting in person may be found in the burgeoning urban renewal programs. Many American cities had made sporadic attempts to deal with blight prior to the United States Housing Acts of 1949 and 1954. Municipalities had also been engaged in programs which in a minor way involved demolition and relocation, such as street and highway construction, public works construction, and similar physical modifications. However, it was not until the emergence of the urban renewal program as we know it today that cities became involved in wholesale and widespread demolition of buildings and residences, with the consequent relocation of businesses and families.

Urban renewal represents not only a new philosophy, namely, that removal and prevention of blight should be a major concern of local government, but it also involves concerns of immediate interest to individual citizens, centering typically around the loss of a lifelong residence. Such a program, vital though it may be to the welfare and economic life of a city, inevitably will come to be viewed as threatening to those immediately concerned, who are all too likely to see only the immediate and short-term detrimental effect it has upon them and upon their direct interests. It becomes easy to ignore the broader long-range community concerns represented in such programs. Here indeed is a prime opportunity for oral reporting by municipal officials.

What can reporting in person contribute? Printed brochures explaining the benefits which urban renewal brings to a city will not allay people's fears. Direct confrontation is essential to the continuation of public confidence, in the face of such a dramatic and potentially threatening change in the physical character of the community. These circumstances demand a series of meetings between the various representatives of the city government and those most directly involved, the residents of the project areas. These people need to be told, in simple and understandable terms, the necessity for the program. The city's appointed spokesmen need to stress the positive aspects of the program.

Direct interaction between speaker and listeners, with feedback from the audience by means of a question-and-answer session following the report, is a crucial agent in this communicative process. Individuals should normally be allowed to express reservations about urban renewal—or whatever topic is being reported—so that the fears they have attached to it can be overtly expressed. Questions reflecting such reservations should be encouraged and then answered with understanding and sympathy.

To repeat, there is fully as much value in the personal appearances of representatives from the local government as in what they say. Such appearances reflect a desire to include the citizens of the community in a participative way in community decision-making. The ultimate decision made may be precisely the same as would have been made without citizen involvement. But the citizenry will now be justified in feeling that they have been consulted and their interests considered judiciously, and thus that their advice has been significant in the decision-making process in their municipality.

Verbal communication directed personally to the governed from the elected or appointed governmental official, accompanied by responsive feedback from the body politic, has always provided a warmly human means of relief from the administrative mechanism of government. The listener is thus encouraged to feel that an invitation to approve and support government action has been issued personally and is therefore to be taken more nearly at face value.

Preparation for Reporting in Person

Whether addressing the annual banquet of the local council of Boy Scouts of America or participating in a panel discussion before the League of Women Voters the principal purpose of the oral reporter is to inform and to educate. The techniques, skills, and information necessary to achieve this purpose depend on the nature of the audience, the subject-matter involved, and the format or type of presentation expected.

Because our focus in this chapter is fairly specific, the range of format or type of presentation is limited generally to formal addresses, lectures, round-table conferences, panels, demonstrations, and forums, or question and answer discussions. On the latter type of public discussion, Thomas F. Maxwell has cautioned:

Public forums can be useful in increasing citizen participation in government if they are carefully planned and are restricted to a specific subject such as a proposed bond issue for public improvements. A public forum which is held for the purpose of discussing municipal government in general has inherent dangers. Even in the most carefully planned public forum, it is difficult to prevent citizens who have a pet peeve from injecting it into the discussion. Public forums which are called for purposes of discussion of the general problems and activities of the municipality are likely to generate much heat and very little light.[3]

Accordingly, even with the forum, the subject-matter, the nature of the audience, and the purpose of the oral presentation can be well known and planned for in advance.

OPPORTUNITIES TO DEVELOP SPEECH SKILLS

Many opportunities to improve the skills of platform expression, both in formal programs or informally, are available throughout the United States. In urban communities, high school, junior college, and university adult education and extension programs abound with courses in speech and public address.

Repeated practice before audiences is fundamental to assure confidence in speech skills. This need can be filled in two ways, which could be alternatives, but preferably should be carried out in succession as ease on the platform increases.

The first is to join one of the many public speaking clubs which meet regularly, perhaps once a month, for dinner, which is followed by speeches by members assigned to address the club on that particular evening. Discussion and criticism of content and presentation follow each speech. Criticism may be made by a selected outside expert or by members of the club, or by a combination of both. The most widely known of such groups are the nationally organized "Toastmasters" clubs, but there are many others, organized around some special vocational or organizational concern.

The Speakers Club of Los Angeles, for example, organized in 1931 by Dean Emery Olson and sponsored by the School of Public Administration at the University of Southern Califor-

[3] Thomas F. Maxwell, "Citizens—The Key to Good Government," PUBLIC MANAGEMENT, August, 1954, p. 174.

nia, provides group practice situations for governmental officials feeling the pressure of the need for personal communication. Originally, many practice presentations in the club's monthly meetings were "dry runs" of actual presentations planned for city councils and other civic audiences by club members.[4]

The alternative is to search out opportunities to speak to community audiences. The first of such public encounters should be with smaller audiences, in relatively informal and relaxing circumstances, if at all possible. Gradually, larger and more formal audiences can be met with increasing self-assurance and ease.

Speech Skills—A Brief Exposition

The literature on public speaking is varied and extensive but a brief review of certain essentials is included in this section. It is our central thesis that any intelligent person can become skilled in oral reporting. Good speakers are made, not born.

Selecting and Arranging Materials for Presentation. A highly useful way to approach preparation of an oral report, whether expository or persuasive, is to think of it as a conversation with a group of listeners. But the conversation is one-way only, posing the difficulty of maintaining audience interest. How, then, in direct reporting, is it best to prepare materials for oral presentation?

The simple answer is to "extemporize" it. The word "extemporaneous" is often used as a synonym for the word "impromptu." In oral communication, however, it has come to have a special meaning. It describes a presentation which allows for maximum planning and preparation of the subject matter, yet retains the directness, the spontaneity, and the consequent increase in listener attentiveness, of highly effective platform communication. Thus, the speaker takes full opportunity to prepare a rationally arranged body of materials, judiciously screened for maximum efficiency in achieving a particular effect on his listeners.

Generally there are four possible ways to

present any speech: it may be impromptu or extemporaneous, or it may be read from manuscript or recited from memory. To illustrate these methods visually, it is helpful to arrange them along a straightline continuum, as shown below, indicating the degree of advance preparation for a speech. It can lead to an awkward presentation that embarrasses the speaker as well as the audience.

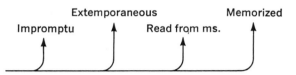

No one, if he can avoid it, should plan to present a speech impromptu, or with little or no advance preparation.

On the other hand, if a speech is read from manuscript, it assumes a rigid form, from which the speaker—or, more accurately, reader—cannot easily digress to adapt to an audience's reactions. Most of us read aloud very badly. Moreover, it is difficult to talk directly to an audience while consulting a manuscript. And if a blackboard or other visual aid is used, it may be awkward to depart physically from the manuscript. The exceptions to the counsel against reading from manuscript are when material must be presented carefully such as on a formal occasion, for testimony of record, or at a time of controversy.

Memorizing is even more hazardous, since the speaker must recall precisely what was on the manuscript, yet present it in a fresh and spontaneous manner. This method of presentation will almost invariably lead to a stiffness of manner and to an excessively fluent language pattern which will not show the speaker at his best.

How then should a speech be presented for most uniformly effective results? Extemporaneously, of course—which is to say that the speaker will talk conversationally to the audience, following a carefully planned pattern of ideas. The precise steps to follow are, in brief form:[5]

---

[4] Emery E. Olson, THE SPEAKERS CLUB OF LOS ANGELES, Civil Service Assembly, Pamphlet No. 4, July, 1936. Often such clubs serve as clearing houses for civic groups seeking speakers on public affairs.

[5] Any one of several standard works on public speaking will expand on this process in a useful manner. See, for example, Milton C. Dickens, SPEECH: DYNAMIC

1. Define purpose in speaking (or response desired from listeners) .
2. Collect materials appropriate to purpose.
3. Select and arrange materials best suited to purpose.
4. Outline speech in written form, using full sentences.
5. Prepare visual aids, as appropriate to purpose.
6. Practice extemporizing (aloud) , using outline as a guide.

Materials to be used in a speech may be developed into a variety of so-called "forms of support," sometimes referred to as "amplifying information," or "supporting detail." Information on a particular subject may be used to expand an assertion, amplify an idea or concept, or support a general line of argument. Usually such information appears as:

1. Statistical data
2. Examples, either
   (a) specific instance (undetailed)
   (b) illustration (detailed)
3. Comparison and contrast, or analogy
4. Testimony
5. Restatement, or reiteration

Graphic structures of accounting formats are frequently used to present comparative numerical data, or results of statistical analyses. Certain budgetary items reported publicly must be presented visually during a speech, to achieve full and immediate comprehension. Examples of topics treated in a talk may be shown in pictorial or cartoon form. Other kinds of information may be visualized more readily than verbalized.

The fundamental form of expression is deductive in nature. That is to say, the speaker progresses from a general statement to specific samples of information. These samplings, or "supporting materials" as we have called them, must be (1) sufficient in number to effect audience comprehension, (2) related closely to the listeners' everyday experience, and (3) truthfully representative of the whole body of information sampled. This latter point is, of course, where honesty in reporting is most likely to go astray.

A general statement or assertion, accompanied by one or more forms of supporting material is what Dickens describes as a "speech unit."[6] Various combinations of these "units" to a maximum limit of five or six, with appropriate transitional materials, can be arranged for reporting the same general topic in a different manner to different audiences.

There are some commonly recurring patterns of arrangement which are "natural" to the treatment of certain topics, of course, such as a chronological sequence to describe an event, a spatial arrangement to describe a physical environment or setting, a cause-to-effect (or effect-to-cause) sequence, or a problem-solution rational progression. These occur so frequently they are referred to as "stock" patterns of arrangement of materials for oral presentation.

Effective introduction of a presentation combines forceful demand for listener attention and provocative focus of this attention on the main ideas to be treated, most particularly to the purpose to be achieved in reporting. A number of time-honored techniques are detailed in the available literature on speech making.[7] The use of humorous narrative is probably the most common. It is employed much too frequently and often with questionable taste, but several others are equally good and can be applied imaginatively to the topic in hand. The speaker, for example, might quote a striking statistic, or repeat a forceful piece of testimony favorable to the view he will espouse.

In the final analysis, however, the individual must develop his own style for introducing a talk effectively. Oftentimes, for a speaker to move easily into the central substance of the report a discreet blending of elements from events which occurred earlier in the meeting, or recent public events, spiced with a touch of wry humor, will do the trick as well as some standard rhetorical device.

The conclusion should achieve a reinforcement of the purpose of the talk by means of a pointed summary of what has been said, or a

---

COMMUNICATION, Second Edition (New York: Harcourt, Brace and Company, 1963) , and Alan H. Monroe, PRINCIPLES OF SPEECH: Fourth Brief Edition (Chicago: Scott, Foresman and Company, 1958) .

[6] Dickens, *op. cit.*, pp. 57–59.

[7] Dickens and Monroe are particularly helpful on this point. See Dickens, *op. cit.*, pp. 145, 152; Monroe, *op. cit.*, pp. 168–171.

FIGURE 34. *Visual aids are almost indispensable for certain kinds of explanations*

strong restatement of the purpose. The exit should be quick and forceful, but neither hurried nor confused.

If we seem urgent in espousing efficiency in the introduction and conclusion of a speech, it should be kept firmly in mind that every second used in this way subtracts from the total time available for the main body of materials to be communicated. Only with an uninformed or hostile audience can a speaker afford to spend much time pre-conditioning his listeners to a properly receptive frame of mind.

This brief treatment of the fundamental elements in selection and arrangement of subject materials pertinent to oral reporting should focus attention on the need for full and careful consideration of the verbal path to be followed in preparing a speech. To prepare his mind properly for conversation with an audience, the speaker must take into account all the alternative routes the verbal treatment of

his report might take, and select that combination of ideas and component detail best calculated to bring full comprehension to the members of the audience.

Visual Aids for Oral Reports. Visual materials are almost indispensable for certain kinds of explanatory talks. The fundamental function of language is to transfer meaning through verbal stimulation. Sometimes, however, language is a hopelessly inadequate and inefficient means of communication. If "one picture is worth a thousand words," then efficiency dictates use of the picture, both to save time and to insure full comprehension by the listener. An explanation of precisely how a tax dollar is spent, or how an agency functions to serve citizens in some specific way, can best be effected through visual stimulation, with accompanying verbal commentary (Figure 34). Visual materials might include maps, charts, graphs, diagrams, pictures, small working models, or even demonstrations with full scale equipment. Common devices to create visual materials might include a portable chalkboard or a paper pad mounted on an easel and an assortment of colored crayons or felt-point pens. Slides and movies are employed where fuller dependence on visual materials is essential to convey the message.[8]

A simple credo for the reporter who is trying to decide whether to use a visual aid would be that if a thing must be *seen* to be *understood,* then it should be *shown,* and talk should be used to clarify and point up relationships in the visual materials. Occasionally, an abbreviated outline on a chart could be used. Often, the visual materials simply make more vivid the facts the speaker wishes to present, and reveal with greater clarity the facts he thinks are most significant to the audience.

When visual aids are to be used in a talk, the manner in which the speaker employs them, or adapts himself to them, becomes quite important. The speaker should retain control of the attention he directs to the visual material. This means getting the attention of the listening audience, then directing it to the precise item or items displayed at the exact moment each item becomes pertinent to the topic discussed. Thus, each chart, graph, or picture should be displayed only at the time attention is invited to it. At the outset of the talk, *no visual material* should be in view. Thus, even when showing movies or slides, when the communicator becomes only a voice in the dark, the speaker should first establish a meaningful context for the visual aid. He should tell the listeners precisely what to expect from the film or slide sequence, then proceed with it in carefully rehearsed fashion, re-emphasizing at the conclusion the message contained in these particular visual materials.

Finally, visual aids may make it possible for the reporter to convey a much more detailed message than would otherwise be possible. They should always be made subordinate to the purpose of the message, else listeners will

be led astray from the purpose, or attention will be distracted from the line of thought the speaker is developing.

The Language of Talking. Nobody is "fluent as a faucet!" This comment, attributed to a speech pathologist who is deeply concerned with the non-fluency of the stutterer, succinctly describes the difference between the language of speaking and of writing. English is a curiously confusing language in which there are some 45 different spoken sounds, but only 26 written characters; or to put it another way, there are some 11 different ways to spell the sound "ee."

Why should this concern a person who wants to talk fluently and cogently to a listening audience? It clearly suggests the hazard in assuming that a written manuscript, read to an audience, will provide the warmly personal, conversational tone essential to holding listener interest. The essential grammatical structure of speech is looser, its vocabulary more fluid and more colorful, than the more rigidly disciplined compression of a well-expressed essay. The speaker must personalize his language, using "we" and "I" profusely to emphasize the close personal identification he feels with his audience. He should use bizarre, provocative, figurative expressions to embellish the ideas he is sharing verbally with a group.

Clarity is not, unfortunately, a simple matter. To illustrate the point, consider the speaker who resorts to an endless string of cliches revolving around an obvious, possibly fatuous point. His language is simple, and the meaning of all he says is clear, but the broad choice of possible meanings left to the listener creates as much vagueness as though every third word were utterly meaningless.

Vocal Variety. Fundamentally, good vocal behavior on the platform is based on "vocal variety." This phrase describes a highly flexible pattern of vocal emphasis involving wide variations of vocal pitch, intensity (or loudness), and rate of speaking, accompanied by frequent pauses. These changes express movement and thus are closely related to the power of a speaker to hold the attention of listeners. Psychologically, movement is the essential ingredient in holding attention. Monotony in any

---

[8] Communication texts usually carry a brief section on this topic. Monroe, *op. cit.,* has a useful treatment, pp. 122–28.

visible or audible form, or repetition of any expressive pattern or physical movement, encourages inattention.

The extreme in vocal variety would be equally distressing, since it would tend to draw attention from the meaning itself. The amount of vigor and variety in the voice should naturally be appropriate to the meaning of the ideas being presented.

The human voice is a marvelously expressive instrument, accurately reflecting human feelings. If ideas are to be transmitted orally, good vocal expressiveness is a fundamental necessity.

How can the layman insure good vocal variety? The answer lies partly in the natural relation of volume level and pitch level in the voice. The human voice will vary through a melodic pattern two octaves or more in breadth, and will range in volume from a whisper to an ear-splitting level. Experiments have shown that when the level of loudness is raised, the pitch level rises. The reverse is of course also true. It has been determined experimentally that the higher the pitch level, the broader the range of melodic change in vocal expression.

Hence, several interactions may be accomplished simply by raising the voice to a higher level of loudness. This makes the voice more sharply audible, demanding attention. It also raises the pitch level, thus widening the melodic range of vocal expression. If the rate of speaking is proper, and occasional pauses and appropriate physical responses accompany it, the speaker has thus attained a marked increase in vocal variety, or improved his expressiveness, simply by raising the loudness level of his voice and projecting his verbal message more forcefully in the direction of his hearers.

Speaking Rate and Pronunciation. The language of the speaker must not only be heard clearly, but it must be uttered in an expressive manner that holds attention and can be comprehended. This means a combination of a comprehensible rate of utterance with precise, clear pronunciation of sounds and syllables.

Rate of speech is a variable matter, determined by the general behavior pattern of the individual. A tense, volatile, quick-moving individual will speak more rapidly than a quiet-mannered, deliberate person. All speakers must pronounce words slowly enough to insure clear pronunciation so that the listener may comprehend fully. If the speaker tries to think of listening ears as receiving microphones, with physiological limitations similar to the electronic limitation of a "mike," a more effective adjustment of rate of speaking will be achieved.[9]

Clear, precise pronunciation is most directly influenced by general jaw movement, and by movements of the lips in shaping the vowels and in articulating the consonants. Vigorous mouth and jaw movement while speaking will materially improve the clarity and precision of pronunciation. Precise articulation is the secret of good vocal projection.

With excellent vocal variety, achieved primarily by raising the volume level of the voice significantly, combined with a judiciously varied rate of utterance, fortified by precise and careful pronunciation, the speaker will encourage attention and facilitate comprehension. Encouragement of good vocal habits will make a speaker a more efficient medium for transmission of a message.

Physical Behavior. The effect on the listener of the posture and gestures of the head and hands of a reporter are an important complement to vocal behavior. Again, well-controlled and vigorous movement attracts and directs listener attention. Responsive facial expression, with vigorous gestures of arms and hands will emphasize meaning in a manner very helpful to full comprehension by a listener.

The core element in soliciting listener attention is, of course, the direct visual contact of the speaker with individuals in the audience. A steady movement of the eyes across the audience, with a brief fixation to center attention on persons selected at random throughout the listening group, invites attention in a basic manner. A crude and mildly negative way to put it would be to say that a listener finds it difficult to be inattentive to a speaker who is looking directly at him. Hence, the maximum amount of speaking time freed from notes or

---

[9] See Grant Fairbanks, VOICE AND ARTICULATION DRILLBOOK. (New York: Harper Bros., 2nd ed., 1960).

manuscript to observe listeners closely is always desirable.

An easy, alert posture, poised but not "ramrod" stiff, is an important part of effective physical behavior while talking. Drooping onto a podium, hands in pockets or clasped in front or behind, and other odd-appearing postures, are a negative and distracting influence on the listeners.

General movements of a definite sort are best utilized to help emphasize climactic points. The chief hazard in moving about on a platform is the possibility of distracting attention from the lines of thought being developed by the speaker. Gestures appropriately punctuating verbal high points serve to reinforce the vocal elements of emphasis in a speech.

Admittedly, nature has endowed some of us more favorably than others to achieve impact on a listener. Some are tall and easy to see from a distance, or have powerful voices easy to hear in the rear of the room, or possess an easy familiarity with a large reservoir of hilarious stories. These are advantages to be utilized if available, but they are not basic to success as a communicator. Some of our finest orators have been unremarkable in all three ways indicated. Any normal, intelligent public official can improve his effectiveness before an audience through conscientious practice and experience.

Multiplier Effect: Optimizing Oral Reporting Opportunities

The effectiveness of a program for municipal reporting in person depends not only on well-trained speakers but especially on the worth and interest of the subject matter or speaker's topic. Almost any service or function of government is substance for a public address and, with a little ingenuity, can be made interesting. Interesting remarks merit receptive audiences.

The Speakers' Bureau

There is an ever-present need for enlarging and expanding the communication network for dissemination of information about the municipality. There is a corresponding need by a variety of groups for qualified and interesting speakers. Systematic efforts to schedule govern-

mental speakers before groups desiring able speakers is one of the more effective ways of expanding the information network of the municipality. Members of audiences who hear a stimulating address on governmental role and function tend to become emissaries by carrying the message to their circle of associates, thus expanding the real audience of the speaker. This "multiplier effect" of reporting in person is basic to effective government. The systematic exploitation of such opportunities by scheduling those who speak on behalf of the municipality is normally a function of a *speakers' bureau* or is handled through *speakers' panels.*

In one metropolitan area, a series of seminars was planned to inform residents of several proposed solutions to metropolitan problems. Despite a vigorous attempt to publicize the seminars, they were not very well attended. Largely the same people attended all the seminars, and those who did attend were already quite knowledgeable about government and the issues involved. The typical man-in-the-street, unsophisticated in his understanding of government, did not attend. This highlights the need to promote speaking opportunities before groups whose members, upon hearing the municipal story, will share it with their friends. A speakers' bureau is a means of creating a demand for information about local government and of providing a mechanism to fill this demand.

Who Shall Speak? Inasmuch as the two principal criteria for an interesting speaker are knowledge of subject-matter and skills in speech, any municipal employee who either has or is willing to acquire such knowledge and skills should be considered for listing on the municipal speakers' roster. Deliberate conscious effort should also be made to include on such a roster those volunteer citizens who are not affiliated officially with the city government but who nevertheless cultivate their interest in maintaining good government. Special effort should be made to include those people who are the thought leaders and who are at the power centers of the community. This is especially true of lay citizens who serve as chairmen or members of municipal advisory committees, bond campaign committees, and similar groups. If they are receptive to the idea, there is merit in including chamber of commerce presidents and managers, service club presidents, local church leaders, and other such people to whom citizens look for direction and counsel. Although some private firms sometimes hire professional speakers, there is not much to commend this approach for a city.

What Shall They Say? From the speaker's point of view the subject should be within his range of experience or knowledge; otherwise he will probably have difficulty in holding the attention of the audience. From the listener's point of view the subject must be related to his interests and the occasion, including the background. The range of topics should include both general and specialized interests and skills. Many groups will want to hear in general about the city government's plans and programs. Other groups will want to know about a particular plan or program. Those speakers who are so inclined should be encouraged to develop special skills in talking about urban renewal, fiscal problems and operations, public works, and other specialized areas. Certain prominent municipal officials may speak on topics of broader social interest because when speaking they will be identified primarily as municipal officials and their effectiveness will reflect favorably upon the city.

Promoting Speaking Engagements. Creating a demand for speakers is a primary function of a speakers' bureau. Audiences for municipal speakers are almost unlimited. A sampling of the broad range of potential audiences includes local civic and service clubs, church groups, evening cultural groups, women's clubs, business and professional organizations, various chamber of commerce groups, educational and fraternal groups, and groups attending various celebrations and dedications. For the active promoter there will be many opportunities at high school and college career days, public service career conferences, trade fairs, panels, specially arranged audiences of elementary and high school teachers of civics and social studies, and as guest lecturers in high school and college classes.[10]

Two principal approaches to such groups are through the mails and personal contact, both of which should be used in a complementary fashion. Additionally, press releases to the news media, both at the time of establishment of the speakers' bureau and with respect to its continuing operation, are of some value.

Mailing lists of appropriate community groups are easily compiled. These should include current officers of the groups, and their program chairmen, and their respective addresses and telephone numbers. Speakers' bureau brochures, indicating the function of the bureau and listing the topics for speeches and the qualifications of speakers, should be mailed to all such groups initially, with a reserve of brochures retained for distribution to those groups who may inquire at a subsequent date. Follow-up personal contacts with presidents of groups and personal interviews with program chairmen are highly effective in stimulating speaking engagements.

The role of employee associations and professional associations in encouraging public addresses on government problems and needs before lay groups is often significant. The Los Angeles County Employees Association maintains a speakers' bureau, from which letters are written to all county department heads inviting them to encourage their employees to undertake such speaking engagements.

As an example of the municipal experience with speakers' bureaus, Las Vegas, Nevada, prepared a booklet, *City of Las Vegas—Speakers' Panel* which initially was distributed to 20 local civic and service organizations. The booklet describes the background of each municipal employee and lists the subjects on which he is qualified to speak. Topics include such subjects as assessment districts, traffic safety, city finance, fire prevention, city parks, crime prevention, the public library, utility problems, and ordinance enforcement.

Supporting Speakers Through Preparation of Materials. A major responsibility of a municipal speakers' bureau is the preparation of current materials for use by speakers. In some cases, entire speeches are prepared, while

---

[10] Promoting communication about government services and careers in the manner suggested here has long

been a feature of the efforts of the Joint College-Federal Service Council of Southern California.

in others the speakers are provided with outlines and illustrative data, as well as specially prepared visual aids. In some instances the bureau collects and catalogs material and serves as a reference library. For individuals listed on the speakers' roster periodic briefing meetings may be held in which the latest information about the municipality's operations and plans is disseminated. Feedback from speakers who have fulfilled assignments should be solicited, indicating attitudes and views of groups to which they have spoken.

Information kits are often supplied to speakers. Such kits for a municipality should be complete and appropriate, including city charter, recent annual reports, recent budgets, and any other significant informative material. Maintenance of such kits with current material and information is important. The Navy Department's Office of Information prepared a U.S. Navy "Pocket Speakers' Guide," which includes 13 cards, each on a topic which navy personnel frequently are requested to discuss. The Standard Oil Company of California has developed for its speakers a brief handbook which is used in a special brief training course for company speakers. Additionally, the public relations staff circulates to the speakers a monthly newsletter with data on speakers, topics, audiences, and platform communication.

Reaching the Hard-to-Reach. It requires constant effort on the part of the mayor, city councilmen, the city manager, and other city officials to make sure that they are reaching all major segments of the community. It is not enough, for example, for the city manager to talk only before service clubs, PTA's, the local chamber of commerce, and other groups that tend to be upper-middle income in nature. He also should seek out organized minority groups, labor unions, boys' clubs, settlement houses, and specialized professional and occupational groups.

City managers and other city officials should get to know their community as well as possible —to learn about its socioeconomic intangibles as well as its physical assets—to learn about its socially and culturally disadvantaged groups. Very few requests for speakers will come to city hall from the "wrong" side of town. City

officials must seek out representatives of these groups so that they can be better known.

THE INTERJURISDICTIONAL IMPACT

Increasingly, urban administrators must consider the metropolitan dimension of local problems. Urbanization and a proliferation of urban government units, with the concomitant interdependence of governments, expand yearly. Increasingly, decisions made by one political unit have a direct and immediate impact upon contiguous and neighboring units. Furthermore, area-wide problems (transportation, air pollution, etc.), which cannot be dealt with effectively by governmental units acting upon them independently, are creating increased pressure on urban management.

Municipal public relations in general, and oral reporting in particular, can play a vital role in the field of intergovernmental relations within metropolitan areas. Granting that Americans seem to prefer a "muddling through" approach to the solving of metropolitan problems, rather than drastic reorganizations, it is likely that the response to metropolitan problems will ultimately rest upon intergovernmental cooperation. This approach has increased in popularity in recent years, largely because it does not disturb existing governmental arrangements within metropolitan areas.

If intergovernmental cooperation is in fact the key to the future, it is important that local governmental officials get to know and respect each other, and learn to work together. Ultimately, given the basic assumptions of democratic government, it is even more important that the constituencies represented by these officials should learn to avoid past suspicions and to sink differences in a common cooperative endeavor.

In effect, then, central city governmental people should make a real effort to address suburban gatherings personally. Suburban governmental representatives should do the same at central city gatherings. Such appearances can and will help greatly in allaying the mutual suspicions which, unfortunately, exist currently in many metropolitan areas. In many such areas, suburbanites view the central city government as an ogre. Appearances by representatives of these governments, at which urban representatives report in a warm, humane, and understanding fashion about governmental problems of the area as viewed from their perspective, should go a long way toward helping to reduce this suspicion and conflict. The converse is obviously true with regard to attitudes held in the central city toward suburban governments.

Again, it is important to stress the *personal* aspect of the reporting. Central city-suburban conflicts have become rather emotional issues in a number of places in the United States and are not amenable to amelioration by written documents. What is needed is the personal touch, supplied by reporting in person.

In one metropolitan area where a meeting was held regarding this problem, two of the participants on the panel were the mayor of the core city of the metropolitan area and a suburban official who was active in a municipal league in the area which excluded the central city from membership. The history of city-suburb relationships in the area was not a bright one. The audience was a denominational high school assembly, with members drawn from the entire metropolitan area.

Despite the past history of city-suburb conflict, both the core city and suburban representatives reflected very reasonable views toward the area's metropolitan problems, and toward each other. As a result, some of the suburban students who had been accustomed to hearing of the city government as an octopus, and some of the city students who had heard of the suburban governments as too small to be anything but petty and selfish in an insular manner, began to modify their points of view.

The changed attitudes exemplified in this experience are a real need if metropolitan governmental units are to cooperate in solving common problems. Effective oral reporting across municipal boundaries can do much toward effecting such an important shift in public attitudes toward the management of their communities.

14

Printing Arts and Publications Distribution

Municipally produced reports, newsletters, informational folders, and other materials can satisfy important public information requirements when their design, production, and distribution are developed with full consideration for their use and ultimate objectives. Municipal publications[1] provide an indispensable part of the public information and reporting program that is met through a wide variety of communication methods and techniques. In contrast to information disseminated through established mass communications media, municipal publications involve the local government directly in all of the specialized processes inherent to the field of communications. Availability, readability, attractiveness, layout, distribution, and other similar criteria will affect the success of the effort. When carefully planned, with full consideration of other communications alternatives, municipal publications provide an excellent way of reaching many publics.

Many problems can plague the agency that decides to produce and distribute its own reports and other materials. However, with care, attention to accepted principles, and recognition of the cost and limitations involved in house-produced and distributed publications, this method of communication does offer great potential for municipal administrators. Intelligent use of the technique, however, requires some understanding of printing methods and publications distribution.

Selecting the Publication

Before selecting a specific communication method for any public information project, several factors should be considered:

The Audience

All communities consist of many "publics."[2] In our highly pluralistic society there are many possible groupings of human beings. Any single individual may hold multiple membership in many groups and therefore may be exposed to many channels of public information and communication. A resident in a metropolitan area must simultaneously be reviewed as a member of many "publics" and as a potential receiver from numerous communication channels. In more subtle and less readily definable ways, the

---

[1] In the publishing and printing industries the term "publications" generally is limited to books, magazines, newspapers, monographs, photographs, maps, and other materials that are announced, advertised, sold, and distributed to the public. They indicate a broader range of interest and distribution than city-issued reports and other materials have. For purposes of this chapter, however, the term "publications" will mean reports, newsletters, informational folders, and other materials that are issued by the city government—primarily for people residing in the community.

[2] See Chapter 5, "The Multitudinous Publics."

population of any community also may be thought of as consisting of people of various educational levels who differ in their ability to receive and interpret information. They also may be perceived as consisting of those who are "thought leaders" and those who are not.

The community may even be multilingual, and there may be a need to think in terms of the foreign language elements in the community, as well as in terms of the political, racial, or religious character of the various community elements.

Intelligently conceived public information activities therefore demand the precise identification of the audience, as well as the structuring of the information to meet their specific requirements and tastes.

AVAILABLE COMMUNICATION CHANNELS

A citizen of a modern metropolitan community is linked to numerous communication channels. Both the metropolitan and the suburban mass media look on him as a customer and client. He may read one or more metropolitan daily newspapers and may additionally receive a suburban daily newspaper and several local weekly or semi-weekly publications. He may listen avidly to several television and radio stations with a broadcast area encompassing the entire metropolitan area and he may also listen to smaller stations serving single suburban areas.

As a member of several formal community groups, he may be linked to further specialized communication channels. As a member of a church, a parent-teachers association, a civic club, a fraternal organization, and a group of local taxpayers, he may be the recipient of specialized publications issued by these groups.

Functionally, his identity as a union member, as the owner of a multiple dwelling unit, as a sportsman, and as an electrician may involve membership in several additional formal groups and a link-up with still other publications and communication channels. He may regularly receive the house organ of his employer, the newsletter or journal of his union, and similar publications of the apartment house owners' association, and of the Sportsmen's Guild. Even without formal membership in a community group, he may subscribe to community newsletters and journals which serve specialized interests.

The concept of a single "public" approachable by a single communication method therefore must be viewed as a fiction rather than fact.

Even when an individual can be identified as belonging to a specific public and as being linked to a specific communication channel, there is no certainty that he can be reached and affected by information transmitted through that channel. A reader of a metropolitan newspaper may confine his attention to the sports section. A television fan may limit his exposure to western dramas. An individual with broader tastes may expose himself to these media in such a random and intermittent way as to reduce the exposure to a level where it lacks practical significance.

The communication methods which are available for reaching any given audience and the degree of audience receptivity to those methods therefore become highly significant variables in the planning and execution of any public information project.

MESSAGE CONTENT AND PURPOSE

The core message and the purposes behind its transmittal also become significant in the selection of a public communication method. The interrelated requirements of the project itself, the "transmitter," and the "receiver" must be considered. For example, some types of civil defense instructions may require a sophisticated understanding of radiological matters by the public. In such a situation, the technical requirements of the public information project may well demand the presentation of highly complex technical information. At the same time, the publics (or receivers) to whom it is addressed may lack technical training in the subject and may also represent widely varying levels of literacy. The message content therefore would require a cultivated simplicity and directness and might demand extensive illustrative and graphic material. This kind of copy normally is not suitable for a daily newspaper, which is in the news dissemination business rather than in the field of public education.

Thus, some other communication channel or channels transmitters would be used.

ILLUSTRATIVE CASES

Undeniably, the agency-produced publication can play an important role in the total agency public information program. The proper integration of such publications into a total program, and into the communication network of a community, has been demonstrated by several successful public information projects.

The Unwelcome Incinerators. When Los Angeles County adopted a ban on all refuse burning in "inefficient" incinerators, its control agency immediately faced several substantial public information problems. One such problem concerned apartment house owners who had incurred substantial costs in constructing incinerator equipment and who now had to abandon use of the equipment or modify it to meet the new legal requirements. Rather than prepare extensive publications of its own on this subject, the control agency prepared a series of illustrated articles which were published in the monthly magazine of the Apartment House Owners Association. A previous check had shown that most of the incinerators which could be modified were operated by members of this association. Following publication of the articles in the association magazine, reprints were prepared in pamphlet form on the control agency's own offset press. The original articles were simply photographed and the image transferred to metal offset plates, thus saving substantial costs for typography. The pamphlet carried a notation stating that its contents originally had been published in the magazine and that the information presented had been screened both by the control agency and the association. Inspectors distributed copies of the reprints to incinerator owners during the course of their routine inspections, and the agency's public information office used them to respond to inquiries concerning the program from apartment house operators. In this public information project, the proper message reached the proper audience in a way designed to heighten its impact, credibility, and receptivity—and at minimum costs to the taxpaying public.

Revenue Bonds for the Marina. In a similar case, a western county provided its electorate with information concerning a forthcoming item on the ballot by publishing a series of feature articles in weekly and semi-weekly suburban newspapers. Involving the issuance of revenue bonds to finance a new marina, this public information project featured well written and illustrated articles concerning the marina. The articles were distributed to weekly and semi-weekly newspapers. Upon publication of the articles, a representative sample of "clippings" from several newspapers was assembled, pasted up in pamphlet form, photographed, and reproduced on an offset press. The cover of the printed booklet gave credit to each of the newspapers in which the articles had appeared, and each article in the booklet carried the masthead of the newspaper from which the "clipping" had been taken. Copies of the booklet were used to respond to public inquiries.

Planning the Publication

Necessary to the success of any municipal publication venture is the planning which precedes the project. At least nine major planning steps must be taken, and at each step important decisions must be made.

Purpose. The purpose of the planned publication must be clearly defined. Is the document designed simply to be instructive, or is it to change existing attitudes? Is it to build public support for a program, or is it to provide details concerning that program to those who will be involved in its administration and implementation? Is its purpose to promote land-use planning and zoning as a city program, or is it to instruct property owners on the proper procedures to follow in requesting a specific zone change?

Audience. Any publication should be aimed at a "target group." The styling of its contents and the reportorial techniques to be utilized in the publication will be determined by the audience to whom it is addressed and their estimated reaction to the message. The nature of the audience may even determine the method of distribution of the publication. The distribution technique may in turn affect the format of the publication.

Quantity. The size of the audience, the length of time the publication will be used, and other similar factors should determine the total quantity of the documents to be reproduced. Knowledge of quantity is essential to selection of the proper reproduction or printing method to be used in the project.

Content. The scope and depth of information to be presented will determine the length of the publication. The nature of the audience and the message will determine the tone, simplicity, and clarity of message to be evidenced by the finished job. Each of these factors will affect the number and kinds of illustrations to be employed, the quality of the printing, and the nature of the layout. At one end of the spectrum is the content of a printed invitation to bid on a city purchase and at the other is the content of an elaborate booklet promoting a bond issue.

Distribution Method. Early in the planning process decisions should be made regarding the method by which the publication will be distributed to its audience. The size and shape of the publication might well be influenced by the method of distribution. If it is to be distributed, at least in part, from existing literature distribution racks, then it must be shaped to meet the design of the racks. Similarly, if it is to be mailed, it should be shaped to meet existing envelope sizes, or special envelopes must be ordered and printed.

Format. The term "format" refers to the shape, size, type, and style of a publication. Before a working "layout" or "dummy" of the publication can be prepared, its format must be determined. Decisions on format are influenced by many factors, including appeal to the reader, method of distribution, printing and paper costs, and other factors. For example, if the specified format requires that each leaf in the publication be 9 by 12 inches in size, and if the only paper available is 17 by 22 inches, substantial costs will be incurred through paper wastage. Only two printed sheets would be possible from each sheet of raw paper stock, with a resulting waste of one strip measuring 4 by 17 inches, and another strip measuring 5 by 18 inches. By changing the format specifications to 8½ by 11 inches, each sheet of raw paper stock would yield four finished sheets and paper costs would therefore be reduced.

Layout. The ultimate blueprint or design for a publication is the layout. A multi-paged layout, having the same number of pages as the finished publication, is also called a "dummy." Whether the layout precedes or follows the editing and the preparation of illustrative material to be included in the publication will depend on the job itself and on the decisions made during the planning process. For example, some annual reports have been produced on the basis of a planned format which assigned a stipulated space to a specific subject. The editorial and illustrative material ultimately assigned to that space was determined by the original format. In still other cases, the editorial material to be included in the publication was produced first, and the format then was structured to meet the requirements of the editorial copy. The publication of a speech made by a city's mayor is illustrative of the last case. Publication of the speech would require a format that provides for inclusion of the full text of the speech, together with appropriate illustrative or explanatory material.

Although a layout or dummy is absolutely essential for the printer to do his job, there is room for argument as to whether a layout is necessary before the text of the publication is written.

Production Details. Decisions must be made on a variety of specific details concerning the finished publication. What printing method will be employed? What type of paper will be used? Will a cover be required for the report, and if so, of what specific nature? What type will be used and what binding method will be employed?

Budget. Interwoven throughout each step in the planning process is consideration of the financial, material, and personnel requirements associated with the job. Some planning must be done so that the general nature of the job can be determined as a basis for final budgeting of the completed publication. Ultimately, however, the assigned budget and planned costs for the project will be decisive in deciding details concerning format, printing methods, paper stock, and the number and nature of the illustrations to be employed.

THE PLANNING PROCESS

Each step in the planning process is interrelated with each of the others. Many persons within the organization may be involved and a variety of personnel skills demanded. An interplay between competing points of view must be provided and an opportunity afforded for adjustments in the total plan as each step nears completion. Decisions as to the final cost of the finished job might well be altered as final planning is completed. For example, several thousand additional copies of the publication could be printed for only a slight increase in the budget approved for the originally planned quantity. If estimates regarding future use of the publication indicate a need, expenditures to meet the increased costs for additional quantities might well be justified.

However, when the final layout is finished, when the printing contract has been signed, and when the material is in the hands of the printer, the time for change is past. Only through incurring additional, and unjustified, costs, can changes be made at this stage of the publication process. Proper job planning will avoid this problem of hurried, last-minute alterations.

Staff Responsibility. A separate and extremely important part of the publication planning process involves the assignment of responsibility for the job itself. Responsibility for supervising the total job, as well as each of its separate parts, must be clearly assigned. Decisions must be made as to whether the entire job will be performed by city personnel and equipment, or whether contract services will be utilized. If parts of the job are to be contracted, then adequate time for bids must be provided. As a general guide to fixing staff responsibility, the following activities might be considered: production supervision; preparation and review of editorial material; preparation and review of art work (photographs and other visual aids) ; preparation of layout; supervision of printing and binding and/or liaison with contract printer; proofing (checking the printed

galley proofs against the original text) ; and distribution of the finished publication.

Only when each of the activities associated with production of the publication has been clearly assigned to a qualified person can the planning process be deemed completed.

Production of Publications

The elements of publishing are fourfold and include paper, typography, printing, and binding. Some knowledge of each component is necessary to the governmental administrator who proposes to "publish a report."

The cost, quantity, and quality aspects of the publication project are relevant to consideration of each ingredient and decisions about any one ingredient may affect one or more of the others. Thus, a decision about the kind of paper stock to be used in the publication will influence the choice of printing methods. Selection of the printing method may influence decisions on typography, and the nature of the selected typography and illustrative material may influence the kind of paper stock that is required.

PAPER

The selection of paper for a publication involves technical judgments and the printer should be consulted on this point. However, eight factors can be considered in reviewing the choice of paper stock:

1. *Cost.* Paper is purchased by the pound and costs range from about 8 cents per pound for newsprint to about 50 cents or more for special papers purchased in small lots.

2. *Proposed Use.* The printing method as well as the types of inks and adhesives to be used may influence selection of paper. One kind of paper is required for spirit duplicating, another for mimeographing, and still another for offset lithography.

3. *Quality.* The quality factor of most importance is adaptability to the printing process which is to be used, but other quality factors include permanence, strength, durability, and opacity.

4. *Surface and Finish.* The appearance of

paper is determined by the nature of its finish and its surface. Papers are known as either laid or woven, and there are many finishes, such as antique, eggshell, machine finish, English finish, supercalendered, glossy coated, dull coated, and coated one-side surfaces. The weight, surface, and finish of paper determine its cost.

5. *Weight.* One characteristic of paper is referred to as its "basis" weight. The designated weight of a particular paper usually refers to the actual weight of a ream (500 sheets) of that paper in a particular size. Since the standard size of paper stocks will vary, a layman can be misled by casual reference to the comparative weights of different papers. Thus, a 20-pound "bond" paper is roughly the equivalent of a 50-pound "book" paper. The difference results from the fact that weights of bond paper are determined on a 17 × 22-inch sheet, while book papers are based on a 25 × 38-inch sheet.

6. *Size.* Paper can be purchased in a variety of sizes directly from stock, and, if the quantity required is large enough, almost any size can be ordered. Usually, however, a 10,000-pound order is necessary to secure a custom size.

7. *Grain.* All machine-made paper has a grain which makes tearing and folding in one direction easier than in the other. Paper usually can be ordered with the grain in either direction.

8. *Color.* Paper is available in a wide range of colors and shades. For example, many shades of "white" are available. Choice among colors and shades will depend on the design of the job.

PRINTING

For purposes of clarity this section on Printing and the next two sections on Office Duplicating and Office Copying are discussed separately because each of the three categories tends to develop its own industrial identification, manufacturers, equipment suppliers, and other distinctive attributes. "Printing" as used here refers to the process of transferring information, usually from metal type or plates, directly or indirectly to paper by high-volume, high-speed, commercial processes. In thinking of "printing" one should think of large-volume work—several thousand copies or more—coupled with a more elaborate kind of job. Letter press and lithographic printing are the major methods that city administrators and their staffs are likely to encounter.

Letterpress (relief) Printing. This method historically is one of the oldest printing processes and is used for printing almost all newspapers and many magazines, books, and other materials. In relief printing the inked type, which is set either by hand or by machine, is applied by pressure directly to paper passed through the press.

Lithographic Printing. This kind of printing, often referred to as "offset," involves two basic principles. First, the printing surfaces, which are almost level with the rest of the plate, are treated to accept a special greasy ink, while the nonprinting parts repel the ink.

Second, lithographic printing is done on a rotary press with three principal cylinders—one with the printing plate attached, known as the plate cylinder; one with a rubber blanket wrapped around, known as the blanket cylinder; and the cylinder that carries the paper to be printed, known as the impression cylinder. The plate cylinder transfers the image to the rubber blanket which is wrapped around the blanket cylinder, and the blanket cylinder then transfers the image by "offset" to the impression cylinder.

Lithographic printing is the same in these two basic principles as the offset duplication discussed below under the heading of "Office Duplicating." Offset printing as used here, however, refers to much larger and more complicated kinds of work involving setting type, making photographic plates by a variety of methods, and printing at high speed and large volume.

Other Printing Methods. Several other printing methods have substantial commercial significance, but will be of little interest to city officials because these methods rarely would be needed. The most important of the other methods is gravure printing, which works on the opposite basis from relief printing. The printing parts in gravure are etched into the plate and are lower than the rest of the plate. These etched portions are filled with ink which is transferred to paper by pressure and suction. Gravure is a difficult and complicated printing method. Thus it is quite expensive and generally is limited to specialized kinds of work such as newspaper supplements and magazines. Other printing methods, such as collotype and silk screen, may occasionally be used for municipal signs and posters.

A Word of Warning. Printing and the allied arts—typography, illustrations, and binding—are very complex subjects. These paragraphs are intended only as a brief indication of the broad approaches to printing, especially in commercial work. Printing, as the term is used here, cannot be equalled for high quality, color fidelity, and quite often for substantial economy where the volume is large. It is, however, very important to secure competent, professional advice both on design typography (illustrations, layout, and related aspects) and production (printing methods, paper selection, and other factors affecting cost).[3]

OFFICE DUPLICATING

Many city publications can be handled more quickly and economically by office duplicating equipment owned or rented by the city government itself. Sometimes this work can be done through equipment housed in the city hall or other city building; or the work can be done outside by a concern generally known in the trade as a "job shop" or a "letter shop." The quality of office duplication can range from the dingy looking stencil duplicated reading lists and syllabi distributed in many schools and colleges to handsome multicolor reports done by offset.

Office duplicating methods provide great potential from the standpoint of efficiency, utility, and economy for most cities, especially smaller cities. The equipment costs are relatively small —from under $100 to a few thousand dollars; space requirements are not excessive; highly trained personnel are not required; and paper, plates, and other supplies can be obtained promptly.

Three basic methods of office duplicating are in use: stencil duplication, fluid duplication, and offset duplication.

Stencil Duplication. All stencil duplicators essentially work the same way. Stencil duplication sheets—usually dubbed "stencils"—are made of a special tissue that has a coating that is impervious to ink. By typing or marking with a stylus, the coating is pushed aside to expose the porous tissue which prints on the duplicating machine. The machine duplicates when the stencil is attached to a cylinder or drum. The term "mimeograph" is often used for the stencil duplicating process; the term came originally from the trade name of the stencil duplicator manufactured by the A. B. Dick Company.

Fluid Duplication. This type of duplicating is done by writing or typing on the face of a special stencil which is backed by an aniline-dye carbon paper. This paper transfers the reverse image of the original impression on the rear of the stencil. The aniline-dye carbon papers are available in purple, red, blue, green, and black. The reverse carbon image on the back of the sheet becomes the master which is placed on a drum of a rotary fluid duplicating machine.

Offset Duplication. As indicated above, offset duplication is based on two principles: (1) that oil and water repel each other, and (2) that the image is transferred from a plate cylinder to a blanket cylinder which in turn transfers, or offsets, to the impression cylinder carrying the paper. Small offset machines can print with plates made by typing or drawing on specially treated paper. For relatively short runs the paper plate (sometimes termed a "master") can be made quickly and inexpensively, and the complete job can be handled in a very short period of time. For longer runs it is possible to make photographic plates either from paper or metal that are capable of quite long runs.

Offset duplicators are larger and faster than stencil and fluid duplicators; they also are more expensive, but they can provide significant

---

[3] A number of books is available on printing methods, typography, publishing, and related fields. Particularly recommended is BOOKMAKING: THE ILLUSTRATED GUIDE TO DESIGN AND PRODUCTION, by Marshall Lee (New York: R. R. Bowker Co., 1965). Chapters 5, 6, 7, and 8 provide a good introduction to composition, typography, plates, printing, and paper.

long-term economy when used for appropriate jobs.

Which Method? Fortunately, the choice of methods and equipment for office duplicating is not nearly as complicated as for commercial printing. Each of the three principal methods has distinct advantages and disadvantages with respect to cost, speed of operation, quality of work, and number of copies desired. Equipment suppliers and salesmen can be quite helpful in providing comparative information on their products, and expert advice often can be obtained from office managers, duplicating equipment supervisors, and other personnel employed by local utility companies and other organizations.

OFFICE COPYING

A wide variety of office copying machines is now on the market at prices ranging (for most models) from less than $100 to a few thousand dollars.[4]

Office copying machines have become widely popular for preparing one, a half-dozen, a dozen, or more copies of memoranda, letters, reports, and other materials. Office copiers, however, should not be confused with the office duplicating machines described above. They generally serve best only when a few copies are needed for internal distribution. When restricted to this kind of use, office copiers can be extremely useful. Office copiers also are used in public libraries to reproduce one or more pages from books, magazines, and other materials.

The costs for office copiers, however, including amortization of equipment, paper, supplies, and employee time are such that they do not lend themselves to large-volume duplicating jobs.

TYPOGRAPHY

Typography is discussed here as "the art of arranging *printed* type."[5] While it is possible to use handwriting for person-to-person communi-

cation, or a typewritten manuscript as the basis for office duplicating, only typography can provide the readability, range of expression, and authority that we take for granted in books, magazines, and other printed materials. Typography is at the heart of printed materials because it provides the basic structure.

Typography has a long and interesting history which reflects both sociological and technological change. The sans serif type faces that we associate with up-to-date advertising can be traced to Greek letters carved on stone in the seventh century B.C. Roman type faces are traced to reliefs carved on Trajan's column in Rome depicting the Dacian wars of 101–102 and 105–106 A.D.

Typography is greatly involved with tradition, but from the layman's point of view the primary consideration should be its use in conveying thought. Words which are set in a type that is very small may discourage reading, and words of great dignity that are set in a flamboyant type will convey an entirely different meaning than was intended. These and other considerations in typography are dealt with in the next three sections on Type Classification, Type Characteristics, and Suitability.

Type Classification. Most references on typography classify types on a historical system that is largely chronological. This is of little use to the layman who is planning a printing job. His concerns are much more practical and include the visual or functional character, readability, availability, and versatility of a given type face.

In addition to size, type usually is classified by historic sequence with a confusing number of variations and exceptions. This system is best left to the typographer and other experts. For the layman the following functional classification is much more useful: roman, abstract, cursive, and decorative.

Roman type shows the classical letters with serifs (fine vertical and horizontal cross strokes) and graduated thick and thin strokes. Roman type is used for the bulk of the material—usually termed "the text" or "body"—in books, magazines, and other materials.

Abstract type looks like the letters are based on mechanical drawing. The letters have

---

[4] An article in ADMINISTRATIVE MANAGEMENT for March, 1964, (pp. 28*ff*.) presents data on 189 office copying machines manufactured or distributed by 38 companies. The listing does not include foreign companies.

[5] Lee, *op. cit.,* p. 78. (Italics in original.)

The type selected should be appropriate

Civic Institutions

CIVIC INSTITUTIONS

The Baskerville family

ABCDEFGHIJKLMNOPQRSTUVWXYZ
Roman capitals

ABCDEFGHIJKLMNOPQRSTUVWXYZ
Roman small capitals

abcdefghijklmnopqrstuvwxyz
Roman lower case

ABCDEFGHIJKLMNOPQRSTUVWXYZ
Italic capitals

abcdefghijklmnopqrstuvwxyz
Italic lower case

ABCDEFGHIJKLMNOPQRSTUVWXYZ
Bold capitals

abcdefghijklmnopqrstuvwxyz
Bold lower case

A method of type classification

Roman

Abstract

Cursive

DECORATIVE

Type measurement

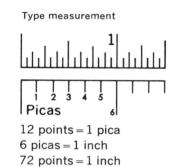

Picas

12 points = 1 pica
6 picas = 1 inch
72 points = 1 inch

FIGURE 35.

straight edges and lines of uniform thickness. Abstract letters are either without serifs (sans serif) or with square serifs of the same weight as the letter (block serifs). Abstract type faces usually are found in advertising, in heads and subheads for book chapters and magazine articles, and uses where emphasis is desired.

Cursive letters are ". . . based on slanted writing with a more or less continuous line. . . ."[6] Italic is the best known form of cursive type, but there are variations.

Decorative type includes "All the faces that have exaggerated characteristics of the other three classes or distinctive features that place them outside the other classes."[7] This covers an astonishing range of type faces for advertising display, college diplomas, public announcements, special certificates, art books, and other highly specialized uses.

[6] *Ibid.,* p. 80.
[7] *Ibid.*

Each of these four groups contains many type faces (the primary unit of classification for type) and some of these type faces tend to cluster in groups. But the important consideration is to consider the function of the type as the vehicle for conveying a message in a printed piece.

Type Characteristics. In typography consideration must be given to types that are suitable for text and display. Text types are those that are used for the text—or body—of books, magazines, reports, and other materials. Display types are generally limited to chapter headings, section and paragraph headings, and similar uses. The distinction is largely one of point size (point sizes are defined below) as a practical matter. It is mentioned here to emphasize the importance of compatibility between text and display types in any printing job. They do not have to be the same type face, but they should look well on the same page.

Printers usually can help resolve this question.

Type Measurement. Some familiarity with type measurement is needed in planning printed materials both from the standpoint of usefulness of the completed work and the printing cost. The point system is used to measure type. It is as follows:

Twelve points to one pica,

Six picas to one inch, or

Seventy-two points to one inch.[8]

The size of each type face is measured by the depth of the metal block on which character is cast. Thus a letter cast in 18 point Times Roman is cast on a block 18 points high. The point size is only an approximate indication of the size of the type face itself. Usually the type size is somewhat larger than the type face.

Printers use a system of picas and points for expressing measurements of type itself, or the "type page" in their terminology. Printers use inches for measurement of paper, illustrations, and margins.

For example, in this book, the type is a 10-point Baskerville on a 12-point body. Expressed vertically, there are six lines of 12-point type to the inch (that is, six picas or 72 points). Each column is 17½ picas in width, and the space between the two columns is 1½ picas. Expressed horizontally, the type page is 36½ picas wide, including both columns of type and the space between the columns.

Suitability. In determining the suitability of a type face for a report or other municipal publication, consideration should be given to several factors.

First some thought should be given to the selection of a type face that is available in appropriate sizes for machine setting. There are two basic methods of setting type: by hand and by machine. This point will not be developed further except to state that hand setting is prohibitively expensive for large amounts of copy. Therefore the type selected should be available for machine setting. In addition, if the job requires it, it should have *italics* and SMALL CAPITAL letters. Also, if the job requires

it, it should be available in a variety of point sizes to provide 6, 7, or 8 point for footnotes and abstracts, 9, 10, or 12 point for text or body, and 12 or 14 point for headings. (Larger point sizes are usually hand set.)

Second, readability should be considered. Some type faces are more readable than others. The point size is an important factor as well as the width of the line in relation to the size of the type face. The amount of leading (space) between lines also affects readability. Nine factors that affect the readability of the page in a book are: type face, point size of type, length of line, leading (space) between lines, page layout (including margins), contrast of type and paper, texture of paper, typographic relationships (headings, body, and other elements on the page), suitability in relation to content.[9]

It is not the intention of these paragraphs to intimidate the city administrator who is planning a printed report. It is intended, however, to point to the importance of readability. Professional assistance is available from graphic artists for the larger and more complicated jobs. For smaller jobs, good printers can be quite helpful.

Finally, suitability itself needs to be considered. This means the appropriateness of the type in relation to the job at hand. An information folder for senior citizens probably should be printed in 11- or 12-point type because older persons often have vision problems. If a folder is being prepared to welcome citizens to new city council meetings, dignity should prevail; cartoons and clever drawings are best omitted. Type faces should not be mixed indiscriminantly in a report; they tend to distract rather than focus attention. Large initials, ornaments, and bizarre arrangements of type should be avoided even if the object is to attract attention. There are better ways typographically to do this.

BINDING

The binding operation encompasses several steps. It begins after the pages have been printed and includes cutting, folding, trimming, gathering, and stitching.

---

[8] The typewriter measurements of elite (12 typewriter characters to the inch) and pica (10 typewriter characters to the inch) have no connection with the point system used in printing.

[9] Lee, *op. cit.,* p. 96.

If possible, the publication should be planned so as to avoid extra expense at this stage of the operation. For example, the two sides of an unfolded sheet of paper make two pages; when folded, a sheet of paper gives the following results:

one fold   = 4 pages
two folds = 6 or 8 pages
three folds = 12 or 16 pages
four folds = 24 or 32 pages

Pamphlets and booklets should be designed around these units, if the cost of adding or cutting out odd pages is to be avoided.

The sheets included in a common fold in a book or magazine are known as a "signature" and usually consist of 32 pages, but may have 8, 16, 24, 32, 48 or 64 pages.

An entire booklet may consist of a single signature, in which case it may be bound by being saddle-stitched (stapled at the top and bottom of the fold).

Books containing two or more signatures may be side-wired (stapled on the sides), or side-sewn. The cover then may be pasted over the entire book by applying an adhesive to the rear of the signature folds.

City publications rarely warrant the expense of the "case binding" that goes into a cloth-bound book. For more important documents, however, cities may wish to use any of a number of kinds of "mechanical binding." This would include the saddle-wire and side-wire publications mentioned above as well as a wide variety of bindings, both permanent and loose-leaf, involving plastic and wire spirals, metal fasteners, metal rings, and metal posts and rods. Although the unit cost is high, mechanical bindings serve a useful purpose for reports that are issued in limited quantity.

Distribution of Publications

Among the primary means for distributing municipally produced reports and publications, at least three are deserving of consideration here. These include the use of circulation racks, direct mail distribution, and distribution in face-to-face situations.

The method of distribution of a report should be decided before the report design has been fixed. Size, weight, shape, color, use of cover illustrations—all of these factors should be tailored to the ultimate distribution method and consideration should be given to the use of more than one method.

CIRCULATION RACKS

The use of circulation racks for distributing governmental reports has become increasingly popular and useful. Many city halls now have a distribution rack in their central lobby and in their public waiting areas. Reports on a variety of subjects can thereby be placed in the hands of those citizens most interested in them. Planning offices may use simple wire racks to distribute inexpensive mimeographed pamphlets which explain the planning and zoning law of the community, how it works, and how a citizen may file a petition for a change of zone or for a variance from an existing zone.

Building departments, licensing offices, and welfare bureaus can place simplified instructions and guides in the hands of their clients and save expensive staff time by use of this method. While a citizen waits his turn at the counter, he can pick up a pertinent city report and have many of his questions answered before his initial contact with city officers and employees.

Perhaps the most extensive governmental use of circulation racks has been made by the Los Angeles County Air Pollution Control District.

Faced with the need for broad public support for the smog control program of the community, the agency entered into an extensive public information program in 1956. As one element in the program, nearly 200 plywood display and literature distribution units were located in banks, public buildings, and transportation terminals. Graphic displays on the smog problem were posted on the boards and free reports and pamphlets were arrayed on distribution racks at the base of the display. Approximately 40,000 publication units were distributed monthly to the public from these racks and a profound change in public attitudes and support for the program was achieved.

Similar distribution techniques have been

used by many local agencies. Pamphlet distribution racks can be made by the city's own personnel, or can be purchased on the open market at modest costs. Inexpensive wire distribution racks are available for use on public counters.

FACE-TO-FACE DISTRIBUTION

Perhaps the most effective way to distribute reports is in face-to-face situations. Interest in the report can be heightened when a personal contact with the reader is made. A report has value only if it is read and used. Citizen interest can be stirred by method of distribution.

In many cities, important municipal publications are delivered, as a civic project, to householders by active community service organizations. Groups like the Boy Scouts, Kiwanis, Lions, and Jaycees frequently are interested in a civic project of this type.

Similarly, public appearances of city officials can be used as a vehicle for distributing pertinent city publications. Speeches and printed reports can be tailored to complement each other, with one increasing the interest in the other and giving supplementary information.

DIRECT MAIL

Of the three primary methods of distribution, direct mail offers the greatest possibility of rapid mass distribution with certainty of delivery. Cost, however, may be a serious handicap to widespread and continuous use of the method and many reports may be wasted by going unread when the householder routinely disposes of all unsolicited mail via the nearest wastebasket. A significant proportion of any community may even be offended by such unsolicited mail and may question the propriety of this type of use of public funds.

On the plus side of the ledger, however, direct mail offers the distinct advantage of permitting rapid distribution of reports to those groups in the community having the greatest need for the information.

Mailing lists can be classified and categorized so as to permit "selective" mailing, and the structuring of public information to meet the unique characteristics and requirements of specific groups in the community.

The alert agency, with a continuing public information program, will maintain a "permanent" mailing list which is periodically revised and brought up to date. The list will be classified and categorized so as to permit its selective use in reaching specific groups with specific mailings. Thus, a portion of the total list will receive all "news releases" of the city; another will receive all technical data on amendments to the building code; while still another will be keyed to receive the mayor's newsletter.

In one large western community, a mailing list of approximately 8,000 names is maintained; the total list is then divided into 18 major categories, plus numerous sub-categories. Each publication of the jurisdiction is keyed to one or more categories on the list. Thus, news releases are mailed to the mass media category as well as to a select category representing the community thought-leaders. Even the mass media category is further classified so as to permit separate identification of metropolitan and suburban daily and weekly newspapers. Additional classifications are devoted to editorial and special-purpose writers, to radio and television personalities, and to other discrete classes of the mass media.

At least annually, each person on the list receives a post card (sent by first class mail) asking whether he or she wishes to remain on the list and whether any address or title changes should be made in the list.

Mail lists can be built in a variety of ways. In large urban or metropolitan communities the listing of all newspapers may present a problem to the administrator interested in launching a new public information program. In such a situation, a variety of nationally distributed references should be consulted. The best known undoubtedly is the *Directory of Newspapers and Periodicals,* published annually by N. W. Ayer and Son, Inc., in Philadelphia. Frequently referred to as *Ayer's Guide,* this reference book is indispensable to any builder of a mailing list. The *International Yearbook* of the Editor and Publisher Company, Inc., of New York City, also is invaluable. Both provide a current list of daily, weekly, and periodical publications in the United States.

Community "chambers of commerce" maintain lists of civic clubs, together with a listing of their officers. These can be tapped for useful and important additions to the mail lists. Provision also should be made for the addition of names to the mailing list through nomination by city employees and officers. Their contact with the public, both personally and through receipt of letters and complaints, provides useful information as to specific personalities who should be included on the lists.

If the list is to have permanence, currency, and continued utility, some employee should be made responsible for its maintenance and use. Typically, this employee will be responsible for receiving all requests from individuals desiring to be placed on or removed from the list, for periodically checking its currency, and for conducting an annual audit of all names on the list. Additionally, this employee may be responsible for ordering and maintaining addressograph plates, or duplicate gummed stickers, for all entries on the list so as to permit rapid and economical mass mailings.

The master list can best be maintained on index cards, readily available to the person responsible for maintaining the list.

The addressing and mailing of reports may be handled manually or through use of labor-saving machinery and techniques, if volume warrants. Two of the more common methods applicable to municipalities are:

Addressograph. This is a special machine which uses an embossed metal plate which prints the address through an inked ribbon. Simple machines requiring manual operation are available, as are power units which automatically feed the plates to the ribbon and imprint the address on envelopes also fed automatically through the device.

Elliott Addressing. This method uses stencils which print much like a miniature mimeograph stencil and which can be cut on a regular typewriter at envelope addressing speed. One address goes on each stencil, and the stencils are filed like index cards.

The size of the mail list, the volume of material to be mailed, the availability of equipment, and the cost will determine which of the many addressing methods is best for any specific application.

Summary

Like any other facet of municipal administration, the performance of a public information activity requires skill, expertness, and an understanding of the variables which can affect the outcome of the effort. Typically, the layman links "public information" with the concept of a printed report and certainly printed publications and reports do have an important role in such a function.

Nevertheless, it is important to outline clearly the purpose of any public information project, to identify with precision the audience which is to be reached, and then to select the most appropriate communication method for the job. If that method is an agency-produced or supervised publication, then further decisions must be made, and all these linked together. They are not discrete and unrelated. The format, design, size, and shape of the report is related to the message and the purpose behind the message. So also are the mechanical aspects of the report linked to selection of the most appropriate reproduction method and to the ultimate means for distributing the document to the desired audience.

15

Organizing for Public Relations

THE PRECEDING CHAPTERS have developed in some detail the philosophy, relationships, techniques and methods of the modern public relations program. To the city official seeking to improve his city government's public relations, the question then becomes one of how to organize to produce the desired results in the most efficient manner possible. How large should a city be before a public relations department is necessary? What about professional public relations counsel? What type of organization is appropriate if professional counsel is not employed? How much will a sound program cost? What results can be expected from the program?

Obviously, no single answer can be given for every city in every circumstance. No single "package" can be applied in every situation and yield the same type of results. In fact, the highly successful program of one city may prove to be of little value in another city. There are, however, certain guidelines which can be observed by the municipal administrator, and the final determination as to the precise type of organization that is best in a given situation must be made by the administrator, in consultation of course with the city council.

Basic Organization

One generalization is that the city with 185 employees should have 185 public relations representatives. And the city with 2,050 employees should have 2,050 representatives. Other facets of the public relations program aside for the moment, no organization and no program are likely to be successful without the basic underlying understanding that *every* employee has, in addition to his primary job assignment, a collateral public relations duty.

The city government's image, as seen by the taxpayer, is an extremely delicate and volatile thing which may be dramatically affected—for better or for worse—by the acts of the city's employees. Only when considered in this light does the great importance of sound public relations training for employees become fully apparent. The approach to insuring good public relations awareness on the part of employees is in part the subject of the following chapter.

A second generalization is that a public relations program of any type must enjoy the full understanding and cooperation of the legislative body, the city council. As the source of all policy, the city council must not only watch its own public relations, of critical importance to the council itself, but must also insist upon sound public relations throughout the city organization.

Regardless of the city, certain public relations measures can be taken, many without incurring any additional expense. The most obvious and important of these is suggested above: public relations conscious employees. Many such measures or elements are not even necessarily thought of as part of a public relations program but are in fact an integral part of the program. Clean, well-organized offices, for example, convey a feeling of business-like efficiency. Modern office machines and field equipment also build a favorable image, as does the courteous driver of a city vehicle.

The examples are virtually endless, as suggested in the preceding chapters.

In brief, the council must take the lead in policy establishment in the area of public relations, just as it does in all other areas of municipal concern. It should establish clear guidelines for the professional staff to follow, and then give the chief administrator sufficient authority to match his responsibility in carrying out public relations policies.

A third generalization is that the chief administrator must not only be "sold" on the importance of the public relations program but must be in the vanguard, assisting the council to develop public relations policy and setting the example himself. He also must inculcate department heads with the importance and philosophy of the public relations program, developing their awareness of the fact that every act of departments or individuals, from refuse collection to plan checking, has its public relations aspects. He must motivate the department heads so that they may, in turn, motivate their employees.

He must instigate training for employees in all areas of public relations and see that training programs are properly staffed, equipped, supported, and attended. He must be in the forefront in development of good press relations, observing the guidelines set forth in earlier chapters. He must be constantly seeking to improve the public's image of the city government through all means at his disposal.

In brief, the chief administrator's obligation for public relations is no less compelling than his obligation for sound public finance, effective personnel systems, and other areas of management. He sets the pace for the entire organization, and if the city's public relations program is lagging, the first place the chief administrator should look for correction is to himself.

The basic organization for conducting an effective public relations program is the entire city organization. No amount of "frosting," frills, or fancy salesmanship is going to develop a good public relations program if services are not sound and the city organization is not aware of and actively working on its public relations responsibilities.

Beyond the Basic

Once development of the basic organization is accomplished—i.e. every employee and official knows his job and his public relations responsibilities—determination must be made regarding what refinements and additions are to be made. There are several ways to organize, and the extent to which a city elaborates on its program in adopting any particular choice is largely a question of its size, available funds, local citizen attitudes, and desire to do as complete a public relations job as possible. The options range from what might be termed the "one-man show" through several stages to the "staff pro."

THE ONE-MAN SHOW

The "one-man show" is used primarily by smaller cities—50,000 population and under. As the name suggests, the public relations program is the responsibility of one man, generally the chief administrator, who is also responsible for preparing whatever formal reports or events constitute the public relations program.

The fact that these responsibilities and execution of the program reside in one man is not to suggest that the end product need be inferior, make-shift, or less effective than other approaches. Many highly imaginative and effective reports and ideas have come out of the offices of administrators who have little or no formal assistance in carrying out the program. Naturally, under a program of this type, the chief administrator should take full advantage of the talents of department heads, and others, not only to lighten his personal burden but also to furnish the diversity of opinions, approaches, and language that results only from cross-fertilization of ideas.

The "do it yourself" approach is an extension of the one-man show. Under this approach, the chief administrator has staff assistance or a particularly well qualified department head who can assume the burden of detail that is inherent in the public relations program. The responsibility still resides with the chief administrator, but he is relieved of the task of conceiving, writing, rewriting, and following through to comple-

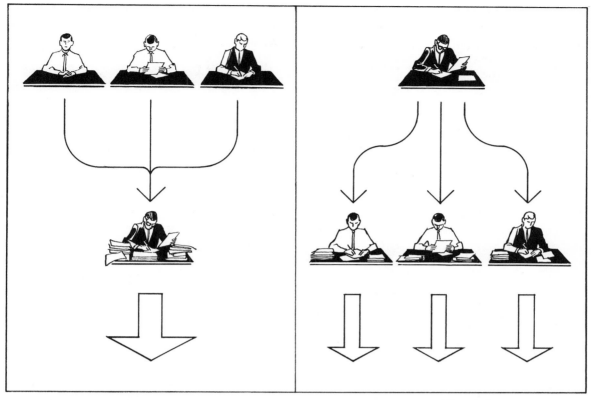

FIGURE 36. *Organization for public relations (Responsibility for the public relations program can range from the "one-man show," usually the chief administrator, to decentralization to departments and use of consultants and professional city staff.)*

tion every public relations project. In general, this approach is feasible for the city of roughly 100,000 to 200,000 population.

This approach permits the chief administrator to retain control over the public relations function and to act as the prime motivating force in the program. The hazards of departmentalization are avoided, and costs inherent in the use of consultants, discussed below, are avoided.

DECENTRALIZATION TO DEPARTMENTS

In some cities, the emphasis is primarily upon the departmental public relations program, sometimes to the exclusion or detriment of any over-all approach for the city government. This is particularly true in two widely divergent types of cities: first, the extremely large city, of perhaps 1 million population and over, and

second, the smaller city in which the chief administrator does not have the inclination, time, or possibly the skills required to develop a truly effective public relations program.

In the first instance, that of the larger cities, individual departments are large and complex enough to justify public information or public relations units of their own. Such units presumably can present the individual department's case more effectively than a centralized department assigned to serve the entire city organization. It is also possible, however, for such a unit to become engrossed in "empire building" and the development of public relations materials which may run counter to the over-all organization's best interests.

Virtually the opposite situation is true in many smaller cities. The chief administrator is faced with the responsibility for operation of the entire organization, often with inadequate staff to perform all the management functions generally considered to be necessary. He may therefore delegate the responsibility for public relations activities, along with a number of other responsibilities, to department heads, with only slight guidance to coordinate the efforts of all departments.

Thus it may be concluded that in the smaller cities at least, the "decentralization to departments" approach and the "one-man show" approach are actually extremes of a single continuum, with many shades of difference between. Both may exist in a single organization, and both may make important contributions to the over-all public relations effort.

THE COLLABORATING CONSULTANT

At some point—and no generalization is possible here—a city may find itself in need of outside professional assistance. This conclusion is not so much a matter of size as of the talents of the chief administrator's staff and the thoroughness and complexity of the public relations job to be done.

A competent, qualified consultant can bring a fresh approach to the public relations job and can save considerable time and many "false starts." In some instances he can, through employment of the techniques of his profession, actually save the city money. As a practical matter, however, the employment of a consultant represents a net outlay of dollars which must be weighed against the final product and its probable effect on the public.

Nor is the consultant a cure-all. Balanced against the advantages of his fresh approach is the fact that he probably has little or no knowledge about the city organization and has considerable learning to do before he can perform any productive work for the organization. Depending upon his degree of sophistication, he may be able to develop a program or single report with considerable "punch" and attractiveness—or he may come up with a proposal that is quite naive in terms of the organization's real problems, progress, and other features. It may require a great amount of orientation and close cooperation by the chief administrator or his representative to

bring the consultant's talents and ideas into harmony with the public relations needs of the organization.

THE STAFF PRO

Principally in larger cities, although cities under 100,000 have been known to use this form of organization, a department of public relations with a full-time director is created. Such a department may be established as a potential answer to a specific problem, or it may simply be to develop a continuing program of improved public relations. This stage of development is generally reached when the occasional services of a consultant become inadequate for the program desired. Often a professional staff is established for the primary purpose of spearheading some specific program, such as attracting industry or promoting a harbor, airport, or other major proprietary facility.

Specifically . . .

How do the five basic types of municipal public relations organizations described above square with actual organizations? Elements of each can be seen in the following city examples, all of which, incidentally, have been winners of the American Municipal Association's annual public relations contest. These examples are not intended to illustrate the five basic patterns above but rather to show how several cities have adapted various elements for successful programs.

ROCKVILLE, MARYLAND

Rockville is a suburban community of approximately 33,000 near Washington, D.C. It is largely residential, although increasing numbers of industrial organizations are locating there. It is a "new" city in the sense that it grew from 2,000 people in 1945 to its 37,000 in 1965. Its socioeconomic status is higher than the average, and it has won All-America City honors twice. Perhaps in part because its five-man city council is young, well educated, and aggressive, Rockville has an especially active public relations program for a city of its size.

Responsibility for the over-all public relations program resides in the city manager, under the general direction of the city council. Day-to-day administration is carried on by a staff assistant in the city manager's office. Its program grew by trial and error over the first few years, according to the city manager, but did not work out because no single individual was charged with responsibility for the program. The services of a consultant were then retained, and this alternative was also found to be less than desirable because of (1) inadequate control over the content of publications produced, (2) inadequate comprehension on the part of the consultant of the intricacies and problems of the organization, and (3) the high cost of the consultant's services.

In 1961, then, the city council assigned specific responsibility for the public information program to the city manager and authorized employment of a staff assistant who was to spend approximately one-half of his time on public information programs and one-half on other administrative duties. A free-lance photographer and a local commercial artist, serving as needed, completed the formal staff. In a relatively short period of time, operation under this organization resulted in a monthly newsletter, an annual report, a citizens' handbook, a program of press and radio relations, special pamphlets and brochures, articles for professional journals, open house, entertainment of foreign officials, and coordination of the public information activities of the city departments.

GLENDALE, CALIFORNIA

Similar in many respects to the Rockville program is that of Glendale, California (126,-205). Glendale borders Los Angeles, and is a balanced city with emphasis on residential development. Glendale's public relations program is a decentralized one in large part, which encourages participation by departments. The city council of course has primary responsibility for public relations, but this responsibility is largely delegated to the city manager. All coordination of departmental efforts and all centralized public information programs emanate from the city manager's office.

The assistant to the city manager carries on the day-to-day development of materials, in-cluding a newsletter, monthly employee relations articles, annual reports, audio-visual reports, special reports, open house type civic displays, routine press relations, a basic booklet entitled *Glendale's Government* (designed specifically for high school civics classes), journal articles, and assistance to departments as required. Roughly one-third of the assistant's time is spent in this type of work, with the remainder being spent on other administrative assignments. No consultant has been utilized by Glendale.

TACOMA, WASHINGTON

Roughly comparable to Glendale in population (147,979) but differing somewhat in organization is Tacoma, Washington. Tacoma has a full time public information officer who is responsible to the city manager. His general assignment is to keep the public informed on city activities. This objective is achieved in many ways, including publication of annual reports, news releases, and a bimonthly employee relations publication.

One of his primary assignments is to supervise the advertising of the municipal transit system, with the objective of stimulating patronage. "In this area alone," reports the city manager, "the PIO has paid for himself many times over by reversing the national downward trend of passengers and saving the city tens of thousands of dollars through an aggressive public relations and advertising campaign."

Tacoma's PIO also acts as the liaison between the city manager's office and the Sister City Committee, serves as the city's representative on many civic committees and organizations, escorts foreign dignitaries, moderates a bi-weekly quarter-hour radio program, and prepares speech materials and related data for various city officials.

NORFOLK, VIRGINIA

Still another variation on the same theme is found in Norfolk, Virginia (305,872). Again the city manager has primary responsibility for the public relations program and delegates the more formalized aspects to his assistant. A local advertising agency is retained, however, for work on specific projects or publications. Preliminary drafts are prepared by the agency and the assistant to the city manager, and the final draft is then reviewed by the city manager. A slightly different approach is used in the development of the annual report, which is generally a newspaper supplement. The art staff of the newspaper assists the city manager's office in the preparation of drafts which are then reviewed by the city manager.

MIAMI, FLORIDA

Miami (291,688) is one step farther in the professionalization of its public relations staff, having its own 41-employee publicity department under the direction of a full-time professional public relations officer. Its emphasis, however, is unusual because it concentrates on tourist promotion, a function which in many cities is carried on by the chamber of commerce. Miami has a well-staffed news bureau under the direction of an experienced newsman. The department has produced several films of the chamber of commerce type and issues literally thousands of articles and photographs each year. Interestingly, the department does not confine its efforts to Miami. Under terms of a contract, it handles publicity for all of Dade County as well.

The department's work in the area of tourist promotion does not preclude an extremely active program in other areas, including coverage of all city functions deemed newsworthy, such as new parking garages, low rent housing, opening of new fire stations, canine police corps, recreation programs, library facilities, and so on. The department also works closely with the chamber of commerce, schools, and other city departments in planning and staging significant community events.

PHILADELPHIA, PENNSYLVANIA

One final example of a highly effective public relations organization is that of Philadelphia (2,002,000). Philadelphia's public relations agency is known as the "office of the city representative," established by the new city charter in 1952. In addition to serving as the director of commerce (with responsibility for promotion of port, airport, industrial development, and conventions), the city representative acts on behalf of the mayor in promoting the city in general. A division of public information operates within the framework of this office under the direction of the deputy city representative. This unit is responsible for the day-to-day operation of the public relations program.

The public information division consists of a chief, a group of information officers, an artist, a photographer, and a production staff. The information officers handle the public relations aspects of special events, radio and television, city-wide promotions, city motion pictures, departmental news, and the preparation of all leaflets, brochures, pamphlets, and monthly newsletters. Information officers are assigned to specific city departments, serving as consultants to the department heads. As such, they sit in on staff meetings and planning sessions in order to provide public relations guidance.

The Philadelphia approach, in brief, is that of the staff professional, with public information officers having at least four years of experience in public information media. Only on rare occasions is outside professional assistance used.

. . . . AND OTHER CITIES

Basic field studies of municipal public relations programs are relatively rare, but one conducted in 1961 brings to light several interesting facts.[1] The study, designed to develop data on the public relations activities of American cities, indicated (in part) that among cities over 30,000 population, most public relations activities were carried on by city departments. Out of 181 replies, 73 cities, primarily with populations between 70,000 and 200,000, left public relations activities to individual departments.

A total of 19 cities had a single centralized office responsible for public relations, with little significant variation among population groupings.

A combined approach—central office and departmental programs—was utilized by 66

[1] Richard Hirtzel, "A Study of Public Relations Activities and Organizations in Governments of Selected American Cities," unpublished master's thesis, Brigham Young University, May, 1961, pp. 15ff.

cities, while the remainder indicated other types of organization or no organization.

It is interesting to note, however, that in response to a question regarding the *ideal* public relations organization, significantly more cities (56) felt that centralization of this function was desirable. Size of staff recommended ranged from one person in the smaller cities to four in the largest cities. Cities in the 400,000 and higher class spent an average of well over $60,000 annually on the public information function, while cities in the 70,000-to-90,000 class spent an average of slightly under $60,000, and cities under 40,000 spent less than $3,000.

Which Is Best?

Of the several alternatives discussed in this chapter, and considering the brief descriptions of several actual municipal public relations units, which is best?

As mentioned earlier in this chapter, no cure-all model for a public relations organization is feasible. One must build the public relations program to fit the populace it is to serve. The successful organization of one city may be inadequate or inappropriate in another, to the detriment of the over-all city organization and program. Features of various programs must therefore be adapted selectively so that the program fits public sentiment, tradition, and the actual need for better rapport between the government and those it serves. The limited guidelines and examples suggested in this chapter should provide a reasonable starting point for city officials contemplating a "beefing up" of the public relations function, but the needs of the individual community always remain paramount.

Characteristically, citizens tend to harbor the belief that no one needs to tell them what they ought to know about their government, that the important facts will be self-evident, and that the presence of a specialist in public relations or public information is immediately suspect. This fact is less true today than it was in the 1940's and 1950's. With the passage of time (and with the increasing complexity that comes with the passage of time), the public information function will be more widely accepted as a necessary operation of government.

In the final analysis, *every* city has public relations, whether formalized or not. The question as to whether its public relations will be good or bad, however, depends largely on the city government's degree of sophistication in approaching public relations problems. The city government in general pays the cost of a good public relations program one way or another: either it may adopt a well-conceived program and pay in dollars and efforts, or it may tend to ignore this critical area of municipal responsibility and pay in loss of good will, community pride, and even more tangible ends.

This is not to say that a good public relations program necessarily means the expenditure of thousands of dollars. A truly good public relations program is more basic than that. It is, as suggested above, inherent in the very services the city government provides its citizens. A good public relations program begins in the minds and attitudes of the public officials and employees concerned; the particular form of organization and the specific type of approach is secondary.

16

Employee Relations and Training

As indicated in earlier chapters, the term "public relations" has several meanings, depending on the specific context. Most persons associate the term with dealings between an organization and its clientele, or its external relations with the public. As pointed out earlier, however, an organization may have more than one public or group with which it relates.

An increasing tendency among students of administrative behavior is to describe organizations as social systems with primary and secondary group classifications. This chapter relies in part upon the traditional classification of external publics, but it treats the traditionally conceived internal public as a social entity. In numerous studies the evidence has been quite clear that the degree of success and harmony achieved among the personnel of an organization constitutes a very important element in the effectiveness of the institution's relations with its external publics.[1]

Employee and Public Relations

Unless there exists an organizational climate that is conducive to healthy and cooperative relations among persons within an organization, effective relationships with persons outside the organization are difficult to maintain.

MANAGEMENT SETS THE TONE

The persons making up the top management level in an organization set the tone of the

organization both for the pattern of interpersonal relationships and for external public relations. In a municipality, the chief administrative officer, the department heads, and their immediate staffs through their policies, attitudes, and actions determine the wholesomeness of the environment within the city's administrative hierarchy. If they demonstrate genuine concern for and strive to foster good human relations among themselves and their subordinates, this will serve to stimulate harmonious relations throughout the city organization.

Effective employee relations must be based on a team approach. Management must practice as well as advocate good personnel policies and procedures, upon which effective public relations with the external public is predicated. Employees owe to each other the same cooperation, respect, and courtesy that they owe to the public. Good habits and attitudes in dealing with the public can be developed by everyday practice with fellow employees.

Often an employee's relation to the team will determine the use he makes of his abilities and capacities. One very effective method of promoting the team approach is to recognize the value of employee participation in program planning and to invite and use suggestions from subordinates regarding city operations. This is not meant to imply that subordinates should be consulted by management on all aspects of administrative policy and decision-making, but merely to point out that a democratic approach to management is the key to good human relations in an organization. Such an approach by management and supervisory

---

[1] John M. Pfiffner and Frank V. K. Mason, "Personnel Management at the Grass Roots," PERSONNEL ADMINISTRATION, XX, May–June, 1957, pp. 25–33.

personnel can inculcate common understanding and cooperation among all employees. Such an attitude can, in turn, serve to promote loyalty and efficiency among the staff.

MAN HAS MANY NEEDS

The essence of the human relations approach to management is the recognition of each employee as a unique person with varying desires, needs, and capacities. In order to achieve satisfaction among employees, management must consider the social as well as the economic needs of the individuals in their respective units. Although the importance of salaries and wages should not be unduly minimized, the monthly pay check serves to meet only one of many needs of employees.

Howard Wilson identifies the following as additional social and psychological needs of persons in organizations:

1. *Need to belong.* Man wants to identify himself with other people; he wants to be part of a group larger than himself.
2. *Need for accomplishment.* Man wants to feel that he is making progress toward worthy goals; goals within his capabilities.
3. *Need for self-esteem.* Each man develops his own sense of worth, his own standard of pride and dignity.
4. *Need for acceptance.* Man must feel that he is accepted by the groups with which he identifies himself.
5. *Need for security.* The interdependence of modern life has sapped the once proud quality of self-reliance. Modern man is insecure and thus needs greater assurance of security.
6. *Need for creativity.* Too often in modern life the skill function has been taken from man and given to machines. Without the chance to be creative, the egos of men suffer.[2]

If healthy internal relations are to be maintained in an organization, these sociopsychological needs must be recognized by management. This means that supervisors at all levels not only must be aware of the needs but that they must demonstrate by their actions that they have a positive interest in the well-being of employees.

Even an awareness of management's concern

for physiological needs may produce beneficial sociopsychological reactions in employees. For example, management should show an interest in employee health standards by providing adequate sanitation, rest facilities, and medical services to the extent feasible. This may exhibit an underlying concern of management for employee welfare which often results in favorable psychological reactions.

If a proper attitude is to be inculcated in the personnel of an organization—an attitude evidenced by pride in work, devotion to duty, motivated effort, and effective performance—then management must demonstrate a genuine interest in employee affairs.

The Importance of Communications

The most effective administrative method by which management can substantiate its interest in employee relations is maintenance of a free and open flow of information among management and subordinate personnel.

The importance of such "two-way" communications to employee relations cannot be overemphasized. For it is only by this type of communications network that an effective interchange of information and ideas can occur in an organization. In practice such a system requires the exchange of differing viewpoints between superiors and subordinates. It may require substantial effort on the part of all concerned to reconcile their differences for the best interests of all the individuals and groups within the total organization.

By practicing "two-way" communication, management can show real interest in employee relations. Through such a system an employee can learn what is really expected of him and how his work fits into total organizational goals.

"Two-way" communication means that not only does information flow upward through administrative channels from subordinates to superiors but that management informs subordinates of events throughout the organization by means of newsletters, conferences, and other media; that employees are encouraged to participate in suggestion programs, and that their

[2] Howard Wilson, "The Psychological Needs of Man," PUBLIC RELATIONS, I, October, 1955, p. 146.

proposals are given careful consideration; that grievance committees are recognized and employee problems resolved; and that employee incentive is recognized and superior performance rewarded.

Particularly important is management recognition of and attention to "feedback" from employees. Sometimes information reported on the grapevine is more revealing than the more formal kinds of information that come to the attention of management through employee grievances and suggestions.

Administrators need to give continuing and careful attention to information that they pick up informally both on and off the job. Often this information can alert administrators to situations that can be very serious with respect to employee attitudes, employee morale, and the effectiveness of management policies. Since employee opinion has such a large influence on public opinion with respect to the city government, it is incumbent on management to do all it can to encourage good employee attitudes.

Employee Opinion Affects Public Opinion

Attitudes and opinions of municipal employees toward the city government are determined largely by their work experience—their relations with fellow workers and supervisors. If an employee feels that he is recognized by his superiors as an individual and not merely as an impersonal element of the machine, if he is respected by his associates, and if working conditions are satisfactory, he will ordinarily have a favorable attitude toward the city as a place to work. In addition to being pleased with his choice of work and employer, the public employee often is highly dedicated in his work and is imbued with the spirit of serving his fellow-man.

Quite the opposite type of attitude may develop, however, if he does not feel that he or his work is of some worth in the organization. If his experience with his associates and superiors is not pleasant, and if he does not feel that he truly is accepted as a member of his work group and the total municipal government, his attitude probably will be negative.

If negative attitudes continue to develop in the minds of employees, it is quite likely that they will soon take the form of opinions which are then expressed and passed on to other persons, both inside and outside the organization. It is only natural that municipal employees should discuss their work with associates, families, and friends. And when such opinions are multiplied hundreds and sometimes thousands of times, it is easy to see why the public's opinion of a city is greatly influenced by what its employees think and say. As Claude Robinson so aptly stated, when pointing out the tremendous impact of employee opinions regarding an organization's public status, "The most powerful influence on a company's community standing is what its own employees think and say about it."[3]

It can be said then that internal employee relations have a direct and significant effect on external relations with the public. Internal employee relations and external public relations are complementary factors in the over-all formulation of public opinion. Although many municipalities and their staffs are recognizing the important part which the internal relations have upon the general public, there still exists an urgent need in many cities for key administrative and supervisory personnel to become more aware of the reciprocal nature of these relationships. They need to devote more attention and time to the development of a human relations philosophy of management that will not only create healthy and harmonious relations inside the organization, but which at the same time will be reflected to the persons outside the organization in the form of many favorable opinions expressed by city employees who, in effect, constitute individual public relations representatives.

Key to Effective Public Relations

No municipality is administered so effectively that it can remain immune from public relations problems. There is always room for improvement in relations with the public.

With effective public relations predicated

---

[3] Glenn and Denny Griswold, editors, Your Public Relations (New York: Funk and Wagnalls Co., 1948), p. 31.

upon the quality of services, the basic orientation of any training program should be improvement of performance. A public relations training program raises false and undesirable aspirations if its goal is the acceptance of the local government entity whether or not that entity "deserves" acceptance. Much more rewarding two-fold objectives for a public relations training program are the continuing improvement of (1) internal procedures for greater effectiveness, and (2) employees' ability to empathize or reciprocate with the external publics. A normal consequence of such a training program will be the better acceptance of the organization by its publics.

Training for better public relations is really a matter of increasing the social awareness of employees. A municipality's employees should not be taught to "be nice" to the public so that the city will gain a better public image. The training rather should be goal-oriented so that employees understand typical citizen actions and reactions and can thus more easily and effectively perform the services for which they are employed.

A municipal public relations training program, then, should be a mutually rewarding relationship in which:

1. An orientation program facilitates the efforts of employees in providing help to the public, especially in directing them to the right place for the right information or service;

2. Continuing attention is given to maintaining high morale among employees who take pride in their work;

3. Participation of employees at all levels is obtained in spotting and correcting public relations problems and in auditing public relations programs for strengths and weaknesses;

4. Key people are trained to lead group meetings and to speak effectively in public; and

5. There is developed and maintained in employees a high interest in

 (a) operating motor vehicles courteously,

 (b) responding courteously on the telephone,

 (c) maintaining attitudes of attention, fairness, and helpfulness in all contacts,

 (d) preparing clearly written and courteous letters, and

 (e) minimizing delays experienced by citizens.

Although the need for more public relations training in municipalities has been recognized for several decades,[4] the practice has fallen far short of the need. A 1962 survey reported in *The Municipal Year Book* showed that only 203 cities in the nation have public relations training for the employees. In many of these jurisdictions, the training in public relations is not recognized as a specific area for training but is frequently integrated into the over-all training program in a rather piecemeal fashion. In some cities certain aspects of public relations problems are considered in the orientation of new employees, in the training of supervisors, or in training of police or fire personnel, but there are still relatively few cities that have formalized public relations training programs.[5]

This review should not be construed as a recommendation for all cities to move immediately into a full-blown public relations training program. To be most effective, public relations training should be part of a larger over-all training program for the municipality. The following guidelines are suggested in the establishment of such a training program:[6]

1. Establish a written training policy.
2. Assign qualified personnel.
3. Develop a training plan.
4. Insist on quality support—personnel, procedures, materials, and facilities.
5. Demand results and require evidence of results.
6. Appoint an advisory committee.

WHO SHOULD BE TRAINED?

Since almost all municipal employees have direct or indirect contacts with the public sometime during their employment, all personnel should be brought into the public relations training program. Some city personnel will require more extensive or specialized training than others, since their duties involve more contact with the public.

Some of the classes of employees who need more intensive public relations training have been identified in earlier chapters and include law enforcement and fire protection personnel,

[4] Elton D. Woolpert, MUNICIPAL PUBLIC RELATIONS (Chicago: International City Managers Association, 1940), p. 23.

[5] International City Managers Association, THE MUNICIPAL YEAR BOOK (Chicago: International City Managers Association, 1962), p. 287.

[6] See Appendix F for elaboration of these six points.

inspectors, receptionists, and public works employees. The extent to which specific groups of employees should be brought into the more specialized phases of the training should be determined by an analysis of the public relations aspects of specific positions. Since operating personnel tend to emulate the behavior and attitudes of their superiors toward the public, managerial personnel should participate actively in public relations training programs.

Whether training classes should involve the personnel from one or more departments or whether they should cut across all departments will depend largely on the size and organizational pattern of the city, the relevance of topics to be considered, and training facilities available. There may be economical advantages in establishing training classes that involve more than one department. Such an arrangement can help persons from different departments to understand each other's problems better and also help to prevent interoffice rivalries.

WHAT SHOULD BE TAUGHT?

In addition to improvement of communications skills, the subject matter of municipal public relations training courses frequently includes materials on (1) organization and operation of the city government, (2) safety and courtesy in operation of motor vehicles, (3) increasing social awareness, (4) effective correspondence, (5) telephone manners, and (6) municipal reports and publicity.

Organization of the City Government. A fundamental part of a public relations training program should involve the history, organization, and operations of the city itself. If municipal employees are to be effective in explaining and interpreting policies, procedures, and activities of their city government, they must first have a good understanding of these factors. If employees understand the past achievements of the city, they are likely to take pride in the city's heritage and to be motivated to maintain high standards of public service.

Safety. Care and safety in one's personal behavior and relationships with others often may have far-reaching consequences. On grounds and in offices the well-being of both individuals and the city is improved with safety in personal conduct and care in orderly arrangement and use of space, equipment, and materials. Courtesy and safety in the use of motor vehicles is especially significant.

Increasing Social Awareness. As discussed in an earlier chapter, employees who have frequent dealings with the public need to take special care in these contacts since public opinion is highly influenced by their behavior and attitudes. Included among such positions are police and fire personnel, inspectors, refuse collection crews, receptionists, and construction workers and their supervisors.

It should be emphasized in training these persons that the factors upon which the public bases its opinion of them and the total city are the manner and attitude they display toward patrons, the quality and quantity of information they furnish, the courtesy and tone of voice used, and personal appearance.

Several sessions should be included on the proper method of answering inquiries and the correct procedures to be used in handling complaints—receiving, routing, notification of corrective action, analysis of causes, and methods to reduce complaints.

Training in this area would not specify how a person should respond ("Laugh here," as some manuals indicate) but rather would illustrate client reaction to a seemingly threatening remark.

Correspondence. Although correspondence is an indirect method of contacting the public, a city is often judged upon the basis of the appearance and tone of letters. Instructions should be given on letter writing, including clarity, accuracy, conciseness, style, punctuation, grammar, and tone. Actual practice should be provided to enable employees to evaluate their own letters so they can improve their letter-writing skill. All letters of course must be neatly and accurately typed and addressed to the appropriate person.

Telephone Manners. The proper use of the telephone is a valuable and important subject for public relations training, as the telephone is used so extensively for communicating with the public. Since the telephone is used by so many city employees at all levels of the organization, training in its proper use should not be limited to switchboard operators.

The major points in communicating with the public by telephone have been discussed previously in Chapter 6, and guidelines have been set forth there. Most telephone companies have developed excellent films on proper telephone usage, and the local branch officials usually are glad to furnish the film and often send a representative to help in training.

Public Information Techniques. Employees who are responsible for public information functions should be given special training. This should include the development of skills in writing news releases, magazine articles, radio and television scripts, and spot announcements. If they are responsible for preparation of municipal reports, they should be given special training in typography, layout, and design of reports, and perhaps photography. If personnel or facilities for such specialized training are not available in the city organization, then an opportunity should be made available for employees to obtain this training at outside educational or other institutions.

RESPONSIBILITY FOR TRAINING

Although training in the larger view is the responsibility of each supervisor, if a formal training program is to be effective, specific responsibility must be assigned for organizing and implementing it. One of the major problems in many governmental jurisdictions which have initiated training programs has been the lack of specific assignments of responsibility for the program. Frequently, instructional assignments are given to individuals on a piecemeal basis and often with little advance notice.

In a larger municipality, over-all responsibility for coordinating the training program may be placed in the personnel office. In smaller jurisdictions, the chief administrator may delegate this duty to one of his assistants. Where possible the city should have a personnel development man full-time. Such a position would be difficult to justify in a municipality with fewer than 1,500 employees, however. It should be emphasized that the training function should be integrated constantly into the whole management process.

In public relations training it is usually advisable to decentralize the actual training function to the departmental level, since specific aspects of public relations will need special emphasis in the different organizational units. This will usually result in the supervisors being given the actual responsibility for carrying out the training program.

This is a logical assignment for supervisors at the lower levels since they ordinarily are in the best position to observe the behavior of employees who have problems in dealing with the public. It is the supervisor who usually must make constructive suggestions to prevent negative reactions from occurring as a result of various contacts with the public.

It is usually advisable to use city personnel as training instructors since they are familiar with the pattern of city operations and potential problem areas. It may be advisable from time to time, however, to obtain outside instructors if the subject is very specialized. For example, it usually is advisable to obtain advisers from the local telephone company to demonstrate the proper use of the telephone. Or members of local business colleges or high schools may be very helpful in training sessions on correspondence. As a general rule, however, the personnel at the supervisory levels, regardless of their titles, should be responsible for day-to-day public relations training.

Training the Trainers. Although the ability to teach others comes quite naturally to some persons, it is not a trait that is common to all. Some supervisors are not "natural born teachers." Yet they may have responsibility for training some or all of their subordinates. If this is the case, special training sessions should be set up for these supervisors. This can often be arranged through the personnel office in larger cities. Where this is impossible, department heads or other staff personnel usually can help in developing some training guides and materials and may also be effective as training instructors for supervisors.

DEVELOPING THE TRAINING PROGRAM

From an over-all view, a municipal public relations training program could be structured into three basic parts.

The first part could focus on socio-organizational relations, which would be concerned with interpersonal relations among operating personnel of the city, and between them and the supervisory and management staff.

The second phase could involve relations with the public. It likely would consider the direct and indirect contacts which municipal personnel have with the public and the critical importance of such contacts in the development of public opinion.

The third phase of the program could demonstrate how employee relations and relations with the public are inter-related and complementary processes in the formulation of public opinion regarding the city government. This could be shown by applying the guidelines developed in the first two phases of the program to practical operating situations. Through discussion and the use of examples of public relations incidents, it would be shown that the effectiveness of relations with the public is directly affected by the internal organizational relations.

METHODS OF TRAINING

The broad scope of topics that need to be included in a municipal public relations training program requires a variety of training techniques and approaches. They are here categorized into two major groupings: (1) individual training, and (2) group training.

As mentioned above, one of the most effective methods for public relations training is through day-to-day supervision and instruction by the employee's supervisor. This type of training may be the most feasible for smaller units, because it can be carried on during the regular course of duties.

Case Method. Specific incidents that have actually occurred can be analyzed by the group as a form of "case study." It is important that such discussions be conducted in an objective manner, so as not to imply personal criticism of the employees involved. If the members of the group are reluctant to contribute their own cases, the instructor may supply cases, either real or fictional.

The basic procedure in the case method is as follows: first, define the problem; second, deter-

mine the facts; third, have the group suggest as many solutions as possible and ultimately select the alternative which seems to be the most reasonable.

Case discussion of this type is thought by many to be therapeutic because employees will tend to compare their own actions with the standards of behavior agreed upon by the group. As Pfiffner has stated: "When each employee has shortcomings pointed out by his own colleagues without the finger of criticism being pointed directly at him, it is thought by some that he will be motivated to follow a more correct behavior pattern in the future."[7]

It is usually helpful to supplement oral group discussion with written materials, such as training guides or manuals. It is important that such documents contain materials that are directly related to the organization, however, and it is best if the materials can be developed within the organization itself.

Role Playing. The technique of role playing involves members of the group acting out parts in real life situations involving problems of human behavior. This technique can be useful in public relations training if it is used in an objective, open-minded manner. It can be used effectively with the case method, by having members of the group act out the various situations. The atmosphere should be permissive, and the objective is to obtain group involvement and participation.

The basic purpose of the role-playing technique is to involve persons in real-life situations so they can see themselves as other persons see them, usually vicariously. This experience may point up some of their problems in human behavior and help motivate them to modify their mannerisms and attitudes.

Lecture Approach. The use of more or less formal lectures can be useful in certain phases of training. In orientation sessions for new employees, it may be the only feasible method for reaching large numbers of employees. Even in these situations, however, most lectures are more effective if supplemented by demonstrations or by visual aids, such as films,

[7] John M. Pfiffner, THE SUPERVISION OF PERSONNEL (Englewood Cliffs, New Jersey: Prentice-Hall, Inc., 1958), p. 483.

flip charts, etc. There should always be an opportunity for questions from the group to clear up any confusion by clarifying or elaborating upon statements made by the speaker.

Occasionally it may be advisable to secure an outside authority to lecture on a particular subject, but, most instructors should be recruited from the local staff.

One of the greatest weaknesses in public relations training programs has been the use of "pep talks," in which some high executive or some outside speaker gives a supposedly inspirational talk on the importance of public relations, or the need for courtesy, etc. If such talks are the basis for additional development and training in public relations, they may have some value. Otherwise they are not worth the time they take.

The role of the employee is largely passive as he has little or no participation in the session. Also, such appeals are usually quite emotional and abstract in nature, and the effect is not permanent. To be effective, a public relations training program must have continuity. Although a didactic approach is part of the training, it seldom leads to behavioral change. Such presentations should be followed by some sort of sensitivity training, stimulating case discussion, role play, incident process, etc.

The Conference Method.   One of the most effective methods for public relations training is the "conference method." The technique involves group discussion under the direction of a training leader.

Although formal presentations may be made by the leader as a part of the session, the basic purpose is to involve the members of the group in the analysis of the subject matter under discussion.

In most conference-type training sessions, the leader should function mainly as a moderator. He should present the problem or subject and then stimulate discussion and suggestions from the members of the group. He should skillfully keep the discussion on the main subject.

In this type of training, the employees are expected to supply a substantial part of the actual training themselves by suggesting solutions to problems, and by self-analysis and comparison of their experiences with that of other employees. There should exist a permissive and democratic atmosphere since many of the topics may be controversial, and the participants may not be in complete agreement on all points.

If, for example, the topic under discussion involved the handling of citizen complaints, the first step might be to determine what types of complaints are most common. The leader should list these on a blackboard so that they can remain in view of the participants throughout the discussion. After there is general agreement on the types of complaints, the leader may then ask for suggestions as to the best procedure for handling such complaints. There will undoubtedly be disagreements or modifications, but the net result will probably be a solution that is better than that which has been used by any single employee.

Interpersonal Effectiveness.   Regardless of the technique that may be used in public relations training, the key to the program's success will depend basically upon the interpersonal effectiveness of the personnel involved. A basic requirement in the learning process is that the persons who are being instructed must understand the instructor and the information being presented before effective learning can take place.

The basic responsibility lies with the instructor to see that he is sensitive to the reactions of the group. This means that the persons being trained not only must receive the message but also must understand the information that is transmitted. Moreover, in order for the instructor to determine whether he is successfully communicating, he must also receive information back from the members of the group. This "feedback" can be in the form of opinions, comments, or questions on subject matter being discussed.

This is why it is so important for the instructor to establish a permissive atmosphere in training sessions so that full and free discussion will permeate the entire group. Individuals then will not hesitate to state their opinions, even if their suggestions appear contrary to those of the majority of the other persons present. Frequently, the optimum solution to a public relations problem can best be determined by synthesizing all the ideas of the persons present.

After he has identified the topic for discussion at the session, and perhaps made some introductory comments, the experienced training leader will usually solicit comments and questions from the group. If the response is not adequate to induce general discussion, the instructor may then pose some questions to the group and initiate discussion in this manner.

The point is that the training instructor should not inject himself into the discussion to such an extent that he discourages or inhibits individuals in the group from participating freely. The leader's basic function in a training session is to introduce the subject, to guide the discussion, and to bring about an often hard-fought-for consensus.

He should, of course, control the discussion and keep it on the subject. It may be advisable or necessary for him to over-rule the opinion of the group from time to time, particularly if he is responsible for the results of procedures or actions, or if he has more experience or knowledge relating to a particular activity.

Free interchange of ideas encourages common understanding, and cooperation may evolve, which constitutes the fundamental requirement for good public relations in municipalities as elsewhere in human organizations.

Status of Public Relations Training

Since relatively few public relations courses specifically related to government are offered by colleges or universities, most of the training in municipal public relations must be done by the cities themselves. In those communities where pertinent courses are available, municipal personnel should be encouraged to take advantage of such offerings as a part of their in-service training.

Although the number of cities throughout the United States which recognize the importance of public relations in-service training is increasing, they are still the exception rather than the rule. This problem is partly due to the lack of adequate in-service training in municipalities in general. As one authority has stated:

"With notable exceptions little is really being done to develop these people from within."[8]

As another authority indicates with regard to the more specialized types of training programs, such as those dealing with public relations, the situation is even worse. "Cities too long have been content to provide only the most elementary forms of in-service training for their employees."[9]

Examples of Public Relations Training

The picture for municipal training in public relations training appears to be somewhat encouraging, however, since the programs which have been established in a number of cities have been very successful and well-received. Some examples of these programs follow:

In Savannah, Georgia, a public relations program has been designated as the "public service training program." The course is structured to provide a basic public relations approach for city employees, and to develop a team spirit. Discussions rather than lectures are used in the four two-hour sessions: (1) the basic principles of public relations; (2) developing better understanding of the public's problems and attitudes; (3) the functions of city departments and the opportunities to provide helpful information; and (4) the role of the individual in public relations. Following completion of the course, it is evaluated by the participants. Each employee is presented with a certificate upon satisfactory completion.[10]

Norfolk, Virginia, conducts public relations training for city employees under the direction of the personnel officer. The course is given to groups of 15 employees and consists of 10 hours of discussions, films, and lectures. Subjects include the city government in relation to the community, complaints, personal appearance, telephone technique, and written and oral communications.[11]

---

[8] John J. Corson, "Better Personnel for Local Government," Public Management, XLIV, February, 1962, p. 6.

[9] Paul Schriever, "Municipal In-Service Training—Performance and Prospects," Public Management, XLIV August, 1962, p. 169.

[10] Public Management, XXXIX, December, 1957, pp. 286–287.

[11] Public Management, XXXVII, July, 1955, p. 153.

Public relations training is a key part of the program in San Antonio, Texas, to improve communications between the city and the public. The program, called the "Training Information Program" (TIP), started in 1959 for 3,500 employees. Every employee is required to attend 30-minute classes held every other week on city time. The over-all planning and preparation of class materials is coordinated by the public information officer and the director of personnel with each department head responsible for the training of his own department. The lesson materials are duplicated and distributed one week prior to each class. The topics that are covered include contacts with the public, courtesy, listening, annual reports, annexation, area service centers, the street program, and the bad effects of gossip upon morale.[12]

Monrovia, California, has developed a special public relations course for all members of the police department. The course is of three weeks duration, with three two-hour sessions held each week on city time. Course content includes lectures and discussions on such subjects as public relations, appearance, bearing, diplomacy, prejudice, conversation, issuing citations, voice and manner of speech, demeanor in the courtroom, and a police officer's private life.[13]

In Denton, Texas, a training program was developed to explore the role of supervisors in public relations. There were four consecutive sessions of one hour each during work hours. The speakers and discussion leaders included two professors from North Texas State College and the managing editor from the *Denton Record Chronicle*.[14]

Cleveland, Ohio, set up a special public relations training course covering the proper use of the telephone and contacts with the public. The personnel department also had printed and distributed to all employees a wallet-size reminder card outlining telephone tips and proper methods to be followed by the employees in their contacts with citizens.[15]

In Westerville, Ohio, a combined public relations-public information program has been used to speed up and improve refuse collection service. In 1959, when the quality of this service had fallen below a satisfactory level, an informal training program was initiated to instruct the refuse collection foremen about the importance of public contacts. Classes were then started for all refuse collection crews and were held during work hours. The sessions stressed courtesy to the public and a clean, neat appearance of uniforms and equipment.

As a result of discussion among all the personnel involved, standard procedures were arrived at for handling general and specific complaints and for providing information about this service. Next, leaflets were provided for the collection crews to distribute to inquirers, and notices to explain why refuse was not picked up. The reasons for nonpick-up were usually that the containers had not been accessible or locked inside garages and no one was at home, or that a vicious-appearing dog was in the yard. After such a notice was left at a residence, a copy was also turned in to the clerk at city hall, who could discuss the matter with the resident, if he should telephone.[16]

An interesting and pertinent example of a guide for public relations training is the booklet, *Interviewing in Social Security*, which was published by the Bureau of Old-Age and Survivors Insurance of the federal Social Security Administration. This federal agency administers the old-age, survivors, and disability program through more than 600 district offices throughout the nation.

The administrative officials of this agency have long been in the vanguard in their recognition of the value of public contacts and interviewing in developing good public relations. Much of the work of this federal agency involves interviewing people of all ages relative to their rights and responsibilities under the Social Security Act. This document was written primarily for the beginning interviewer in the agency for use in in-service training. It is an aid to the development of interviewing skill, and it utilizes actual case histories of the agency to

[12] PUBLIC MANAGEMENT, XLII, July, 1960, p. 154.
[13] PUBLIC MANAGEMENT, XLI, November, 1959, p. 257.
[14] PUBLIC MANAGEMENT, XLIII, March, 1961, p. 68.
[15] PUBLIC MANAGEMENT, XXXVIII, May, 1956, p. 108.
[16] PUBLIC MANAGEMENT, XLII, February, 1961, p. 37.

illustrate the more, and less, effective techniques of successful interviewing of a tremendous cross-section of the American public.[17]

Guidelines For Training

As illustrated in the above examples, each training program in public relations should be structured to fit the specific needs of the particular agency or jurisdiction involved. There are certain basic factors or criteria, however, that should be kept in mind in the development of any public relations training program.

1. Establish training objectives, taking into consideration both the needs and the resources available.

2. The scope and content of the training program should be prepared well in advance of the actual training sessions.

3. All personnel who will be involved in the program should be encouraged to participate in the development of its scope and content.

4. Training classes should be held quite frequently, but they should be relatively brief so as not to become a detriment to personnel in terms of requiring an unreasonable amount of time away from regular duties.

5. Training sessions should be held during regular working hours.

6. Responsibility for specific training topics and sessions should be assigned to individuals, and they should be given sufficient time to prepare for the sessions.

7. Visual aids, such as films, slides, flipcharts, etc., should be used frequently to supplement lectures and discussions.

8. Occasional "ventilation sessions" should be held to enable individual employees to discuss their specific problems and "gripes." This enables employees to get things "off their chest," and group discussion may help to solve such problems.

9. Training assignments should be rotated among all those persons who are capable of conducting sessions. Sessions should be set up also for training the trainers.

10. Results of training sessions should be summarized and condensed in the form of training guides or manuals for future classes. Such documents should list the subject-areas, include examples of pertinent situations, and set forth some guidelines. Care should be taken that such guidelines are not stereotyped or stilted and that they relate to the particular department or unit involved.

11. Training sessions should generally be conducted on a rather informal basis so as to encourage free discussion and interchange of ideas. The training leader should coordinate and guide the session rather than attempt to dominate it. But he should summarize the conclusions for the benefit of all, and he should be sure that general agreement exists on various conclusions reached.

12. Every opportunity within the superior-subordinate relationship should be utilized for training purposes. Most frequent reliance will be upon such techniques as coaching, counseling, job rotation, understudy, and special assignments.

13. Provide for continuing evaluation of both needs and the adopted training program itself.[18]

---

[17] Elizabeth de Schweinitz, Karl de Schweinitz, INTERVIEWING IN SOCIAL SECURITY (Washington, D.C.: Government Printing Office, 1961), p. vii.

[18] See Appendix G for an example of an evaluation form used by one municipality for its formal public relations training sessions.

Appendix A

Suggested Code of Ethics and Creeds
for Municipal Officials and Employees

Be it resolved [enacted] by the Council of the City of _____ that the following be a "Code of Ethics for the Public Service of the City of _____."

1. DECLARATION OF POLICY

The proper operation of democratic government requires that public officials and employees be independent, impartial, and responsible to the people; that governmental decisions and policy be made in the proper channels of the governmental structure; that public office not be used for personal gain; and that the public have confidence in the integrity of its government. In recognition of these goals there is hereby established a Code of Ethics for all officials and employees, whether elected or appointed, paid or unpaid. The purpose of this Code is to establish ethical standards of conduct for all such officials and employees by setting forth those acts or actions that are incompatible with the best interests of the city and by directing disclosure by such officials and employees of private financial or other interests in matters affecting the city. The provisions and purpose of this Code and such rules and regulations as may be established are hereby declared to be in the best interests of the City of _____.

2. RESPONSIBILITIES OF PUBLIC OFFICE

Public officials and employees are agents of public purpose and hold office for the benefit of the public. They are bound to uphold the Constitution of the United States and the Constitution of this State and to carry out impartially the laws of the nation, state, and municipality and thus to foster respect for all government. They are bound to observe in their official acts the highest standards of morality and to discharge faithfully the duties of their office regardless of personal considerations, recognizing that the public interest must be their primary concern. Their conduct in both their official and private affairs should be above reproach.

3. DEDICATED SERVICE

All officials and employees of the municipality should be loyal to the political objectives expressed by the electorate and the programs developed to attain those objectives. Appointive officials and employees should adhere to the rules of work and performance established as the standard for their positions by the appropriate authority.

Officials and employees should not exceed their authority or breach the law or ask others to do so, and they should work in full cooperation with other public officials and employees unless prohibited from so doing by law or by officially recognized confidentiality of their work.

4. FAIR AND EQUAL TREATMENT

a. *Interest in Appointments.* Canvassing of members of the council, directly or indirectly, in order to obtain preferential consideration in connection with any appointment to the municipal service shall disqualify the candidate for appointment except with reference to positions filled by appointment by the council.

b. *Use of Public Property.* No official or employee shall request or permit the use of city-owned vehicles, equipment, materials, or property for personal convenience or profit, except when such services are available to the public generally or are provided as municipal policy for the use of such official or employee in the conduct of official business.

c. *Obligations to Citizens.* No official or employee shall grant any special consideration, treatment, or advantage to any citizen beyond that which is available to every other citizen.

5. CONFLICT OF INTEREST

No councilman or other official or employee, whether paid or unpaid, shall engage in any business or transaction or shall have a financial or other personal interest, direct or indirect, which is incompatible with the proper discharge of his official duties in the public interest or would tend to impair his independence of judgment or action in the performance of his official duties. Personal as distinguished from financial interest includes an interest arising from blood or marriage relationships or close business or political association.

Specific conflicts of interest are enumerated below for the guidance of officials and employees:

a. *Incompatible Employment.* No councilman or other official or employee shall engage in or accept private employment or render services for private interests when such employment or service is incompatible with the proper discharge of his official duties or would tend to impair his independence of judgment or action in the performance of his official duties.

b. *Disclosure of Confidential Information.* No councilman or other official or employee shall, without proper legal authorization, disclose confidential information concerning the property, government, or affairs of the city. Nor shall he use such information to advance the financial or other private interest of himself or others.

c. *Gifts and Favors.* No councilman or other official or employee shall accept any valuable gift, whether in the form of service, loan, thing, or promise, from any person, firm, or corporation which to his knowledge is interested directly or indirectly in any manner whatsoever in business dealings with the city; nor shall any such official or employee (1) accept any gift, favor, or thing of value that may tend to influence him in the discharge of his duties, or (2) grant in the discharge of his duties any improper favor, service, or thing of value.

d. *Representing Private Interests Before City Agencies or Courts.* No councilman or other official or employee whose salary is paid in whole or in part by the city shall appear in behalf of private interests before any agency of the city. He shall not represent private interests in any action or proceeding against the interests of the city in any litigation to which the city is a party.

A councilman may appear before city agencies on behalf of constituents in the course of his duties as a representative of the electorate or in the performance of public or civic obligations. However, no councilman or other official or employee shall accept a retainer or compensation that is contingent upon a specific action by a city agency.

e. *Contracts with the City.* Any councilman or other official or employee who has a substantial or controlling financial interest in any business entity, transaction, or contract with the city, or in the sale of real estate, materials, supplies, or services to the city, shall make known to the proper authority such interest in any matter on which he may be called to act in his official capacity. He shall refrain from voting upon or otherwise participating in the transaction or the making of such contract or sale.

A councilman or other official or employee shall not be deemed interested in any contract or purchase or sale of land or other thing of value unless such contract or sale is approved, awarded, entered into, or authorized by him in his official capacity.

f. *Disclosure of Interest in Legislation.* A councilman who has a financial or other private interest in any legislation shall disclose on the records of the council or other appropriate authority the nature and extent of such interest. This provision shall not apply if the councilman disqualifies himself from voting.

Any other official or employee who has a financial or other private interest, and who participates in discussion with or gives an official opinion to the council, shall disclose on the records of the council or other appropriate authority the nature and extent of such interest.

6. POLITICAL ACTIVITY

No appointive official or employee in the administrative service shall use the prestige of his position in behalf of any political party.

No appointive official or employee in the administrative service shall orally, by letter, or otherwise, solicit or be in any manner concerned in soliciting any assessment, subscription, or contribution to any political party; nor shall he be a party to such solicitation by others. Such appointed officials and employees shall not take an active part in political campaigns for candidates.

No official or employee, whether elected or appointed, shall promise an appointment to any municipal position as a reward for any political activity.

7. APPLICABILITY OF CODE

When a councilman or other official or employee has doubt as to the applicability of a provision of this Code to a particular situation, he should apply to the authority on ethical conduct constituted for the implementation of this Code for an advisory opinion and be guided by that opinion when given. The councilman or other official or employee shall have the opportunity to present his interpretation of the facts at issue and of the applicable provision(s) of the Code before such advisory decision is made. This Code shall be operative in all instances covered by its provisions except when superseded by an applicable statutory or charter provision and statutory or charter action is mandatory, or when the application of a statutory or charter provision is discretionary but determined to be more appropriate or desirable.

8. SANCTIONS

Violation of any provisions of this Code should raise conscientious questions for the councilman or other official or employee concerned as to whether voluntary resignation or other action is indicated to promote the best interests of the city. Violation may constitute a cause for suspension, removal from office or employment, or other disciplinary action.

Suggested Creed for Councilmen

As a City Councilman I believe:

That the proper operation of democratic government requires that public officials be independent and impartial in their judgment and actions; that government decisions and policy be made in the proper channels of the governmental structure; that public office not be used for personal gain; and that the public have confidence in the integrity of its government and public officials.

And that the realization of these ends is impaired whenever there exists, or appears to exist, an actual or potential conflict between the private interests of a governmental official and his public duties. The public interest requires ethical standards with respect to official conduct.

Therefore, as a City Councilman of the City of _____ I assert my solemn belief that the primary responsibility for maintaining a high level of ethics among city officials and employees falls upon the Council as the governing body elected by the people:

Consequently, as a Councilman, I believe it is my duty to:

1. Respect the importance of American ideals of government, of the rule of law, of the principles of public administration, and of ethical conduct in the performance of my public duties.

2. Represent and work for the common good of the people of my city and not for private interest, assuring fair and equal treatment of all persons, claims, and transactions coming before me in my official capacity.

3. Refrain from accepting gifts or favors or promises of future benefit which might compromise or tend to impair my independence of judgment or action as a Councilman.

4. Learn the background and purposes of major ordinances before voting.

5. Faithfully perform my duties as a Councilman by attending all sessions of the Council and of its committees of which I am a member, unless unable to do so for some compelling reason or disability.

6. Help the Council maintain the highest standards of ethical conduct by refusing to approve breaches of public trust or improper attempts to influence legislation and by being willing to vote to censure or otherwise discipline any Councilman who willfully violates the duly established rules of conduct for Councilmen.

7. Disclose all sources of income which may represent a substantial conflict of interest with my duties as a Councilman and to disclose the nature and extent of my interest as an officer, agent, member, or owner of any business entity or other association which is subject to regulation by the city, such disclosure to be made to the proper authority established for that purpose.

8. Refuse to represent private interests before city agencies or in the courts, except as may be my duty toward constituents, such service to be rendered without compensation, and refuse to accept or engage in any employment incompatible with my public duties.

9. Disclose any private interest I may have in legislation before the Council or to refrain from voting when such interest is in substantial conflict with my public duties.

10. Refrain from disclosing confidential information concerning the city government.

Suggested Creed for Administrative Officials and Employees

As a municipal official or employee I believe:

That the proper operation of democratic government requires that public officials be independent and impartial in their judgment and actions; that government decisions and policy be made in the proper channels of the governmental structure; that public office not be used for personal gain; and that the public have confidence in the integrity of its government and officials.

And that the realization of these ends is impaired whenever there exists, or appears to exist, an actual or potential conflict between the private interests of a governmental official and his public duties and that the public interest requires ethical standards with respect to official conduct.

Therefore, as a public official or employee of the City of _____ I assert my solemn belief that I have a responsibility to the people of _____ to do all in my power to maintain the integrity of their government.

Consequently, I believe it is my duty to:

1. Respect the importance of American ideals of government, the rule of law, the principles of public administration, and ethical conduct in the performance of my public duties; and to be efficient, courteous, and impartial in the performance of those duties, assuring fair and equal treatment of all persons, claims, and transactions coming before me in my official capacity.

2. Work in full cooperation with other public employees in promoting the public welfare, recognizing that my private interest must always be subordinate to the public interest.

3. Make decisions conscientiously in compliance with public law and policies of the City Council,

and subordinate my personal views to the requirements of law, my oath of office, and the regulations of the agency in which I perform my public duties.

4. Be scrupulously honest in handling public funds and in the conservation of public property, never using any funds or property under my care for private benefit of myself or others.

5. Never accept or engage in employment incompatible with my public duties.

6. Refuse to represent private interests before city agencies or in the courts in any matter involving the interests of the city as a party or in which my official position is a consideration.

7. Disclose all sources of income which may represent a substantial conflict of interest with my official duties and to disclose the nature and extent of any personal interest in a business entity engaging in any transaction with the city in which I may be involved in my official capacity as a public official or employee.

8. Refrain from disclosing confidential information concerning the city government.

9. Refrain from accepting gifts or favors or promise of future benefit which might compromise my independence of judgment or action as a public official or employee.

Appendix B

Code of Professional Standards
for the Practice of Public Relations

The Code of Professional Standards for the Practice of Public Relations is adopted by the Public Relations Society of America to promote and maintain high standards of public service and conduct among its members in order that membership in the Society may be deemed a badge of ethical conduct; that public relations justly may be regarded as a profession; that the public may have increasing confidence in its integrity; and that the practice of public relations may best serve the public interest.

1. A member has a general duty of fair dealing towards his clients or employers, past and present, his fellow members and the general public.

2. A member shall conduct his professional life in accord with the public welfare.

3. A member has the affirmative duty of adhering to generally accepted standards of accuracy, truth and good taste.

4. A member shall not represent conflicting or competing interests without the express consent of those concerned. . . .

5. A member shall safeguard the confidences of both present and former clients or employers and shall not accept retainers or employment which may involve the disclosure or use of these confidences to the disadvantage or prejudice of such clients or employers.

6. A member shall not engage in any practice which tends to corrupt the integrity of channels of public communication.

7. A member shall not intentionally disseminate false or misleading information and is obligated to use ordinary care to avoid dissemination of false or misleading information.

8. A member shall not make use of any organization purporting to serve some announced cause but actually serving an undisclosed special or private interest of a member or his client or his employer.

9. A member shall not intentionally injure the professional reputation or practice of another member. However, if a member has evidence that another member has been guilty of unethical, illegal or unfair practices, including practices in violation of this Code, he should present the information to the proper authorities of the Society for action in accordance with the procedure set forth in Article XIII of the Bylaws.

10. A member shall not employ methods tending to be derogatory of another member's client or employer or of the products, business or services of such client or employer.

11. In performing services for a client or employer a member shall not accept fees, commissions or any other valuable consideration in connection with those services from anyone other than his client or employer without the express consent of his client or employer, given after a full disclosure of the facts.

12. A member shall not propose to a prospective client or employer that his fee or other compensation be contingent on the achievement of certain results; nor shall he enter into any fee agreement to the same effect.

13. A member shall not encroach upon the professional employment of another member unless both are assured that there is no conflict between the two engagements and are kept advised of the negotiations.

14. A member shall, as soon as possible, sever his relations with any organization when he believes his continued employment would require him to conduct himself contrary to the principles of this Code.

15. A member called as a witness in a proceeding for the enforcement of this Code shall be bound to appear unless, for sufficient reason, he shall be excused by the panel hearing the same.

16. A member shall co-operate with fellow members in upholding and enforcing this Code.

Appendix C

City of La Habra, California
Use of the Service Request Form

USE

Use a Service Request for an external matter originating from a citizen, requiring attention by a City department. This request serves as:

A work order to the department responsible for the proper handling of the matter.

A record of the volume and intensity of requests for services.

A record of the volume of the workload in comparison with the capacity of the department under the current budget.

All requests for service are referred to by the name. Never call such a request a "complaint."

PAPER

Use printed "Service Request" forms.

Use the white sheet for the original, and the pink and yellow sheets for the second and third copies.

NUMBER OF COPIES

Prepare each Service Request in triplicate.

FILL IN PRINTED FORM COMPLETELY

Be sure to get the name, address, and telephone number of the person making the request. Place this information at the top of the form.

Fill in your name and department, and the date.

Give a short summary of the request.

After "Details" list any further information given by the person making the Request.

After "Referred to" type the name of the department to which the request is to be referred for action.

DISTRIBUTION

Send the white (original) copy to the office of the City Administrator.

Send the pink and yellow copies to the department which is to handle the request.

ACTION TAKEN

As soon as the appropriate department has completed the action, the pink and yellow copies of the Service Requests are to be filled in.

Be sure that a description of the action taken is given after "Report."

The Service Request should be dated and signed by the person fulfilling the request.

DISPOSITION OF COPIES

As soon as the pink and yellow copies have been filled in, indicating completion of the request, the pink copy should be forwarded to the Office of the City Administrator. The yellow copy is to be retained in the files of the department which acted upon the request as a record of work performed.

What's Wrong with Committees

Time consuming, boring and poorly managed committee meetings are inexcusable in our present-day pace. Correct procedures can be learned. But as long as some of these problem-solving boards remain offensive, many capable people will reluctantly accept such assignments. Low esteem of these meetings is well illustrated by a United States Senator who says that a committee is nothing more than a small group of uninformed persons who prove the unnecessary unwillingly.

In this survey, staff members in business, professional institutions and organizations who have had wide experience as committeemen were interviewed. Top level executives who usually preside in meetings were excluded. When asked about their impressions of committee participation, many employes offer sharp attacks while others acknowledge that such work is fruitful.

First, a majority of individuals interviewed believe that a monopolizing chairman or committeeman (sometimes the employer) is the major objection to committee participation. Little respect for individual opinions or opportunity for a fair group decision is evident. This self-centered type of monologue and control ignites sparks of resentment and misunderstanding among participants. Mental rigidity and too much traditional thinking suppress the possibility of new ideas. Inevitable recourse to this repression is an unwillingness to accept ultimate decisions.

A second complaint among those queried is the disregard of the time element in many meetings. They needlessly start late or run long overtime.

A third criticism is leveled at discussions which waver from the problem under consideration. In some meetings there is rambling and repetition of ideas, some of which have been previously decided. That the unskilled presiding officer ever accomplishes anything seems to be the direct accusation.

These views remind us of Mrs. Kettering, who said, "Isn't it wonderful that Lindy flew across the ocean by himself?" To which her husband, the financier, replied, "Yes, but it would be more remarkable had he done it with a committee!"

In the investigation, various personnel disclose that excellent committee work is accomplishing results in a number of industrial and professional organizations. In the rewarding sessions presided over by a neutral and objective official everyone contributes freely in a democratic manner. Here there is more incentive for participation since the individual feels his services are of value. In these lively meetings a willingness to serve on committees is noted.

It was observed throughout interviews that few of those quizzed has had training for committee work. Therefore, aim of this study is to supply some processes for improving committee proceedings so that people will want to serve in the best interests of an organization.

It may be helpful at the outset to define the committee as:

A small group of persons appointed or elected as planning units to do essential tasks that cannot be done as well by one person or a larger organization.

Advantages of committees are many. In business, research shows that a majority of top executives prefer to place their very important policies before their staffs. One assistant estimates that as much as a quarter of his employer's time is spent in seeking help in his decision making. Professional organizations likewise place much emphasis on group problem-solving. By using this democratic procedure everyone in the organization profits. They can:

1. Place in the hands of the group their most difficult obstacles.

2. Use the group as a workhorse for finding needed information.

3. Insure more success in decision making.

4. Lay the foundation for a successful conference involving many people.

5. Keep the supervisor or organization from bogging down with detail.

6. Investigate, discuss and recommend suitable action.

7. Operate on the premise that several minds are better than one.

8. Share confidential ideas and policies.

9. Offer a freer flow of ideas than can larger groups.

10. Pool ideas of authorities, experts and laymen.

11. Have an instrument to delegate responsibilities.

12. Spot more errors in a plan than can one individual.

13. Help train inexperienced personnel in decision-making.

14. Reach decisions which will carry more weight.

15. Ascertain truths which become more evident in the competition of minds.

16. Derive less criticism of policies.

17. Increase morale of the organization.

To delegate a project to a poorly chosen committee is an unfailing way to kill a motion, delay solution of a problem or pave the way for misrepresentation. A case in point was the report that a committee was formed for which no chairman had been named. As a result, no one took it upon himself to call meetings. One member made the decisions for the group year in and year out. This created poor morale among the others.

A qualified chairman should be chosen to see that work is done systematically. His role is so important that he can easily make or break the committee. He is responsible for the success of the meeting. Following qualifications, therefore, must be considered carefully:

1. Is proposed chairman too autocratic in his attitude?

2. Is he a laissez faire leader who allows group to talk about irrelevant matters?

3. Is he one who can guide group work in a minimum of time?

4. Does he understand human beings and their wants?

5. Has he the ability to stimulate others to work together?

6. Is he able to interpret correctly feelings of others?

7. Can he convert a person-centered group into a task-centered group?

8. Can he be patient and listen carefully to someone else?

9. Is he one who is likely to impose his wishes on the group?

10. Can he be impersonal and refrain from favoritism?

11. Is he one who is apt to manipulate others' statements?

12. Does he seek views of *all* present?

13. Has he ability to accept suggestions?

14. Does he handle people with tact? Is he informal and friendly?

15. Is he willing to learn?

16. Does he familiarize himself with problems to be solved?

17. Does he have respect for opinions of other people?

18. Is he able to take group intelligence and release it?

19. Does he realize that even an expert doesn't know all the answers?

20. Does he understand that people are satisfied if they have a part?

21. Is he one who will follow through with their decisions?

A staff official recalls the instance when a person had been appointed to a committee as a reward for special services. It was observed that this member did not make a single remark in the four years he belonged to an important policy-making group. Another administrative assistant complains that committeemen who have too much to say and too little to offer are irritating to others. This lack of contribution from participants and many other shortcomings should cause those concerned to choose responsible people. Some principles to note in participants are:

1. Are they individuals who will study problems with an open mind?

2. Are they punctual and will they come to meetings regularly?

3. Can they listen intelligently?

4. Are they well-informed individuals?

5. Can they avoid temptation to railroad the group?

6. Do they have a spirit of investigation and inquiry?

7. Are they capable of working together?

8. Do they have respect for attitudes of others?

9. Have they a positive attitude?

10. Are they interested in a given project?

11. Do they have a suitable background for the problem?

12. Will they allow others to talk?

13. Do they represent different points of view about a problem?

14. Do they abide by decisions of the majority?

Most people interviewed feel that business-like procedure is essential. They are impressed with convenience, comfort and punctuality in meetings.

Some inviting circumstances or inducements for your committee meeting may include any number of factors. They are:

1. Determine carefully the objectives of your meeting.

2. Select a favorable time for your meetings. Consult the group.

3. Agenda should include a carefully and briefly worded list of items for consideration.

4. This agenda should be mailed well in advance. Follow it in the meeting.

5. Invite *all* members to come to the meeting.

6. A short reminder often helps attendance.

7. Start on time and announce the time for closing. Stick to this announcement.

8. Introduce those not known to the group. Otherwise, get to the problem at once.

9. If there appears to be solo performances of any length, allot each member in turn a time limit on his remarks.

10. Plan to have someone write solutions on the blackboard.

11. If yours is a permanent committee, use rotation system which calls for staggered terms of office. Inexperienced members can bring new ideas, yet lean on experience of others.

12. Special assignments for certain individuals

and recording the attendance could help to keep members coming to each meeting.

13. Do not meet too often in regularly scheduled meetings unless there are a sufficient number of pressing problems.

If the chairman does not have an outline or does not adhere to any logical sequence of ideas, he probably will have a meeting which wanders about considerably. This is described among those who serve on committees as consuming too much valuable time and provoking impatience. Hence, a blueprint or a plan of some kind should be followed in order to secure maximum results in a minimum of time.

There are various possible outlines. They may be followed informally and, of course, flexibility is in order. Some items may be omitted. Committee proceedings should be painstakingly tailored to a particular group. Following plan has several merits and is suggested:

1. State problem briefly and clearly. (You could write it on the board if you sense that it is a little involved.)

2. Define problem so there is agreement as to the phase or limitations of the question. (Don't spend much time or offer any solutions here.)

3. Briefly discuss the seriousness of the problem. (Are there people or conditions concerned? What are the losses? Any dangers?)

4. Invite possible solutions from *everyone*. (Suggest recording these on blackboard so they will be remembered.)

5. Choose a common solution. (Try to scrutinize advantages and disadvantages of each one and select most acceptable. Ask *each* member for his opinion.)

6. Make plans as to how the preferred solution can be put into effect. (Personnel involved, finance, material, time, place, etc.)

Researchers have found that normally individuals in small groups have a feeling of wanting to work together toward some goal. They are disturbed when serious disagreement exists. When queried about this problem some of those interviewed thought that there are no sure-fire methods of reaching agreements, but they are more likely to occur if certain conditions prevail. Some of these are:

1. People should have a clear understanding of what is to be decided and understand one another. Be specific not general in your comments.

2. Preconceived judgments need to be omitted from the discussion.

3. Careful listening should be maintained.

4. Personal comments or name calling should not be allowed.

5. A positive approach is needed.

6. Select people who have an open mind to work together.

7. Have an impartial chairman.

8. Facts, sound information, illustrations, and statistics need to be used.

9. Leader should check frequently for areas of agreement.

10. These points of accord should be stressed.

11. Completion of part of the work toward compromise should be accepted.

12. Free exchange of ideas should be sought by chairman.

13. Exacting summaries need to be made by presiding official.

14. Haste is an enemy of objectivity, so do not try to press items along too fast before any group.

In reaching decisions a committee usually depends upon common understanding, compromise or assent in solving problems. One of the most glaring errors made by the presiding officer is to draw incorrect conclusions. One employe says that on too many occasions the time-worn phrase, "We are agreed upon," was used when there were obviously those who were decidedly in opposition to the chairman's remark. To allay this mistake the chairman should ask each individual if he agrees to the conclusion as it has been stated. Researchers note that the secret ballot is often different from the voice or hand vote. Therefore, the written method would be more valid.

If the committee cannot make a decision because of a tie vote, the chairman may need to cast the deciding ballot. On the other hand the problem which may be too "hot" to handle at a given time, may be deferred to a later date. Final decision may also be placed in the hands of the larger organization or in the hands of an outside authority commonly called an arbitrator.

Throughout committee meetings there should be an accurate recording of the business transacted. This is normally done by a secretary or recorder. When the group meets periodically these notes should, of course, be transferred to a permanent copy for approval by the membership. In this way accuracy can be maintained. The record of business can be scrutinized by those interested at any later date. This process frees the chairman from recording efforts and he may more fully concentrate on his responsibility of guiding the group.

If you are called upon to give an oral report of committee findings, speak it extemporaneously as you would a speech. Outlines are helpful and the following one can be used effectively:

1. Statement of the problem. (Make it short and clear. Example—Several complaints have been received about parking.)

2. Conclusions reached. (Upon investigating you find that parking is bad.)

3. Tell us how the investigation was made. (Experts consulted? Persons interviewed? Facts and statistics gleamed?)

4. Offer recommendations. Be certain to recognize alternate ones to remain completely objective. If you are before the larger organization, offer the preferred solution in the form of a motion at the conclusion of the report.)

After the committee's work is done, the chairman may gain added insight regarding his work if he requests unsigned written evaluations. Future meetings may greatly benefit from these suggestions.

Giving recognition to those who did outstanding work pays dividends. Informing the membership of any action taken upon their recommendations and thanking them personally for contributions would be conducive to further cooperation and willingness to serve on committees.

By Milton J. Wiksell, Associate Professor, Department of Speech, Michigan State University. Reprinted with permission from May 3, 1957, issue of *Sales Meetings* magazine.

Appendix E

Public Relations Policy Statement,
Los Angeles Police Department

Subject: Activation of Chapter Three, Volume One, of the Department Manual

Effective: Immediately

Purpose: This order is issued to activate Chapter Three, Volume One, of the Department Manual. This chapter, entitled "Community Relations," sets forth principles and policies to be followed by all employees of the Department.

1/000 GENERAL

005. *Police Commission—Executive Power.* The rule making power of the Police Commission is prescribed in the City Charter, Section 78, which is quoted in part:

• "Sec. 78. The board of each department shall have the power . . . to supervise, control, regulate, and manage the department and to make and enforce all necessary and desirable rules and regulations therefore . . ."

010. *General Provisions.* The objectives, principles, policies, procedures, rules, and regulations set forth in the Manual of the Los Angeles Police Department and in the Tactical Manual are guides to the actions of employees of the Department.

1/300 COMMUNITY RELATIONS

305. *Community Relations—General.* Community relations, insofar as it relates to the Police Department is the sum total of the attitudes, impressions, and opinions of the public in its relationship with the Department.

The mutual advantages of a friendly relationship between the people of a community and their police force should be widely understood and more fully appreciated. The success of a police force in the performance of its duties is largely measured by the degree of support and cooperation it receives from the people it serves. It is of paramount importance, therefore, to secure for this Department the confidence, respect, and approbation of the public. The cultivation of such desirable attitudes on the part of the public is dependent upon reciprocal attitudes on the part of this Department. These policies designed to enhance good public relations anticipate active participation therein by every member of the Department.

There is a personal satisfaction derived from the proper performance of police duty. Public service is one of the noblest professions, and it is never nobler than when rendered to the weak and the uncertain.

The principal factors involved in determining relationship between this Department and the public are:

• Police Service—the attitude of the police toward the people of the community, and their deportment and efficiency in the performance of their duties.

• The Public—the attitude of the people toward the police and law enforcement in general.

• Ethnic Composition of the Community.

• News Media and Public Information.

310. *Police Service.* The most important factor in gaining the good will and confidence of the people is in fostering among members of the Department an attitude of courtesy and objectivity toward the people with whom they come in daily contact.

It is also important that the Department, individually and collectively, demonstrate the knowledge, technique, and capacity to provide the type of police service which the people have a right to expect.

Each member of the Department must be imbued with an esprit de corps, and be prepared by study, training, and self-discipline to meet the responsibilities of police service. Self-confidence, so essential for accomplishment, comes from experience gained through the diligent performance of duty. Courtesy, patience, and tact are characteristics of the experienced, competent policeman.

The judicious policeman most correctly reflects the policy of the Department. To most people the individual policeman is representative of the entire Department. To transients and visitors he is the public representative of the City. His demeanor and deportment in dealing with the public create impressions either favorable or unfavorable to himself, the Department, and frequently to the City.

A policeman must realize that his activities are matters of particular interest, not only to those with whom he has direct dealings, but also to the general public. This is so because his official duties are closely related to practically every phase of community life.

He must, therefore, train himself to habits of acceptable conduct that will merit public approval. The courage he displays in moments of danger, or his calm objective approach at the scene of disorder, instantly evokes admiration. His sympathetic interest in caring for children or in rendering aid to the injured, aged, or infirm begets sincere affection. The inquiring visitor or the inadvertently erring motorist will usually manifest feelings of gratitude for a courteous explanation. Firmness, devoid of any personal feelings or use of unnecessary force, in effecting arrests or performing other necessary police duty will merit respect, even of the offender.

It is not sufficient that officers do a professional job of law enforcement. It is of equal importance that everyone be convinced that such is the case.

All citizens object to the use of language that offends their person, race, or religion. Verbal abuse is as demoralizing to human dignity as physical abuse. Everyone is entitled to be treated with respect and dignity.

310.05 *Policy.*

• The personal conduct of each member of the Department is the primary factor in promoting a program of desirable public relations. Tact, patience, and courtesy shall be strictly observed under all circumstances.

• A police officer is a public official representing all of the people. He shall maintain a professional attitude and demeanor which will not in any manner communicate any personal prejudices.

• Superior officers shall by example demonstrate, and shall instruct subordinates in proper deportment and desirable attitudes, in their dealings with the public.

• Members of the Department shall avoid behavior such as would tend to bring about criticism of the Department. Their conduct, whether on or off duty, shall be such as to merit the respect and confidence of the people.

• Officers shall diligently perform their duty with professional dignity. They shall not convey an attitude of subservience or servility.

• Each officer shall perform his duty fearlessly and impartially keeping uppermost in his mind that he is the guardian of the people's constitutional guarantees and civil rights, as well as the protector of their lives and property.

315. *The Public.* The public we serve, for the most part, is composed of peaceful, hard-working, law abiding people. The criminal element comprises only a small fraction of the population. While enforcement of numerous regulations is necessary to insure the safety, health, comfort, and convenience of all the people in an urban community, violation of such regulations does not necessarily indicate criminal tendencies, and enforcement should ordinarily be sought along educational and cooperative lines.

The regulation of crowds is a daily experience in the more congested sections of the City. Problems of greater complexity arise in policing special events and situations involving exceptional community interest. While the proper policing of crowds includes the formulation of plans designed to meet contingencies, the most important factor in routine regulation is to obtain the cooperation of the crowd itself. This can be accomplished best by persuasive methods. A suggestion will frequently prove more effective than an order. While the average individual or group may resent a domineering attitude on the part of a policeman, and be quick to assert constitutional rights, the same individual or group will often comply with a courteous direction.

The people naturally look to their police force for security in their person, homes, and property. Modern concepts of social police service include, not only programs for youth and traffic safety, but also active participation during emergencies such as a flood, earthquake, and other major disasters.

Various organized groups, and individuals, interested in promoting religious, racial, national, or civic programs play an important part in community life and tend to crystallize public sentiment. Being interested in the community, they can render material assistance to the police in the control of undesirable and anti-social elements. Their worthy objectives should be understood by, and receive the cooperative interest of commanding officers. This does not mean the granting of official recognition or favors contrary to the practice and policy of the Department.

315.05 *Policy.*

• Commanding officers shall acquaint themselves with the organized groups and individuals within their respective commands interested in promoting religious, racial, national, or civic programs. They shall learn the identity of key persons, the objectives or primary purposes of such organizations, and shall keep informed of their current interests.

• Initial contacts with these organizations or individuals shall be made by commanding officers in person. Subsequent contacts shall be made by commanding officers of divisions in person, insofar as possible, but may be made by superior officers. Contacts will be made as frequently as possible, and without unnecessary delay when the assistance of this Department is requested. Where possible, commanding officers of divisions shall attempt to achieve a mutual understanding and confidence between such groups and this Department.

• Petitions, committees of protests, appeals for assistance, and letters or other forms of complaint, shall be given prompt personal attention and careful study by commanding officers. Every effort shall be made to correct improper conditions or if proper to render the assistance requested.

320. *Ethnic Composition of the Community.* The cosmopolitan character of our population is reflected in the several distinctive racial and national sections or areas of the City. Religious, national, and racial prejudices, although ordinarily dormant can be aroused to action with little provocation. An ordinarily trifling incident can become extremely serious when it involves a racial or religious aspect. Crowds form quickly where there is a commotion, and false rumors spread by excitable persons or by professional agitators, may quickly generate an explosive situation.

Under such circumstances the patience, tact, and resourcefulness of the policeman are put to the severest test. Above all he must not lose his temper. Self-restraint and a calm demeanor, even when confronted with great provocation, increase the effectiveness of the policeman. Prompt dispersal of a threatening crowd is of the utmost importance. Assistance should be summoned immediately. A firm, assured manner is essential for success when dealing with a hostile crowd. Physical contact with persons should be avoided where possible. Force should not be resorted to unless absolutely necessary, and then only to the extent and degree necessary. Rival groups shall be treated impartially. Officers shall seek the services of citizens of both sides to persuade the participants to disperse.

For members of this Department, mere knowledge of the constitutional guarantees of racial equality and religious liberty will not suffice. Every member of the Department, individually and collectively, must recognize these principles, and at all times, by official and personal conduct, demonstrate such recognition. The mutual respect, tolerance, and good will existing among members of this Department comprising all races and creeds, is in itself a worthy example. Officers should be especially alert to detect and prevent situations or conditions conducive to racial or religious tensions. Discrimination, derogatory remarks, or provocative actions involving racial or religious groups require prompt attention.

Every citizen has the right to police protection on the basis of need. Police field deployment is not social agency activity. In deploying to suppress crime, the Department is not interested in why a certain group tends toward crime. The police are interested in maintaining order. The fact that the group would not be a crime problem under different socio-economic conditions and might not be a crime problem tomorrow, does not alter today's tactical necessities. Police deployment is concerned with effect, not cause.

320.05 *Policy.*

•Members of the force assigned to duty in areas of the City in which well defined racial, national, or religious groups are present, shall carry out the Department policy of just, impartial, and reasonable enforcement for all. Officers shall be aware of the problems that exist in these areas and take appropriate, affirmative action to correct them. Through these actions officers shall attempt to eliminate any impressions of police indifference or neglect. In his daily contact with the people the policeman shall avoid all derogatory comments.

•Commanding officers of divisions in areas inhabited by various racial groups shall cultivate the acquaintance of responsible community leaders and groups, to better ascertain the police needs of the area and to solicit cooperation and support. . . .

•Special interest shall be shown in inter-racial and inter-religious problems of places of worship and schools. Commanding officers of divisions concerned shall maintain close liaison with the heads of these organizations and shall give personal attention to their problems. Officers shall be alert to similar problems which might arise in other areas such as on the streets and at recreational facilities.

•All people may have prejudices; however, a police officer must learn to distinguish between his right to hold personal opinions as a citizen and his sworn duty as an officer. While his right to hold his beliefs as a citizen is inviolate, any manifestation of prejudice while acting as a member of the Police Department cannot be tolerated.

325. *News Media and Public Information.* The news gathering media performs an important service for the public, which should be clearly understood by police officers. It is a function of the news media to keep the public informed on matters of public interest, including the activities of departments, officials, and employees of the city government.

While police officers must exercise discretion with respect to information of a nature that cannot and should not be divulged, it is equally important to promptly release to representatives of the news media such information as is permissible.

Cooperation with accredited representatives of the news media and other accredited publications is extremely important in promoting good public relations. A cooperative attitude and a courteous explanation, when necessary, will usually result in a more desirable presentation of the facts from the police viewpoint.

325.05 *Policy.*

•News media shall be notified when an event being investigated is of such a spectacular or unusual nature as to stimulate general community interest.

•A designated Department employee shall be responsible for maintaining close liaison with members of news media. He shall facilitate their obtaining accurate information in matters concerning the Department.

•Information shall be released to the news gathering media, except information which would interfere with the investigation of a case.

•Unarraigned prisoners shall not be interviewed by members of news media except in exceptional cases with the approval of the Chief of Police.

•Prisoners shall not be compelled to be photographed by members of news media.

W. H. PARKER
Chief of Police

Special Order No. 33
December 5, 1963

Appendix F

Fundamentals of a Productive
Training Program

Six Steps for a Productive
Training Program

1. *Establish a written training policy*—see that the whole staff understands and uses it.

2. *Assign a qualified individual*—of appropriate rank or grade, staff responsibility for training and see that he gets and gives the kind of help that will get the job done.

3. *Develop a training plan*—which is an integral part of the overall operating plan, and see that this plan is systematically checked for its ability to meet operating needs. This indicates a system of quality and quantity control.

4. *Insist on qualified personnel*—and best procedures, materials and facilities available being used in carrying out the training plan.

5. *Support the program*—demand results and require evidence of results in terms of problems solved.

6. *Appoint Advisory Committee*—composed of top management representatives to help guide the progress of the training program.

POLICY

1. Is it related specifically to the operating problems of the installation?

2. Does it fix responsibility for training by: (a) making operating officials responsible for training operations within their respective divisions, departments, branches and sections; (b) making a member of the staff responsible for inspection advice, assistance, and staff supervision of the training program?

3. Does it establish standards and procedures for training such as: (a) Determining training needs? (b) Selecting trainers? (c) Selecting trainees? (d) Determining course content? (e) Selecting training methods? (f) Maintaining training records?

4. Is the policy known and understood by every member of management?

ASSIGN QUALIFIED INDIVIDUAL

1. Does he have the necessary qualifications of education experience, personality and ability to to get the job done?

2. Does he command the respect, confidence and cooperation of the management group?

3. Does he attend staff meetings so he knows the problems of the installations present and anticipated?

4. Does he guide the formulations of the training program and help keep it current and up to date?

5. Does he assist operating officials in their training activities such as: (a) developing qualified training representatives, job instructors, and conference leaders? (b) using the best training procedures materials and facilities for training?

6. Does he provide staff supervision for quality, for organization and scheduling of training measures?

7. Does he assist operating officials in evaluating the effectiveness of their training program?

8. Does he receive and prepare reports on training so that administration knows what training is going on and how successful it is?

9. Does he follow up training to see that it is being used?

DEVELOP A TRAINING PLAN

1. Is it based on the specific needs of the installation?

2. Is it kept up to date?

3. Does it provide for qualified, trained personnel to do the training?

4. Does it provide for job analysis as a basis for instruction?

5. Does it provide that a training timetable be maintained by each supervisor?

6. Does it provide that a proved training method be determined for every job?

7. Does it provide basic training for all employees?

8. Does it provide for management conferences on current and future problems?

9. Does it take account of training facilities outside the installation?

10. Does it include methods of reporting and evaluating training?

INSIST ON QUALIFIED PERSONNEL AND FACILITIES

1. Are these qualified trainers in sufficient number to provide: (a) on-the-job training? (b) class instruction or training conferences? (c) management conferences?

2. Has adequate space been set aside for training conferences?

3. Have adequate training aids been developed or secured to fit the specific operating problems?

SUPPORT THE PROGRAM

1. Is evaluation of the training program made through: (a) production records? (b) individual performance records? (c) cost records? (d) breakage or waste records? (e) accident reports? (f) turnover records? (g) absentee records? (h) health records? (i) complaints?

2. Does evaluation of the training program have its source in the opinions of the operating officials?

3. Is evaluation of the training program made through those receiving the training?

CONCLUSION

1. If the answers to the above questions are yes, then a training program should produce desired results. If in any instance the answer is no, the necessary steps are self-evident.

Suggested Training Policy

OBJECTIVES

1. An integrated comprehensive training program that provides training for the development and maintenance of an effective work force, to include training for executive management, for supervision, for job skills, for health and safety, for up grading, for orientation, for morale, and for both long range and immediate needs.

2. Sufficient freedom in the application of basic training policies to permit quick and proper adaptation to local and changing conditions.

LINE RESPONSIBILITY

1. The responsibility for developing the personal abilities of the work force is a line function and part of the management responsibility in each supervisory category.

2. It is the responsibility of management and all subordinate supervisors to exert aggressive leadership in the training program and to train or provide for training needed by the individuals under their direct supervision.

3. Line officials must inventory the jobs for which they are responsible, including their own, to ascertain skill requirements, inventory the skills of personnel available for these jobs and compare the two. Deficiencies noted should constitute the basis for training both for immediate and long-term goals.

4. Line supervisors must analyze each repetitive task under their direct supervision in order to standardize its procedure thus standardizing the training necessary for the task.

5. Management at each level must select suitable individuals to supervise and conduct if necessary such training as is necessary to match job requirements with personal abilities.

6. Reporting in connection with the training program is necessary for the purpose of evaluating progress against inventoried needs.

7. Operating officials must appoint an aggressive leader of sufficient prestige to activate, coordinate and supervise the training program to meet specific determined needs within the company division, department, or section which ever the case may be.

STAFF RESPONSIBILITY

1. The responsibility of a training department is staff in nature, i.e., inspection and advice based on gathered facts.

2. The training department must maintain a close and cooperative relationship with operating officials.

3. The training department must give constructive advice on solution of operating problems by means of training; must assist in the determination of training needs; must advise as to effective training plans, procedures and methods and must aid in the maintenance of a high quality in all training programs.

4. The training department must advise and assist in securing and developing competent instructors, course content, and instructional materials, in adapting training procedures and subject matter to new operating problems and changing needs; in appraising the results of training; in maintaining effective cooperation with outside agencies engaged in training activities and arranging for the services of such agencies when necessary.

5. The training department must provide assistance in training persons in operating divisions who have been selected on a part time basis to serve as training coordinators, training supervisors or job instructors.

ORGANIZATION

1. The chief operating official, through the director of industrial relations and training department must formulate company wide training programs and policies and audit training activities at each echelon to the extent necessary to assure compliance towards company wide objectives.

2. Each subordinate line official must appoint a training representative to serve either on a full or part time basis as the need indicates.

3. Requirements of each job and capacities of persons available for each job must be inventoried at least once each 6 months.

4. Suitable arrangements must be made to

provide adequate facilities and training for discovered deficiencies on a continuing basis.

PROCEDURE

1. In providing training, the jobs to be done must be clearly defined by positions; standards of performance must be established; actual training required to develop this performance must be designated; the individuals to be trained must be carefully selected; training courses must be decided on; training time required to enable an employee to accomplish performance standards must be determined; individual progress reports must be maintained and the results of training must be continuously appraised.

Desirable Qualities of a Training Supervisor

1. Ability to plan, organize, coordinate, and conduct large scale training programs.
2. Good health and appearance.
3. Extensive experience in business and industrial management or processing work.
4. Knowledge in the techniques of industrial engineering.
5. Thorough knowledge in conference methods.
6. Education equivalent to a college degree.
7. Ability to analyze people and situations.
8. A strong sense of supervisory responsibilities.
9. Sense of humor.
10. Skill in writing reports.
11. Ability to speak effectively.
12. Skill in managing his own time.
13. Ability to command respect.
14. Willingness to shoulder responsibilities.
15. Thorough knowledge of the staff function.

Desirable Qualities of Division Training Coordinator

1. General all-around knowledge of division activities.
2. Authority to command respect.
3. Ability to get along with and understand people.
4. Ability to organize and conduct conferences.
5. Ability to speak effectively.
6. Sense of humor.
7. Skill in techniques of gathering pertinent data.
8. Ability in problem solving techniques.
9. Skill in conducting work simplification and safety meetings.
10. Skill in writing reports.
11. Knowledge of the fundamentals of management engineering.
12. Skill in managing his own time.

Desirable Qualities of Department Job Instructor

1. Extensive knowledge of department functions.
2. Specific and extensive job knowledge.
3. Knowledge of Job Instruction techniques.
4. Knowledge of problem solving techniques.
5. Skill in conference methods.
6. Respect of fellow workers.

Planning a Training Program

These 40 steps were drawn up by the Northern Ohio Chapter of the American Society of Training Directors. They were published in the June, 1951, issue of *Factory* in an article by M. J. Murphy. A few revisions have been made to relate the steps more specifically to the government service.

PRELIMINARY APPROACH TO TRAINING

1. *Be sure you know what kind of training you are talking about.* You need the right kind for your particular purpose so that it will do the job you have to do.
2. *Study the kinds of benefits you can get from training.* Here are some things it can do: cut learning time, overtime costs, waste, absenteeism and turn over, accident rate, grievances; improve methods and systems, quality of work, communication with employees; increase employees' job interest and satisfaction; make employees versatile; lighten load on supervisors.
3. *Don't expect to do it all yourself.* Plan with the people involved. Basic responsibility rests with the people in charge of the line functions.
4. *Never expect to finish the training job.* Constant follow-up is needed to see how the trainees are using what they learned. How can you help, review, stimulate? Growth of the individuals will continue after training.
5. *Go out and see what other agencies are doing.* Study the kinds of programs they have. Gather sound principles and good ideas.
6. *Find out what kinds of training there are.* Here are a few types: induction of new employees, on-the-job information, intern, supervisory, presupervisory, refresher, executive department, safety, technical, new skills.
7. *Obtain qualified assistance.* Collect good reference materials. Get help from your headquarters or staff office, other agencies. Consider outside speakers.
8. *Assign the responsibility for the program to some one person.* He won't do the whole job, but will see that it gets done, working with the others concerned.

LOCATING TRAINING NEEDS

9. *Consult with as many people as possible.* This means administrators, supervisors, and employees.

10. *Study the records for clues.* For example: records on turnover, absenteeism, work products, error rates, grievances, quality, accidents.

11. *Study all divisions.*

12. *Consider plans for expansion.* Expansion will mean the hiring of new employees and the promotion of some old employees to positions as supervisors. As a result, the need for organized training may be increased.

13. *Check each training need systematically.* Here is a suggested checklist:

What is the need?

Is this need immediate? Is it permanent or temporary?

Where was it first spotted?

Does it apply anywhere else?

What causes it?

Should it be handled by itself or combined with another need?

Should anything else be done before this need is taken care of?

What kinds of employees are needed? (Position, experience, ability)

What degree of skill needs to be developed?

How many people or jobs are involved?

What are the ages of the employees?

How will this affect training?

How much time is needed for training?

Can I decide now about the probable cost of training?

Can I decide anything now about who can and should do the training?

Is there anything else to do or check?

14. *Summarize your findings.* You need information to help you plan ahead.

15. *Review your summary with key people.* Check with key divisional and operating personnel to be sure your ideas are practical.

16. *Keep your plans simple.* You can't do everything at once.

LAUNCHING A TRAINING PROGRAM

17. *Know your training methods.* Here are some of the suggested methods: individual instruction, job rotation, problem solving, practice and drill, group instruction, lecture, demonstration, conference, written instruction, and oral directions.

18. *Start one project at a time.*

19. *Use the simplest method.* Don't sacrifice effectiveness to ease of instruction, however. Consider visual aids.

20. *Pick your instructors carefully.* Consider supervisors, experienced employees. Use people who are interested in the project.

21. *Train your instructors.* Knowledge of the subject matter is not enough. Trainers must understand training principles.

22. *Establish teaching outlines.* They insure coverage of subject matter, logical presentation, and digestible units.

23. *Make plans for evaluating your training.* Arrange before you start to keep necessary records, develop follow-up.

24. *Clear all arrangements.* Get people, space, and equipment lined up. Clear general plans with management.

SETTING UP INDUCTION TRAINING

25. *Pick the right topics.* Induction training should slant more toward orientation to the agency and division than toward specific job information.

26. *Decide who should induct.* Supervisors should do some. Specialists can do technical subjects.

27. *Spread induction training out.* Don't try to concentrate it into one large session. Give it over a period of time, and the employee will assimilate more information.

28. *Avoid "over-selling".* Discuss problems and problem areas as well as the good aspects of the organization.

29. *Don't underestimate induction training.* The early weeks are critical ones for a new employee. Induction training can do yeoman service in allaying fears and misgivings, and can help the employee reach the point of maximum production sooner.

SETTING UP ON-THE-JOB TRAINING

30. *Don't overload your supervisors.* They have considerable responsibility in regard to normal operations without being unduly burdened with a training program. Give consideration to appointing experienced employees as job instructors.

31. *Train instructors to teach.* Success of training depends upon the instructor's ability to teach.

32. *Be sure supervisors have instruction training too.* Supervisors will always have some instruction work to do, and they will have to supervise on-the-job instructors in their sections. They must, therefore, understand training techniques.

33. *Give instructors incentive.* The position of instructor should be a privilege and not a position that no one else wants. It should have some prestige value.

34. *Get agreement on methods.* Be sure the work methods taught are the accepted methods. Straighten out poor methods before training starts.

35. *Follow up on-the-job instruction.* Check on the progress of trainees either by inspection or through the use of reports.

SETTING UP SUPERVISORY TRAINING

36. *Let your supervisors help you plan.* Not only will you get useful ideas, but the supervisors will be more receptive to training if they have a part in planning it.

37. *Know the basic goals you are aiming for.* Don't be confused by the variety of supervisors' duties. Concentrate on: knowledge of responsibilities, agency policies, practices, officials; manage-

ment skills-methods, planning, costs, standard analysis; human relations skills; technical skills.

38. *Concentration on the proper training goals.* Take one thing at a time. Attend to the greatest need first.

39. *Give new supervisors special study.* With new supervisors you may want to combine orientation with some other type of training. Give presuper-visory training.

40. *Use a variety of methods.* Consider on-the-job training, conferences, extension courses, outside readings, etc.

From First Annual Management Conference, Sacramento (California) State College, March 9, 1957. Conducted by Neely D. Gardner and Lloyd M. Smith.

Evaluation of In-Service Training Course
in Public Relations

We would like to know what you think of this course.

The reason the course was given was to help you do a better job—for yourself and for your City. Did the course do the job? Your honest and critical evaluation is invited.

Please put a circle around the answer that best describes your attitude.

DO NOT SIGN YOUR NAME.

I. COVERAGE

How completely do you feel the various aspects of the subject of PUBLIC RELATIONS were covered? | Quite Complete | Average | Inadequate

II. INTEREST

A. Did you find the subject matter of interest? | Quite Interesting | Average | Dull and Boring

B. Did you find the presentation of the subject matter interesting? | Quite Interesting | Average | Dull and Boring

III. LEADERSHIP

Was the leadership given throughout the course adequate? | Very Good | Adequate | Inadequate

IV. VALUE

A. Was your participation in the course of any value *to you personally?* | Very helpful to me | Some Value to me | Little Value to me

B. Do you believe this course has any value for the average City employee who has a position involving public contact? | Very helpful to average Employee | Some Value | Little Value

(Your comments on points below may be put on opposite side of this sheet)

V. In your opinion, what was the best single feature of the course?
VI. What would you say was the *weakest* or *poorest* feature of the course?
VII. What suggestions can you offer to improve the Public Relations Course when it is offered again to other City employees?
VIII. If you have any suggestions to improve relationships between your City and the public it serves, your comments will be appreciated.

Selected Bibliography

Items have been selected primarily on the basis of their interest and usefulness for local government administrators. They are listed in alphabetical order by author's name or, where the author is not known, by the publishing organization. Most out-of-print items are available in the larger college, university, and public libraries.

Most of the items have been annotated by the staff of the Joint Reference Library by checking JRL resources and those of the University of Chicago Library and the Chicago Public Library. The remaining items have been annotated by direct quotation from Scott M. Cutlip's *A Public Relations Bibliography,* second edition, 1965. (Reprinted with permission of the copyright owners, the Regents of the University of Wisconsin; published by the University of Wisconsin Press.) The latter annotations are indicated as follows: (Cutlip)

The original compilation of this bibliography was done by Desmond L. Anderson, the editor of this book. The Joint Reference Library annotated most of the entries and checked all entries for editions, publishers, and other bibliographic details.

Readers seeking further information are referred to Cutlip's *A Public Relations Bibliography* which is comprehensive, completely annotated, and up to date.

Three professional and service organizations are of value for local government administrators seeking first-hand help in the public relations field:

The National League of Cities, 1612 K Street, N.W., Washington, D.C., 20006, is the federation for 47 state leagues of municipalities and also provides direct membership for larger cities. Many of its member services are in the public relations area, and it has a standing committee on municipal public relations. NLC sponsors an annual public relations competition for cities, and the entries are retained in reference files for loan to city officials on request.

The National Public Relations Council of Health and Welfare Services, 257 Park Avenue South, New York City 10010, primarily serves governmental and private health and welfare organizations, but its services are available also to other public and private, nonprofit groups. Particularly recommended is its "How-To-Do-It" series of pamphlets on writing and editing, illustrations, exhibits, annual reports, and public information programs. Membership includes a biweekly public relations newsletter, special publications and kits, and a professional inquiry service by mail.

The Public Relations Society of America, 845 Third Avenue, New York City 10022, is a professional organization of public relations practitioners, primarily from private business. It operates an information center and has chapters in many parts of the United States.

ADRIAN, CHARLES R. and others. *Social Science and Community Action.* (East Lansing: Institute for Community Development and Services, Michigan State University, 1960.) 55pp. Papers by Charles R. Adrian, Peter H. Rossi, Robert A. Dahl, and Lloyd Rodwin; the latter three on finding ways to apply accumulated relevant knowledge of the various fields of higher education to public policy issues which confront American urban society.

ALBIG, JOHN WILLIAM. *Modern Public Opinion.* (New York: McGraw-Hill Book Co., 1956.) 518pp. (out of print.) Revision of 1939 work, giving comprehensive treatment of psychological processes involved in public opinion, its measurement, etc. (Cutlip)

ANGELL, NORMAN. *Let the People Know.* (New York: Viking, 1943.) 245pp. (out of print.) Aim is to present and answer questions, doubts, and misgivings about the war, its causes, origins, and outcome —for the average citizen.

ARONFREED, EVA. "Public Relations as a Function of Local Government in the United States," in International Union of Local Authorities, *Local Government in the United States of America.* (The Hague: Martinus Nijhoff, for the Union, 1961.) 133pp. pp. 71–90. If one or more suggestions in this article were undertaken, public relations as a municipal function would be recognized as a device to inform citizens and to ascertain their attitudes.

————. "Understanding Municipal PR." *Public Relations Quarterly,* Fall, 1960, pp. 2–10. General review of PR for city governments: values, political dangers, requirements, goals. (Cutlip)

BACKSTROM, CHARLES H., and GERALD D. HURSH. *Survey Research.* (Evanston, Illinois: Northwestern University Press, 1963.) 192pp. A guide for students and professionals, discussing the goals, techniques, and abuses of survey research. Presents a model survey. (Cutlip)

BAKER, MADELINE. *Careers in Municipal Public Relations.* (Washington, D.C.: National League of Cities, 1965.) 9pp. Brief report on purposes of municipal public relations, employment opportunities, and educational requirements.

BANFIELD, EDWARD C., and JAMES Q. WILSON. *City Politics.* (Cambridge, Massachusetts: Harvard University Press and M.I.T. Press, 1963.) 362pp. Views city government as a political process. Day-to-day workings of city government in U.S. are best understood by looking at the differences of opinion and interest within cities, at issues that arise out of the differences, and at ways institutions function to resolve or fail to resolve them.

BAUS, HERBERT M. *Public Relations at Work.* (New York: Harper & Brothers, 1948.) 242pp. (out of print.) Book is in four parts: publics of public relations, fundamentals, telling the story, and agencies of public relations.

BELL, WENDELL, RICHARD J. HILL, and CHARLES WRIGHT. *Public Leadership; A Critical Review With Special Reference to Adult Education.* (San Francisco: Chandler Publishing Company, 1961.) 242pp.

BERELSON, BERNARD, and MORRIS JANOWITZ (eds.). *Reader in Public Opinion and Communication.* (New York: Free Press, rev. ed., 1966.) 788pp. Selections cover theory, formation and impact of public opinion on public policy; theory of communication; communication media, content, audiences, and effects; relation of public opinion and communication to democratic objectives; and research methods.

BERNAYS, EDWARD L. *Public Relations.* (Norman: University of Oklahoma Press, 1963.) 374pp. Deals with public relations history; includes case studies.

BEVERLY HILLS, CALIFORNIA. *Public Relations Training Manual.* (Beverly Hills: Office of the City Manager, 1962.)

BIDDLE, WILLIAM W. *The Cultivation of Community Leaders.* (New York: Harper and Brothers, 1953.) 203pp. (out of print.) Preliminary record of continuing experiment to discover and develop human potential in community environment.

BRIGANCE, WILLIAM NORWOOD. *Speech: Its Techniques and Disciplines in a Free Society.* (New York: Appleton-Century-Crofts, 1961.) 576pp. Based on concept that speechmaking grew out of man's first attempts at self-government, that it is inherent in a free society, that a course in speechmaking ought to be based on this concept, and that speech training in a free society essentially is at variance with that in countries where governments are sustained by thought control.

CANFIELD, BERTRAND R. *Public Relations: Principles, Cases, and Problems.* (Homewood, Illinois: Richard D. Irwin, 4th ed., 1964.) 622pp. College text which covers public relations theory and problems for industrial, commercial, and private, non-profit organizations.

CANTRIL, HADLEY. *Gauging Public Opinion.* (Princeton, New Jersey: Princeton University Press, 1944.) 318pp. (out of print.) Essays on setting the issues, interviewing, sampling, opinion determinants, and applications of techniques to a specific problem.

CHAPIN, RICHARD E. *Mass Communication: A Statistical Analysis.* (East Lansing: Michigan State University Press, 1957.) 148pp. (out of print.) Issued in microfilm in 1955 as thesis, University of Illinois, under title: "An Evaluation and an Interpretation of the Statistics Relating to the Mass Communications Industries." Evaluates and interprets statistics for newspapers, books, magazines, radio, television, and motion-picture industries.

CHILDS, HARWOOD L. *Public Opinion.* (Princeton, New Jersey: Van Nostrand Co., Inc., 1965.) 376pp.

CHASE, STUART. *The Tyranny of Words.* (New York: Harcourt, Brace and World, 1938.) 396pp. One of the early and stimulating discussions on communication of ideas. Primer on semantics.

COX, DAVID M. "How Much Public Relations in Government?" *Public Administration Review,* Summer, 1961, pp. 136–40. Public relations of a local unemployment compensation office are examined as a case study. Whatever public relations problems appear are centered around the customer-employee relationship where the employee is the key figure.

CROSBY, ALEXANDER L., *Pamphlets—How To Write and Print Them.* (New York: National Public Relations Council of Health and Welfare Services.) This short pamphlet is a model. The author practices what he preaches.

CUNNINGHAM, JOHN T. "Evaluating Public Relations Effectiveness." *Public Relations Journal,* January, 1962, pp. 21–23. Set detailed objectives and carefully audit each program. (Cutlip)

CUTLIP, SCOTT M. *A Public Relations Bibliography.* (Madison: University of Wisconsin Press, 2nd ed., 1965.) 305pp. Complete revision of 1957 edition which represented first full-scale effort to provide a complete catalog of vast amount said and written about public relations. This edition, updated through 1963, includes 5,947 annotated entries divided into 74 categories. Contents are indexed by author and by subject. Used extensively in preparation of this bibliography.

CUTLIP, SCOTT M., and ALLEN H. CENTER. *Effective Public Relations.* (Englewood Cliffs, New Jersey: Prentice-Hall, 3rd ed., 1964.) 512pp. Focuses on the role of the practitioner as a specialist in communications, an analyst of public opinion, and an advisor to administrators. Ecology and evolution of public relations are discussed.

DAHL, ROBERT A. *Who Governs? Democracy and Power in an American City.* (New Haven: Yale University Press, 1961.) 355pp. One of three examples of the study of community power structure included in this bibliography. The other two are by Hunter and Presthus. Dahl studies the concept of political pluralism in New Haven, Connecticut.

DEFLEUR, MELVIN L., and OTTO N. LARSEN. *The Flow of Information: An Experiment in Mass Communication.* (New York: Harper and Brothers, (1958) 302pp. (out of print). What we know about the effects of mass communication.

DEJEN, JEAN. *Visual Presentation Handbook.* (St. Petersburg, Florida: The Oravisual Co., Inc., 1959.) 105pp. (out of print.) Discusses practical techniques for using visuals, such as charts, slides, models, etc., in combination with a live talk made before an audience.

DEXTER, LEWIS A., and DAVID M. WHITE. *People, Society, and Mass Communications.* (New York: Free Press, 1964.) 595pp. The editors present readings on social aspects of the revolution in communications technology and preface the readings with extended interpretation and comment.

DICKENS, MILTON C. *Speech: Dynamic Communication.* (New York: Harcourt, Brace and Co., 2nd ed., 1963.) 433pp.

DIETRICH, JOHN E., and KEITH BROOKS. *Practical Speaking for the Technical Man.* (Englewood Cliffs, New Jersey: Prentice-Hall, Inc., 1958.) 310pp.

DOOB, LEONARD W. *Public Opinion and Propaganda.* (New York: Henry Holt & Co., 1948.) 600pp. New edition "in preparation," Shoestring Press, Hamden, Connecticut, winter, 1966.

FLESCH, RUDOLF. *The Art of Plain Talk.* (New York: Harper and Brothers, 1946.) Trail blazing book in readability movement.

HENRY, ALBERT C., and EDWIN W. WEBER. *A Handbook for the Preparation of an Annual Municipal Progress Report.* (Kingston: Bureau of Government Research, University of Rhode Island, 1963.) 28pp. Includes checklist for judging the quality of municipal reports.

HUNTER, FLOYD. *Community Power Structure: A Study of Decision-Makers.* (Chapel Hill: University of North Carolina Press, 1953.) 297pp. A study of the reputational kind of power leadership in an unidentified city of half a million population. See also entries for Dahl and Presthus elsewhere in this bibliography.

INTERNATIONAL CITY MANAGERS' ASSOCIATION. *The Municipal Year Book.* (Chicago: The Association, annual.) Provides annual review of developments in municipal public relations with particular attention to municipal annual reports.

IRION, FREDERICK C. *Public Opinion and Propaganda.* (New York: Thomas Y. Crowell Co., 1950.) 782pp. (out of print.) Places emphasis on content and function of public opinion in U.S. Strives to describe all aspects in this field. Book tends to be elementary. (Cutlip)

GOURLEY, G. DOUGLAS. *Public Relations and the Police.* (Springfield, Illinois: Charles C Thomas, 1953.) 123pp. (out of print.) Surveyed are the relations presently existing between the police and the public; brings out factors that have resulted in present public attitudes toward the police.

HAIMAN, FRANKLIN S. *Group Leadership and Democratic Action.* (Boston: Houghton-Mifflin, 1951.) 309pp. (out of print.) Balances theory and practice—the philosophical-scientific background and the techniques of group leadership.

HARLOW, REX F. *Social Science in Public Relations.* (New York: Harper & Brothers, 1957.) 203pp. (out of print.) Through a survey of scientific information, an attempt is made to bring forces of social science and public relations closer together.

HARLOW, REX F., and MARVIN M. BLACK. *Practical Public Relations, Its Foundations, Divisions, Tools and Practices.* (New York: Harper and Brothers, rev. ed., 1952.) 422pp. In three parts: I—Foundations of public relations; II—Divisions of public relations; III—Tools of public relations. (Cutlip)

HARPER, ERNEST B., and ARTHUR DUNHAM (eds.) *Community Organization in Action.* (New York: Association Press, 1959.) 543pp. Readings primarily for graduate and undergraduate students; drawn mainly from field of social welfare.

HAYAKAWA, S. I. *Language in Thought and Action.* (New York: Harcourt, Brace and World, 2nd ed., 1964.) 350pp. Standard guide to semantics, the science of the meaning of words.

HIRTZEL, RICHARD. "A Study of Public Relations Activities and Organizations in Governments of Selected American Cities." Thesis for master's degree at Brigham Young University, 1961.

HOLCOMB, RICHARD L. *The Police and the Public.* (Springfield, Illinois: Charles C Thomas, 6th printing, 1964.) 40pp. Discusses the many ways in which good will can be cultivated by the administrator and the individual officer. The reasons for following proper procedures in dealing with people are clearly explained.

JANOWITZ, MORRIS, and others. *Public Administration and the Public—Perspectives Toward Government in a Metropolitan Community.* (Ann Arbor: Bureau of Government, University of Michigan, 1958.) 140pp. Analysis of empirical investigation of public perspectives toward specific administrative agencies and administrative aspects of government in general.

KATZ, ELIHU, and PAUL F. LAZARSFELD. *Personal Influence.* (New York: The Free Press, 1955.) 400pp. Study of decision-making in marketing, fashion, movie going and public affairs. Study found personal influence is a more significant factor than influence stemming from the mass media. The introductory over-view of the two-step communications process is most valuable. (Cutlip)

KEITH, JOHN P. *Public Relations Program for a Citizen Committee.* (Austin: Bureau of Municipal Research, University of Texas, 1950.) 74pp. Provides guidance to those citizens wrestling with problems in governmental affairs.

KELLEY, STANLEY, JR. *Professional Public Relations and Political Power.* (Baltimore: Johns Hopkins Press, 1956.) 247pp. Role of public relations man in contemporary American politics and the consequences of his activities for our political life.

KEY, V.O., JR. *Politics, Parties and Pressure Groups.* (New York: Thomas Y. Crowell, 5th ed., 1964.) 738pp. Includes an extensive treatment of pressure groups, as well as a discussion of violence, bribery, and education as political techniques, matters not usually dealt with in the texts. Best work on this subject. (Cutlip)

———. *Public Opinion and American Democracy.* (New York: Alfred A. Knopf., 1961.) 566pp. An analysis of the bearing of public opinion on American government.

KIDD, PAUL E. *Public Relations for West Virginia Municipalities.* (Morgantown: Bureau of Governmental Research, West Virginia University, 1960.) 28pp. Presents procedures and practices in municipal public relations from all parts of the U.S.

LEE, MARSHALL. *Book Making: The Illustrated Guide to Design and Production.* (New York: R. R. Bowker Company, 1965.) 400pp. Covers (1) book design, including typography, illustrations, etc., and (2) book production, including planning and scheduling work, purchasing materials and services, and coordinating book manufacture and distribution. Chapters 5–8 provide an excellent introduction to composition, typography, printing, and paper. Includes extensive bibliography.

LESLY, PHILIP, (ed.) *Public Relations Handbook.* (Englewood Cliffs, New Jersey: Prentice-Hall, 2nd ed., 1962.) 901pp. Compendium of best instructive information now available on phases, types, and aspects of modern public relations.

LEYS, WAYNE R. *Ethics for Policy Decisions.* (Englewood Cliffs, New Jersey: Prentice-Hall, Inc., 1952.) 428pp. First the author reviews the leading systems of ethics and shows how various philosophers achieved the points of view that are most relevant to the kinds of practical issues that are faced today. Second, Leys applies philosophy's questions to selected policy issues in government and industry in an attempt to improve and systematize practical judgment.

LIPPMANN, WALTER. *Public Opinion.* (New York: Harcourt, Brace, 1922.) 427pp. (Also New York: Free Press, 1965, paperbound.) One of the classics in the field, still widely read and quoted. Valuable for discussion of barriers to communication in our society. (Cutlip)

MacDONALD, JAMES C. *Press Relations for Local Officials.* (Ann Arbor: Institute of Public Administration, University of Michigan, 1950.) 50pp. Covers wide variety of situations encountered by municipal office holders in dealing with the press. (Cutlip)

McCAMY, JAMES L. *Government Publicity.* (Chicago: University of Chicago Press, 1939.) 275pp. Detailed study of government information during peak of New Deal. Out of print, but still invaluable reference for this area of PR. Most detailed, specific book yet available. (Cutlip)

McCORMICK, THOMAS G., and ROY G. FRANCIS. *Methods of Research in the Behavioral Sciences.* (New York: Harper and Brothers, 1958.) 244pp. (out of print.) Written primarily for graduate students, particularly candidates for master's degrees. Method is presented "serially," from the initial decision to do research to the selection of the problem and, subsequently, step by step through publication of findings.

MATTHEWS, LEMPI K. *Making the Most of Your Annual Report.* (Chicago: Public Personnel Association, 1963.) 76pp. Guide to compilation, writing, illustrations, layout, and working with the printer. Although intended for preparation of personnel reports, principles explained are applicable to general municipal reports.

MICH, DANIEL, and EDWIN EBERMAN. *Techniques of the Picture Story:* (New York: McGraw-Hill Book Co., 1945.) 239pp. (out of print.) Textbook on technique and procedure of picture editing. (Cutlip)

MILLER, CLYDE R. *The Process of Persuasion.* (New York: Crown Publishers, 1946.) 234pp. (out of print.) Applied psychology in use of persuasion. (Cutlip)

MINNICK, WAYNE C. *Art of Persuasion.* (Boston: Houghton-Mifflin, 1957.) 295pp. Reviews social science research as it applies to speeches. Describes factors determining human behavior and their part in persuasion. (Cutlip)

MONROE, ALAN H., and DOUGLAS EHNINGER. *Principles of Speech.* (Chicago: Scott, Foresman and Company, 5th brief ed., 1964.) 345pp.

MORRIS, CHARLES W. *Signs, Language and Behavior.* (New York: Prentice-Hall, 1946.) 365pp. (out of print.) Signs and symbols. Includes bibliography. (Cutlip)

NATIONAL FIRE PROTECTION ASSOCIATION. *Public Relations Manual for Fire Departments.* (Boston: The Association, 1966.) 40pp. Comprehensive treatment of the how and why of public relations, citing many case histories of successful programs.

————. *The Individual Firemen's Responsibility in Public Relations.* (Boston: The Association, 1960.) 20pp. Explains role of individual fireman in his department's public relations.

————. *Sparky Project.* A program initiated by NIPA in 1954 to bring fire safety teaching to children, which has additionally many public relations benefits. Folders, inspection blanks, comic and coloring books, membership kits, and teaching materials are among the many *Sparky* publications available on request.

NATIONAL MUNICIPAL LEAGUE. *The Citizen Association: How To Organize and Run It.* (New York: The League, 1958.) 64pp.

————. *The Citizen Association: How To Win Civic Campaigns.* (New York: The League, 1963.) 64pp.

NIELANDER, WILLIAM A., and R. W. MILLER. *Public Relations.* (New York: Ronald Press, 1951.) 398pp. Intended primarily as a textbook for college courses. (Cutlip)

OLMSTED, DONALD W. *Social Groups, Roles, and Leadership.* (East Lansing: Institute for Community Development and Services, Michigan State University, 1961.) 55pp. Introduction to sociological and social psychological view of social groups, roles, leadership, and related terms; summarizes some key problems and issues.

PETRULLO, LUIGI, and BERNARD M. BASS. *Leader-*

ship and Interpersonal Behavior. (New York: Holt, Rinehart, and Winston, 1961.) 382pp. U.S. Office of Naval Research sponsored symposium which brought together psychologists known to be conducting research on leadership.

PFIFFNER, JOHN M., and FRANK P. SHERWOOD. *Administrative Organization.* (Englewood Cliffs, New Jersey: Prentice-Hall, Inc., 1960.) 481pp. Gives equal attention to the traditional framework of organization structure and to the behavioral orientation that has come to the fore in recent years. Attention is given also to the social setting for organizations in the U.S.

PHILLIPS, WALTER M. *Toward a New Program of Public Information and Ceremony by the City Government of Philadelphia.* (Philadelphia: Office of City Representative, 1956.) 40pp. A four-year-report on Philadelphia's pioneering municipal PR program. (Cutlip)

PIMLOTT, J.A.R. *Public Relations and American Democracy.* (Princeton, New Jersey: Princeton University Press, 1951.) 265pp. (out of print.) Visiting British information man takes a close, hard look at American public relations. Valuable critique on our PR practices. Part II deals with public relations practices in federal government and in a sense updates McCamy's work. (Cutlip)

POLSBY, NELSON W. *Community Power and Political Theory.* (New Haven, Connecticut: Yale University Press, 1963.) 144pp. Purpose is to ascertain the state of scientific knowledge about power and policy-making in local communities. Book grew out of a study of New Haven, Connecticut.

PRESS, CHARLES (compiler). *Main Street Politics, Policy-Making at the Local Level.* (East Lansing: Institute for Community Development and Services, Michigan State University, 1962.) 150pp. Survey and review of periodical literature since 1950.

PRESTHUS, ROBERT. *Men At the Top; A Study in Community Power.* (New York: Oxford University Press, 1964.) 485pp. A general volume on the system of social relationships which makes up power structure in communities. See also entries for Dahl and Hunter in this bibliography.

REDFIELD, CHARLES E. *Communication in Management: The Theory and Practice of Administrative Communication.* (Chicago: University of Chicago Press, rev. ed., 1958.) 314pp. An orderly, systematic presentation of problems, techniques, and basic difficulties of communication. Making and implementing decisions relies very heavily on an optimum system of information handling throughout an organization.

RICE, LARRY A. "A Public Information Program for Walla Walla, Washington, under New Council-Manager Government." Master's thesis, University of Kansas, 1960.

RIDLEY, CLARENCE E., and HERBERT A. SIMON. *Specifications for the Annual Municipal Report.* (Chicago: International City Managers' Association,

1948.) 52pp. (out of print.) The pioneering effort to develop meaningful standards for preparation of reports.

RIKER, WILLIAM H. *The Study of Local Politics.* (New York: Random House, 1959.) 126pp. Manual of field research in political science, prepared especially for undergraduate students with no background in research methods.

ROGERS, LINDSAY. *The Pollsters: Public Opinion, Politics, and Democratic Leadership.* (New York: Alfred A. Knopf, 1949.) 239pp. (out of print.) A criticism of political opinion polling. (Cutlip)

ROSENAU, JAMES N. *Public Opinion and Foreign Policy.* (New York: Random House, 1961.) 118pp. (paperback) Perceptive analysis of influence and opinion, the opinion-policy continuum, opinion makers, and channels of opinion circulation. Helpful for understanding the dynamics of opinion as part of the governmental process.

ROSS, MURRAY G. *Community Organization: Theory and Principles.* (New York: Harper and Row, 1955.) 239pp. Basic process and theory for evaluating community programs. Useful book. Includes bibliography. (Cutlip)

RUBIN, BERNARD. *Public Relations and the Empire State: A Case Study of New York Administration.* (New Brunswick, New Jersey: Rutgers University Press, 1958.) 357pp. Using New York state as an example, author examines public relations as a function of modern democracy. Useful guide to PR in state government. . . . (Cutlip)

RUHL, ELEANOR S. *Public Relations for Government Employees.* (Chicago: Public Personnel Association, 1953.) 32pp. (out of print.) Small pamphlet outlining in simple, general terms some of elements of public relations practices. Oriented toward civil service employees at all levels. (Cutlip)

SCHETTLER, CLARENCE. *Public Opinion in American Society.* (New York: Harper and Row, 1960.) 534pp. Introductory college text, emphasizing sociology and social psychology. (Cutlip)

SELLTIZ, CLAIRE C., and others, editors, *Research Methods in Social Relations.* (New York: Holt, Rinehart, and Winston, rev. ed., 1959.) 622pp. Excellent introduction to research with specific chapters on various techniques and problems. (Cutlip)

SCHWARTZ, ALVIN. *Evaluating Your Public Relations.* (New York: National Public Relations Council of Health and Welfare Services, 1965.) 52pp. Shows the range of approaches and procedures that can give the reader a better sense of direction.

THORNDIKE, E. L. *Your City.* (New York: Harcourt, Brace and Company, 1939.) 207pp. (out of print.) A three-year statistical study of 301 American cities. The conclusions about the quality of life, the causes of differences, and the ways and means of making all our cities a better place to live in are often startling and opposed to popular doctrines.

WALL, NED L. *Municipal Reporting to the Public.* (Chicago: International City Managers' Association, 1963.) 71pp. Working manual with specific and practical suggestions for city officials, particularly for the general annual report. Contains 88 illustrations carefully chosen to augment points in the text.

WHEELER, PAN DODD. *How To Make Reports.* (Knoxville: Municipal Technical Advisory Service, University of Tennessee, 1957.) 42pp. Discusses general principles of municipal report preparation.

WOLPERT, ELTON D. *Municipal Public Relations.* (Chicago: International City Managers' Association, 1940.) 50pp. (out of print.) Major aspects of public relations are covered clearly and concisely.

WHYTE, WILLIAM H., JR., and the editors of *Fortune. Is Anybody Listening? How and Why U.S. Business Fumbles When It Talks with Human Beings.* (New York: Simon and Schuster, 1952.) 239pp. (out of print.) Collection of articles by Whyte and *Fortune* editors which first appeared in that magazine. Provocative; widely discussed, quoted, and disputed. Basic reading. (Cutlip)

WILLIAMS, ROBIN M., JR. *American Society: A Sociological Interpretation.* (New York: Alfred A. Knopf, 2nd rev. ed., 1963 reprint, copyrighted 1960.) 575pp. Analysis of social relations, beliefs, and values that characterize people in the U.S.

List of Contributors

The persons who have contributed to this book are listed below in alphabetical order with a brief review of experience, training, and major points of interest in each person's background. Most of these persons have written books, monographs, reports, and articles; information of this kind has not been included.

DESMOND L. ANDERSON (Editor, Chapters 1 and 2) is Associate Dean, School of Public Administration, University of Southern California. He has been with the University of Southern California since 1950 in a number of teaching, research, and administrative capacities, including Assistant Director and Director of the Civic Center Campus, Assistant Dean and Associate Dean of the School of Public Administration, and Chairman of the University Senate. For 15 years he has served as a training and management consultant to the state of California and to a number of local governments in that state. He has been active in several professional societies and has served on the National Council of the American Society for Public Administration. Dr. Anderson's educational background includes bachelor's and master's degrees from Utah State University and the doctorate in public administration from the University of Southern California, with dissertation concentration on the administration of higher education.

ARTHUR A. ATKISSON, JR. (Chapter 14) is Assistant Chief Deputy Air Pollution Control Officer for the Los Angeles County Air Pollution Control District. He entered government service as an engineer with the Bonneville Power Administration and has been with the Air Pollution Control District in several capacities since 1955. He has served as a consultant to several governmental jurisdictions on air pollution and governmental administrative problems and is a part-time faculty member at the School of Public Administration, University of Southern California. He holds a bachelor's degree from Lewis and Clark College and the master of science degree from the University of Oregon. He currently is a candidate for the doctor of public administration degree from the University of Southern California.

ROBERT B. CALLAHAN (Chapters 6 and 16) has been at the California State College at Los Angeles since 1960 and is Associate Professor of Government, Director of Peace Corps Projects, and Director of Admissions. From 1950 to 1960 he was an administrator and consultant for a number of federal, state, and local governments and in 1959–60 was Assistant Director of the Civic Center Division, University of Southern California. He also has

served as a consultant to the Peace Corps in Washington, D.C. He holds two bachelor degrees, a master's degree, and a doctorate in public administration—all from USC.

ROBERT M. CHRISTOFFERSON (Chapters 12 and 15) is City Manager of San Dimas, California. From 1956 to 1965 he was assistant to the city manager of Glendale, California, and has been in his present position since February, 1965. He holds a bachelor's degree from the University of California at Santa Barbara and received his master's degree in public administration in 1956 at the University of Southern California. In 1955 he held a Coro Foundation Internship in Public Affairs in San Francisco and in 1955–56 he was an administrative intern with the city of Beverly Hills, California.

G. DOUGLAS GOURLEY (Chapter 9) is Chairman, Department of Criminology, and Acting Dean, School of Fine and Applied Arts, California State College at Los Angeles. He was a member of the Los Angeles Police Department for 20 years, from 1937 to 1957, and rose through the ranks to the post of Inspector in charge of patrol forces for one half of the city. While a member of the Los Angele police force, he served as an instructor in police science and administration at the Civic Center Division of the School of Public Administration, University of Southern California. He has been at California State College at Los Angeles since 1957. He holds the master's degree in public administration from the University of Southern California and is a Fellow of the American Society of Criminology.

ROBERT J. HUNTLEY (Chapter 4) is Director of Real Estate Development for Alpha Beta Acme Markets, Inc., San Leandro, California. He was Administrative Officer (city manager) for La Habra, California, from 1959 to 1964, and prior to that time had served three other California cities as city administrator of Santa Paula, administrative assistant in Beverly Hills, and research technician in Los Angeles. He holds a master's degree in public administration from the University of Southern California and has taught courses in public administration at several colleges and universities.

GARTH N. JONES (Chapters 5 and 8) is Associate Professor, School of Public Administration, University of Southern California, and currently is serving as chief of party on a USC contract in Pakistan. He has been at the University of Southern California since 1961. Prior experience includes three years with the department of political science, Brigham Young University; five years as a public administration advisor with the International Cooperation

Administration; and several research and consulting assignments with the Utah Foundation, the U.S. Department of Agriculture, the Utah Municipal League, the Pennsylvania State Department of Internal Affairs, the Trust Territory of the Pacific Islands, and other agencies. He holds a bachelor's degree from Utah State University and master's and doctor's degrees in political science from the University of Utah.

KENT M. LLOYD (Chapter 3) is Assistant Professor of Public Administration, University of Southern California. He received his bachelor's degree from Brigham Young University in 1955 and his master's in public administration from Wayne State University in 1956. From 1957 to 1961 he was a teaching and research assistant at Stanford University and has been at USC since 1961. He received his Ph.D. from Stanford in 1963 with major work in political science. He has been a consultant to several governmental, educational, and private organizations in management and executive development.

DAVID MARS (Chapter 13) is Associate Professor of Public Administration, School of Public Administration, University of Southern California. He was on the faculty of the University of Connecticut from 1952 to 1960, and has been on the USC faculty since 1961. During this time he also has held a variety of research and consulting assignments with the Mercer County (New Jersey) Industrial Commission, the Connecticut Tax Study Commission, and the Metropolitan Study Commission (Milwaukee). From 1963 to 1965, he served on a USC Technical Assistance Team in Brazil under contract with the Agency for International Development. He holds bachelor's, master's, and doctor's degrees from Rutgers University.

GALE L. RICHARDS (Chapter 13) is Professor of Speech and Chairman, Department of Speech and Drama, Arizona State University. He has been on the faculty at Drake University and the Universities of Akron, Nevada, Southern California, and Washington. He also has been a consultant and training specialist in management communications for many public and private organizations. He received his bachelor's degree from the University of Akron and his master's and Ph.D. degrees from the State University of Iowa.

HARVEY W. WERTZ (Chapter 7) has been Field Secretary for the Los Angeles City Council since 1953. He has had extensive background in journalism, including service with several federal government agencies, a news service, two St. Louis newspapers, and several private organizations. He also has been a professional manager for political campaigns and in the late forties was co-founder and co-publisher of the *Sherman Oaks Sun*, Sherman Oaks, California. He holds a bachelor's degree in journalism from the University of Missouri and a master's degree in journalism from Columbia University.

ROBERT F. WILCOX (Chapters 10 and 11) is Professor of Political Science and Director, Public Administration Center, San Diego State College. He has been with San Diego State College since 1950. Earlier experience includes service with the United Press, the Office of War Information, and the Haynes Foundation. In 1957–58 he was a visiting professor of public administration at Thammasat University, Bangkok, Thailand, and has served on the National Council of the American Society for Public Administration. He holds bachelor's, master's, and doctor's degrees from Stanford University, as well as a master's from Columbia.

Index